France and the
American Tropics
to 1700

France and the American Tropics

to 1700

Tropics of Discontent?

Philip P. Boucher

The Johns Hopkins University Press
Baltimore

Dedicated to my so-supportive wife, Mary,
my children Mandee Countess and Andrew and Alexander Boucher,
and my grandson Henry Countess

The Johns Hopkins University Press
2715 North Charles Street
Baltimore, Maryland 21218-4363
www.press.jhu.edu

Library of Congress Cataloging-in-Publication Data

Boucher, Philip P., 1944–
France and the American tropics to 1700 : tropics of discontent? /
Philip P. Boucher.
p. cm.
Includes bibliographical references and index.
ISBN-13: 978-0-8018-8725-3 (hardcover : alk. paper)
ISBN-13: 978-0-8018-8726-0 (pbk. : alk. paper)
ISBN-10: 0-8018-8725-9 (hardcover : alk. paper)
ISBN-10: 0-8018-8726-7 (pbk. : alk. paper)
1. Caribbean Area—History—To 1810. 2. West Indies, French—
History. 3. French—Caribbean Area—History. I. Title.
F2161.B68 2007
972.97'00441—dc22   2007018704

A catalog record for this book is available from the British Library.

All figures except the map on page 14 are courtesy
of the John Carter Brown Library at Brown University,
Providence, Rhode Island.

Contents

Preface

The writing of history is a collective enterprise. The present work, a general history of a complex subject, is more indebted to scholars past and present than is the typical academic monograph. Only in small patches of the immense quilt that is the story of France and the American Tropics can the author claim some originality. In a general history, one can only arrange or rearrange some pieces of a large mosaic. As Michel de Montaigne observes: "One man may have some special knowledge at first hand about the character of a river or a spring, who otherwise knows only what everyone else knows. Yet to give currency to this shred of information, he will undertake to write on the whole science of Physics."[1]

The premise of this book is that knowledge of the intertwined history of France and the American Tropics is far from common, and yet is a subject that deserves more scholarly and public awareness. At one stage, the title was "France and the Greater Caribbean," and at another "France and the Circum-Caribbean." I rejected a trendier title such as "France and the Atlantic World," which would be misleading, because the better-known French enterprises in the North Atlantic are not considered here. Because this volume also contains material on French activities in various regions of Brazil and in "Florida," the present title seems appropriate.[2] The Circum-Caribbean is its main focus, however, just as it was for seventeenth-century French merchants, corsairs, buccaneers, colonists, and metropolitan officials.

In scholarly circles today, archival citation is vital to academic success. The reader will see below references to archival materials that I have used for past projects, and the text also uses manuscript sources that other historians have cited. I properly acknowledge those scholars, something which is not always done adequately (student readers may not be aware that some historians cite archival sources they have gleaned from secondary sources without mentioning the latter). Archival materials help scholars identify factual errors that have all too frequently been repeated down the generations. One purpose of this book is to stimulate

interest in French colonial and commercial projects in the regions outside continental North America, and to make readers aware that so much
work remains to be done.

Scholars are fortunate to have available rich mines of printed primary
materials on this volume's subjects. Seventeenth-century missionaries
and promoters of colonization left behind much of this wealth. Few eighteenth-century missionary accounts exist, but secular writings of promoters, merchants, and scientists abound. The great work of the Dominican Father Jean-Baptiste Labat, which this volume heartily exploits,
covers the decade after 1695, although not published until 1722. The is-
land-born (Creole) lawyer Médéric Moreau de Saint-Méry compiled a
marvelous six-volume collection of laws and other materials about the
islands, as well as a magnificent history of the French part of Hispaniola,
or Saint-Domingue.[3] The reader will soon become aware of how dependent this volume is on these seventeenth- and eighteenth-century
sources. I thank the former director, Norman Fiering, and the superb
staff of the John Carter Brown Library in Providence, Rhode Island, especially Susan Newbury and Susan Danforth, for making the reading of
these printed sources such a pleasant task over many years of research.
The library is also the source of this volume's illustrations.

Between the French Revolutionary era and the end of World War II,
French historians did yeoman work in assembling and printing collections of primary resources related to the colonial history of the Caribbean. Compilations of laws, ministerial correspondence, and guides to
the archives and to the literature more generally made possible modern
studies of the Antilles, and U.S. scholars, notably Stewart Mims and
Charles Cole, also published important books.[4] French scholars and ge-
nealogists provided detailed biographies of long-forgotten "founding
fathers" such as Pierre Blain (or Belain) d'Esnambuc and Commander
Philippe Longvilliers de Poincy. I dutifully note these contributions. I
have little sympathy to the modern tendency of citing only the most recent authors, even when some of these are basically derivative from earlier historians. Do those who engage in this sad habit care that their work
may thus be forgotten by a next generation of historians?

Despite all the resources noted above, there are huge gaps in our
knowledge of French activities in tropical America in the seventeenth
century. The period from the 1680s to the 1700s, in particular, deserves
much more attention, as do topics such as the status and condition of island women. True, the recent books of James Pritchard and Bernard

Moitt have started to fill that void.[5] What Montaigne advises his reader about the general condition of historical knowledge, that "even if all the reports that have come down to us concerning the past . . . were known to some one person, it would be less than nothing in comparison with what is unknown,"[6] is true of the subject of this volume.

In his laudable book *Colonialism and Science: Saint-Domingue in the Old Regime*, James McClelland discusses at some length the "invisibility" of the history of ancien régime Saint-Domingue in English North America. He rightly takes to task many noted historians for their ignorance of this most important eighteenth-century colony. However, what he has to say about eighteenth-century Saint-Domingue can be applied to all of France's Caribbean colonies, and for both the seventeenth and eighteenth centuries. McClelland himself proves the point by making numerous errors and advancing shallow generalizations when he discusses the seventeenth-century background. For example, he has the Dominican Father Raymond Breton as a Jesuit; he has the important chronicler and natural historian Dutertre as Jacques rather than Jean-Baptiste; and he renders the Dominican bon vivant Labat as Labatt, a mistake the Rabelasian good father might have pardoned had he been familiar with the Canadian brewery.[7] McClelland's reliance on general histories, some a half-century or more old, that are too often unreliable points to the need for the present book.

In fact, it is legitimate to ask whether enough work has been done to permit a useful survey of France and the American Tropics at this time. I think so, and in large part because of significantly increased recent interest in at least aspects of the larger topic.[8] In 1972, William Eccles, the preeminent historian of New France (Acadia, the Saint Lawrence Valley, the Great Lakes, and the Illinois and Mississippi river basins), published his fine survey *France in America*, which contains a brief but then reasonably up-to-date sketch of the French West Indies, with a heavy emphasis on economic and social issues. He brought out a second edition in 1990, which thoroughly incorporated advances in historiography related to New France, but left intact the material on the Caribbean.[9] The later work of Gabriel Debien, including his 1974 synthesis on slavery in the French islands, and the writings of Lucien Abenon, Yves Bénot, Paul Butel, Jacques de Cauna, Michel Devèze, Léo Elisabeth, Carolyn Fick, Charles Frostin, Arlette Gaultier, David Geggus, Christian Huetz de Lemps, Gérard Lafleur, Jean Mettas, Anne Perrotin-Dumon, Jacques Petitjean Roget, Pierre Pluchon, Jean-Pierre Poussou,

Christian Schnakenbourg, Etienne Taillemite, and David Watts, among others cited below, thus do not appear in Eccles's bibliography. My work is in particular heavily dependent on the research of Abenon, Elisabeth, Lafleur, and Petitjean Roget on the history of Martinique and Guadeloupe. These authors have shed much light on the slave trade, the plantation regime, African American responses, and the special circumstances of female slaves, among other topics. Eccles's book *The French in North America* (1998) retains errors of fact and interpretation on the French West Indies.[10] To say that later editions of his general work are out of date as concerns the West Indies is not meant in disrespect to an admirable, even great, historian, but to show the need for a broader, up-to-date synthesis.

The reader must trust that in addition to the primary sources deployed, I have striven to select the most reliable secondary sources on which to base the following story. "The bees steal from this flower and that, but afterwards turn their pilferings into honey, which is their own," Montaigne observes.[11] The critics will have the final say about whether what follows resembles honey. To change the metaphor, my goal is to present the reader with the equivalent of a fine bottle of wine blended from a variety of good grapes. Not perhaps a truly great wine, for my talents are much too modest for that, and there are mountains of unexplored primary manuscript sources, but one that is decently full-bodied, that will age tolerably well for five to ten years, and that will afford the consumer moments of pleasurable satisfaction. In addition, I hope that doctoral students will come to recognize the untapped potential of this not uninteresting topic and will use this work as an introductory tool.

This book is a composite product in another, very important sense. I would never have undertaken this project without the encouragement and support of many colleagues. And this support has been far more than verbal or rhetorical. Especially in a general survey such as this, there would be little chance of keeping factual errors down to an acceptable level and interpretative analysis within reasonable scholarly norms in the absence of expert criticism. I have been most fortunate in that James Pritchard, Sue Peabody, Carla Pestana, Alisa Petrovich, as well as the graduate students in Brett Rushforth's doctoral seminar at the College of William & Mary, have reviewed all or part of what follows. Students in two master's level graduate classes involuntarily read the manuscript and commented on it. My wife, Mary, a high school U.S. history teacher, was kind enough to read the manuscript to point out what needed clarification; but this volume owes her much more than that. I am indebted as well to the book's copy editor, Peter Dreyer. The remaining errors of fact are, of course, my own, as are interpretations that may strike some readers as fanciful, wrong-headed, or even outrageously erroneous, the result of my occasional unwillingness to listen to advice.

I also thank my colleagues in the history department at the University of Alabama in Huntsville (UAH) and my dean Sue Kirkpatrick for believing that this book would eventually come to fruition, and the UAH Humanities Center, founded by my dear colleague Johanna Shields, for financial support of research trips over the long years of its preparation. A final word of thanks goes to my advisor at the University of Connecticut, Edmund (Tedd) Dickerman, who taught me what I know about the art of historical thinking and who long ago encouraged this book.

I hope that this work will allow scholars and students of the Atlantic World to acquire greater familiarity with the French part of that world. To facilitate students' access to this work, I have attempted to restrain the impulse to footnote every statement, while providing adequate documentation for doctoral students and faculty colleagues. My editor and great friend Jackie Wehmueller and her colleagues at the Johns Hopkins University Press decided that posting the bibliography to my web site, www.philipboucher.com, would keep the book to manageable length. My son Andrew Boucher kindly constructed this site for his old man. At this web site, the interested reader will also find two drafts of chapters on French representations of the American Tropics between 1500 and 1700 excluded from this volume for reasons of length.

I apologize in advance if I have left out of the bibliography writings deemed indispensable by their authors; materials that should have been included will be added at my web site. I have also attempted to use a relatively informal style of presentation, which will not please some of my stodgier colleagues.

Allow me to conclude by thanking all of those past and present whose researches and writings have contributed to an understanding of a very interesting, if often unhappy, part of the human saga. No doubt, they have undertaken their labors for a variety of motives—ideological zeal, political or material interest (in the latter category, academics, in part), familial interest, curiosity, or a combination of these—but the product is almost always of some value if used carefully. In four decades of my researches, my predecessors and contemporary scholars have often been stimulating and usually humane company; included in that group are

some seventeenth- and eighteenth-century writers whose views on slavery, women, lower-class whites, and the environment the modern world
and I find abhorrent. If the following pages bring a distillation of their
remarkable labors to a wider audience, and a recollection of their contributions, my labor will have been rewarded.

French Colonial and Commercial
Companies Discussed

Compagnie de Saint-Christophe (Company of Saint-Christophe, currently St. Kitts), 1626–35

Compagnie rouennaise du Cap du Nord (Company of the North Cape, that is, the north bank of the Amazon to the Orinoco), 1633–51

Compagnie du Cap Vert et du Sénégal (Company of Cape Verde and Senegal), 1633–64

Compagnie des Isles de l'Amérique (Company of the Islands of America), 1635–51

Compagnie de la terre ferme de l'Amérique ou France équinoctiale (Company of Equatorial France, that is, Guiane), 1651–54

Compagnie de l'Amérique méridionale (Company of Equatorial America, or Guiane), 1656–57

Compagnie de Guiane (Company of Guiane), 1663–64

Compagnie des Indes occidental françaises (Company of the French West Indies), 1664–74

Compagnie du Sénégal (Company of Senegal), 1673–79; reorganized, 1679–81

Compagnie de Guinée (Company of "Guinea," that part of central West Africa later known as the "Slave Coast"), 1685–96

France and the
American Tropics
to 1700

Introduction

In August 1791, slaves in Saint-Domingue took advantage of the political turmoil besetting that most renowned of plantation islands and launched a revolt. After many twists and turns of fortune, this rebellion led to independent Haiti, which held a muted celebration of its bicentennial on January 1, 2004. Along that road to freedom, the insurgents, assisted by yellow fever, prevented a French army from snuffing out their resistance and thus inter alia persuaded Napoleon to sell Louisiana to the new American Republic in 1803. The events and social conditions leading to the Haitian Revolution—and the inability of other enslaved masses to follow suit—are relatively well known thanks to C. L. R. James, David Geggus, Carolyn Fick, and, most recently, Laurent Dubois, among others, writing in many languages (see www.philipboucher .com). Some histories of France and the Caribbean in the early modern era (i.e., the sixteenth through eighteenth centuries), such as that edited by Pierre Pluchon, make generalizations about the Caribbean colonies on the basis of the eighteenth-century sources, which are far more plentiful than earlier ones.[1] The relegation of the sixteenth and seventeenth centuries to a background function is detrimental to understanding their particular evolution, something this volume intends to correct.

A chief contention of this volume is that the history of French activities and possessions in tropical America before 1700 is little known in continental North America; not by the general public, not by students, not by scholars, and not even by specialists of France overseas before the Revolution. Multiple reasons explain this neglect: the nineteenth-century decline of the Caribbean islands as economic powerhouses; the meager number of descendants of European colonists still living in these regions who might have a greater incentive and sentiment to probe the colonial era—descendants of slaves are understandably more attracted to the period of abolition and its aftermath; the smallness of the islands' current academic and historical infrastructure; and the impoverished state of local archives for the earlier periods, owing to hurricanes, earthquakes, political upheavals, and insect damage, among other things. A startling comparison of this relative neglect is with the state of knowledge of former French possessions in continental North America, from the Saint Lawrence to the lower Mississippi. French descendants in continental North America, of whom I am one, number many millions, the cadre of interested academics is large and enthusiastic, and local archives are quite rich and reasonably well preserved (this was written prior to Hurricane Katrina in 2005, which did damage to some archives in New Orleans). However, another impediment to greater interest in the colonial era of the French Caribbean in the English-speaking world is the unavailability of a reliable general history of these regions before the eighteenth century. The present book attempts to provide such a survey.

This volume takes the story to 1700 (a contemplated second one may continue it to 1789). Other than for the practical purpose of producing a manageable book, one that students and scholars peripherally interested in the topic might actually read, 1700 is an excellent stopping point. By 1700, only Martinique among the French islands had developed a relatively mature plantation regime, and that not to the same extent as English Barbados or Jamaica, with their higher slave to planter ratios. Wars had ravaged French Saint-Christophe (St. Kitts, or Saint Christopher), the original and for many decades the most prosperous French colony, and Guadeloupe and especially Guiane (Guiana) lagged behind Martinique for different reasons. Although Guadeloupe possessed more arable land than Martinique, the latter had better harbors at Saint-Pierre and at Fort Royal, so ships from Europe and West Africa stopped there first. Except for Cayenne, the waterlogged coast of Guiane and its stultifying climate made colonization difficult and unpleasant, when not deadly. Other French possessions such as Sainte-Lucie (Saint Lucia), Saint-Martin, and Saint-Barthélemy were little developed before 1700.

After 1700, however, Saint-Domingue, the western part of Hispaniola that is now Haiti, plunged headlong into the sugar revolution, and Guadeloupe made significant strides in the same direction. The French slave trade finally got off the ground after 1700, in part because France's new ally Spain granted a contract (*asiento*) to French traders to supply Spanish America. By the 1730s, the classic plantation regimes dominated the French Greater Caribbean, although the smaller islands and Guiane continued to lag behind. The type of society now known as the plantation complex characterized much of the French West Indies by the

1730s, and it has been well described in a phalanx of works by prominent French- and English-language scholars.[2] The burgeoning economic importance of these plantation islands after 1700 for the first time made them a high priority in Bourbon foreign policy. (The term "plantation islands" is far preferable to "sugar islands," because the French produced a variety of crops. In the seventeenth century, tobacco and indigo were the chief alternatives to sugar; in the eighteenth, cotton and especially coffee supplemented sugar production.) That was clearly demonstrated during the War of the Spanish Succession (1702–13) and in the wars of 1744–48, of 1756–63, and of the American and French Revolutions.

Chapter 1 examines the geography, topography, climate, and flora and fauna of the Greater Caribbean, as well as the cultures of their indigenous inhabitants, the Island Caribs. The Carib world forever changed as a result of its invasion by the French, accompanied increasingly by their enslaved West Africans. A host of European and West African diseases converged in the Caribbean, with dangerous consequences for Native Americans and very serious ones for Europeans and Africans. In a crude Darwinian sense, it might seem, because of their demographic dominance in most Caribbean islands, that Africans and their African American descendants were better equipped to deal with this disease environment. However, this dominance was only assured in the nineteenth century after the abolition of slavery, when black populations finally achieved a surplus of births over deaths. Both willing and unwilling colonists found themselves transformed through encounters with the tropical environment and its indigenous peoples.

Chapter 2 examines a variety of French efforts to smash Iberian hegemony in the Americas prior to France's establishment of colonies in the Lesser Antilles in the 1620s—and why the French failed to do so. Often labeled with such dismissive phrases as "false starts," the background endeavors examined in this chapter deserve the extensive coverage it gives them.[3]

Chapters 3 and 4 provide a narrative of what is called here the "frontier" or "settlement" era, from the 1620s to the 1660s. This period is *not* treated as a prelude to the classic plantation regime model, but instead as an era that had a whole variety of possible outcomes. In Chapters 5 and 6, the structure and character of society in the frontier era are analyzed in relation to other early American societies ("American" is always used here in the broad sense of the Americas as a whole).

My approach is to devote space to all the islands' inhabitants—Island

Caribs, land-owning free settlers (*habitants* in island parlance), indentured servants (*engagés*), the gradually increasing number of "African"
slaves from various geographic and ethnographic backgrounds, and, at
this early period, the few people of mixed blood (called *gens de couleur* in
the islands).[4] It is understandable—considering that their major focus is
to explain slave rebellion and emancipation in the Greater Caribbean, or
"Circum-Caribbean," an area stretching from the north bank of the
Amazon to the mouth of the Mississippi and the Florida Peninsula—that
most modern historians of the region are predominantly interested in
slavery, the slave trade, and the status and condition of Africans and
African Americans, and the *gens de couleur*. But surely the contemporary
European populations of the islands should not be ignored or marginalized in modern historiography, as if in retribution for how eighteenth-
and nineteenth-century and even twentieth-century Western historians
neglected non-Europeans, not to mention their neglect of female and
lower-class European male habitants.

Chapters 7 and 8 return to a chronological survey of what I call the
"pre-plantation complex" era, that is, the period from the 1660s through
the 1690s. The term "pre-plantation complex" serves to indicate that,
despite the growth of sugar, plantation agriculture, and the gradual dominance of African over European labor, the transformation was gradual
and should not be imagined as having been inevitable for all Caribbean
islands, or for all areas within any one island. Attention needs to be paid,
as well, to the partially successful effort of the French monarchy under
Louis XIV (r. 1661–1715) to assert control over island developments.

Chapters 9 and 10 examine the economic and social history of this
pre-plantation complex era. The Conclusion briefly provides a glance at
a projected sequel volume, which will depict an eighteenth-century era
in which French would-be millionaires strove at any cost for quick
riches, a roller-coaster ride up to a summit of delirious fortune for some,
but for the great majority, a plummeting down to economic and social
despair. Massive, brutal, and wasteful importation of Africans characterized this era and accounts for the long-term Africanization of the
Caribbean islands. Also in part responsible for these changing tides of
fortune and misfortune was the islands' ever-increasing involvement in
France's imperial wars, fought not only in Europe but worldwide.

The balance of this Introduction introduces the reader, especially
students and general readers, to a variety of thematic and methodological
issues. As employed below, the terms "Circum-Caribbean" and "Greater

Caribbean" recognize that the coast of northern South America from the Amazon Delta to the Orinoco was an area of—often feverish—French maritime activity. The region was then considered complementary to the island colonies. In fact, writers of that era treat the island of Cayenne on the coast of French Guiane as just another Antillean island. French activities and colonial projects south of the Amazon were also sufficiently important to merit space in this volume.

To write a general history of France and tropical America during the ancien régime cuts against the grain in several ways. First, general narrative history is not much in vogue, especially among scholars of the Circum-Caribbean, whose major concern has been, rightly, the social history of the plantation complex. So why write one, especially when a general account is such an onerous task? Upon starting research for my doctoral dissertation almost forty years ago, my progress suffered from not having available the kind of book I hope this will be. General narratives then available, by such scholars as Herbert Priestley and Nellis Crouse, were helpful faute de mieux, but they were already dated and hardly touched on economic and social issues. Cobbling together a survey of tropical French America from specialized French- and English-language sources was then (and still is) time-consuming and frustrating. In addition to the secondary literature, I have read and employed just about all of the primary printed sources and have done research on specific topics in the French archives in Paris and, more recently, in Aix-en-Provence. Scholars even in closely related areas of Atlantic World studies today know little about the French Caribbean before the later eighteenth century, and some have encouraged this project to gain easier access to the subject. The recent intense interest in Saint-Domingue in the era of the Atlantic revolutions (ca. 1770s–1820s) has not yet promoted much interest in the earlier period.

Why write a book on just the *French* Circum-Caribbean in an age of transnational scholarship, and concerning a region whose scholars justly, if sometimes rhetorically, emphasize pan-Caribbean perspectives? Some colleagues will criticize this project on this very issue, considering it "Eurocentric." Some decades ago, Gordon K. Lewis argued that "it is misleading to seek to understand the Caribbean in European terms, as so much of the traditional metropolitan scholarship has vainly attempted to do. The region's history is not just the overseas history of France or England or Holland; so to see it [as such] is to indulge in ethnocentric distortion."[5] In principle, I recognize the validity of and empathize with

Lewis's perspective. Some answers to this legitimate concern come to mind: once again, the French Circum-Caribbean before the Age of Revolution is nearly terrae incognitae to English-language scholars.[6] Even distinguished Caribbean specialists very familiar with the English and Spanish Caribbean are less than sure-footed in the French materials. And why should they not slip occasionally, since easily accessible secondary sources are even more than usually flawed? Even the beautifully illustrated and generally valuable catalogue of a major exhibit about the islands at the Musée de l'histoire de France in 1992 contains such errors as the English colonizing Barbados before Saint Christopher (p. 46), calling Martinique and Guadeloupe Leeward Islands (p. 46), and attributing a document illustrating the deeds of the Compagnie de la terre ferme (Guiane) of the 1650s to the 1635 Compagnie des Isles de l'Amérique (Company of the Islands of America), created to exploit the Windward Islands (p. 39).[7] A useful survey of the French colonies, which this volume hopes to provide, might thus assist scholars one day to produce the great pan-Caribbean historical chef-d'oeuvre.

The paucity of English-language scholarship on the French in tropical America is well demonstrated by the commendable vogue of collections of essays on Caribbean topics. A few scholars, David Geggus, John Garrigus, and Léo Elisabeth among them, have had to do yeoman work to get contributions on the French Caribbean included in such collections. Finally, I would note that some of my students who wanted to learn more about this topic were frustrated by the lack of a convenient starting point.[8]

Surprisingly, the unavailability of narrative histories of the Caribbean in French is almost on a par with that of equivalent English texts. To be sure, there are lengthy older accounts of particular islands and texts that emphasize social and economic history, as my volume makes obvious. Breezy overviews of the Caribbean as a whole, such as Michel Devèze's 1977 book *Antilles, Guyanes, la mer des Caraïbes, de 1492 à 1789*, are useful, if a bit superficial.[9] If a satisfactory narrative did exist in French, my travails would have been much mitigated.

Although the narrative chapters below concentrate on French projects in the Greater Caribbean, in the thematic chapters, the treatment of such issues as French–Native American relations, patterns of emigration and settlement, the European impact on the natural environment, the character of French colonial government, and the particular French evolution of plantation slave society is comparative in the broadest geographical sense of an Atlantic World approach; that is, to the best of my ability. Atlantic World literature is voluminous and shows no signs of scholarly fatigue.

The period of revolution and abolitionism in the French Caribbean (say 1770–1850) has attracted some excellent North American scholars recently. Although in listing them I risk excluding others (who may review this volume), Laurent Dubois, Carolyn Fick, Robert Forster, John Garrigus, David Geggus, Gwen Hall, Lawrence Jennings, James McClelland III, Sue Peabody, Alyssa Sepinwall, Gene Stewart, and Dale Tomich have all helped English-language scholars better understand this complex era. However, most of these scholars are interested in ancien régime colonial society primarily as a springboard for understanding the revolutionary era. Aside from Dubois, Forster, Geggus, and Peabody, they are not particularly concerned with the metropolitan political context of colonial evolution. In my volume, the destruction of the ancien régime in France and the French Caribbean are epilogue, not center stage. No historian can or should ignore outcomes, but they can lead to historical tunnel vision.

The methodological difficulties inherent in attempting to evaluate historical societies on their own terms and not simply as predecessors to a more modern world can be illustrated by my use of the phrase "pre-plantation complex era" to describe the decades between 1660 and 1700. On the one hand, during these decades, the larger French Caribbean islands did move sporadically but steadily toward a society dominated by large plantations, especially those making sugar. We can see here the embryo, or perhaps the adolescence, of the plantation complex of the middle eighteenth century. In retrospect, such an evolution takes on the character of inevitability. To fail to remember that other outcomes were possible is to impoverish historical study.

To take one, stark example, there were times, especially between 1691 and 1696, when Spanish and English attacks almost destroyed Saint-Domingue, and other islands, such as Saint-Christophe, suffered such a fate at other times. Beyond this type of contingency, scholars must examine what structural factors led to or did not lead to the development of plantation complexes in the Caribbean. Why, for example, did seventeenth- and eighteenth-century Spanish Santo Domingo and Cuba not develop mature plantation regimes? They certainly had the climate, large amounts of arable land, and the harbors necessary for such a transformation, as indicated by the sudden emergence of nineteenth-century

Cuba as a sugar behemoth. Obviously, they lacked other key economic, social, and political stimulants, possessed earlier by both the English and French islands. Here it is sufficient to say that a combination of capital and labor shortages in the context of the much larger Spanish American empire kept the Spanish islands backwaters until the Haitian Revolution of the late eighteenth- and early nineteenth centuries promoted the development of alternative producers of sugar.

It is also fair to say of most contemporary scholars that their primary purpose is to reach the world of their peers, with the knowledge that someday their researches and discoveries may eventually reach a larger public. Having long shared it, I fully understand that perspective. However, there is also a legitimate need to cast our nets wider. I can only hope that specialists will be indulgent of my shamelessly baiting my net with some of the juiciest, best-known quotations, anecdotes, and illustrations. Nonspecialists encountering these for the first time will perhaps, like young fish, more readily take the bait. Expert colleagues will also need patience when commonplaces of the discipline are explained to a more general readership. Surely they can understand the impulse to write a book for more than a few score fellow scholars, close relatives, and friends? (At family gatherings, my siblings pretend that they are having trouble getting to sleep and then make a big show of toting one of my academic writings up to bed.) Perhaps when traversing familiar ground in this work, colleagues will come across curious byways, or at least unfamiliar anecdotes and materials with which they can lard classroom lectures.

Readers may be surprised that the remarks above about the relative economic success of the French slave-based regime are not immediately accompanied by reference to the utterly odious aspects of such societies. In later chapters, readers will find abundant materials that illustrate the dark character of this regime and of many who profited from it. And though the injuries and injustices to slaves far exceeded those leveled at Native Americans and white indentured servants, this book will amply demonstrate the social frustrations of the great majority of island inhabitants, of whatever "race"—there is no biological logic to dividing humanity along "racial" lines, notwithstanding its power as a social construct— and of their often similar responses to poor conditions. Furthermore, even many profiting from this regime apparently lived lives of quiet or drunken desperation and social isolation, plagued by the insecurities of war, natural disasters, chronic indebtedness, and, most of all, by life-limiting diseases.[10] So, given these documented social pathologies, what could possibly justify the eye-catching question mark in this book's subtitle, *Tropics of Discontent?*

Although some scholars consider Caribbean slavery "a monstrous distortion of human society," characterized not just by unusual physical cruelties but also by an abysmal degradation of life,[11] the view of French Caribbean society depicted here is *slightly* less bleak. Nonspecialists deserve a clear exposition of my perspective. The proper context in which to evaluate French societies in tropical America prior to 1700 is that of early colonial life in the Americas, of conditions in pre-1700 Europe, and, insofar as my preparation allows, of the relevant areas of sub-Saharan West Africa. To be sure, most masters in French islands were far from humane, most Europeans were indentured servants, not masters, and slaves were far from "content" with their lot; they expressed resentment in a variety of ways, discussed below. Life for the vast majority of people in that era was hardly as depicted in the rustic paintings of a Peter-Paul Rubens or a François Boucher, or in idealized eighteenth-century representations of plantation society. Perhaps only Hieronymus Bosch could have done justice to illustrating the misery of most human beings in most places in the early modern world.

In the past four decades or so, a large body of scholarship has well established that a large majority of early modern Europeans lived lives not irreconcilable with Thomas Hobbes's famous dictum about the life of natural man being poor, nasty, brutish, and short. Despite the valorous efforts in seventeenth-century France of people such as St. Vincent de Paul and the Sisters of Charity, the number of poor probably increased. There was among the privileged an increasing tendency to blame the poor themselves, thus auguring one modern worldview. In this respect, things became only worse in the next century with the declining zeal and thus charitable activities of French Catholicism and the ascendancy of secular, capitalist values little compatible with sentimentality about the "dangerous masses." Common French islanders in the seventeenth century at least did not have to submit to the oppressive taxes of the metropolis—the *taille*, or hearth tax; the hated *gabelle*, or salt tax; and mandatory tithes. Blood-sucking tax farmers and others of the stealthy financier elite were mercifully absent from the colonies. And, at least for much of the seventeenth century, lawyers were persona non grata in the islands, and some there considered buccaneers and freebooters to be defenders of the people.

In the colonies, people were de facto freer than at home; anyone wishing to know the limitations of French "absolutism" (a popular topic today among U.S. historians of France) should study the Caribbean colonists' attitudes to obedience to the king. This volume argues that the French state was less directive of colonial development in the French Caribbean than is usually portrayed.[12] As later chapters argue, it is true that Louis XIV and his chief minister, Jean-Baptiste Colbert (1619–1683), made significant if limited strides in asserting royal authority. For just one example, island officials repeatedly but vainly argued that the French part of the exposed condominium island of Saint-Christophe be exchanged for an English island. Louis's glory (*gloire*) would not allow this to happen.

French migration across the Atlantic in the early modern era was comparatively small. Global estimates suggest a figure of 60,000 to 100,000 leaving for the Americas in the years 1500–1760, as compared to 746,000 British subjects, 678,000 Spaniards, and even 523,000 from thinly populated Portugal. France at the time had the largest population by far of any European state, some eighteen to twenty million. Only the Dutch, with some 20,000 migrants, trailed France among the big five imperial powers. It should be noted that more than half of the French migrants probably either died during the experience or returned home.[13] These broad demographic figures are an important context for what follows. Chapters 5 and 9 explore these issues in detail.

On another issue, social historians of New France and New England have depicted positive conditions for the growth of European populations there, a claim that cannot be made for the tropical colonies. Still, the available data do not prove or even strongly indicate that the life expectancy of island French immigrants and native-born Creoles was any lower than the admittedly miserable figure for the average contemporary Frenchman. True, newly arrived individuals from France did have to overcome a seasoning period during which malaria and, after 1690, yellow fever took a heavy toll.

Very little is known of the first Africans who involuntarily came to inhabit French possessions in the American tropics. The French slave trade was negligible before 1700, which means that the growing numbers of seventeenth-century slaves arrived on Dutch or English ships, or by sale through a motley crew of agents, not excluding buccaneers and Island Caribs. No evidence exists that these Africans were not from the beginning treated as perpetual slaves. Some evidence suggests that Africans reached demographic parity with Europeans at Saint-Christophe, Martinique, and Guadeloupe by the 1660s, and that the ratio was about two to one by 1700. The great majority of African and African American (Creole) slaves in the later decades of the seventeenth century belonged to the small minority of Europeans who established capital-intensive sugar or indigo works. Nevertheless, neither these prosperous planters (in eighteenth-century parlance, *grands blancs*) nor their African slaves dominated island life to the extent that they did by the second third of the eighteenth century. Chapters 5, 6, 9, and 10 explore these social issues in greater detail and make the case that life for seventeenth-century slaves was not as stultifying and oppressive as it would be for their successors. This does not mean that it was not stultifying and oppressive.

This volume argues that in many but not all ways colonial society before the triumph of the plantation complex was relatively healthier and less brutal than during the eighteenth century for most groups, with the notable exception of the declining Island Carib population. It is also claimed herein that whites born in the islands were physically healthier and psychologically less insecure than hard-living, fast-dying young male emigrants from France. "Professionals"—many of them, to be sure, self-proclaimed—such as surgeons and skilled workers in the building and other trades had more opportunities in the islands than those who stayed in France. Similarly, African American Creole slaves were healthier and perhaps less overtly discontented than newly arrived slaves, the so-called *bossales*, or "salt water" Africans, who were quick both to die and to escape (the French terms *marrons* and *marronage* are widely used in scholarly circles for escaped slaves). Among Creole slaves, domestics and especially male skilled workers were better off materially than field hands, and not a few were able to acquire their freedom either legally or de facto. Slaves in the tiny towns were perhaps better off than plantation hands. Were all African American slaves worse off than all bonded folk in West Africa or than those Africans transported over long distances to Muslim markets in North Africa or points further east?[14] Most historians would say yes, some unequivocally. Although at present we are not well equipped to answer these questions definitively, they should be posed. How "hellish" island life was in the seventeenth century depends then on what it is being compared to. I argue that in many ways most islanders, white or black or colored, were better off in earlier times than in the more prosperous eighteenth century. In short, not all islanders were equally unhappy all the time, given a realistic spectrum of what then constituted "happiness."

This book will introduce the reader to France's efforts to establish a presence in the American Tropics. There, the French lived in a raw, fast-moving world, and a large majority of them had wanted neither to come nor to stay, at least not in any permanent sense. But sometimes they did stay, although too often not for long, given the high mortality rates among newcomers. As regards deplorable human behavior, which we shall encounter only too often when discussing labor conditions, political and legal repression and the follies of war in the French American Tropics, I shall attempt to shed light on it—that is, to finish the maxim, to understand injustice but not excuse it, especially injustice that contemporaries deplored.

CHAPTER ONE

At the Dawn of French Colonization
The Greater Caribbean

France's commerce and colonies in the American Tropics dominated its Atlantic interests during the ancien régime. After French colonization of various Caribbean islands in the 1620s, exports to and imports from them increasingly dwarfed those of France's other American colonies, Acadia, New France, and Louisiana. Although in terms of economic importance, Canada was not just "a few acres of snow," as Voltaire famously quipped, the value of its furs, cod, and other less important exports paled in comparison to that of tropical plantation produce—tobacco, indigo, cacao, coffee, cotton, and, most important of all, sugar. To establish France's tropical empire, therefore, officially supported expeditions attempted to erect fortified garrisons on the fringes of the reputedly vulnerable Spanish and Portuguese possessions.

Comparing continental North America with the islands of the Greater Caribbean (including Cayenne in Guiane) in geographical, topographical, and ecological perspective, this evaluation of their relative worth appears paradoxical. How could these small tropical islands yield far greater rewards than the incomparably larger and potentially richer lands of the continent—especially given that privateers and pirates marauded throughout the Caribbean region? Some observations about the geography, topography, climate, and flora and fauna of these islands may shed light on this question, which is a central focus of this book.

The Natural Environment

Although Guiane is on the margins of the Caribbean world, its history is tightly linked to that of the French Lesser Antilles (the Iles du vent, or Windward Islands). In part, this connection was due to the sixteenth-century French interest in exploiting dyewoods, especially brazilwood, and tropical exotica, such as parrots. In the High Middle Ages, the term *braise* referred to dyeing textiles, hence the name the Portuguese discoverers gave Brazil, where they found brazilwood and logwood, both used to dye cloth with a prized reddish tint. Ships engaged in that trade,

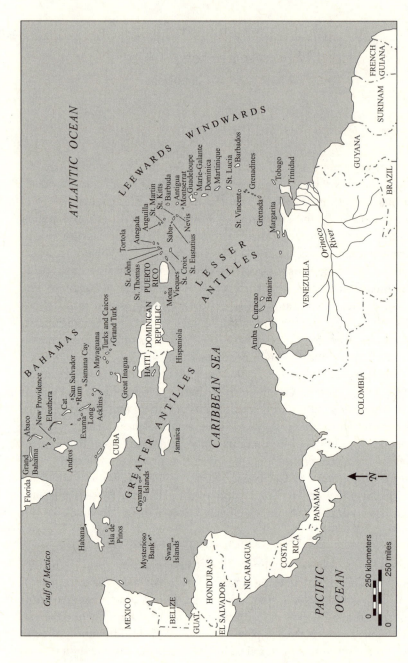

The Greater Caribbean as it is today.

or corsairs preying on Iberian commerce, found that currents and winds promoted a return to Europe via the Antillean and Bahaman island groups. The Guiana current sweeps ships northwest from the hump of Brazil, past the mouth of the Amazon, and along the Guiana coast to Trinidad and Tobago. At that point, a northerly current sweeps sailing ships to Saint Vincent and the Grenadines, then northwest to Saint Lucia (Sainte-Lucie), Martinique, Dominica, and Guadeloupe. The ability to take on fresh water and provisions along this route fostered its use.

In the seventeenth century, French slavers heading west from the African coast usually chose to cruise northwest toward the Orinoco before crossing to the Lesser Antilles. Along the swampy, seasonally rainy Guiana coast of some 200 miles claimed by France, there were only a few sites to anchor and go ashore, the most hospitable being the island of Cayenne, which provided safe harbor and high ground on which to construct fortifications. Local Cariban-speaking Indians, whom the French called Galibis, were willing to trade provisions, hammocks, and tobacco, if treated with care.

Sailing up the major rivers of French Guiane (i.e., heading east to northwest, the Oyapock, the Approuague, the Cayenne, the Sinnamary, and the Maroni), seventeenth-century sailors hoped to discover the legendary El Dorado residing in his fabled golden city of Manoa. However, upriver camps did not benefit from the sea breezes that modestly alleviate the intense heat and moisture of the coastal climate. Fearsome rapids and waterfalls denied European vessels significant access to the rain forest interior. Tropical diseases made life extremely hazardous for unacclimated settlers. Malaria was perhaps the most important killer in the seventeenth century, and yellow fever in the eighteenth. Although the region is at least not afflicted by the hurricanes and earthquakes that make life precarious for Antilleans, French Guiane, with only about 200,000 people, is even today the least densely populated area of the Caribbean basin, closely followed by its neighbors Suriname and Guyana.[1] The distance from Cayenne to Martinique, the closest significant French island settlement, is about 1,200 km. While it was relatively easy for sailing ships to go from Cayenne to the Windward Islands, the reverse was not the case; at a minimum, three weeks were necessary.

The Caribbean islands divide into the eastern Lesser Antilles arc and the Greater Antilles (Puerto Rico, Hispaniola, Jamaica, Cuba) to the west. The name "Antilles" probably derives from medieval cartography, which postulated the existence of islands of Antilia to the west of the Azores. In the seventeenth century, the French established settlements in the western third of Hispaniola and the neighboring island of Tortuga, jointly called the colony of Saint-Domingue (currently Haiti). The small and numerous Bahama Islands lie to the north of the Hispaniola-Cuba axis, scattered like splotches on a Jackson Pollock canvas.

Although it usually took about a week to reach the northern coast of Saint-Domingue sailing westward downwind from the Windward Islands, it could take a month or more to return against the wind. Thus, like Cayenne, Saint-Domingue evolved in isolation from the other French islands. The character and quality of life differed significantly from island to island. French colonists in the Windward Islands shared Saint-Christophe (today St. Kitts) and Saint-Martin with their rivals the English and the Dutch, respectively, and thus lived in a state of heightened military insecurity. Guadeloupe had serious difficulties acquiring slaves legally, basically because Martinique evolved as the main economic and political center, and the smaller islands were even worse off in this respect.[2] Moreover, in assessing these differing island situations, one cannot only consider legal trade. Smuggling so pervaded the Caribbean that the official statistics, in any case notoriously unreliable for this era, mask island conditions as much as they reveal them. Borders were highly permeable in the early modern Caribbean.

Whereas Martinique and, to a lesser extent, Guadeloupe did move in the direction of a predominantly plantation regime starting in the 1660s, large parts of these islands and the smaller islands subsisted on the production of tobacco and foodstuffs, small-scale farming, ranching, woodcutting, trading with Island Caribs (a factor usually overlooked), and the coastal trade (*cabotage*). As long as the supply of African slaves was uncertain, that is, until after about 1715, the supremacy of sugar was delayed. The development of French possessions in the American Tropics was anything but uniform or constant.

Similarly, one must distinguish among three distinct and isolated parts of Saint-Domingue. The southern peninsula remained little developed until the late eighteenth century, with an economy centered on smallholdings, intra-island trade, and smuggling. Only after 1760 did this region develop significant plantation agriculture. In the eighteenth century, the northern region became the Elysian Fields of sugar planters (and the Hades of slaves), and its capital, Cap François (familiarly, Le

Cap; currently, Cap Haïtien) was among the brashest of nouveau riche American cities. The western sector that joined the two areas contained river valleys ideal for sugar if irrigation systems were built; after 1750, Port-au-Prince (the current capital of Haiti) became the colonial capital. But it took a sea voyage of two or more weeks to reach it from Le Cap and even longer to reach Les Cayes, the administrative center of the south. Not until the 1780s were rudimentary roads available to travelers.[3] From the 1730s on, in the previously undeveloped mountain interiors of the western and southern districts, the rapid development of coffee plantations created new types of capitalist enterprise and new conditions for both masters and slaves. To reach the nascent French settlements in what was then called Louisiana (today's southern Alabama, southern Mississippi, and Louisiana proper), ships from Saint-Domingue had to sail some 1,200 miles.

These island groups emerged in the past twenty-five million years as a result of a variety of geological processes; the Greater Antilles because of the mountain building geographers call uplift, and the younger Lesser Antillean islands as a result of volcanic activity. The names Greater and Lesser are well deserved, because the former cover about eighty thousand square miles, compared to about two thousand three hundred for the latter. Haiti today, roughly comparable to French Saint-Domingue, is slightly bigger than the state of Maryland and covers 27,750 km^2 (10,694 sq. miles), with 1,570 km (roughly 976 miles) of irregular coastline. Until the early eighteenth century, buccaneers and privateers found it a safe haven. Martinique and Guadeloupe (including dependent islands), the largest French Windward Islands, occupy only 1,103 km^2 (426 sq. miles) and 1,709 km^2 (660) respectively.[4] Our smallest state, Rhode Island, occupies 2,706 km^2 (1,045 sq. miles). The Hawaiian island of Oahu, at 1,575 km^2 (608 sq. miles), is slightly larger than Guadeloupe proper (Guadeloupe and Grand-Terre, without its former dependencies). Other French-influenced islands are much smaller. The first settlement at Saint-Christophe occupied less than 129 km^2 (about fifty sq. miles). Saint Lucia is an island of 606 km^2 (234 sq. miles), Grenada, 350 (135 sq. miles), and Saint-Christophe 176 (68 sq. miles).[5] South of Martinique, Saint Vincent, the site of sporadic French settlements from the later seventeenth century on, measures 381 km^2 (147 sq. miles). Somewhat smaller than Martinique and Guadeloupe, Dominica (790 km^2, or 305 sq. miles) lies some fifteen miles north of

Martinique, and was much fought over by the Island Caribs, French, and English.

Geologically, there are two arcs in the Lesser Antilles, with an outer arc of much older, relatively low-lying, volcanically inactive islands. Erosion gradually wore down their peaks to less than 1,000 feet. Barbados, the eastern island of Guadeloupe named Grande-Terre, Marie-Galante, Antigua, Anguilla, Barbuda, Saint-Barthélemy, Saint-Martin, and Saint-Croix at the northwestern end are part of this arc.[6] The southern part of Martinique, Saint Lucia, and Grenada are also evidence of the older arc, and these islands therefore had more complex habitats, supporting human life, as well as flora and fauna. These islands have a limestone core, and the processes of erosion created coral reefs around them. Mangrove swamps harbored rich supplies of fish, shellfish, and manatees. The older northern islands get little rain and have scant fresh water, in part because of their relatively flat character and their location far removed from the continents. Sugar or other staple crop production was difficult on these islands, although as the cases of Antigua and Grande-Terre, Guadeloupe, demonstrate, not impossible.

The inner arc of the Lesser Antilles consists of active volcanic islands, which look like mountains that have emerged from the sea.[7] Their summits reach almost to 6,000 feet. In recorded times, the volcanoes on the French islands were quite active from the 1690s to the first part of the twentieth century. The worst single disaster occurred with the eruption of Mont Pelée on Martinique, which destroyed the island's major urban center, Saint Pierre, in 1902.[8] At the end of the twentieth century, the catastrophe at Montserrat occurred when the Soufrière Hills Volcano there erupted. Although volcanic activity does occur in the Greater Antilles, it is less significant there, but earthquakes are more of a problem.[9]

The climates of the French-occupied islands varied significantly, although all lay in the Tropics. The northern and western parts of Saint-Domingue, except for the Artibonite river valley, receive only moderate amounts of rain today, approximately fifty inches annually.[10] Because the extent of forest cover plays a role in amount of rainfall, the figure was presumably somewhat higher centuries ago. Periodic droughts (five in the Cap François area in the eighteenth century) produced misery but also promoted extensive public irrigation works.[11] On the other side of the wet central mountains, the southern peninsula is drier and hotter. The uplands of the French islands, and more than 50 percent of Saint-

Domingue, lie above 500 meters and were not opened up until coffee plantations emerged in the 1730s.[12] Martinique, Dominica, and Guadeloupe receive between seventy-and eighty-six inches of rain annually today and do not have as distinct a dry winter season as does Haiti. In higher elevations, up to about 2,000 feet, these islands nurture rain forests. Chroniclers constantly refer to the perennial springtime there, because rain forest trees do not lose their foliage, as do the coniferous woods of the temperate zones. The sheltered leeward, generally western side of these islands (called Basseterre in French), the lands first settled by Europeans, receive significantly less rain than the windward side (called Capesterre) of the central mountains. Small, relatively flat and dry areas include the Grenadines, Marie-Galante, the Grande-Terre island of Guadeloupe, and the southern tip of Martinique. No French island, except parts of Grande-Terre, enjoyed the unique advantages of nonvolcanic Barbados, whose rich-soiled plateau ensured adequate rainfall for the growing of sugar.

Many French islands were subject to earthquakes, but none as spectacular as that which destroyed Port Royal, Jamaica, in 1692. Alexandre Moreau de Jonnés documents six earthquakes in the seventeenth century, the first in 1664, sixty-five in the eighteenth century, and forty-three in the first half of the nineteenth. The lack of evidence for much of the seventeenth century suggests that six episodes is almost certainly an undercount. Affecting the French islands were those of 1664 at Martinique, 1684 at Saint-Christophe, and in 1691 on various islands of the Lesser Antilles, as well as Saint-Domingue.[13]

About two-thirds of rainfall in the Caribbean islands occurs during the "hot" months from July to December (it is especially heavy from mid August to mid October); about one quarter of that total is the result of hurricanes. (Our word "hurricane" comes to us via Spanish from the Hispaniola Taíno aborigines' Arawak term *hurikane*.) On average, the French Windward Islands are in the direct path of many Atlantic hurricanes in the season running from June to the end of November or later. In some years, only one or two hit land; in others, ten or more do.[14] Contemporary accounts, even blatantly propagandistic ones, usually fail to conceal their horror at the devastation these storms wrought. For example, in 1650 a storm smashed twenty-eight ships at Saint-Christophe.[15] One older source estimates the number of hurricanes as six in the sixteenth century, eighteen in the seventeenth, and thirty one in the eighteenth. The lower estimate for earlier centuries is likely the result of inadequate documentation. Of those Moreau de Jonnés could document with certainty, eight storms occurred in July, fifteen in August, eleven in September, and nine in October.[16] These hurricanes' destructive impact was a major reason for the triumph of large planters, who could more readily finance rebuilding efforts. The gut-wrenching fear of total crop loss and devastation of home and infrastructure accounts in part for the gold rush mentality of so many settlers.

Although contemporary observers praised the presumed fertility of islands verdant with thick vegetation and majestic trees, in fact, tropical soils are "extremely vulnerable to fast and massive erosion, once the protective cover of natural vegetation has been removed."[17] Settlers ignorant of these ecological facts hastily carved out farms (*habitations*). Because soil-destroying tobacco was their main crop, the ecological damage was even greater than might otherwise have been the case.

Contemporary propagandists also vaunted an island climate of perpetual warmth, moderated by cooling sea breezes, colloquially called the northeast trade winds. Due to the equatorial current, the temperature of the Caribbean Sea varies less than two degrees summer to winter. Along the leeward coasts of the Windward Islands, where most Europeans lived, temperatures vary very little by season and average from the high seventies to the lower eighties Fahrenheit. Near sea level, temperatures almost never fall below sixty degrees and rarely rise over ninety. In higher altitudes, cooler temperatures prevail, and when one approaches the tops of the higher mountains, jackets and sweaters are comforting.[18] Propagandists usually failed to mention the perennial high humidity of the coastal climate, never less than 70 percent.

The hottest months in the Lesser Antilles are August through October, and the mildest December through February. The most variable months are March, May, June, and October. April and November are the months closest to the mean annual temperatures. The most humid months are July to December, with October the worst, at 98 percent humidity. The mean humidity is in the eighties. Of course, there are significant variations within these islands, depending on ground level, relationship to prevailing winds and other factors. The best harbor in the Lesser Antilles, Fort Royal (today Fort-de-France), Martinique, also probably had the most dismally hot and humid climate.[19]

Climatic alterations between wet and dry seasons profoundly affected the rhythms of colonial life. The rainy season runs from July through November, with September and October the wettest months.

December through May are drier, especially March and April. All planters of crops, but most especially of water-hungry sugarcane, had to adapt to these realities.

A number of factors make problematical any evaluation of the original natural resources of the seventeenth-century islands. First, although some early voyagers describe them in Edenic terms, in fact, the Island Caribs, and no doubt even earlier aborigines, had had a significant impact on the islands' environment, in ways to be discussed in the next section. Second, the Spanish and other Europeans made their mark on the environment during the sixteenth century, the Spaniards by their ubiquitous practice of introducing pigs and goats to assure fresh supplies of barbecue. (Our word "barbecue" derives from the Hispaniola Taínos' Arawak language, in which it referred to wooden grids used to grill foods.) Europeans also slaughtered large numbers of sea turtles. Almost invariably, contemporary authors give the impression that turtles were available at all seasons. Europeans traded as well with the aborigines both for valuable turtle shell (*caret*, from a particular variety) and to satisfy collectors' craze for parrots and other tropical exotica.

Finally, contemporary accounts naturally emphasize useful animals and plants and those to be avoided at all costs. Propagandists painted the climate or flora and fauna of rival colonies in dark hues. The poisonous snakes of Martinique were no doubt dangerous (the fer-de-lance and coral snake were the most feared), but some accounts falsely portray them as insatiable pursuers of men in order to lure French colonists to rival islands.[20]

Writers praise the natural resources of tropical America, real or imagined, and laud the health and strength of the large-bodied indigenous Island Caribs. Contemporary accounts speak of the gastronomic pleasures to be derived from turtle hunting and the delights of iguana trapping. Iguana was better than chicken, and as good as veal, some claimed. Considered a fish, manatee could satisfy stomachs and consciences on Fridays and during Lent. The agouti, a rodent related to the guinea pig, was the size of and supposedly tasted as delicious as French hares. Multitudes of birds, all delicious, including pigeons, doves, and aquatic fowl, were there for the taking. At night, pursuers of land crabs found as many as they could eat. Another major source of fresh food came from the rivers and the surrounding sea. Accounts describe dozens of edible fish, as well as shellfish such as oysters and the conch, the latter unfamiliar to the French. For dessert, snacks, or to make preserves for family and friends at home, native fruits, especially the universally praised pineapple, and citrus fruits flourished in this tropical paradise. Such depictions of a cornucopia of delights often occur, however, in accounts that elsewhere refer to early French colonists dying of hunger.[21] And no one could hide the fact that the islands contained none of the big game animals—deer, moose, elk—that might have whetted the appetite and hunting urge of French readers. At best, feral pigs might provide sport.

Not surprisingly, there was unchecked speculation about gold and silver mines and precious stones. The seemingly endless tropical forests contained valuable trees such as brazilwood. The acacia and the mahogany provided excellent wood for carpentry. The resin of the lignum vitae (*Guaiacum officinale*), sometimes used today to treat rheumatism and gout, was then thought to be a cure for syphilis. The dried roots of the sarsaparilla and sassafras plants passed as remedies for a variety of maladies, including venereal diseases. Many species of turpentine trees and gum trees provided useful resins. The Island Caribs used a species of gum tree to fashion their large canoes, or pirogues.

Most seventeenth-century accounts did not attempt to camouflage the "annoyances" and "irritations" of life in these lands completely. Missionaries wrote most such accounts. Although they promoted colonization as essential to evangelizing the indigenous population (usually called *sauvages*, a term often used in a more or less neutral sense of "wild" men, or, more negatively, *barbares*), missionaries were not averse to informing their readers about their fatigues and sacrifices. They found island "vermin"—ranging from burrowing chiggers to the tormenting swarms of huge mosquitoes—especially exasperating, and although they could not adapt to the native lifestyle, they were aware of aboriginal means of warding off insects, such as sleeping in hammocks above a smoky wood fire and daily application of annatto-based grease (rocou or *roucou*).[22] Also, it was impossible to hide the fact that missionaries in their "seasoning" period suffered fevers (malaria perhaps) and other illnesses described in vague terms. Their readers heard all too often about the deaths of blessed missionary colleagues. On balance, though, most of these authors insisted that island life was far more enjoyable than metropolitan readers assumed; and it was getting better every year as frontier conditions receded.[23]

The Human Environment:
The Island Caribs, or Kalinago

All seventeenth-century writers, from perspectives ranging from the propagandistic to a few who found little to praise about island life, had to deal with the reality that fierce Kalinago—Island Caribs—inhabited the major islands the French settled.[24] These supposedly insatiable man-eaters were among the most publicized indigenous American groups in Europe. Columbus and most Spanish commentators saddled the Caribs with the most negative image of any contemporary native people.[25] As a result, French promoters of these islands and the missionaries sent to convert the *sauvages* found it imperative to moderate the traditional representations of Hispanic authors widely translated into French. In doing so, the missionaries presented a great deal of ethnographic information (mixed with misinformation and, of course, filtered through French cultural lenses) about these peoples. The Dominican Raymond Breton was the crucial figure, both for his work on these peoples' languages and for his influence on fellow Dominican authors, especially Fathers Jean-Baptiste Dutertre and Jean-Baptiste Labat, as well as on the principal lay commentator, Charles de Rochefort. Who were these Island Caribs? What was the character of their relationship with the Spaniards and other Europeans? Why had they acquired such a monstrous reputation?[26]

Although the French authors cited above went to great lengths to refute traditional stereotypes about Island Carib culture, they unsurprisingly viewed it through the prism of French (and, for most, Catholic) cultural attitudes. For example, little is known about Carib spiritual beliefs, other than such generalities that they believed in benign and malignant spirits (*chemin* and *maboya*), that they had two or three souls, one of which (located in the heart) went to heaven, and that shamans (*boyés*) had powers of divination and healing. Most missionaries simply dismissed Carib religion as idolatry, with the recognition, however, that knowledge of how the devil tyrannized over them would assist evangelical goals. All seventeenth-century information about Carib lifestyles must be interpreted based on modern ethnohistorical methods. Unfortunately, the little archaeological work done on Carib sites after the appearance of the Europeans makes reliance on contemporary accounts more than usually necessary.[27]

The first question, that is, who the Caribs were in an ethnographic sense, is surprisingly difficult to answer and the source of much controversy.[28] The traditional view has a venerable source, the writings of a French missionary who had more familiarity with these people (at least those of the island of Dominica) than any other European ever did. Raymond Breton, who had an unrivaled comprehension of Island Carib languages, related what Caribs had told him (or what he thought they had told him) about their origins—to wit, that their ancestors had been Galibis (Caribs or Cariban-speakers) from the Guiana coast. Parties of male warriors in great pirogues raided northwest up the Lesser Antillean chain, killing and eating the males and enslaving the women.[29] To Breton, such origins perfectly explained his impression that male Carib warriors among themselves and on certain occasions spoke a special language. Women and children spoke an Arawak-based language. Many contemporary facts reinforced this interpretation. Island Caribs still undertook long voyages to ambush their Arawak enemies in Trinidad and on the South American mainland. There, they often joined mainland Caribs in wars of revenge. Fellow Dominican writers, able to profit from Breton's manuscripts,[30] believed that Caribs had reached Saint-Christophe in the northwestern Lesser Antilles soon before the Spaniards appeared in the Caribbean.

Only in the past fifty years have anthropologists, archaeologists, and especially linguists poked holes in the Breton orthodoxy. Notably, Douglas Taylor, the modern dean of Island Carib cultural and linguistic studies, first noted that Breton's dictionary demonstrates in fact that Carib men spoke primarily an Arawak language, with only a sprinkling of Cariban words used in ritual ceremonies.[31] Even though Taylor does not dispute the substance of Breton's conquest scenario, others have. Scholars have pointed to the fact that Caribs of other islands had other, more or less dissimilar origins myths.[32] Some archaeologists claim to find no signs of disruption at pre-Columbian sites, which casts doubt on the traditional story. Other scholars argue that there is no clear ethnic difference between the Arawaks of the Greater Antilles and the Caribs; the latter, less developed economically and politically, simply found the richer Arawaks tempting targets for raids and assimilated captives. When Columbus first encountered the Arawak-speaking Taínos of Hispaniola, they convinced him that "Caribs" were a monstrous, cannibalistic, alien people. After a series of hostile encounters with these aborigines, Spaniards had every reason to perpetuate and constantly reinforce this ethnic division.

There is no simple resolution to this controversy. Perhaps Carib men migrated to the islands and forcibly persuaded the previous populations (called Igneris by Caribs) to submit to their leadership. In such a speculative scenario, these warriors would then have instilled their militaristic values into male offspring in ritual ceremonies, especially during the ordeal of the rites of puberty, and otherwise gradually discarded their Cariban language. After all, both boys and girls first learned the Arawakan language of their mothers, with young males from puberty forward acquiring a Cariban pidgin. But then why did the Dominican Caribs insist that their ancestors had conquered the islands? This may not be a serious problem since, according to French sources, Caribs were notorious braggarts about their military valor and past conquests. The same sources' insistence upon the traditional alliance with the Galibis tends to support some modified version of Breton's story. These groups seem to have evolved a trans-Caribbean Cariban-based pidgin to promote trading and strategic contacts.[33] With the coming of Europeans, Caribs quickly incorporated Spanish and French words.

Further masking the issue of ethnic origins is the roughly 130-year interval between the first Carib contacts with Europeans and Breton's extensive stay at Dominica.[34] Spanish archival sources indicate that some Taínos of the Greater Antilles sought refuge from Hispanic dominance in the Lesser Antilles, presumably preferring to live among their reputed enemies rather than under European oppressors. Probably other Taínos, mainly females, fell captive to Carib raids at Trinidad and Puerto Rico. These Arawak-speaking wives/slaves would presumably have reinforced that component of the Carib linguistic brew. Perhaps these kidnappings (which also included Spaniards and African slaves) were intended to alleviate population losses due to Spanish slave raids and the probable although undocumented losses to European diseases. Some scholars speculate that the relative isolation of the Kalinago allowed them time to recover from epidemic episodes and to acquire some immunity to the infamous Indian-killing diseases.[35]

The impact of Spanish slave raids on the post-Columbian distribution of the Caribs is not well known. When Englishmen later came to occupy several Lesser Antilles islands, especially Barbados and Antigua, no Caribs lived there. Yet they had done so in earlier times and continued to visit them to gather food, medicinal plants, and materials such as flint and clay. Had the Caribs evacuated these islands because their topographies made them easier targets for Spanish slavers? Such security concerns probably explain high-density Carib populations on mountainous Saint Vincent, Martinique, Dominica, and Guadeloupe. Nevertheless, Caribs considered exploitation of such islands as Antigua and Marie-Galante as essential to their survival.[36]

Our understanding of Island Carib culture is made difficult because the first serious European observers described it some 130 years after the Caribs' first contact with Europeans. These indigenous peoples saw the advantages of European iron tools, fishhooks, knives, and weapons and used a variety of means, from theft to barter, to obtain them. Let the reader imagine felling fifty- to sixty-foot trees without axes in order to fashion pirogues. The arduous work of hollowing out the interior of the log using controlled fire, followed by scraping away the ash with conch shell, was transformed by hatchets, axes, and other iron tools. On long sea journeys, Caribs used sails adapted from Europeans. They fancied European copper pots, although not necessarily for their intended purpose, and treasured glass beads and other "trinkets." European spirits were coveted to supplement their cassava beer (*ouicou*), brewed by village women, who after chewing leftover cassava pancakes—their spittle unleashed the fermentation process—mixed them with other ingredients.[37] Caribs also accepted some Old World food plants, for example sugarcane, millet, and Angola or pigeon peas (*Cajanus indicus*); in the seventeenth century, they raised poultry, not for food, but for trading. They killed and sold wild pigs.[38]

It is difficult to gauge the influence of Spanish, African, and Arawak prisoners on Island Carib culture. In some ways, Caribs were remarkably resistant to outside influences, most notably in their preservation of native religious beliefs in the face of Christianity; in other ways, they assimilated much. By 1600, for example, they were rigging their pirogues with sails.[39] By no later than the mid seventeenth century, they were speaking a pidgin (called *baragouin*, or jabber, by the chroniclers) that used French, Flemish, and especially Spanish words.[40] Their villages then included Caribs and Arawaks, African slaves, European prisoners, and a mixed (*méti*) population of uncertain dimensions. Caribs targeted white women and children, especially English ones from such islands as Antigua. In 1640, a party of Dominican Caribs captured the pregnant wife of Governor Thomas Warner and her two children. Just as in con-

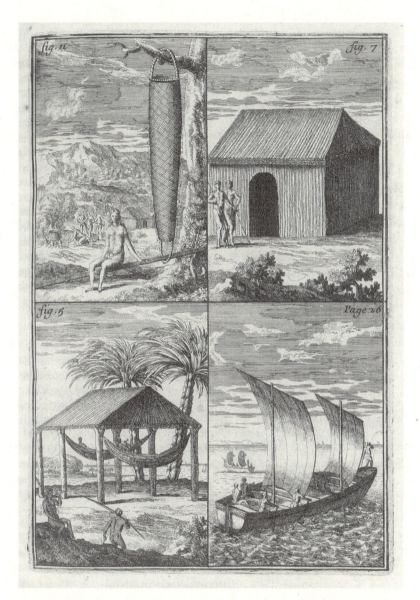

Carib woven basket, lodge or longhouse (*carbet*), hammock, and canoe with sails. From Sieur de Laborde, *Voyage qui contient une relation . . . des Caraibes*, in *Recueil des voyages*, ed. Henri Justel (Paris, 1674), 26.

tinental North America, such children were rapidly assimilated. The most famous example of this cultural mixing (*métissage*) was the "Black Carib" population of Saint Vincent, which became historically visible toward the end of the seventeenth century.

These cultural assimilations make knowledge of precolonial Carib culture problematical. However, one certainly cannot accept the facile solution of John Locke by ignoring the later French sources in favor of the first Spanish descriptions, notably that of Peter Martyr d'Anghiera. In Locke's view, Spanish authors captured Carib culture prior to significant contact with Europe. Based on prejudiced sources that had only fleeting, violent contacts with Island Carib culture, Martyr's evocative book was the locus classicus for the horrible reputation of these peoples.[41] Martyr never set foot in America.

Almost all contemporary sources described the Island Caribs as medium- to heavy-fleshed, well-proportioned people. It is not surprising, given their physical environment and their way of life, that they possessed great stamina running on land and swimming at sea. Their seminaked state allowed viewers to witness their practice of scarification and their use of various body paints. They viewed the human body as a work of art. To complete this picture, Carib men and women proudly wore the hair on their head very long but otherwise despised body hair; for certain rituals or as a penalty for certain punishments, both genders shaved their heads. They thought hirsute European males unbearably ugly.

Caribs' agility in their pirogues and smaller canoes and their skill as bowmen drew admiration from European observers, who noted that these *sauvages* exhibited stoical courage, "satanical" wiliness, and great patience in their long voyages to attack their enemies. On these sea odysseys, they went without food for extended periods. Their pirogues were so well designed that capsizing at sea occurred without loss of goods or provisions. They showed no fear whatsoever of sharks or any other creature.

On heavily populated islands (e.g., Dominica, Saint Vincent, Martinique, Guadeloupe), the Carib population lived in more or less autonomous villages of from 100 to 150 people under a headman (called captain by the French).[42] The village headman owned a large war pirogue, which he commanded on Carib raids. On occasion, a headman might have such exceptional prestige as to exert some sway over lesser chiefs, not in the European sense of command and control, but rather to head councils to adjudicate disputes. Only for military purposes would

Romanticized view of a Carib man and woman. From Jean-Baptiste Dutertre, *Histoire générale des isles Antilles* (Paris, 1667–71), 2: 356.

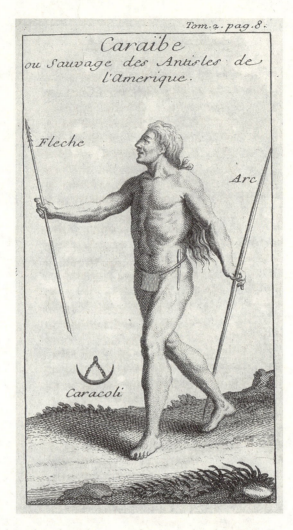

Long-haired Carib male without scarification or lip plug. From Jean-Baptiste Labat, *Nouveau voyage aux isles de l'Amérique* (Paris, 1722), 2: opposite 8.

one or more Carib villages choose a temporary war leader, who did command obedience.

Within each village, a number of smaller, conical-shaped huts surrounded a central lodge or *karbay* (*carbet* in French), where the men gathered for important occasions.[43] The headman maintained up to six wives, a sign of great prestige as well as wealth and one important rea-

Carib female. From Jean-Baptiste Labat, *Nouveau voyage aux isles de l'Amérique* (Paris, 1722), 2: opposite 11.

son for raids on enemies; other warriors had two or three. Some wives of important men lived in other villages and on other islands. Men alternated time with wives on a monthly basis. The current wife was responsible for feeding and caring for her husband. Missionaries, while disapproving the practice of polygamy, expressed amazement that these multiple wives got along so well.

Although each village, and indeed each man (called *Carib*, or brave warrior) in the village, was free and independent, Caribs from the same and different islands gathered together for clan-related events such as rites of puberty, marriages, and funerals. When a Carib died, the relatives would never believe it without seeing the deceased buried in a sitting-up or fetal position under the *carbet*, along with his possessions and sacrificed servants or slaves. But, most notably, when the call went out to discuss whether a raid should be undertaken, Caribs gathered for one of their famous *ouicous*. Once heavily laced with alcoholic beverages, these normally laconic people worked themselves into rages against enemies old and new. Elderly women recounted ancient insults against the people and the valorous deeds of past warriors, and called upon the men to revenge the wrongs. Preserved fat and bones of defeated enemies were apparently gnawed in rage. Supposedly, the women called upon the fighters to bring fresh prisoners to be the objects of torment and serve as the entrée for a communal feast, after being dispatched by a *boutou*, a flat war club about four feet long, decorated on both sides.[44] Each Carib and each village was free to join or not join the proposed sortie; nevertheless, Caribs believed that an injury to one of them by an enemy was an injury to all.

Caribs from different islands often convened for great voyages to the mainland, sustained during the long days of rowing by pinches of snuff. They might choose one or two captains, one to pilot the fleet and another to lead the attack.[45] Caribs did not eat during the day while on a voyage, believing that if they did so, the pirogue would not go. In the evening, they consumed dried cassava, iguanas transported live, and barbecued fish and crabs prepared by a few women accompanying the raid. The warriors used the tactic of surprise to capture their enemies alive; if successful, they kept the women and children as slaves and dispatched the men in a highly ritualized ceremony. According to many sources, the victors consumed the victims; however, no author was an eyewitness to such man-eating.[46]

The anonymous contemporary author of *Un Flibustier français dans la mer des Antilles, 1618–1620*, edited by Jean-Pierre Moreau (1990) records that during some French freebooters' 1619–20 stay at Martinique there was only one man eaten during the ten months he was there; but all too typically of such accounts, he does not claim to have witnessed the event. His account of the ceremony could have been taken from earlier ones. The most trustworthy seventeenth-century writers agree that

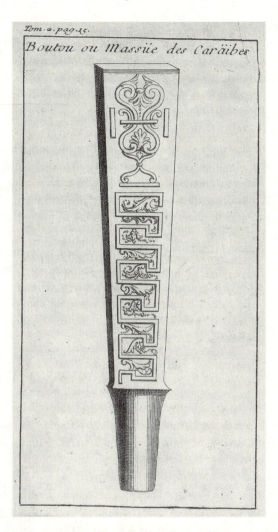

Carib war club (*boutou*). From Jean-Baptiste Labat, *Nouveau voyage aux isles de l'Amérique* (Paris, 1722), 2: opposite 15.

Europeans no longer had to worry about being the pièce de resistance of a Carib feast. According to one source, the Caribs' detestation of salt supposedly made Christians unpalatable to them.[47] Only their Arawak enemies received that treatment, although none of these authors explicitly states he was present at such a ceremony. The smoked limbs seen by contemporaries were probably the objects of symbolic cannibalism, during which Caribs may have gnawed them in a ritualized frenzy.

In peacetime, the Carib male lived like a king surrounded by females, who were treated like slaves, or so missionary observers claimed. Of course, some of these women *were* slaves. The indignation European clerics so often expressed about native males' mistreatment of their females is ironic given the priests' own misogyny. After he awoke, the Carib male whiled away the time before sunrise playing his flute, made from the leg bone of an enemy, and then went with his family for a swim in the river. Upon his return to his hammock, his current wife then dried him and slathered him with *roucou*. The main meal of the day followed, normally cassava griddlecakes, made from the manioc flour of the bitter yucca root.

The Carib method of grating the root to extract potentially fatal dosages of prussic acid was among their greatest gifts to Europeans, although in partial compensation, the latter's iron griddles eventually replaced Carib stone ones. These flat cakes, though relatively tasteless, when dried could be used many months later, and European sailors soon carried them on board ship for food.

Caribs always ate fresh cassava cakes seasoned with a hot red pepper sauce (too fiery for most European taste buds), into which had been stewed land crabs, fish and shellfish, small birds, iguanas, snakes, and agoutis, which were commonly also barbecued. This hot pot did not elicit favorable comments from European observers, who were, however, expected to partake of it when visiting a *carbet*. The Caribs did not eat the feral offspring of the pigs the Spanish had left to breed, but they barbecued their flesh for sale to Europeans.[48] They never drank or talked when eating and thought Europeans rude and barbarous for doing so. And since Caribs never ate when drinking alcoholic beverages, they became drunk far more quickly—but then that was the purpose.

After the communal breakfast, Carib males lounged in their hammocks smoking and then made wooden objects, baskets, combs, and fishing gear.[49] They then might decide to go hunting or fishing or to tend to their upland gardens with their families. A companion might be asked to go along on the hunt but was under no obligation to do so. According to contemporaries, Caribs excelled at fishing and hunting. Ingenious in the extreme, they fished with both lines and nets, dove to sea bottom for shellfish, such as conch, poisoned rivers to kill or stun fish, and used arrows and spears in shallow waters.[50] On an island such as Saint Vincent, which was relatively untouched by outsiders, they could hunt European-introduced wild goats and pigs, native agoutis, and the staple land crabs.[51] Upon their return, the males dropped their game or catch by the canoe without a word, and their wives took it back to the village and readied it for eating. After their morning trip to the garden, wives also prepared manioc flour and beverages, as well as vegetables such as sweet potatoes, potatoes, Carib cabbage, and Angola peas. In addition, they spun cotton, made hammocks and rocou dye, fashioned calabashes, and waited on their husbands and children in a never-ending day of labor.[52]

The well-meaning but naïve missionaries, who considered hunting and fishing recreational and aristocratic activities, were appalled by Carib males' insouciant, "lazy" lifestyle, even when they understood the dangers of ocean fishing and hunting on snake-infested islands.[53] They did not know that Carib males performed intense labor in the months prior to the dry season. They practiced what is called swidden agriculture, clearing seasonal plots by cutting and burning the plant cover. To prepare for planting at the start of the wet season, they cut down trees, which were burned once dry. Since this slash-and-burn method quickly exhausted the thin island soils, males frequently had to clear new gardens.[54] Some gardens were adjacent to the village, but others were well upland or on other islands to guard against enemies or because of unfavorable climactic conditions. The men also cut trees at this time for pirogues and canoes, as well as posts for their great lodges, and crafted a variety of objects from conch shell for daily use. They made weaponry for war and hunting, as well as lines for fishing. They produced manioc grates, cotton belts, basketry, and wooden bowls, some of which they exchanged with Europeans for knives, hatchets, and spirits.[55] They constructed the central village lodge (*carbet*). Sources differ on whether men or women fashioned the pottery. With the coming of the dry season, Carib women started the planting of cassava, sweet potatoes, pineapples, melons, sugarcane, pimentos, cotton, and tobacco. Some sources also mention Old World yams, citrus, and bananas, another example of the process of borrowing.[56] For a man to sow seeds was regarded as ludicrously counterproductive, because Carib myth connected women's fertility with the fertility of the earth.

With the conflicts of the colonial era in mind, it should be emphasized that Caribs roamed far and wide among the islands, for example, hunting turtles at Tobago and iguanas on Antigua. They fished in the most abundant waters, such as those around the Grenadines, Antigua, Barbuda, and other nonvolcanic islands wreathed in rich mangrove swamps; they also hunted manatees along those coasts. Flint for tool making and clay for pottery were often found on islands not formally occupied. They traded for desiderata such as green stones from the Amazon region and flakes of jasper, used for grating cassava roots. They traded hammocks, foodstuffs, parakeets, turtle shell, and tobacco to friendly Europeans for hardware, textiles, crystal beads, and the like.[57] They collected herbs and medicinal plants from all the islands. In sum, they drew resources from all the islands and thus reacted hostilely to foreign efforts to occupy them.

Most missionary authors expressed little admiration for the way Carib males undertook their most arduous task—the fashioning of pirogues.[58] While hosting a round of libations, the prospective boat owner inquired in an offhand way whether any of his companions would assist him. Since only prestigious captains or headmen had the right to build these large dugouts, they usually attracted volunteers. A date was set (typically early in the dry season) for the group to meet at the site of the tree (usually a logwood or gum tree) selected by the owner. To Europeans, it seemed to take forever to cut down the tree, even with European hatchets, and finish all other tasks needed to complete the vessel. Once the prirogue was ready, days were required to drag it on rollers from the uplands to the sea. By no means did the group work on a daily schedule. Weeks or even months were "wasted" between the various stages of completion. Consumption of alcoholic beverages accompanied the steps of production. European observers did not comprehend that the cut log had to dry before fire became effective as the hollowing agent. Finally, with the semi-finished boat at the shore, the headman and his family finished the craft. Days of feasting preceded the launching.[59]

Thus the Carib male hunted and fished, fashioned and repaired weapons and tools, and occasionally built huts or made canoes and pirogues. Was that it? Writers ignored the economic aspects of Carib raids and trading, even though they comment on how these brought Indian, European, and African slaves to Carib villages, as well as looted metal goods and textiles. But even though Carib males "worked" far more hours than assumed, their labor was not the semi-coerced product of political or economic agents, as was the case in Europe.

Contemporary accounts claim that Carib females lived in drudgery, or according to some classically trained authors, endured lives similar to those of helots bound to Spartan masters. Not only did women minister to their husbands' needs, but they did all of the agricultural labor, except that performed by slaves. Carib gardens, however, in general required little maintenance, so that for security reasons, they were planted at some distance from riverside villages adjacent to the sea. Indeed, Caribs also planted gardens on adjacent islands, for example, on uninhabited Marie-Galante. Vegetables and cotton were sowed at the beginning of the rainy season and checked only periodically thereafter. So, just as with hunting, agriculture occurred in islands not containing Carib villages. Caribs searched for woods, medicinal herbs, and raw materials wherever they might be found. They collected the rich fish and shellfish resources at the older, low-lying coral-rimmed islands. Turtles and manatees could be found only in certain areas, for example, off the beaches of Tobago. What I have elsewhere called the Carib "commuter" economy, a hunting, gathering, and primitive agricultural one, became a source of much contention when it came into contact with European perceptions of "civilized" economic activities.[60] The Caribs could never accept the idea of exclusive use of island resources.

Carib family life evoked European responses ranging from outrage to scornful laughter. Upon marriage, formerly sexually free women ("libertines" to the missionaries) found their bodies jealously guarded property; that is, if wives became pregnant during a year of trial marriage. If not, they tried again for another year with another prospective husband, and then with a third. Infertility was a horrible fate, and such women lost all communal privileges becoming barely tolerated pariahs. Even the suspicion of adultery by a married woman might lead to a mortal blow of the husband's long club (*boutou*).[61] Proof of adultery led at least to the casting off of the wife, the public humiliation of having her hair cut, and the right of any male to fornicate with her. Male adulterers had to endure a thirty-day fast, followed by eight days of public whippings and admonitions, but were finally fully reintegrated into society.[62]

Carib wives birthed children without much apparent fuss or pain, and a new mother immediately returned to her arduous chores, while the father retired to his hammock "pretending" birth pain for a period of forty days (a practice called the couvade), which Europeans thought imbecilic. In dramatic contrast to contemporary European swaddling, Carib infants had total freedom of movement, and their parents never corrected them or controlled their desires, or so said contemporary accounts. (Among some native peoples of continental North America, uncles rather than parents disciplined children.) The missionaries admitted that children were respectful to their parents and observant of community mores, although writers pronounce themselves befuddled as to how this could be the case without discipline.

All commentators agree about Caribs' hospitality. They expected to be hospitably received as well, and not to be refused their requests for gifts. To receive guests, Carib men wore multicolored feather head-dresses, sported a gold ring in each ear, and either gold or silver rings in the nostrils to accompany their famous lip plugs. The exposed parts of the body were decorated with black or red lead-oxide-based paints. (Some Europeans naturally thought as a result that the men looked like devils.) A shoulder cloak of feathers of birds of prey or jaguar skins and leggings below the knees made of bands of cotton cloth completed the ensemble. Armed with bow and arrow and a wooden club, the Carib male was then ready to party with his guests.[63]

Although the Caribs' nudity and lack of "table manners" provoked mostly negative reactions among Europeans, what the latter found most upsetting were Carib religious practices. This was not so much because of their polytheistic beliefs and "superstitions"—these were to be expected—but because of the "stubbornness" with which they were maintained in the face of Christianity. French missionaries regularly equated the powerful Carib spirit Mabouya, who ate the moon during eclipses, Caribs believed, with the devil. To be sure, Caribs quite willingly accepted baptism to please the priests and to receive the little accompanying presents. In fact, some individuals found the sacrament so satisfying they wanted repeat performances, but few of them would alter behavior inconsistent with the new religion. According to the author of *Un Flibustier français*, the Carib paradise was analogous to the sensible European peasant legend of the bounteous land of Cockaigne, a place of utter plenty and sensuality. In the Carib case, this heaven was a mountain of warm cassava cakes, through which flowed rivers of cassava, manioc beer, and sweet potato spirits, and in which Caribs had endless supplies of their enemies to consume and hordes of black slaves to serve them.[64] Especially irritating to Carib men were the "unreasonable" Christian restrictions on polygamy and sexual "libertinism." Given the economic and military aspects of their culture, there was no point in insisting that they live in permanently settled communities.[65] Father Dutertre admits that some three decades of work by Breton and fellow Dominican missionaries had yielded at most twenty serious Carib Christians.[66]

Both in terms of its flora and fauna and its human inhabitants, the Greater Caribbean was an exotic place to French explorers, pirates, merchants, and colonists. However, they did not sail and maraud in these waters out of sheer curiosity. The hated Spaniards had sensationally exploited tropical America, garnering riches that fueled their campaigns to dominate Europe and especially their French neighbors. French monarchs and their subjects could not afford to leave Spain in peaceful possession of the American Mediterranean.

CHAPTER TWO

French Challenges to Iberian Hegemony in America up to 1625

In 1493, Christopher Columbus established the first European settlement in America on Hispaniola (the island today shared by the Dominican Republic and Haiti), the focus of Spanish colonization until Hernán Cortés's invasion of Mexico (1519–21). There, and subsequently in Cuba, Jamaica, and Puerto Rico, Spanish conquistadors exploited, enslaved, and, unintentionally, with the assistance of Old World diseases (principally smallpox, measles, tuberculosis, influenza, and dysentery), drastically reduced the Arawak-speaking aborigines.[1] Conquistadors raided surrounding islands in the Bahamas and Lesser Antilles for slave labor to replace the declining Taínos, and from 1511 on, they imported African slaves. By the 1530s, significant parts of Hispaniola, especially the northwestern and western regions that would eventually become French Saint-Domingue, had returned to wilderness; but one now overrun by feral cattle and pigs.

With the astonishing exploits of Cortés and the ruffian Pizarro brothers in Peru, European readers came to regard America in a new and more favorable light. The "New World" witnessed a gold rush fever that would last through much of the sixteenth century. Spaniards flocked there and, using the Greater Antilles as base camps, launched frenzied expeditions in all directions to uncover other golden kingdoms.

Notwithstanding this reorienting of Spanish imperial impulses to the mainland, colonists at Puerto Rico and after 1570 at Trinidad initiated sporadic and mostly unfriendly contacts with Island Caribs. Spanish raiders even launched invasions of the Lesser Antilles for punitive reasons, to rescue captives, and to enslave Caribs. To refresh Spanish convoys sailing westward, stops at Guadeloupe, Dominica, or Martinique for water and provisions became routine, despite frequent Carib hostility. Jean-Pierre Moreau has extensively documented these relations, although he may underestimate the amount of cautious trade between these enemies.[2] Bad news from the Indies has more likely survived in the archives than good.

Unlike Henry VIII's England and Spain's still loyal Lowlands provinces (modern Belgium, the Dutch Netherlands, and Luxembourg), France under the Valois dynasty battled the hegemonic claims of King Charles I of Spain (r. 1516–1556), simultaneously Holy Roman Emperor Charles V (r. 1519–1556), in a series of wars. By the 1520s, it was evident to northern Europeans that Spain's conquest of Mexico had filled its treasury, and its subsequent domination of Incan Peru only increased the reputation of America as a storehouse of gold and silver. At the same time, Portugal's sparsely occupied territory of Brazil, with its dyewoods and parrots, attracted French merchants.

This chapter examines French reactions to Iberian claims of ownership of the Americas. French privateers terrorized Iberian shipping, while more peaceable merchants supported efforts to establish fortified garrisons astride strategic points of Iberian America. In the end, these efforts did little more than harass the Iberians, who responded by destroying French garrisons weakened by internal conflicts between Catholics and Protestants (Huguenots) and lack of sustained royal support. The failure of these efforts shaped French colonization in the American Tropics during the seventeenth century.

The Spanish refused to allow other Europeans into their American preserve, especially after metallic riches started pouring in. The sensational news of Aztec and Incan treasures whetted other European appetites, especially those of Spain's hard-pressed enemies. That primarily meant France, which contested Spain's imperial ambitions in Italy and elsewhere. The French king François I (r. 1516–1547) vociferously refused to honor Iberian pretensions to a monopoly on America. In an oft-quoted anecdote, he reputedly asked the Spanish ambassador to produce Adam's will leaving the Americas to Iberians. He insisted that legitimate claims to areas overseas depended on de facto occupation, not on grandiose papal grants.[3]

Not only did François support voyages searching for a northwest passage to Cathay (the Orient), the expeditions of Giovanni da Verrazano, Jacques Cartier, and Jean Roberval, but during these years of almost continuous war, he unleashed privateers in the Caribbean. (A privateer obtained a letter of marque—effectively, license to plunder the enemy—from a recognized sovereign or his representative in return for conveying all his booty to a given port and sharing the profits with his patron, who usually took 10 percent.) The great Norman port of Dieppe, with its renowned school of navigation and its dynamic ship outfitter (*armateur*) Jean Ango, happily implemented the king's will. As early as 1523, Ango's captains captured two ships containing looted Aztec treasure.

With the renewal of war in 1552, King Henri II (r. 1547–1559) in turn provided letters of marque to privateers. The famous François Le Clerc, whom the Spanish called Pié de Palo, or Wooden Leg, resembled the later English sea dogs in his daring and his hatred of the Spanish. Not only did the French privateers prey on shipping, they captured Spanish settlements for ransom. These predators, primarily from the Norman cities of Rouen, Dieppe, Honfleur, and Le Havre, but also from the Basque region, were by the 1550s more and more likely to be French Calvinists, or Huguenots, who especially hated the Spanish champions of international Roman Catholicism. The fortress city of La Rochelle, on France's mid-Atlantic coast, which was increasingly Protestant, joined in.

Like their Viking ancestors, the Norman raiders were ready to assume the role of traders given the right conditions. Although the penalties for trading with the enemy were severe on paper, and sometimes in reality, Spanish settlers were always short of European manufactured goods, such as textiles, ironware, and brandy, and being perennially starved for labor, they were especially willing to take chances if the smugglers also brought African slaves. So it is not surprising that Norman archives attest to many ships armed for the African trade, offering textiles, ironware, and brandy in exchange for gold and ivory.[4] Not until the Treaty of Cateau-Cambrésis of 1559 secured peace between exhausted France and Spain did the Norman thrust decline, although the treaty affirmed the principle of no peace beyond a line west of the prime meridian in the Atlantic and south of the Tropic of Cancer, where fighting would not automatically lead to war in Europe. Religious conflicts in France were about to consume Normandy's and indeed all of France's energy.

When François I's successor Henri II died in a freak jousting accident in a tournament celebrating Cateau-Cambrésis, a long series of religious conflicts ensued. These pitted a growing and determined Huguenot faction led by the Admiral Gaspard de Coligny and the Bourbon prince Henri of Navarre (the future Henri IV) against the ultra Catholics led by the powerful Guise family. Inevitably, the Norman ports were heavily involved and, although raids on the Caribbean did not cease, they declined in frequency from the 1560s to the 1590s.

The first French ship arrived in Brazil in 1503 and returned with the son of a local chieftain, Essomericq, who purportedly lived in France until his death at the age of ninety-five, leaving fourteen children. From the 1520s on, the coast of Brazil was the principal focus of legitimate French American trade, aside from the northern fisheries, and some Caribbean raiders also participated in the Brazilian dyewood trade before 1560.

French, primarily Norman, merchants established close contacts with various Tupi-Guarini-speaking peoples, especially the tribes known collectively as the Tupinambá, who cut and transported the dyewood to the coast in exchange for European axes and other ironware, textiles, and brandy. The wood yielded a reddish dye especially sought after for the Rouen textile industry. The Normans left young boys (*truchements*) among the Native Americans to learn the language and act as trade facilitators. Apparently, many "went native," to the point of taking common law wives and, some observers claimed, of engaging in cannibalism.[5]

This swarm of French traders alarmed the titular rulers of Brazil, the Portuguese, who in the 1530s launched a drive to colonize it by large grants of territory to captain-donataries. Some regions, such as the future sugar provinces of Bahia and Pernambuco in northeastern Brazil, attracted settlers, but the coast was too long to impede the lucrative French commerce. By 1550, one Portuguese source claimed, 100,000 cut brazilwood trunks awaited French ships.[6] It was a French effort to establish a permanent settlement in the south, however, that galvanized serious Portuguese development there.

The 1550 reception of Henri II and his much-neglected wife Catherine de' Medici at Rouen—then by far France's busiest port, and its second biggest city, with 70,000 inhabitants—was a spectacle worthy of a Hollywood impresario.[7] Desperate to reverse a royal ban on their Brazilian trade, the city magistrates orchestrated a simulated battle between Tupinambá warriors and their Indian enemies, starring some fifty actual Brazilians and two hundred experienced Norman veterans of Brazil, who dressed down for their roles, so to speak. The royal couple, separately entertained, apparently expressed wonderment, and the exotic affair launched something of a fad in Atlantic ports. The near nudity of the participants apparently caused little stir, and it would scarcely have bothered a king famously charmed by representations of his mistress Diane de Poitiers bare-breasted as the goddess Diana. Henri, known also for his love of the exotic—he maintained a zoo of African animals—and of mock combat, succumbed to the enchantment of this gala.[8]

These events, as well as renewal of war with Spain in 1551, place in context the first French "colonial" ventures south of Canada. Expeditions to Brazil and Florida in the decade between 1555 and 1565 failed disastrously, with dramatic results for all subsequent efforts in the Caribbean basin. Ex post facto arguments about the reasons for these failures became inextricably bound up with the emerging religious hostilities. A veritable polemic ensued, which long obscured the narrative of events and the causes of failure to the participants and subsequent historians alike.[9]

There is a clear difference between the related but ultimately different processes of raiding and trading and those of settlement and colonization. Trading overseas required authorization from some state authority in the form of a passport, and, to distinguish it from piracy, raiding in wartime required a letter of marque. Colonization, defined as the creation of permanent settlements in another land, or at least the intent to do so, depended more heavily on royal approval. Only official charters could legitimize and regularize property relations in a colony and establish a legal framework for life. Also, the state (or crown) had to sanction, inter alia, the building of fortifications and declarations of war and peace with the aborigines. A French king might or might not be involved in the financing or coordinating of such enterprises, but colonization always was at least a semi-public affair. Governments naturally also wanted their share of any loot.

The establishment of fortified posts either to provide logistical support for military action or as entrepôts for trade with aboriginals lay somewhere on the spectrum between raiding and trading and colonization. Such enterprises typically had an all-male, heavily military composition, and established outposts in areas not particularly hospitable to food production. Even though historians have discussed the Brazil and Florida episodes as failed colonization efforts, it may be more helpful to view them as the establishment of fortified outposts whose goals were temporary in character. To be sure, had they been successful, such outposts might have been the embryos of further colonization.

The only clear motives for the 1555 French expedition to Brazil were to challenge Iberian claims to monopoly, to facilitate French trade along that coast, and to explore an overland route to the recently publicized treasures of the Incas. The latter motive seems geographically improbable to the modern eye, but South America was not then well known in France. Clearly, Henri II and later Admiral Coligny—the office of admiral of France was lucrative, because he ruled on passports for all ships leaving or entering France and shared in captured prizes—wanted to strike at the Iberians in their rich American lands, and apparently a number of proposals fermented after the renewal of war with Spain late in 1551. Henri also authorized corsairs to attack Spain in the Caribbean and elsewhere. A Spanish colonial official complained to Holy Roman Emperor Charles V that the French were "so powerful in these seas that a bird cannot fly without being seen [by them]."[10]

In 1555, Nicholas Durand de Villegaignon, vice-admiral of Brittany, a tough-minded knight of Malta (formally, the Knights of the Order of St. John of Jerusalem), led an expedition of some 600 men to Brazil.[11] A colony cannot be established with men alone. The king supported the plan with money and the loan of two ships. Probably, Coligny had less to do with the expedition in the initial stages than is usually assumed. This project was not intended to establish a Huguenot refuge overseas, certainly not by the fiercely orthodox Catholic monarch, not by an admiral of France occupied with other matters and who had not yet declared for Calvinist reform, and not by Villegaignon, who, although a one-time acquaintance of Calvin's at the University of Orléans, had ties to the fervently Catholic Guise family.[12] True, Villegaignon had long espoused reform of a corrupt church hierarchy. His chaplain, André Thevet, chronicler of the expedition's first months, was a Franciscan friar selected by the powerful cardinal of Lorraine, a prominent Guise. Probably, only a minority of Villegaignon's recruits sympathized with anti-papal Reformed Christianity (or perhaps with any form of Christianity), but religious divisions were not rigid at that time. The traditional but flawed idea that the enterprise intended to establish a Protestant refuge emerged only as part of a fierce debate in the 1560s and 1570s about which side had "lost" Brazil.

That Villegaignon's primary aim was to establish a fortified entrepôt to protect the dyewood trade is supported by the fact that he chose the site of the future Rio de Janeiro, which was so far to the south as to be an inconvenient place from which to attack the Spanish in the Caribbean. Sailing northwest to the Caribbean was in any case difficult because of the currents. Villegaignon's selection of the island of Guanabará, which had little fertile soil or fresh water, for his entrepôt is equally curious. No doubt, defense motivated this choice, not surprising for a knight of an order storied for its garrison island of Malta, which held back the Turkish Islamic tide. Did Villegaignon and his patrons in this secretive affair hope to create a powerful naval base from which to launch attacks on the weakly defended western coast of South America? Ville-gaignon did dispatch two reconnaissance expeditions north and then south toward the Rio de la Plata (between what are now Argentina and Uruguay). He initiated the construction of fortified posts in both direc-tions to support the extensive French commerce along a coast increas-ingly occupied by the Portuguese. Another hypothesis is that a strong naval base there would be able to threaten the legendary Portuguese East Indies' fleet.

The authoritarian, puritanical Villegaignon also feared, no doubt justly, that his men, who included a number of forcibly transported pris-oners (*forçats*), would be difficult to discipline. These coerced and con-scripted laborers, perhaps infected by tales of conquistador millionaires, might be lured into the interior to discover golden cities; or worse, to pursue native women, who, according to legends dating back to Amerigo Vespucci's popular letters, knew nothing of sexual restraint.[13] In later writings, Villegaignon depicted these aborigines as brutish animals.[14] His efforts to set his men to grinding work on fortifications and his harsh discipline naturally caused grumbling among people so far from home, who no doubt soon desired nothing other than to return there. Worse was to come.

Although Villegaignon dispatched his nephew to France to seek as-sistance, it was less than hoped for. Besieged by renewed war with Spain, Henri II could send only some 300 more men, six women, and provi-sions.[15] Some colonists and local French veterans of the logwood trade rebelled against Villegaignon and persuaded the disease-ridden coastal Tupinambá that Villegaignon had made them sick. Desperate, Ville-gaignon apparently wrote to John Calvin requesting support from Geneva and French Calvinists. Fourteen of the latter, including Jean de Léry, the future chronicler of the resulting episode, arrived at Guanabará in 1557 (since they stopped at Coligny's château before setting sail, his involvement can be assumed). According to Huguenot critics, Ville-gaignon warmly welcomed them. But he soon sparked religious polemics with his insistence on the Catholic doctrine of transubstantiation, anath-ema to Calvinists, who believed communion to be a spiritual remem-brance of the Last Supper, whereas Catholics believe, of course, that the bread and wine of the mass, while retaining their external physical ap-pearance, are transformed into the body and blood of Jesus through the medium of the priestly celebrant. If the Protestant version is trustworthy, Villegaignon's dogmatism was the doctrinal equivalent of waving a red cape in front of a bull. The Calvinists and some others were exiled to the mainland to live among the Tamoyo Indians (a Tupinambá tribe) until return passage to Europe could be secured. Five Calvinists returned to Guanabará rather than face the Atlantic Ocean in a crude boat. Two accepted Catholicism under duress, and the three who would not were shoved off a cliff into the sea. Hearing news of discontent at court, in 1559, Villegaignon returned home with assorted curiosities, including fifty Indians, to attract colonists and missionaries to his struggling colony. At just that time, the Portuguese were gearing up to liquidate "Lutheran pirates" who threatened their vital interests in Brazil and, perhaps, their famed East Indies' treasures.

Villegaignon found France in political and religious flux. Henri II negotiated a peace with Spain's Philip II (r. 1556–1598) at Cateau-Cambrésis in 1559. Admiral Coligny had converted to the Reformed religion after his capture in battle in 1557, although he did not publicize that fact until 1561. With peace, Henri II broadcast his intent to rid France of Huguenot "heretics" and thus was uninterested in reinforcing a colony reputed to harbor these outlaws; however, his accidental death changed everything. Not able in these circumstances to get support for Guanabará, Villegaignon remained in France and soon became involved in the religious struggles that would torment France for thirty years. He sided with his patrons the Guise family and the ultra Catholics and engaged in a war of pamphlets over who was responsible for the Brazilian fiasco. In effect, he agreed with the Protestants that he had staunchly maintained Catholic orthodoxy at Guanabará, blaming them, of course, for weakening and undermining the enterprise. Hindsight was clearly at work here, for how else to explain Villegaignon's letter to Calvin, the pope of Geneva? Villegaignon was probably covering his tracks.[16]

The Portuguese destruction of the French fortress at Guanabará in 1560 did not discourage Coligny when he reentered the good graces of the monarchy after the death of Henri and then that of the sickly François II (r. 1559–1560).[17] The ten-year-old Charles IX (r. 1560–1574) succeeded, and his wily mother, Catherine de' Medici, became regent. Coligny's star gradually ascended in the 1560s, and by 1570, he had become the indispensable Huguenot leader. However, in 1562, he could not count on royal support of overseas activities, because Catherine feared angering the Spaniards over what she viewed as less than critical issues. Coligny and other Huguenot leaders apparently believed, however, that an anti-Hispanic crusade overseas would unite all except the most "papist" French and thus mitigate religious differences.[18] This and no doubt other motives explain Coligny's promotion during 1562–65 of a primarily Huguenot outpost in "Florida," astride the crucial shipping lanes of the annual Spanish treasure fleet. He knew Philip II could not tolerate this breach of his claimed monopoly in such a strategic region.

Coligny probably did not have as a primary goal the use of Florida as a Huguenot refuge, as many have argued, because the rapidly growing Reform movement instilled hope of triumph in France itself. The nearly all-male composition of these expeditions, except for the last, also argues against the refuge thesis, and indeed calls into question the appropriateness of applying the term "colony." The personnel were much more appropriate to a conquistador or corsair operation than to a permanent settlement, although artisans and a few women accompanied the 1564 and 1565 expeditions. It is doubtful that participants believed they had committed to a permanent stay overseas.

Led by a respected Norman captain, the Huguenot Jean de Ribaut, a scourge of Spain, the first reconnaissance expedition left before religious war broke out in 1562. Ribaut sailed directly across the Atlantic in order, he claimed in his 1563 account, to give the Spaniards no pretext for reprisals. However, his 150 mostly Huguenot men were armed to the teeth. Making landfall near the future site of Saint Augustine in northeast Florida, Ribaut cruised up the coast claiming lands for France and establishing friendly relations with indigenes. Before returning to France, he left between twenty-six and thirty volunteers at Charlesfort (on present-day Parris Island, South Carolina), the remains of which were located in the 1990s. This opening gambit appears to have been a brilliant success.[19]

Ribaut's crew returned to a France engulfed in religious combat, and they participated in the failed Huguenot effort to lift the royalist Catholic siege of Dieppe. Ribaut took refuge in London and wrote his account, which ironically played a role in arousing English interest in "Virginia." Neither he nor his patron Coligny, hard pressed by Catholic forces, could send help to Charlesfort. Having in typical fashion alienated the local indigenes, their sole source of food, the desperate colonists constructed a rickety vessel and sailed home in extraordinary misery. According to accounts, episodes of survivor cannibalism occurred among these starving men.

After a truce in the religious wars in 1563, Coligny wished to follow up the earlier expedition, and with Ribaut imprisoned for refusing to help the English colonize Florida, he chose René de Goulaine de Lau-donnière to lead a new venture. Ribaut's deputy on the first expedition, the Huguenot Laudonnière, took the now traditional southern route through the Lesser Antilles with some 300 people, including four women. In an augur of things to come, his men undermined the initial hospitality of the Island Caribs at Dominica by stealing food from their gardens. Carib poisoned arrows hastened their departure. The expedition headed to the Saint John's River, near present-day Jacksonville, Florida, where the Indians had graciously received the earlier expedition. An interpreter in 1562 had heard from them that the legendary golden city of Cibola lay not far inland. The French also searched for the legendary river Jordan and its fountain of youth, products of the Spaniards' fertile imaginations.

The ensuing story is one all too familiar to historians of European imperialism. After building Fort Caroline, named optimistically after the indifferent monarch Charles IX, Laudonnière proved unable to make settlers out of his would-be conquistadors.[20] Shortages of supplies made them dependent on Indian allies (Timuacans), the price of whose support was French participation in their sundry local wars, and whose surplus of maize was insufficient to feed the French.[21] A bout of what may have been malaria further sapped the small settlement. Laudonnière's men, some of whom had criminal records, only wanted to search for gold, silver, and gems, and, not locating any, they turned their sights south to the Spanish Caribbean. Given their background and prevailing ideas about venturing to America, their actions hardly surprise. Laudonnière was unable to prevent desperadoes from taking ships southwards to plunder Spaniards. But the hunters soon became the hunted, and after capture and undergoing the usual coercion, they indicated the location of the French fort. These pirates undermined Catherine's claim to the Spanish ambassador that the expedition's purpose was only to settle unoccupied territory. Soon enough the news reached an enraged Philip II, who designated an experienced sea captain, Pedro Menéndez de Aviles, to lead the empire in striking back.

Menéndez had gained fame fighting French corsairs. In 1549, he had bested and killed Jean Alphonse, famous for his role as pilot in the Roberval expedition to Canada in the 1540s; for good measure, he killed Alphonse's revenge-minded son in another engagement.[22] Named captain-general of the Indies fleet, Menéndez in 1558 fought unsuccessfully to resupply Spanish forces in Flanders by capturing the harbor of Calais. Successfully defending against him there was the intrepid Huguenot captain Ribaut.[23] In the early 1560s, Menéndez's son Juan, captain of a fleet leaving New Spain for home, disappeared in a storm in the Bahamas channel. A desire to search for his son and Philip's interest in hunting down French "Lutheran" pirates resulted in a contract (*asiento*) commissioning the father as *adelantado* of Florida. Charged with assuming control and developing "Florida," Menéndez's most important duty was to root out Gallic trespassers mercilessly.[24]

Meanwhile, Ribaut had arrived back in France, and Coligny engaged him to convoy hundreds of civilian recruits to Fort Caroline. Numerous delays allowed news of Menéndez's preparations to reach Coligny, persuading him to change the character of the French expedition. About 500 heavily armed soldiers now joined the civilians.[25] Perhaps the difficult combats of 1562–63 had turned the admiral's thoughts toward establishing a Huguenot refuge, but as a minority of the expedition's participants professed Catholicism, there was no religious litmus test applied. Although aware of Menéndez's preparations, Ribaut spent fifteen days meandering along the Florida coast. No one exactly knows why, and we have only Laudonnière's hostile account blaming Ribaut for the French debacle.[26] Meanwhile, storms had dispersed Menéndez's large fleet, and he arrived in Florida with only five ships.[27]

At Fort Caroline, Laudonnière and his desperate people had received a temporary reprieve when the famous corsair and slave trader John Hawkins found the colony and relieved it with fresh supplies. Elizabeth I had requested him to do so on his return from a raiding and trading expedition to Spanish America. Hawkins gifted his French co-religionists with a boat to return to France. As they prepared their departure, however, which included dismantling the fort, Ribaut's ships appeared on the horizon.[28]

The usually accepted denouement to the Florida affair is not necessarily historically accurate. Shortly after Ribaut's arrival at Fort Caroline, the would-be imperial avenger Menéndez appeared. He sailed into the midst of Ribaut's fleet outside the sandbar at the Saint John's River outlet. Ribaut cut his cables and escaped to sea. Menéndez withdrew his forces to Saint Augustine's harbor, where he frantically built fortifications of mud and wood. Ignoring Laudonnière's pleas, Ribaut assembled almost all the soldiers and set off in pursuit of Menéndez. Confronted with the latter's rudimentary fortifications, he then gave chase to some ships Menéndez had dispatched to Cuba, but a sudden tempest wracked and dispersed the French fleet.[29] Menéndez boldly marched his men north in extremely stormy conditions through swampy land and attacked Fort Caroline, achieving complete surprise; of some 150 French there, only Laudonnière, the well-known artist Jacques Le Moyne de Morgues, the future chronicler of the expedition Nicholas Le Challeux, and a few others escaped to tell the story. Protestant accounts, hyperbolic if not totally untrue, claimed that men, women, and babies were all put to the sword.

Ribaut's ships had all capsized, and the survivors were stranded in three groups at Cape Canaveral and the Matanzas and Ponce de Leon inlets. Informed by native allies, the Spaniards located Ribaut and scattered shipwrecked survivors. According to the French Protestant version of events, Menéndez coldly massacred all the prisoners, except the Catholics, despite vague promises not to do so. Of approximately 1,000 French in Florida, probably three-quarters perished; according to Protestant historiography, they perished as martyrs. Recently, historians have successfully challenged this. It seems that fewer than half died at Spanish hands.[30]

This affair became a cause célèbre in some French circles, especially when the weak king and Catherine felt unable to redeem French honor at the cost of war against Spain. Huguenot accounts by Laudonnière and Nicholas Le Challeux painted a grisly story of Spanish barbarism and contributed much to the idea of irredeemable Hispanic brutality, or what is called the Black Legend.[31] Although only Le Challeux (not present at the massacre) told the tale of Ribaut's head (or, alternatively, his facial mask) having been dispatched as a trophy to Philip II, it was endlessly repeated in Huguenot and anti-Hispanic propaganda.[32] Protestants, and some moderate Catholics, advertised these stories of Spanish perfidy to attack Philip and his French Catholic allies. When the Catholic captain Dominique de Gourgues of Gascony led raids on weak Spanish forts in Florida with a crew of mainly Huguenot seamen, they exacted terrible eye-for-eye revenge based on the sensational French accounts. Combined with the Brazil debacle, whose embers were rekindled by André Thevet's bitter anti-Calvinist account (1575) and the almost immediate riposte by Jean de Léry (1578),[33] ideological war raged over who was responsible for France's humiliations overseas.

The legacies of these expeditions and the bitter debates that ensued between Catholic and Huguenot polemicists undermined France's colonial prospects for decades or longer. First, although Huguenots scored points in these debates, their enthusiasm for America as a possible refuge diminished. Some came to believe that these overseas efforts had been misguided in the first place, because every man was needed for the struggle at home.[34] To the chronicler of the Florida fiasco, Le Challeux, God had punished his people for abandoning home and country.[35] The Edict of Nantes of 1598 seemed to secure the Huguenots' future place in France. Although Huguenots as individuals would later establish themselves in the Americas, and notably in the Caribbean area, this minority lost interest in America as a refuge because of the sixteenth-century failures. Thus, Huguenots never played the crucial role in the French colonies that Calvinists such as the New England Puritans and Pilgrims did in the development of English America.

A second consequence of the mid-century disasters was to promulgate the notion that the French character was not appropriate to colonization. Frenchmen were brilliant sailors, explorers, corsairs, and adventurers, it was argued, but too mercurial for the lengthy labor required to reap the fruits of colonization. To cite only one example, the Huguenot minister of Henri IV (r. 1589–1610) Maximilien Béthune, duc de Sully declared that the French did not possess "either the perseverance or the foresight" to sustain colonial projects.[36] Seventeenth-century advocates of colonization beat their heads futilely against this received wisdom, and future French colonial setbacks would make it a self-fulfilling prophecy. Although modern historians look askance at explanations emphasizing supposedly innate national characteristics, contemporaries took it for granted that they profoundly influenced historical actions and opportunities.

Ebbs and Flows: From the 1570s to the 1610s

It has often been asserted that a hiatus in French maritime activities occurred after the Florida debacle until the beginning of the seventeenth century, and there is a grain of truth in that. After all, bursts of religious war alternated with cold war truces down to 1598, when the Edict of Nantes concluded religious peace. Because the Huguenot faction usually held a weaker hand in these years, and because it controlled many of the maritime ports, proposals for colonial adventures must have appeared diversionary to Huguenot leaders. Nevertheless, trading and raiding activities continued, especially during truces. Evidence indicates a continuing interest in African commerce, as demonstrated by a famous episode in 1571. A Dieppe vessel unloaded a cargo of African slaves at Bordeaux, which galvanized the *parlement* of Guyenne to free them, based on its famous judgment that "there are no slaves in France."[37]

Just as the failure of the Cartier-Roberval expeditions to the Saint Lawrence in the 1530s and early 1540s did not mean the end of fishing voyages to the region, the liquidation of Villegaignon's colony did not mean the demise of the Brazil dyewood trade, merely a shift away from Portuguese Rio de Janeiro to northeastern Brazil. For example, a La Rochelle expedition in 1581 explored the Paraíba area of northern Brazil.[38] Rouen merchants, who had dominated French-American exchanges up to the 1570s, did reduce their investments in this area. However, Gayle Brunelle argues convincingly that they employed Spanish merchants or naturalized French agents in Seville to trade their linens "legally" to Spanish America in return for dyes, hides, and, of course, silver.[39] In continental North America, French traders and corsairs, who often rested and refreshed themselves in the river mouths of what would one day be the Carolinas and Georgia, started a lucrative exchange with the local aborigines. The commodity they desired, sassafras bark, brought a high price in Europe because of its reputation as a tonic against the ravages of syphilis.[40] Finally, some twenty to thirty, mostly Huguenot corsairs per year departed for the "Indies" in these decades of nominal peace with Spain.[41] Any injury to Spaniards in America would make Philip's continuing support of the Guises more difficult. The proceeds helped finance the Huguenot Cause in these difficult years.[42]

A minor revival of state involvement in Atlantic projects ensued after a religious truce of 1576. The last Valois king, the eccentric, perhaps unstable Henri III (r. 1574–1589), usually favored a coalition of moderate Catholics and Huguenots. The death of the Portuguese king Sebastian without heir in 1578 created a struggle for the succession, which Philip II won, leading to a Hapsburg union of Spain and Portugal that lasted until 1640. In 1579, two years after Francis Drake left on his famous voyage pillaging Spanish treasure around the world, Catherine de' Medici designated her cousin Filippo Strozzi to sail on a secret mission to Brazil with the title of French viceroy of that land. In 1582, he led a strong fleet of fifty-five ships and an international force of 6,000 men to the Azores to support Don António, the prior of Prato, the pretender to the Portuguese throne resident in those islands.

"Western designs" were in the air in Protestant Europe, and a host of propaganda works appeared in these years, including numerous translations of Bartolomé de Las Casas's fiery condemnation of his fellow Spaniards for their vicious treatment of Native Americans. And can it be pure coincidence that Jean de Léry's history of Villegaignon in Brazil first appeared in 1578? As it transpired, a Spanish fleet caught and defeated Strozzi in the Azores, and the victorious Spanish commander, Álvaro de Bazán, marqués de Santa Cruz de Mudela, treated Strozzi and other prisoners, mostly Catholics, in the manner of Menéndez. Lacking any official French protection, the mortally wounded Strozzi was simply thrown overboard from a Spanish ship.

With Philip firmly on the Portuguese throne, an opportunity had passed, but the 1580s nonetheless saw intense French activity in the area of Brazil north of Pernambuco, where the French established alliances with the Potiguar, another Tupinambá tribe. That area and farther north to Maranhâo were sites of continuous French trading.

When the Huguenot leader Navarre became legal if not uncontested heir to the French throne in 1584 (Henri III remained without male offspring), the last and worst phase of the religious wars unfolded. The House of Guise and international Catholicism could not tolerate a Bourbon prince of the Huguenot faith on the throne. With the Spanish naval buildup in the mid 1580s in preparation for the Armada against England, French maritime forces stayed close to port. In 1588, Navarre offered Elizabeth maritime assistance against the Armada.[43]

Bloody and bitter years of internecine conflict, marked by the assassinations of leaders such as Henri III, consumed France and quite naturally produced a decline in maritime activity.[44] Henri IV, when he came to the throne, faced a powerful and determined Catholic League (organized 1585), supported covertly and then overtly by Spanish gold and troops. By converting to Catholicism in 1593, by his charisma, and by a liberal use of bribes he could not afford, the able Henri slowly reconciled his opponents and rallied his countrymen to war again Spain in 1595. Three years later the foes of a hundred years' war (1494–1598) concluded the Treaty of Vervins just months before Philip's death.

Although his parsimonious minister Sully expressed doubt about colonial projects, Henri IV attempted to stimulate fresh ventures in many parts of the world as part of a plan to rebuild the French economy. In the American Tropics, the focus was the region between northeastern Brazil and the Orinoco River. Discussions at Vervins about America had been unfruitful, resulting in a "we agree to disagree" official silence. But like his predecessors, Henri acted on the premise that lands not colonized by the self-proclaimed owners were open to the taker.

Since the Portuguese continued to fortify much of the Brazilian coast and treated captured French merchants as pirates, the regions adjacent to the wide mouth of the Amazon alone remained secure to French traders. In 1602, the French king commissioned René Montbarrot as lieutenant general of "Guiane," who in turn dispatched the Huguenot Daniel de La Ravardière and other veterans of Brazil to explore the area. La Ravardière's 1604 reconnaissance expedition of some 400 men included the king's collector of natural curiosities, Jean Mocquet, and was deemed promising.[45] In 1605, La Ravardière received the commission of lieutenant general "of America, between the Amazon and the island of Trinidad."

Why the interest, even fascination, with Guiana then and for many decades later? Although his was a voyage of reconnaissance, La Ravardière left some men along the coast to plant tobacco, which signals one reason. First introduced from Spain into France in the 1550s by Jean Nicot (hence the genus *Nicotiana* and our word "nicotine"), the smoking addiction gathered pace slowly but steadily, and by the early 1600s, the leaf fetched a promising price. After the addicted smoker Sir Walter Ralegh undertook a voyage to Guiana in 1595, his propaganda account of it created something of a sensation.[46] Ralegh claimed that the golden king El Dorado reigned in the city of Manoa not far up some Guiana river. This mythical city appears on all maps of that era. El Dorado and Manoa started to compete for celebrity with Potosí, the famed silver mountain of Peru. What a panacea Manoa's conquest would be for the sorry state of the French treasury. The search for tropical dyewoods, as well as the newer attraction of sugarcane, must also be considered as motives. La Ravardière's expedition also searched for an American type of aloe (*Agave americana*, the so-called American aloe), supposed to be a cure for migraine headaches, and brought back 70,000 pounds of it.[47] The strategic potential of an area straddling the Iberian possessions is apparent. The heightened English and Dutch activity in the Greater Caribbean, stimulated also by the growing volume of Brazilian sugar reaching Europe, also piqued French interest.[48]

La Ravardière explored the possibilities of trade with various indigenous groups. An intelligent man, he refused the repeated requests of a powerful Yapoco chief to join in a war against his enemies the Galibis (mainland Caribs) in order to explore potential benefits of trade with the latter. Despite this refusal, the chief allowed his nephew to sail with the French, and the nephew continued on to France. As the expedition's chronicler Jean Mocquet tells the story, the young Indian quickly tired of life in France and managed to get passage back to South America. However, the ship went to Maragnan (Maranhaô), a long way from his Guiana home. He caught a ship back to France, only to be seized by pirates. Somehow, he reached France and went to see Madame de La Ravardière in the western part of France.

He was well received, but one day Madame asked for his assistance in retrieving a pig, which had fallen into the château's moat, but he refused what he considered a servile task. Gravely insulted when Madame said harsh words to him, our picaresque hero shipped from La Rochelle to Paris. There, he encountered his old acquaintance Jean Mocquet, who arranged a visit with the young king Louis XIII. Our knowledge of his exotic odyssey ends with his return to La Ravardière's estate.[49]

Named lieutenant general of Guiane after his return, La Ravardière embarked on another reconnaissance in 1609 but focused this time on the Brazilian coast. It is not certain why he did so, but in any event these territories claimed by Portugal (whose king was the Spaniard Philip III, r. 1598–1621) were much closer to the rich sugar coast from Pernambuco south to Bahia (San Salvador). Portuguese Brazil was in the middle of a sugar boom in 1610, making it certain that the Iberians would respond to French encroachments. La Ravardière's goal apparently was to stake a claim somewhere in or near the Amazon River valley.[50]

While the project was in its infancy, the seemingly indomitable Henri IV fell to the knife of a fanatical Catholic cleric in 1610. Succeeding was the eight-year old Louis XIII (r. 1610–43), the product of a loveless marriage of that aging gallant Navarre with Marie de Médicis.[51] The neglected Marie raised Louis as a strict Catholic, and although she reaffirmed the Edict of Nantes, she also entered into marriage negotiations with Philip III in 1612 to gain the hand of the Hapsburg princess for her son. Huguenots and other haters of Spain were displeased.

Perhaps because of these events, the proposed expedition took on a more distinctly Catholic and evangelical flavor. Marie renewed the office of La Ravardière on condition that he include Catholic associates, of whom the most important was Admiral François de Rasilly.[52] In 1611, Rasilly recruited Henry de Harlay, sieur de Sancy, reputedly rich as

Croesus. The admiral also appealed to the Capuchin fathers for missionaries to convert aborigines. He met with an enthusiastic response, with some forty monks volunteering. These Capuchins were a reformed, very strict branch of the Franciscan order, which had emerged in Italy (1536) at the dawn of the Catholic Reformation. Along with the Jesuits, the Capuchins were shock troops in the movement to heal the Catholic Church and restore it to its universal dominance. Also like the Jesuits, these friars took their evangelical mission seriously; unlike the Jesuits, they disdained material goods, even sandals. Marie de Médicis supported the Capuchin mission despite her perennial shortage of funds, which suggests that at least in 1611 and 1612, committed Catholic supporters of the project did not anticipate the fierce Iberian opposition to come.

In 1612, Rasilly, La Ravardière, and Sancy conducted an expedition to the large island in the Bay of Maranhâo, some 300 miles south of the Amazon, which contemporary Frenchmen called Maragnan (currently, Ilha de Marejó).[53] There, at Saint Louis (currently, Sâo Luiz), the French constructed a fort adjacent to villages of the diseased remnants of those old Indian allies the Tupinambá, who had fled from their perennial Portuguese enemies. Reconnaissance expeditions sought to locate grounds suitable for growing sugarcane and tobacco. Rasilly and La Ravardière pursued an enlightened policy toward their Indian allies and intervened to settle tribal disputes. In his inaugural speech to the indigenes, Rasilly insisted that the sole purpose of the expedition was their salvation.[54] The outlook appeared bright for the establishment of a vital colony.

Meanwhile, Rasilly and a sick Capuchin, Claude d'Abbeville, returned to France (late 1612) to generate support, bringing a load of dyewood, the usual exotica, such as parrots, and six Indian protégés. (It should not be supposed that the latter had been kidnapped; although Jacques Cartier kidnapped Iroquoians in the 1530s, in general, the French eschewed the practice, whereas the English engaged in it for centuries.) Rasilly choreographed a brilliant spectacle at Paris. The young Louis XIII and his mother took part in the very public baptism of the three young *sauvages* who survived the ordeal of the trip and the climate. The Tupinambá captain Itapoucou harangued the king and the court. Published letters and, in 1614, Claude's interesting book extolled the land, the equatorial climate—a veritable Eden—and the innocent Tupinambá awaiting salvation. In all, some fifteen books, pamphlets, and letters were written to promote this expedition. Apparently, the queen-regent had as yet no reservations, and to support eleven more Capuchins at Maragnan and send reinforcements, she found 18,000 livres.[55] The surviving Tupinambá were made chevaliers de Saint Louis (knights of St. Louis) and returned to their homeland, accompanied by French brides.[56]

In 1614, storm clouds gathered on the horizon. The very publicity that excited Paris elicited increasingly vocal protests from Madrid and Lisbon. A Portuguese force under Jerônimo de Albuquerque started preparations for a riposte. At court, to resolve desperate financial problems and growing tensions between Huguenots and pro-Hispanic Catholics, Marie de Médicis found it necessary to call a meeting of the Estates-General, which dissolved in bitter name-calling. The Jesuit-led first estate, the clergy, could not win the registration of Tridentine decrees, that is, those passed long ago by the Council of Trent (1545–63) but not accepted by the French national (Gallican) Church. Far from alleviating confessional disputes, the Estates meetings gave them a public forum presaging a renewal of armed conflict.

Events at Maragnan mirrored those at home. Disputes arose between the Capuchins and the Huguenot commander La Ravardière, and most of the former quit the colony. Their loud complaints at court undermined Marie's support. But it was the Spanish marriage that led to royal withdrawal of support. This new hostility resulted in the order to destroy the Capuchin Yves d'Evreux's newly printed book about the colony; more important, the colonists were now on their own.[57] In a badly planned maneuver, La Ravardière's force, including 2,000 Tupinambá bowmen, attacked the Portuguese, but they were badly rebuffed.[58] A truce was called, and both sides agreed to consult their respective courts about how to proceed. Largely abandoned by Native American allies and despairing of receiving support from France, La Ravardière capitulated at the end of 1615. So the last major French colonial project in what is now Brazil ended ignominiously. The feared La Ravardière, as great a hater of Spain as Sir Walter Ralegh and probably a greater threat, languished in jail at Lisbon for four years. The French court did not lift a finger to help him. In 1624, Louis XIII named him lieutenant general for lands between the Amazon and Trinidad, but La Ravardière burned his bridges by joining the Huguenot rebellion against the king.

Preludes to Colonization, 1615–1625

During and after the fiasco at Maragnan, small groups of Frenchmen without publicity or support from the court attempted to establish themselves along the Guiana coast, especially on the island of Cayenne. Shadowy evidence places some French there before 1620, probably to plant tobacco. By some reports, mainland Carib Indians, whom the French called Galibis, destroyed their fort.[59] In 1623, a Huguenot group led by Jesse de Forest, under the auspices of the newly created Dutch West India Company (1621), tried but failed to settle at the Oyapock River. A remnant of this colony was later involved in the founding of New Amsterdam, the future New York City.

Almost simultaneously, some Normans settled at the Sinnamary River, but after antagonizing the Galibis, they found a retreat on the Lesser Antillean island of Saint-Christophe (now St. Kitts).[60] There they lived in relative peace with other European squatters and a small Carib population. These Guiana fugitives would before long (1625) give succor to a badly damaged ship and crew of fellow Normans led by Pierre Blain d'Esnambuc, the "founding father" of the French Antilles. He found Saint-Christophe charming, got on well with the English leader, Thomas Warner, and resolved to return to Normandy to recruit servants and capital.[61]

French corsairs on many occasions had rested and refreshed themselves in the Lesser Antilles. Jean-Pierre Moreau and other scholars have documented significant numbers of these episodes. One 1610 contract was signed between a ship captain of Le Havre and his associates for trade with the Indians of Trinidad, Martinique, and Tortuga, opposite modern Haiti.[62] Trinidad at this time was a large supplier of tobacco to northern European interlopers; indeed, Englishmen called tobacco "Trinidado." Spanish archives contain alarming reports about the frequency of French (as well as Dutch and English) activities at Trinidad.[63] Especially at Trinidad and Tortuga, French shippers could easily turn from Indian barter to trading with Spaniards or to raiding Spanish coastal shipping.

The leaders of the first colonial expedition to Saint-Christophe had extensive experience in Caribbean waters. In a contract of 1619 between d'Esnambuc and a Rouen *armateur*, the former received a commission as a privateer to scour the seas from West Africa to Brazil and beyond.[64] In 1624, Urbain de Roissey was "cautioned" to pay customs duties on fifty-four "casket, pipes and barrels full of sugar." He had most likely robbed a Portuguese ship to obtain this amount of the white gold.[65] These corsair jaunts were not precursors to colonization, but in the 1620s d'Esnambuc and his backers saw an opportunity to plant tobacco and take advantage of rising prices for the weed. Colonization meant transporting free colonists and indentured servants and planting food crops at Saint-Christophe.

By the early 1620s, growing Huguenot antagonism toward the French court, deemed too submissive to Spain, stimulated corsair enterprises out of the Norman ports and La Rochelle. At the very same time, Puritan outrage at James I's execution of Ralegh (1618) after his failed voyage to Guiana generated a wave of English prowling in the Caribbean. Simultaneously, international religious tensions accelerated dramatically in the years 1618–21, when the Austrian and Spanish Hapsburgs declared war on Calvinists in Bohemia and the upper Rhine and renewed the struggle with the Dutch Netherlands. Both English Puritans and French Huguenots understood the gravity of the situation, but their pro-Spanish monarchs refused to become involved.

When d'Esnambuc and Roissey debarked at Le Havre (Normandy) in 1626 with a cargo of Saint-Christophe tobacco and the usual exotic curiosities, they fortuitously encountered agents of Armand du Plessis, Cardinal de Richelieu, the chief minister of Louis XIII from 1624 to 1642. These servants of the cardinal were François de Rasilly's brother Isaac (also a veteran of Maragnan, 1612–16), who advised Richelieu on maritime affairs, and Jean Cavelet, a local merchant client of Richelieu's. They provided the captains with access to the minister, who was then engaged in a project for maritime reform and renewal. Although circumstances prevented him from showing overt hostility to Spain, the cardinal's anti-Hapsburg proclivities made him receptive to colonial projects in the "Spanish Caribbean." D'Esnambuc and Roissey not only wanted official protection; they needed legalization of their land claims. Soon they and Richelieu joined ranks to form a small, little-publicized, semipublic chartered company, Compagnie de Saint-Christophe, to colonize Saint-Christophe and adjacent islands.[66]

D'Esnambuc and Roissy returned to Normandy and Brittany to recruit colonists (*habitants*) and indentured servants (*engagés*). In the difficult economic decade of the 1620s, the recruiters had few problems signing up some 500 servants, especially because the captains already knew many of them. After a long and difficult voyage, the ships arrived at Saint-Christophe in 1627. The French had come to stay in the Caribbean; the precolonial era was over.

From early in the sixteenth century on, French mariners became familiar with the exotic world of the Caribbean, with its strange flora and fauna and even stranger indigenous inhabitants. Pirates and privateers traversed the waters of the American Tropics in search of Iberian prizes. These French marauders put ashore on a variety of islands and along the mainland to careen and repair their vessels and to take on fresh water and viands, such as turtles and feral pigs. Some others did so after suffering ship damage. These European intrusions only marginally affected Caribbean lands, except for the unknown impact of Old World diseases on the Island Caribs.

For almost a century prior to successful colonization in the Greater Caribbean, with or without official support, Frenchmen challenged Iberian claims of hegemony in the Americas. Privateers in search of prizes; more prosaic merchants in search of trade with indigenous populations for dyewoods, sassafras, tobacco, tortoise shell, and showy birds such as toucans; adventurers seeking to establish fortified outposts on the margins of Brazil or in the strategic location of "Florida"; all these maritime endeavors and more characterized the hundred years preceding French occupation of part of the tiny island of Saint-Christophe starting in 1625. They provide the proper context for the emergence of a French Caribbean.

CHAPTER THREE

Frontiers of Fortune?
The Painful Era of Settlement, 1620s to 1640s

The early years of colonization are always agonizing ones, albeit subject to romantic retrospection by the grateful descendants of rugged pioneers. If "strange" peoples inhabit the desired site for settlement, as was the case with most islands in the Greater Caribbean region, conflict almost always overwhelms any initial intent of friendly cohabitation. French colonists, unfamiliar with the Tropics, had to endure "starving times." A different disease environment took a toll, not least psychological, induced by the unfamiliarity of illnesses and the lack of known remedies. The attempt to plant colonies when the mother country was enduring exceptionally trying times exacerbated the pains of the colonial project. All these conditions prevailed during French colonization of tropical America.

This chapter examines France and its embryonic colonies from the 1620s through the 1640s, when the French monarchy sought to develop Caribbean colonies. Louis XIII inaugurated semi-official colonial and commercial company monopolies over various areas and trades in the Atlantic world, a cheap method of inspiring colonial and mercantile development while maintaining royal suzerainty. At brief intervals in the 1620s and 1630s, Cardinal Richelieu also used his power and patronage to stimulate colonial and commercial activity. The monarchy awarded patent letters of lieutenant general to company-appointed governors of various lands, thus holding them responsible for military and security affairs. The king insisted that the Custom of Paris, the preferred royal legal system, be employed in the colonies. Monarchs initiated the sending of missionaries (principally Dominicans, Capuchins, and Jesuits) to evangelize the indigenes and serve Catholic colonists. However, the French Bourbons had only limited success in controlling colonial developments, although arguably more so than did the early Stuart kings of Britain (James I, r. 1603–1625; Charles I, r. 1625–1649).

Island colonists proffered obeisance to Louis XIII (r. 1610–1643) and then to the young Louis XIV (1638–1715; r. 1643–1715) as well as to their famous ministers, Cardinals Richelieu (1624–1642) and Mazarin (1643–1661), but their lives testified strongly to their desire for freedom. Miserable conditions in France, the state priority given to European wars and negligible enforcement tools, given the long distances separating Paris and the Caribbean, undermined efforts to enforce the royal will. A weak royal navy and irregular mercantile contact between French and Caribbean ports made communications difficult throughout the century. Thus, the traditional thesis—that state control characterized French colonization, as opposed to a more laissez-faire English model—needs reevaluation.[1]

Louis XIII and Richelieu: Policy and Pragmatism, 1624–1642

Richelieu's maritime and colonial initiatives were only one aspect of his drive to valorize the Bourbon dynasty. The cardinal deemed reputation to be the bedrock of a powerful, respected monarchy. Threats to the crown's internal stability, such as those by the rebellious Huguenots (1620–29) or by over-mighty nobles, had to be crushed without pity. Harassment of French coastal commerce had to be punished, and thus Richelieu started building the modern French navy.[2] The humbling of Hapsburg Spain was his ultimate goal, which explains his support for Caribbean colonies. He had only peripheral interest in their economic potential—tobacco, turtle shell, parrots; rather, he viewed Caribbean settlements as a means to threaten the fabulous American treasures of Philip IV (r. 1621–1665), which fueled Spain's imperialism in Europe.

When Richelieu became first minister in 1624, threats in Europe were uppermost on his agenda. At this stage of the Thirty Years' War (1618–48), the Austrian and Spanish Hapsburgs had made significant progress against Protestants in the Netherlands and in the Holy Roman Empire. The nonhistorian might assume that the successes of his fellow Catholic Hapsburgs would have caused Richelieu great joy, but that was far from the case. France had fought "Hapsburg encirclement" for over a century, and only the most zealous of French Catholics rejoiced in Hapsburg triumphs. A serious Huguenot revolt prevented French intervention against the Hapsburgs. The most Richelieu could attempt in the 1620s was to contest Spanish control of the crucial Alpine passes, the lifelines (or chokepoints, from a French perspective) of Spanish armies on their way to the Netherlands. But even these initiatives enraged devout French Catholics (*les dévots*), so the cardinal constantly had to reassure Louis XIII. Richelieu also had to overcome troubles with the Huguenots, whose legal right to maintain fortified strongholds made them formidable. The walled city of La Rochelle on the Atlantic coast was the powerful center of French Protestantism.

In 1626, Richelieu initiated a reform program focused on the revitalization of the French navy and, more generally, of France's maritime commerce. Richelieu's advisors, such as the knight of Malta Isaac de Rasilly, painted a somber picture. Only one French ship in the Atlantic could challenge the heavyweight Spanish galleons or the sleeker English men-of-war. Foreign corsairs attacked French merchantmen within sight of their home ports. Barbary pirates savaged French Mediterranean commerce with impunity. The paralysis of maritime France meant that merchants found it safer to engage foreigners, especially the English and Dutch, to handle French commerce. The Dutch transported French salt and wines to the Lowlands and the Baltic and were the real owners of many commercial firms in France's ports, with French nominal owners serving as their agents. The Dutch East and West India Companies were the envy of Europe.

Richelieu moved as quickly as he could in tradition-bound France to overcome these weaknesses. Offices of state were routinely bought and sold, thus becoming the private property of powerful individuals, and Richelieu had the crown purchase the office of the Admiralty of France, which controlled the Atlantic and Channel ports (the west, or Ponant, as opposed to the Mediterranean, or Levant). Simultaneously, Richelieu adopted the title of *grand maître et surintendant de la navigation* (grand master and superintendent of navigation), which gave him authority over maritime France.[3]

Without a strong navy, dreams of colonial empire were chimerical. A navy is not built with legal documents, however. Over the next decade, the cardinal ordered surveys of port facilities, authorized funds for upkeep of shipyards, and issued new naval regulations. He imported skilled workers, ordered ships from the Netherlands, and revitalized French shipbuilding. By 1642, he had increased the naval budget from one and a half million *livres tournois* (hereafter l.t.) to around seven million, giving France some forty galleys in the Mediterranean and fifty large, bluewater ships in the Atlantic.[4] In the short run, however, for the successful siege of La Rochelle in 1628, he was fortunate to get assistance from the Knights of Malta and from the Dutch, the beneficiaries of surreptitious French support against Spain. When the 1629 Peace of Alais reduced Huguenot independence and removed the threat of La Rochelle corsairs, Richelieu could move forward with his naval program.

Many other problems also plagued France in the crucial years 1629 and 1630, however. Armies loyal to the Austrian Hapsburgs routed the German and Danish Protestant opposition and reached the Baltic. The French and Spanish were conducting proxy wars for control of vital Alpine passes. To make matters worse, in 1628, the untried English King Charles I (r. 1625–49) declared war on France, which lasted four years. Within France, in 1630, a major coup against Richelieu by zealous Catholics nearly succeeded. After this close call, his position became much more secure. Soon thereafter the good news arrived that Sweden's dynamic King Gustav Adolph, secretly subsidized by French gold, had landed in the Holy Roman Empire to oppose the triumphant Hapsburg imperial forces.

Richelieu's highest priority in the 1630s was to engage the Habsburgs in a continentwide struggle. He could not, as the Dutch did, pursue a Periclean defensive strategy on land combined with an aggressive naval and commercial policy on the high seas.[5] Nevertheless, naval and colonial assaults on the reputedly vulnerable Spanish Americas promised significant payoffs. After all, Dutch West India Company squadrons under Piet Heyn had captured the fabled Spanish treasure fleet off Cuba in 1628 with staggering profits. Such a result would have been a quick fix for a French royal budget overly dependent on corrupt financiers, whose insatiable greed was also increasing social tensions.[6]

The cardinal had many connections with naval personnel; for example, his uncle Alphonse du Plessis had participated in the Maragnan colony led by François de Rasilly and including Isaac de Rasilly. The Rasillys, fiercely loyal to Richelieu, were heavily involved in overseas France. The minister opened his ears to schemes to expand France's horizons. His personal connection with the Compagnie de Saint-Christophe (1626–35) of Pierre Blain d'Esnambuc and Urbain de Roissey has been noted in the preceding chapter. Moreover, his advisors, especially Isaac de Rasilly, had grandiose dreams of matching the successes of the Dutch East India Company (established 1601) and the initial promise of the Dutch West India Company (1621).[7]

Richelieu shared their premises and the goals of the system known subsequently as "mercantilism," which held that a country should seek to obtain a greater share of the world's wealth; gain cheaper access to raw materials and markets; increase manufactures; and employ otherwise useless vagabonds. These policies were meant both to increase France's wealth and to harm its enemies. State-chartered companies of the Dutch type that could weld together France's capital and skills seemed a perfect solution for French trade problems, because a state in constant warfare in an age of spiraling military costs could not finance colonial ventures. "We must . . . create huge companies, force the merchants to participate, and accord them great privileges," Richelieu wrote in his *Mémoires*.[8]

French merchants were content with their petty transactions and helpless in face of corsairs, the cardinal complained. So twice in 1627, Richelieu granted charters and trade monopolies over all of France's maritime trade. Naturally, these giant (on paper) chartered companies aroused bitter opposition from excluded merchants. Still in a precarious domestic and international position, Richelieu retreated. Instead, he granted charters to smaller companies targeting specific overseas areas (e.g., New France, the Antilles, Guiana, Senegal, and Madagascar).

Chartered companies influenced the development of France overseas. They were different from the traditional merchant associations for maritime commerce in that the king or his representative accorded them official sanction. Privileges were granted on the premise that chartered companies would engage in high-risk enterprises that would not bear immediate fruit, and that they were to realize noncommercial crown goals. Thus, to ensure that investors had an opportunity to profit, a lengthy monopoly was legitimate. In return, the companies recognized their official relationship to the king and accepted state tasks. The state usually did not contribute capital, although its officials sometimes did so in their private capacities.

Different types of companies evolved. Predominantly commercial companies targeted particular overseas regions for specific trades. The same merchant house, Rosée, Robin of Rouen, received a monopoly for the trade of Senegal and Guiana (the latter a vague term referring to the whole coast between the Amazon and Orinoco rivers). A company of Saint Malô merchants received the rights to "Guinée." These companies received rights to property, on which they established fortified entrepôts (e.g., Saint-Louis on the Senegal River and the island of Cayenne in Guiane). They sent commercial agents there and, in the case of Cayenne, company servants to grow tobacco. The main goal of the Compagnie de Cap du Nord, however, was to exploit its commercial potential by trading with the indigenes for their natural products, for example, dye woods, medicinal plants, and tropical exotica. Establishing colonies, with their higher overhead costs, was not in these companies' interest.

Only when colonists were needed to produce desired staple commodities such as tobacco, cotton, indigo, and sugar did chartered *colonial* companies emerge. In such cases, the state granted property rights, monopoly trading rights for a certain number of years, and other privileges, including the right to maintain private armies and navies. In turn, the company accepted royal sovereignty through the king's right to appoint a lieutenant general and, sometimes, judicial officials. Companies agreed to transport a specific number of colonists, to support missionaries, and to fight the king's wars if called upon. The Compagnie de Saint-Christophe, among others, was of this type.

One may distinguish among chartered colonial companies on certain bases, the most important being the character of a company's relations with the state. Such relationships ran the gamut from minimal government control to active interference, including appointment of directors. The latter type did not occur in the era of Richelieu and Mazarin; only after 1664 would Jean-Baptiste Colbert pioneer this model of hands-on state supervision. In the era of the cardinals, a number of companies had sporadic contacts with royal officials. The Compagnie de Saint-Christophe and Guiana companies of the 1650s fall into this category. Except for a French fleet sent to Saint-Christophe in 1629, Richelieu and his key associates had little to do with the colony.[9] However, the situation changed in 1634–35. Importuned by d'Esnambuc's lieutenant, Pierre Liénard de l'Olive, to expand the French presence to Guadeloupe and beyond, the cardinal decided on the eve of war with Spain to reorganize the company, expand its capital, and prepare it to be a more aggressive force in the Caribbean.

Although he and a number of royal officials had invested in the Saint-Christophe company, Richelieu began promoting increased capital for the "new" Compagnie des Isles de l'Amérique (Company of the Islands of America), which he managed through a quartet of trusted officials, headed by François Fouquet. Other dignitaries in the Compagnie des Isles were the merchant capitalist Jean Rosée of Rouen and Captain Jacob Bontemps of Dieppe; however, only six of the fifty-seven associates were *armateurs*, or ship outfitters.[10] Many of the rest no doubt invested to curry favor with Richelieu.

The cardinal had another motive for re-forming the company. Unlike its predecessor, the Compagnie des Isles had a strong evangelical purpose. Apparently, there had only been a couple of secular priests (as opposed to regulars, or monks who followed a rule—*regula* in Latin) in the islands before 1635. Had the hard-nosed Richelieu suddenly been moved to pity at the sad religious state of the island *sauvages*? Perhaps, but a review of the political context suggests other motives. The Compagnie des Isles received its charter just four days after France and the Protestant Dutch sealed an alliance to make war on Catholic Spain. Naturally, this pact produced murmurs among French *dévots* too "naïve" to understand the ultimate good that would result from a French victory over Spain. Fortunately for Richelieu, France had a strong ally in Pope Urban VIII (r. 1623–1644), who feared that a Hapsburg victory would turn the papacy into that dynasty's humble servant. So the pope received Louis XIII's request to dispatch Dominican missionaries to the islands favorably, thus tacitly revoking traditional papal support for Iberian claims to a monopoly in the Americas. How could pro-papal French Catholics protest the establishment of a company that supported evangelism in the American Tropics? Or a company whose charter specifically stated that all emigrants had to be orthodox Roman Catholics? This silencing of Catholic critics was a masterpiece of Richelieu's statecraft.

The directors of the Compagnie des Isles were moderately diligent in their conduct of business; for example, in the early 1640s, they paid ship captains the passage fee for indentured servants, who were to repay it in tobacco. Fouquet before his death in 1640 occasionally received an audience to brief the cardinal about company progress. However, unlike Colbert and other future naval secretaries of state with more specialized briefs, Richelieu supervised all governmental bureaus and conducted foreign policy during a dangerous war. Even though the decline of Spain had by then begun, it is more apparent in hindsight than it was to contemporary Parisians, who were uncomfortably close to the heretofore-invincible Spanish infantry. Understandably, Richelieu could not closely scrutinize colonial matters in such turbulent times. In any case, the Compagnie des Isles proved unable to send out more than a handful of ships, thus allowing the Dutch to gain a near monopoly of island commerce.

In the year of his death, 1642, Richelieu authorized a revised charter for the Compagnie des Isles to extend its monopoly. Was this an official stamp of approval for a company under whose aegis a reputed 7,000 people lived in the islands?[11] Or was it that the company investors had not yet received any significant return and thought an extension would revive hopes and commitment? Or did the promising start of sugar manufactures at Barbados inspire the greed of some company directors?[12] Unfortunately for them, the immediate future would bring nothing but bad news.

The Agonies of Settlement:
The Caribbean, 1620s to 1640s

Few documents describe the first years of settlement. The colonists were unlettered men, not intellectuals or diary writers. The few secular priests did not record their experiences. Thus historians rely primarily on the admirable histories of Father Jean-Baptiste Dutertre, who heard oral accounts of the early years and had available most government records then surviving in writing his magnum opus of 1667–71.[13] His account cannot usually be checked against other evidence, nor is it invariably reliable. For example, he has the English Governor Thomas Warner and d'Esnambuc arriving at Saint-Christophe on the same day in 1625, a pleasing but fanciful legend.

The trying first experiences of the French settlers might well arouse pity in the reader. Of some 1,200 migrants who sailed to Saint-Christophe, only 350 survived in 1629. Around 350 died on board, upon arrival, and during the "seasoning" period; others may have fled to join brigands in the western Caribbean. These events took a terrible toll, both physically and in morale. But readers might reconsider their pity when considering the joint Anglo-French "sneak attack" in 1625 on a Carib longhouse (*carbet*), resulting in a massacre of indigenous men, women, and children.[14]

By 1627, Warner and d'Esnambuc concluded a treaty splitting the island. The English took the middle part, with the French at the ends. The treaty committed both "nations" to peace, but also to mutual assistance against Spanish and Carib threats. Renewed five times before 1662, the concord between these ancient enemies succeeded remarkably, which does not mean that there were not periods of tension.[15]

Then, in 1629, a traumatic event almost ended the French (and English) settlement. Shortly after a French fleet had left Saint-Christophe to prowl in the western Caribbean, a Spanish force chased the English and French off the island and burned everything not transportable. Though the refugees straggled back from neighboring islands, a discouraged d'Esnambuc was ready to give up when a Dutch ship appeared, provided supplies on credit, and promised to return and take whatever tobacco could be made ready. The Dutch captain, part of an aggressive invasion of the Spanish Caribbean, kept his word; the colony had found its savior. By the early 1630s, some five hundred settlers and fifty-two African slaves (forty men and twelve women) were engaged in tobacco production.[16] In 1635, according to Dutertre, French officers at Saint-Christophe led hundreds of armed slaves in a campaign to terrify their English neighbors.[17] If correct, this demonstrates significant growth in the early 1630s.

Although some African slaves labored on Saint-Christophe from the beginning, the Norman freeholders returned to their native province to recruit indentured servants (*engagés*) among relatives and friends. It was customary for lower- and even middle-class families to apprentice their children to neighbors. However, a substantial difference separated apprentices from indentured servants; masters of the latter had the right to sell the contracts. However, early indentured servants were usually known to their masters and apparently treated reasonably well for what became a customary three-year term.[18] Life as an *engagé* was likely the norm for most early French colonists. The value of the usual 300 pounds of tobacco awarded at the end of one's contract sufficed to start a farm (habitation), often done in partnership with another ex-servant, or to pay for return passage. The plunge in tobacco prices by the late 1630s made setting up on one's own habitation much more difficult, however. In any case, most of these servants had no intention of emigrating permanently, and many returned to France.[19]

Island population and production steadily grew, but the Compagnie de Saint-Christophe did not share in the profits. Island profits were meant to be distributed giving the company 40 percent, with another 40 percent going to producers who were technically company employees. D'Esnambuc and Roissey shared the rest. When this formula proved totally unrealistic, as happened wherever it was attempted in the Americas, the company settled for a 100 pounds of tobacco per head per year, called the capitation levy. Given the current high price of tobacco and the government's levy of a thirty *sols* per pound duty on foreign leaf (1629), this would have been a good bargain if the colonists had consistently paid.

Not only was the tiny island of Saint-Christophe shared with superior numbers of Englishmen, but tobacco quickly exhausts land not "fattened." Some French colonists looked greedily at the larger islands of Martinique, Dominica, and Guadeloupe to the southeast. Hoping to obtain rights from the company to settle one of these islands, d'Esnambuc's lieutenant, Pierre Liénard de l'Olive, returned to France in 1634. At Dieppe, he joined forces with a lawyer, Jean du Plessis d'Ossonville. In Paris, their proposals precipitated Richelieu's re-formation of the Saint-Christophe company. Soon about 500 recruits, mostly *engagés*, were located in Normandy. Accompanied by Dominican missionaries, l'Olive and du Plessis then set out for the Windward Islands.

Meanwhile, not wishing to be excluded from the larger islands, d'Esnambuc led 150 men including his nephew Jacques Dyel du Parquet to reconnoiter rugged, snake-infested Martinique. D'Esnambuc wrote to Richelieu that its occupation would give France "a great advantage over Spain." He also suggested removing the Saint-Christophe French settlers to Dominica to prevent English occupation of it.[20] So, practically at the same time, two distinct colonizing groups invaded these Island Carib strongholds. A trying time for all commenced.

No reliable estimate of the precolonial Carib populations of these larger Windward Islands exists. Up to this point, Old World epidemic diseases had apparently not had a devastating impact on them. Contemporaries give the impression that these islands were densely populated. Certainly, various Europeans had had sporadic contacts for over a century with Island Caribs, which made possible transmission of smallpox, measles, influenza, and other Eurasian killers. Yet the early French chroniclers depict the Caribs as robust and healthy. Does that simply mean that these indigenes hid their dead so as not to expose weakness?

Historians have recently connected social conditions in Native American populations to susceptibility to epidemic disasters; claims as to the universal vulnerability of all Native American populations to Old World diseases are increasingly disputed.[21] Colonial disruption of traditional Native American societies, oppressive labor systems, and especially malnutrition probably made aboriginal peoples, such as the Arawaks of the Greater Antilles, far more susceptible to epidemiological disasters. Island Caribs resisted fiercely colonial exploitation. Their healthy lifestyles, in combination with raiding neighboring peoples for female captives, apparently kept their population relatively dense. However, growing contacts with Europeans and their African captives after 1635 likely took an increasing toll.

Despite memories of the 1625 massacre, Island Caribs did not immediately oppose the French landings. Civil relations with the 150 heavily armed veterans of Saint-Christophe lasted until the French erected a fort on Martinique at a place they named Saint-Pierre, when a Carib frontal assault resulted in the latter's bloody defeat. Guerrilla skirmishes continued, but governors du Pont and then du Parquet (in 1637, after his uncle's death) concluded a truce based on a division of Martinique, with the leeward coast in French hands. A dangerous moment occurred in 1639 when du Parquet arrested an important Carib chief, Kayerman, because Caribs had freed two of their people detained in a habitant's cabin (*case*). Despite being held in irons, Kayerman escaped, only to die of a viper's bite.

Tensions remained high for some time.[22] However, du Parquet and the Carib chiefs resolved their differences, leading to a decade of peace. He was firm but fair with them. They often visited the French for trade and to get small presents. When visiting them, du Parquet painted himself *à la sauvage* with annatto dye and prepared his hair Carib-style, but he never relinquished pistol or sword.[23]

Du Parquet has enjoyed an enviable reputation. Contemporary sources describe him as generous to all visitors and prospective colonists. He did not apply the capitation tax to new colonists. He resolved disputes quickly, fairly, and at no cost to the parties. Much to the habitants' content, du Parquet firmly rejected company efforts to install a civil judge. Finally, he was a brave leader of the island militia. Even his later enemy Philippe Longvilliers [or Lonvilliers] de Poincy, lieutenant general of the French islands from 1638 on, had nothing but admiring words to write about him to the company.

Settlement did not proceed nearly as smoothly at Guadeloupe. The 1635 expedition carried about 500 men, mostly indentured servants, and four Dominican priests. At first, when the colonists had trade goods, relations with the Caribs were cordial enough. Pierre Pelican, one of the Dominicans, noted his kind reception. With their normally laconic tongues loosened by the good father's brandy, these Caribs thanked him for chasing away their "evil spirits" (*mabouyas*). As time passed and their provisions dwindled, the utterly unseasoned colonists, helpless in a strange environment, grew desperate. Carib gardens with their yucca roots, sweet potatoes, and pineapples were too tempting. After the death of du Plessis, l'Olive launched attacks that put his colonists in a terrible situation. Only the ability of black slaves to kill feral pigs saved some colonists from starvation. The Dominicans warned l'Olive not to imitate the Spaniards, who "were reputed to be cruel for putting to death

VISITE DES SAVVAGES AVX FRANÇOIS.

Le Clerc. f.

Caribs visit a French settlement. Note the hammock and the dugout canoe
(pirogue). From Jean-Baptiste Dutertre, *Histoire générale des isles Antilles* (Paris,
1667–71), 2: 395.

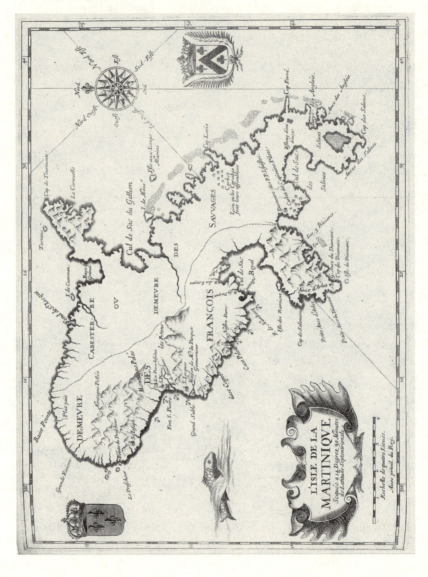

Martinique. From Jean-Baptiste Dutertre, *Histoire générale des isles Antilles*, 1: opposite 100.

the inhabitants of Peru."[24] Dutertre frankly blames his countrymen and l'Olive for the terrifying war that ensued.[25]

D'Esnambuc having died in 1636, the company needed to appoint a new governor of Saint-Christophe, and the king a lieutenant general. At the request of the Knights of Malta Commander de La Porte, Richelieu's uncle, the company offered the governor's position to René de Beculat, sieur de La Grange Fromentau. The latter at first accepted the position, but financial concerns subsequently led him to suggest in his place Philippe Longvilliers de Poincy, a knight commander of the order of Malta with experience as vice-admiral of Brittany. La Grange was to serve as Poincy's second in command, and the latter loaned him money to establish himself on Saint-Christophe. Poincy's appointment as lieutenant general removed him somewhat from company control. He arrived early in 1639, and his tempestuous career there lasted until his death in 1660.

Only help from Saint-Christophe allowed Guadeloupe to survive the Carib wars. Poincy had ulterior motives for sending assistance. He had sent an agent to Paris to plead for removing his colony to Guadeloupe. The commander encouraged armed men to leave for Guadeloupe by canceling their indebtedness. Two hundred men, led by the experienced and able Major de Sabouïlly, fought hard to prevent equally determined Caribs from destroying the Guadeloupe settlement.[26]

Peace did not come until 1640–41 and the surprising arrival of a new governor, Jean Aubert, the agent Poincy had sent to Paris. Aubert immediately brokered better relations with the Caribs. He exiled the colonists whom the Caribs most detested. He swapped hostages with indigenous chiefs, especially "Captain" Baron, who sent his son. The governor assigned men to learn the Caribs' customs and language and sent a French gunner to support Captain Baron in an attack on Trinidadian Arawaks.[27] Most Caribs agreed to remove to the windward half of Guadeloupe proper, to Grande-Terre, or to neighboring Dominica.[28] From these islands, Carib dugout canoes could make landings on hazardous, windy coasts to stage guerrilla attacks.

The Compagnie des Isles backed its evangelical rhetoric with modest financial support for missionaries, who helped the settlers maintain a semblance of tradition and orderly lives. At Richelieu's request, four Dominicans first settled at Guadeloupe, and then obtained a concession on Martinique. Dutertre, the great chronicler of the Antilles, who had been well prepared for island life by his earlier career as a mar-

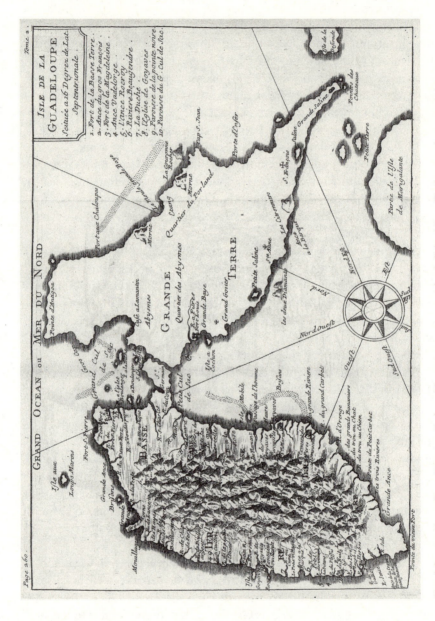

ISLE DE LA
GUADELOUPE
Scituée a 16 Degrez de Lat.
Septentrionale

1. Fort de la Basse Terre.
2. Anse du gros François.
3. Fort de la Magdeleine.
4. Anse Vadelorge.
5. Vance Recrey.
6. Riviere Beaugendre.
7. La Duché.
8. Uglise de Goyaves.
9. Paroisse de la pointe noire.
10. Paroisse du G.ᵈ Cul de Sac.

GRAND OCEAN ou MER DU NORD

GRANDE TERRE

BASSE TERRE

Guadeloupe. From Jean-Baptiste Labat, *Nouveau voyage aux isles de l'Amérique* (Paris, 1722), 2: opposite 223.

iner and soldier in Dutch service (explaining his generally pro-Dutch, anti-Spanish perspective) was soon to join them. Two Capuchins came to Saint-Christophe in 1635. The king himself strongly favored these friars; the Capuchin Father Joseph was a key confidant of Richelieu's.[29] Upon du Parquet's appeal, Jesuits consented to serve on Martinique. They soon spread to Guadeloupe and, after 1651, to Saint-Christophe, whose proprietor, Poincy, owned a number of their spiritual writings.[30] Some Dominicans, notably Raymond Breton, went on mission to the Caribs of Dominica; Jesuits would also soon attempt their conversion on Saint Vincent, southeast of Martinique. Although unsuccessful, these missionaries arguably helped in the establishment of more humane French treatment of Caribs. The *sauvages* perhaps thought of the priests as hostages to good French conduct.

Without bishops or traditional parishes, these regular clerics under-took the parish duties of secular priests. Since the colonists had not risked their lives to pay tithes, the company directors provided mission-aries with free passage, land, and servants. In time, those servants would primarily be African slaves, and the regular clergy, except for the Ca-puchins, came to be among the most successful plantation owners.[31] However, these clerical orders could never supply enough priests, and all were palpably discouraged by indigenous recalcitrance and the priests' high rates of mortality. The Jesuits did expand their missions in the 1650s, and in 1658, they succeeded in persuading the *parlement* of Paris to register letters allowing the black-robed Jesuits to have missions anywhere in the Americas.[32]

Another hopeful sign for islanders was that some powerful Parisians became interested in their well-being. In 1639 and in 1644, the Com-pagnie des Isles sent virtuous, chaperoned young women to marry colonists; most were welcomed with open arms.[33] In 1638, supposedly overcoming some misgivings, Louis XIII legitimized the enslavement of Africans for island use.[34] The same year, the king named a lieutenant general (called general in the islands), as was his privilege. Poincy, by far the highest-ranking Frenchman to set foot in the islands, arrived in early 1639, accompanied by twenty-four bodyguards. He did not conceal his access to the mighty Richelieu. Like Villegaignon, Poincy ruled in an au-thoritarian fashion; unlike the tyrant of Guanabará, however, he was not unduly puritanical or dogmatic. Despite having served with Isaac de Rasilly and other fellow knights in the bitter siege of Protestant La Rochelle, Poincy got along well enough with the Huguenots on his is-

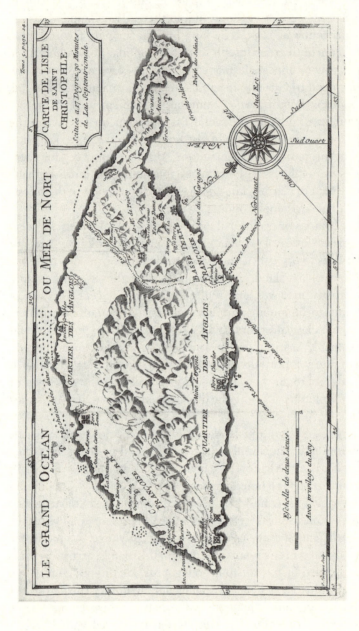

Saint-Christophe, with a depiction of Lieutenant General Philippe Longvilliers de Poincy's villa on a hill overlooking Basse-Terre on the east side of the island ("Logis de Mr. de Poincy"). From Jean-Baptiste Labat, *Nouveau voyage aux isles de l'Amérique* (Paris, 1722), 5: 14.

land.[35] He had no qualms about undermining the Compagnie des Isles by dealing extensively with Dutch merchants; after all, were they not then France's allies? His sporadic efforts to interfere in the affairs of Guadeloupe and Martinique alienated their governors.

The new colonists at Guadeloupe and Martinique intended to make their fortunes in tobacco. For reasons beyond their understanding, tobacco prices plummeted some 80 percent by the end of the 1630s.[36] Poincy signed an accord with his fellow strongman Thomas Warner to stop growing tobacco, indeed to uproot existing plants, until the price rose. The ensuing discontent of the habitants was not allayed when Poincy started to build his remarkable fortified château high above the town of Basseterre in southeastern Saint-Christophe. He justified the expense to the company by declaring that it would intimidate neighboring English settlements; since cannon also protected the entry from the town of Basseterre below, one might wonder whether potentially mutinous colonists were not equally on his mind. Poincy and other governors soon experimented with other crops, first indigo and then sugar, but these were difficult years.

Perhaps 10 percent of the habitants at Saint-Christophe were Huguenots, and the company admonished Poincy about his religious tolerance. François Le Vasseur, an experienced Huguenot military engineer who had been in the islands since 1624, was quite close to Poincy. Hearing of a weak English garrison established on the strategically important island of Tortuga, opposite Hispaniola, Poincy deputized Le Vasseur to lead about fifty Huguenots to conquer and settle the island. Poincy agreed to allow religious toleration there but did not report this to king or company. Le Vasseur persuaded about fifty buccaneer hunters roaming the coast of Hispaniola to join his Huguenots. The English at Tortuga put up little resistance.[37]

Le Vasseur proceeded to construct now-legendary fortifications to protect not only against all foreigners but against mutinous elements. This would-be king of Tortuga—which he ruled tyrannically for a decade—now forgot that the profits were supposed to be shared with the king of France, the Saint-Christophe company, and especially the ever-avaricious Poincy, whose efforts to control him he skillfully parried. Le Vasseur taxed all trade and split the prizes corsairs brought to his port. Moreover, he also soon showed his true Huguenot colors by persecuting Catholics.

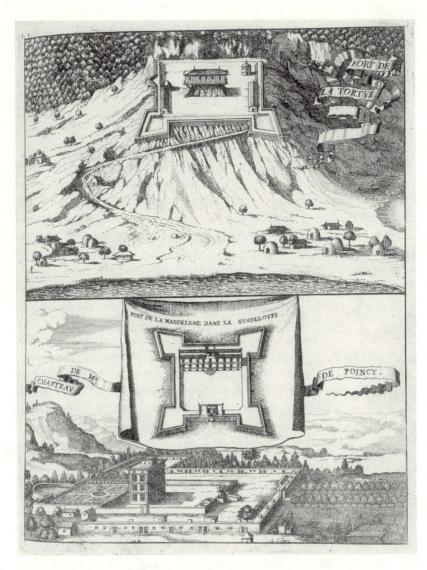

Depiction of the fort at Tortuga and Poincy's villa on Saint-Christophe "Chasteau de Mr. de Poincy"). From Jean-Baptiste Dutertre, *Histoire générale des isles Antilles*, 1: opposite 168, mistakenly labeled 468.

Divergent Paths: France and the Antilles in the 1640s

Bad times for France did not commence with the deaths of Richelieu (1642) and his master Louis XIII (1643), but conditions worsened considerably during the regency of Anne of Austria and with the emergence of a new, very different first minister, Jules, Cardinal de Mazarin (1643–1661). Louis XIV was only five. Neither the Hapsburg-born Anne nor the naturalized Italian cardinal-minister instilled much respect or fear in France's haughty powerful nobles (*les grands*). At enormous cost, French armies fought simultaneously in the Low Countries, along the Rhine, and in Catalonia.[38] One phase of the war ended in 1648 with the Peace of Westphalia, but fighting the stubborn Spaniards continued eleven more years, until the Treaty of the Pyrenees (1659). Anne and Mazarin used desperate means to keep armies in the field.

One may distinguish among the natural and political causes of social misery in 1640s France, although these inevitably intersected. In much of seventeenth-century Europe, colder and wetter weather patterns meant declines in harvests and outbreaks of famines. Malnutrition produced greater susceptibility to epidemic diseases, and endemic diseases also preyed on weakened bodies. Perhaps the century's worst food crisis occurred in 1648–53.[39] Increasing rural poverty took its toll on the towns with the decline in demand for manufactured goods. Inevitably, desperate people took to the roads, thievery no doubt increased, and the upper classes expressed growing anxiety.

In these difficult decades, a desperate government added political misery to natural disasters by seeking to raise revenues. Basic taxes were increased on the order of 300 or 400 percent.[40] Revenues did not, however, go up correspondingly. Tax evasion and fraud simply increased. Officials did everything they could to reduce the tax exemptions of nobles, and even to reduce the number of self-proclaimed nobles; in turn, aggrieved nobles used means fair or foul to extend their exemptions. Many so resented government pressure as to stir up local rebellions against Paris.[41]

Social anxiety in face of this turmoil did translate into greatly increased charitable activities. This era witnessed the good works of the future saints Vincent de Paul and François de Sales and of various orders of nuns (most notably the Sisters of Charity).[42] But others of the privileged classes, even as they perhaps contributed to these charitable works, were bloodsuckers to the poor. The privileged profited from a political system that combined legal inequality and massive corruption. Always in financial difficulties, the French monarchy had devised expedient measures in wartime that became permanent, among them the sale or venality of bureaucratic and judicial offices, and worse (for taxpayers), after 1604, the right to pass these down in one's family. As private property, these offices could not be liquidated without compensation. Thus the people came to support thousands of functionless, parasitic officials. The state's various taxes, almost all falling on the poorest 95 percent, were "farmed" out to private syndicates of financiers. In return for immediate, up-front money, these tax farmers then attempted to squeeze the maximum out of people. Inevitably, those government officials letting out the contracts received kickbacks; Mazarin himself often took the lion's share, not that he was the first official to do so. Finally, to make up for continuous shortfalls, the government sold bonds (*rentes*), which often had to pay exorbitant interest rates to find takers; by the 1640s, the following years' revenues were pledged to pay off the *rentiers*, that is, those who had purchased these bonds. Officeholders, tax farmers, financiers, and *rentiers* thus came to control the economic and, indirectly, the political power of France. Corruption and greed reigned in seventeenth-century France, and commoners paid.[43]

From the mid 1630s right down to 1648, unrest, killings of tax collectors, and localized revolts plagued France.[44] The five-year upheaval known as the Fronde started in Paris in 1648 because of elite outrage at arbitrary decreases of interest rates on government bonds. Soon the great nobles, like buzzards in hope of carrion in the form of pensions and titles, joined in the hunt for the Italian red bird, Mazarin. Now Anne, Mazarin, and government loyalists such as the attorney-general of the Paris *parlement*, Nicholas Fouquet, and the cardinal's new steward (*intendant*) of his household, Jean-Baptiste Colbert, had to cope with both foreign and civil war.

These events had an immediate impact in the maritime and colonial arena. After 1642, lines of authority in the navy became unclear. Richelieu's nephew, the duc de Brezé, became *grand maître et surintendant de la navigation*, but he was only a titular figure. Later, Anne herself took the office. In 1644, the duc d'Amville received the office of viceroy of America, but he showed little interest in it. César, duc de Vendôme, one of Henri IV's bastards and a perennial pain in ministers' necks, received the revived office of the Admiralty of France (*Ponant*), but his interest in maritime affairs was purely fiscal. Later, Nicholas Fouquet, a crucial figure in the Compagnie des Isles, would claim with some justification that he alone had attempted to keep France's maritime interests alive through various colonial companies. On top of this administrative uncertainty, funding for the navy declined drastically after 1642, from some seven million l.t. to less than a million. When the dwindling navy could not even protect France's Mediterranean coast from Spain's fleet or Channel shipping from English corsairs, the Caribbean colonies could hardly expect to see royal ships.

Island governors sought to increase their own prosperity and that of their colonies as best they could. That meant cooperation with the Dutch, while giving lip service to the Compagnie des Isles. Not only did the king heavily tax colonial produce but Dutch freight charges were substantially lower than French ones, and their manufactured products were cheaper.[45] Governors Poincy, du Parquet, and, after 1643, at Guadeloupe, Charles Houël all built up estates based on their prerogatives, especially the capitation tax and first choice of African slaves. Only the Dutch could make slaves available, market the colonies' produce, and provide credit. For example, Poincy contracted with a Dutch firm at Middleburg to supply his island's needs.[46]

The colonies became part of the Dutch commercial empire, which suited the colonists. The burghers of Vlissingen, or Flushing, now a port city of the modern Dutch province of Zeeland, even called the French island habitants "their planters." Dutertre says that the richest colonists at Martinique bought the title of bourgeois from certain Dutch cities, thus acquiring protection in case of a Franco-Dutch war.[47] The same author notes that French shoes cost 100 lbs of tobacco (or 45 l.t.), making them far more expensive than the Dutch equivalents. The high French duties on colonial commodities also directed trade flows to the Lowlands.[48] Dutch and Portuguese Jewish refugees from Brazil in the 1650s provided the expertise to launch a substantial sugar industry.[49]

Political discord wracked the colonies in the early 1640s. Poincy alienated many habitants at Saint-Christophe with the vindictive persecution of one Des Marets, accused of undermining the commander's authority. When Des Marets's wife freed him from prison by getting the guards drunk, Poincy's rage could be satiated only by their blood. Threatened with war, Warner returned the doomed Des Marets from refuge in the English sector.[50] Poincy also quarreled viciously with his lieutenant governor, La Grange, resulting in the latter's loss of his property and forced exile. The commander gave himself and his cronies a monopoly of all island imports and exports, enraging the colonists, who had always enjoyed free trade with the Dutch. Fortunately, he backed away from this ill-conceived policy.

In 1642, the Compagnie des Isles decided to send sixty African slaves and from forty to fifty indentured servants to establish a large sugar works, to be run by one of its directors, Charles Houël, son of the financier Louis Houël, sieur de Petit-Pré and an investor in the Compagnie de la Nouvelle-France. To the bitter surprise of Governor Aubert, Houël, who as manager of the new enterprise was to receive 20 percent of its profits, unexpectedly arrived in Guadeloupe the following year with a commission as governor.[51] A habitual troublemaker, Houël persecuted Aubert with such ardor that the latter sought refuge on Saint-Christophe, where Poincy appointed him militia captain. Poincy's enraged reaction—the supercharged baroque era prized intense emotionality and passion—to Houël's haughty refusal to recognize his authority no doubt explains his kindly reception of Aubert.

The Compagnie des Isles was obviously displeased with this state of affairs. The weak regency no doubt emboldened colonial potentates. The Poincy-Houël contretemps sharpened when the latter visited Paris with a brief against the lieutenant general. Disgruntled colonists at Saint-Christophe had also made their complaints known in France. Poincy's outrageous conduct, in combination with his dealings with the Dutch, weakened his written explanations of his conduct. The company tried to replace the man who paid the least lip service to its sovereignty. When the regent Anne cooperated and named one of her favorites, Noël Patrocles de Thoisy, as Poincy's successor, she provoked a colonial Fronde in 1645–46. Poincy wrote a letter to the company suggesting he would comply with the change, but, frightened by what he was hearing about attitudes in Paris, he subsequently decided not to relinquish his position.

Preparing for Thoisy's arrival, Poincy buttressed his support by flattering important habitants and liberally distributing food and wine to commoners. Those whom the commander could not trust, he purged. He was able to get his militia of some twelve companies of two hundred men each to back him by raising the specter of real company rule. He also gained the support of Sir Thomas Warner. In return he pledged to support the royalist Warner in the event that a Parliamentary force appeared (by 1645, Oliver Cromwell had largely defeated Charles I's supporters in the English Civil War). A civil war soon ensued, with du Parquet backing Thoisy and Houël fence-sitting, after initially welcoming the new lieutenant general. Poincy's disobedience to royal orders and his alleged mistreatment of du Parquet's nephews explain the latter's anti-Poincy stand.

Poincy decisively won the struggle. After du Parquet led a raid on the northwestern part of Saint-Christophe and captured Poincy's two nephews, the outraged commander routed du Parquet's men and those habitants of Saint-Christophe who had joined him. Warner then treacherously delivered du Parquet to Poincy, who imprisoned him. The general conducted a reign of terror against perceived opponents, not failing to confiscate the property of those exiled. He removed the influential Capuchin friars for offenses ranging from their support of the unfortunate Thoisy to their assertion that the children of baptized slaves should be free.[52] Poincy owned many hundred Africans, and such clerical interference in master-slave relations was therefore intolerable to him.[53]

Thoisy cooled his heels at Guadeloupe, where Houël soon schemed to undermine his authority. The naïve Thoisy goaded the Guadeloupe governor to ever more outrageous conduct by his compromising, even conciliatory, conduct. Meanwhile, at Martinique, colonists used this conjunction of events to stop paying taxes to the company and to refuse the authority of the pusillanimous Thoisy. Company stores at Martinique fell prey to looters. French island society was disintegrating into chaos.[54]

The denouement of this almost comical affair was that the situation became so unstable in Guadeloupe that Thoisy fled to Martinique, where he was initially well received. Houël tormented Thoisy's supporters, and especially the Dominicans, with whom he quarreled interminably over l'Olive's generous grant of land to them. After a meeting between Houël's representative and Poincy, the general sent some 800 men to Martinique. Thoisy issued orders to oppose them, but local residents conspired with Poincy's lieutenants to arrest Thoisy as part of a deal to exchange du Parquet for Poincy's nephews. So it transpired. Soon, Thoisy was the house prisoner of the man he had been meant to replace. Poincy spirited him in the middle of the night onto a ship leaving for France.[55]

Recently, historians of France have criticized the traditional view that the seventeenth-century monarchy established an authoritarian, absolutist system. Instead, they argue, kings slowly increased their authority over local officials and power brokers by carrot-and-stick policies. The king won some rounds and lost others, but never admitted defeat. The increase of central authority proceeded in fits and starts, and only at a very gradual pace. In the context of colonial governance, the general picture was even less favorable to the monarchy. Anne and Mazarin were unable to do anything about Poincy's insult to royal authority; they had few ships, less money, and greater and closer insults to deal with. Unaware of Thoisy's arrest, they dispatched secret letters (*lettres de cachet*) that allowed Poincy to remain as lieutenant general for one year to wrap up his affairs. In effect, the letters admitted that calumnies against Poincy had led to Thoisy's appointment.[56] In the end, the commander got off almost scot-free, except for paying Thoisy 90,000 pounds of tobacco.[57] What suffered in the islands was royal authority. Only a few years later, in 1651, Thomas Hobbes would publish his encomium of the absolutist state, *Leviathan*. In this case, the French Leviathan slunk back into the mud temporarily to catch its breath.

Sizing up the situation, the company directors decided to liquidate. Even without the political disaster, their failed effort to promote sugar cultivation left them some 260,000 l.t. in debt.[58] With the possible exception of du Parquet, company governors clearly treated their own interests as far more important than the company's.[59] When the company offered to sell the islands, the governors, especially Houël, who had sunk company capital into sugar works, were eager purchasers. In 1650, du Parquet, the company's golden boy, bought Martinique, Ste.-Lucie, and Grenada and the Grenadines for 60,000 l.t.[60] In Paris to sign the contract, this loyal governor twice appeared before the king, who rewarded him with the title of lieutenant general of Martinique and its dependencies. Although the company remained so angry with Houël that it refused to have his name on the contract, he and his brother-in-law Jean de Boisseret d'Herblay together purchased Guadeloupe, Marie-Galante, and their dependencies in 1649 for about 83,000 l.t.[61] Despite being out of favor in Paris and with his superiors at Malta for ignoring orders, Poincy in 1651 persuaded the knights to buy the French parts of Saint-Christophe and claims to Saint-Martin, Saint-Barthélemy, and Saint-Croix for 120,000 l.t.; and to leave him as commander there with a promotion to *bailli* (bailiff).[62] This amazing man, whose name lives on through the Poinciana tree, the colors of whose showy scarlet flowers resemble those of the robes of the knights of Malta, even effected a reconciliation with Paris. The proprietary period of the French islands commenced.

The two initial decades of French colonization in the Greater Caribbean may be deemed a success despite all of the failures and human miseries. By 1649, significant numbers of colonists inhabited Saint-Christophe, Guadeloupe, and Martinique. The economic and demographic vitality of the following decade led to expansion to other islands such as Saint-Croix, Saint-Martin, Saint-Barthélemy, Marie-Galante, Grenada, and Sainte-Lucie. Much to the horror of Island Caribs, the French were on the move. Grave consequences ensued.

CHAPTER FOUR

Frontiers of Fortune?
The Era of the Proprietors, 1649 to 1664

When Louis XIV and his de facto colonial minister Jean-Baptiste Colbert decided to force the island proprietors to sell out to the new Compagnie des Indes occidentales françaises, or French West India Company, in 1664, they depicted the islands as suffering from stunted development and incessant political turmoil under proprietary rule.[1] Many historians have too easily accepted this skewed, self-serving portrayal, which this chapter seeks to correct.

The new proprietors moved quickly to attract immigrants and attempted to make good their claims to neighboring islands. Lieutenant General Philippe Longvilliers de Poincy sent expeditions to Saint-Croix, which he considered a very desirable island. Disease killed his dream of expansion there. He had better success on the small islands of Saint-Martin and Saint-Barthélemy (St. Barts), sending his nephew Robert to assert French rights to the former. Robert made an agreement with Dutch colonists to share the island based on a condominium agreement similar to that of the English and French at Saint-Christophe.[2] The energetic Charles Houël colonized Marie-Galante, at first without antagonizing his Island Carib friends at Dominica. Du Parquet sent colonists to Grenada and Sainte-Lucie to the south of Martinique. This policy of expansion suggests growing numbers of colonists living on the main islands, which is attested to by all contemporary chroniclers.[3] They also attest to the military preparedness of all men and "boys carrying guns."[4]

Fortunately, detailed studies of indentured servitude by the late Gabriel Debien show that two intense periods of *engagé* recruitment for the islands occurred during these decades, and thus buttress the impressionistic evidence of contemporary writers. That these were years of hunger and unrest in France was perhaps not coincidental.[5] However, it may be that the allure of the Tropics, with their prospect of quick, perhaps illicit gains also played a role. The propaganda of the proprietors promising good, strong government and fair, free justice may have persuaded some colonist candidates. According to Jean-Baptiste Dutertre, islanders who knew "the current state of France" considered themselves "happy."[6]

Although significant colonial population growth almost certainly characterized this era, there were no censuses at that time; not that later official censuses are rigorously accurate, far from it. One current scholar arrives at a figure of 13,000 French and 16,000 African slaves in the islands by 1660 by splitting the difference between the lowest and highest estimates of the chroniclers.[7] As there were probably not many more than 3,000 colonists each at Martinique and Guadeloupe in the early 1660s, 13,000 may be on the high side. True, Saint-Christophe was the most populous island at this time, but we do not know how many French lived on their share of this tiny island. In any case, if the 1642 estimate of 7,000 inhabitants of all races is at all accurate, then the population had increased significantly by 1660. Perhaps the best evidence for growth is the program of expansion noted above.

Though a large number of *engagés* left France in this era, their mortality rates were most likely high, and many survivors returned to France at the contract's conclusion.[8] Contemporary missionary accounts attribute high mortality rates to the brutal workload greedy masters placed on indentured servants. Modern commentators would also emphasize their susceptibility to a new disease environment, especially *Plasmodium falciparum* malaria, transferred by the bite of the female *Anopheles* mosquito, which was especially prevalent on Martinique and Guadeloupe (but not Saint-Christophe). Yellow fever may have reached Guadeloupe in the later 1640s. Modern estimates are that malaria killed at least one-quarter of adult immigrants to these islands.[9] Father Pierre Pelleprat mentions widespread sickness at Saint-Christophe in 1653–55 but provides few details.[10]

Contemporary observers generally give high marks to the proprietors, with the exception of Houël of Guadeloupe, who was an enemy of the influential Dominican writers. To be sure, Poincy's relative tolerance of French and foreign Protestants caused dismay among Catholic clerical writers. Except for certain militia officers and clerics, the habitants paid the governors a capitation 100 pounds of tobacco per annum for themselves and each of their workers. Houël insisted on 200 pounds, as well as duties on commerce. When in 1660 (year of his death), Poincy attempted to substitute 100 pounds of more expensive sugar, only the fact that he was obviously dying prevented a revolt. No *taillage*, salt tax, tithes, or inheritance tax on land burdened the habitants; they were li-

A sugar mill. From Jean-Baptiste Dutertre, *Histoire générale des isles Antilles*, 2: 122.

able only for the capitation. The absence of metropolitan fiscal burdens also meant that colonists did not consider themselves as peasants and as solely taxable. Proprietors administered justice freely, with few bribes corrupting the system, and there were no lawyers. Poincy and his council met under a large tree in Basse-Terre and swiftly administered justice without any fees.[11] All males over fourteen did militia duty, but they thereby had the right to carry firearms and swords. Their military prowess guaranteed that the authorities treated them with respect.[12] Most governors, most famously Poincy, had an open-door, open-table policy for the officers and gentlemen of the island, especially on Sundays after Mass. No wonder writers like Dutertre depict this as something of a golden age for free habitants.[13]

Although sugar planting had taken root in Saint-Christophe by the early 1650s,[14] the year 1654 was a watershed one in the history of the French Caribbean. Boatloads of Dutch and Portuguese Jewish refugees, some 600 with 300 slaves and sugar-mill equipment from the Pernambuco area of Brazil visited the French islands. They were warmly welcomed by Houël, who had previously failed to produce competitive white sugars, and some stayed on at Guadeloupe and showed the French how to make good sugar.[15] Du Parquet, angry that Jesuits had initially persuaded him to reject the fugitives, also welcomed them. Perhaps the good fathers were worried about competition, because they owned a large sugar works at Martinique in 1660. Dutch merchants supplied slaves on credit, which was critical to the transition to sugar. Fortunately for the French habitants, the strained relations between the Dutch and English during these years of the first (1652–54) and second (1664–67) Anglo-Dutch Wars meant that Dutch slavers found a better reception in French colonies.[16] For better or worse, the French islands had begun a long transition from the small farmers' provision and tobacco farms to the all-consuming sugar and slave regime.

Slowing the advance of big plantation agriculture was the final effort of the Island Caribs to stop French expansion. Skirmishes had been occurring since 1649, when French from Martinique attempted to settle Grenada. Initially, they had made a pact with a local captain, Kaierouane, based on false French promises that their hastily constructed fort was intended to protect against an imminent English invasion. Soon, the permanence of the French presence became clear to the Caribs, especially those of neighboring Saint Vincent. Besieging the small French fort, the Caribs attempted to smoke the French out by burning hot peppers.[17]

Alerted by a Dominican Carib, du Parquet and sixty men surprised some Grenada Caribs during one of their inebriated rituals; in an infamous episode, the cornered Caribs jumped to their deaths off a cliff (thereafter called the *morne des sauteurs*, or cliff of jumpers) rather than surrender. Sporadic conflict continued for years afterwards.[18]

Du Parquet then dispatched a force to establish a foothold on rugged Sainte-Lucie to the southeast of Martinique. To head the effort, he chose the sieur de Rousselan, who had the advantage of having a Carib wife and thus had good relations with the *sauvages*. Rousselan established his fort near present-day Castries. The next four years were peaceful and productive. However, Rosselan's death and the continuing French-Carib conflict throughout the archipelago meant trouble for his successor, who was slaughtered along with ten family members.[19]

Meanwhile, a Carib band from Dominica destroyed Houël's tiny colony on Marie-Galante; after a few of the culpable Caribs had been killed, peace returned. In 1654, Caribs of Saint Vincent, alarmed by du Parquet's advances south and especially the conflict on Grenada, launched the final struggle by killing two Jesuit missionaries and then proceeded to attack the French on Sainte-Lucie. Upset at assaults from Martinique, Saint Vincent Caribs besieged a small number of French on Grenada, who survived only because of the fortuitous arrival of some 300 men from a failed expedition to Cayenne (see below).[20] The vigorous du Parquet dispatched large militia forces against Saint Vincent until a truce was agreed to in 1655. However, tensions remained very high, and when du Parquet executed ten Caribs for "crimes" committed during the previous conflict, a powerful indigenous invasion of Martinique ensued, which almost succeeded. Fighting alongside the Caribs were escaped African *marrons*, or maroons, perhaps slaves brought from Brazil (typically, slaves forced from familiar environs were more likely to escape as a protest against an unknown new situation). Only the arrival of Dutch ships saved the colony. Dutch sailors ended the Carib siege of du Parquet's fortified house. However, the refugees from Brazil suffered many losses, and survivors returned to the Netherlands.[21]

A brief truce occurred prior to the culmination of this five-year struggle. After the death of du Parquet in early January 1658,[22] no one could control the habitants' determination to remove the Island Caribs from Martinique. After coldly killing the great Carib Captain Nicolas and some of his men at Saint Pierre, an "assembly of notables" decided to drive the Caribs from Capesterre.[23] The subsequent fighting included an attack in 1659 on the French at Grenada by the Dominica Carib band of "Indian" Warner, the son of Governor Thomas Warner of Saint Christopher by a Carib mistress, an enigmatic figure who first enters the historical record here.[24] After more skirmishes, Poincy produced an alliance of English and French governors whose purpose was to end the war and confine the remaining Caribs to Dominica and Saint Vincent, in what are called reservations today. Presumably, the exhausted Caribs saw the omens and, through the good offices of two missionaries, they put their marks on a treaty. By 1660, all fighting had ceased, and the islands could thus share the fruits of peace with the mother country.[25] New lands now became open for incipient sugar planters, who perhaps dreamed of emulating the successful du Parquet habitation, La Montagne, which in 1660 employed twenty-eight white servants, eighty-seven African adults, and forty-six African children.[26]

The Guiane Riddle

In hindsight, the intense French interest in the "wild coast" of Guiana (spelled "Guiane" in the seventeenth century) before 1660 is surprising. Of the approximately 1,500 to 2,000 French adventurers to this swampy, disease-ridden coast in these years, *none* remained by 1660. Chapter 2 outlines some of its attractions—it was seen as the gateway to El Dorado, possessed natural wealth such as dyewoods, offered land for growing tobacco, indigo, and sugar, and could serve as a launching pad for strikes against the Iberian colonies. In Isaac de Rasilly's 1626 memoir to Richelieu, Guiane was lauded as the most desirable site for a French colony in the Americas.[27] During the 1640s and 1650s, Guiane became a magnet for the missionary drive of the French Catholic Reformation, that zealous movement so familiar to historians of New France. Thus, a combination of secular and religious motives and delusions, as well as economic and political distress in France, drove colonizing activities between the Amazon and the Orinoco.

Sporadic earlier efforts to establish settlements having failed, in 1633, Cardinal Richelieu granted a charter to the Norman firm of Rosée, Robin, with a ten-year trading monopoly, in return for transporting Roman Catholics and supporting Capuchin missionaries.[28] The same firm in the same year not coincidentally received a charter for the trade of Senegal, once again in return for supporting Capuchins. The Compagnie rouennaise du Cap du Nord established a small fort at Cayenne in 1636, and two Capuchins arrived in 1637.[29] Richelieu had strategic goals for this establishment, because the winds and currents allowed easy access to Spanish Caribbean holdings, and his displeasure at its paltry progress led him in 1638 to transfer the privilege to Captain Jacob Bontemps, a company director and associate of the Compagnie des Isles de l'Amérique. Bontemps agreed to transport between 1,000 and 1,200 Roman Catholics and to maintain the Capuchins, whose strict vows of poverty made them low-cost missionary friars.

Bontemps's company made little progress in peopling Cayenne and a site at the Maroni river,[30] so no doubt it was with pleasure that it received a request from the Paris-born, socially well-connected Charles Poncet de Brétigny to lead some 300 colonists to Cayenne. Louis XIII made Brétigny lieutenant general for Guiane, and he turned out to be another Villegaignon. Many of Brétigny's "colonists" were, in fact, vagabonds or prisoners, as Villegaignon's had been at Guanabará. At Cayenne, Brétigny organized the all-male troop into militia companies, worked them for ten hours a day in the brutal tropical climate, and tried to prevent them from going off hunting or fishing. Like Villegaignon, too, he promulgated ordinances minutely regulating all behavior, and decreed that "heretics," if uncovered, be burnt alive. He quarreled with everyone, including some of his officers, and he imprisoned four Capuchins.[31] A tawdry civil war combined with disputes with the local Galibis Indians undermined the colony. Eventually, some fortunate colonists found refuge in Suriname, then subsequently in the French islands, where they told terrible tales about Guiane. The less fortunate had few regrets when Brétigny fell to Indian arrows. Thus, with the death of the "tyrant," ended the first major French colonial expedition to Guiane.[32]

Unaware of these events, the company sent reinforcements in 1646; the aroused Galibis killed them. Then, in 1648, came another, little-known botched expedition under the authority of a baron d'Ormeilles. Of two ships sent, one captain quarreled with the governor, La Fontaine, and did not proceed to Guiane. The other ship deposited the governor and twenty-two men on shore and brought the other colonists to Martinique. The governor and his men disappeared.

Even more bizarre episodes ensued. In the midst of the Fronde, a Parisian group published a pamphlet announcing the formation of a "Company for America." It appealed to investors by promising great profits, but did not specify the location of the proposed colony. Soon, however, an act of association indicated that royal letters patent had nullified the rights of the Compagnie rouennaise du Cap du Nord, which was criticized for tolerating Protestants and for failing to convert the aborigines.[33] The principal investors, important figures, were made known, and their participation gave an élan to the enterprise. Thus was born the Compagnie de la terre ferme de l'Amérique ou France équinoctiale, or Company of Equatorial France.[34]

In its three-year history, this ambitious company launched a sustained propaganda campaign, created at least the framework for a truly national company, dispatched the largest French expedition to America up to that time, and did all of the above without strong government support. Had it succeeded in its goals, it might have transformed the character of French colonial endeavors. Instead, its spectacular failure eventually pushed France in the direction of greater state supervision of colonization. Who were the men who organized this company and what were their goals?

As is too often the case, we have only limited knowledge from which to draw inferences. What is clear is that this company did not have ties with Fronde rebels, as some historians have inferred from the pro-Guiane publicity of the playwright Paul Scarron, a noted polemicist against Mazarin.[35] Scarron, the poet Jean de Segrais, and the celebrated courtesan Ninon de Lenclos announced their intention to emigrate to Guiane, whose climate, they said, would heal the crippled Scarron.[36] In reality, key company figures included people close to the regent, Anne of Austria, a zealous supporter of missions, and to the pious niece and heir of Cardinal Richelieu, the duchesse d'Aiguillon. These powerful connections explain how the company received letters of patent through the king's council. Overt *frondeurs* could hardly have expected such a favor, or that of the regent supplying troop escorts for the expedition as it proceeded down the Seine through a dangerous Paris. Anne and the young Louis XIV formally received the expedition leaders downriver at the château of Saint-Germain-en-Laye. A staunch royalist and longtime supporter of missionary work, the duchesse d'Aiguillon gave her protection to the expedition at Le Havre prior to its embarkation for the Wild Coast.[37]

The public documents of the Compagnie de la France équinoctiale strongly suggest a powerful religious motive for its expeditions. Indeed, its religious impulse seems to have been stronger than that of any other French colonial company. All participants took a formal oath that their religious duty to implant Christianity among the *sauvages* constituted the principal reason for their involvement. "We have concluded that the most useful and most solid means was to sustain this evangelical mission by the establishment of a French colony in that place," they declared.[38] Besides the duchess, a key figure in the company was the Sorbonne theologian Abbé Marivault. Naturally, as the company explained, people could not be expected to uproot themselves without some guarantees concerning their ability to live well in a "new world." Life would be "incomparably easier" for those who went.[39] These motives were in no way contradictory for that era, because it was gospel that missions to the *sauvages* required a colonial base for support and protection. This message, initiated in the Brazilian expedition of 1612–16, had been constantly reinforced by the yearly publication of Jesuit *Relations* of their New France missions.[40]

Most likely, the Compagnie de la France équinoctiale was backed by the powerful, secretive Compagnie du Saint-Sacrement (Company of the Holy Sacrament), one of the principal agents of the French Counter-Reformation, which had close ties to prominent spiritual leaders such as Vincent de Paul and was very interested in missions. The Compagnie de la France équinoctiale reflected the intense religiosity that drove the Compagnie du Saint-Sacrement, which attracted individuals holding high public office. It may be coincidental but many of the company directors were such officials. Pierre de La Boulaye was general-secretary of the Marine; the first director Jean de Bragelogne, the intendant of justice at Orléans between 1641 and 1648, was perhaps the most prestigious Frenchmen up to that point to migrate overseas. He had a number of ties directly and through his family to the Counter-Reformation.[41]

The support of powerful people and the sad conditions of France during the Fronde no doubt explain the large number of company recruits. More than one-third and perhaps one-half of an estimated 500 to 600 recruits paid their own passage, and thus would receive large grants of land, some with attached letters of nobility. Considering past recruitments, the success of the company is astonishing. Most of the remaining recruits were likely indentured servants, but there is no evidence of forced transports. No doubt, as the chronicler and participant Abbé Biet caustically complains, there were too many good-for-nothing valets of directors and too many soldiers, and not enough carpenters, fishermen, and farmers. Still, this was a promising group of colonists, and included about ninety women. Quite clearly, the directors rejected the Villegaignon/Brétigny model, and they formally declared that any director responsible for the loss of a company ship chasing Spaniards would have to pay for it. This was to be a new day for France Outre-mer. The organizers knew what had gone wrong previously.

The company also demonstrated innovation in its organizational structure. Two councils, one in Paris and one at Cayenne, were to govern in concordance. Although utopian, given the distances involved, this structure was a response to excessive direction from France and a corresponding colonial resistance to such control. Also by 1653, the company attempted to go national, establishing offices in major provincial cities. One of its propaganda documents had "tear out" sheets, which potential directors, habitants, or indentured servants could send in. These documents indicate ambitious company goals.

Had it not been so tragic in the loss of human lives, what happened to the expedition might be considered farcical. Its spiritual leader, Marivault, drowned in the Seine while attempting to pass from one ship to the other to settle a dispute. For unknown reasons, the ships did not obtain the necessary permission from Admiral Vendôme to leave France. A long delay at Le Havre meant that supplies intended for Cayenne were consumed. Then at sea, the directors became fearful that the leader, Lieutenant General Le Roux de Royville, was behaving like Brétigny, and they promptly assassinated this Norman nobleman. The usual sicknesses and deprivations associated with putrid food and barely potable water tormented passengers on an exceptionally long voyage; only ten escaped illness.

At Cayenne, the directors soon engaged in civil conflict with one another. At one point, the factions signed a formal treaty of peace. At another, an African public executioner (*bourreau*) was assigned to remove the head of a condemned plotter. Other plotters were set ashore on a deserted island, ironically presaging the future infamy of Devil's Island.[42] Soon enough, once again, the colonists became entangled in disputes with the Galibis, and their lives became as insecure as those of their cousins simultaneously being tormented by Iroquois at the garrison island of Montréal. After barely one year, the remaining hundred or so colonists either fled to the neighboring English settlement at Suriname or accepted an English captain's offer of transport to Barbados.[43] This ignominious failure constituted the worst single French colonial disaster between Ribaut's Florida and the Kourou (once again Guiane) debacle of 1763–64.

In France, meanwhile, the Compagnie de la France équinoctiale launched a new round of propaganda. The military engineer Jean de

Laon d'Aigremont, who had returned to France shortly after the colonists had gone ashore, published an account that explained in more realistic, utilitarian terms the natural advantages of Cayenne.[44] The company distributed an attractive poster that depicted the landing of the first expedition at Cayenne in a highly idealized fashion. Cleared fields ready for sowing, friendly natives with gifts, and the orderly disembarking of the colonists are featured. The accompanying text touts the delicious attractions of the site and promises the poorest of Frenchmen that the company will transport them free of charge and provide them with supplies until the first harvests.[45] Another such piece was Paul Boyer's *Veritable relation* of the 1643 colony, which simultaneously promoted the wealth of Guiane and savaged the tyrannical behavior of Brétigny; thus it may have been intended as an indirect defense of the company directors responsible for Royville's assassination. Worth noting is the fact that Boyer dedicated his volume to Jean-Baptiste Colbert, then the steward of Mazarin's household. It is known that Mazarin invested in a Madagascar company in the 1650s. Did he or Colbert purchase stock in the Compagnie de la France équinoctiale as well? The company prepared a second expedition and promised potential investors further sailings.

Although it was not yet known in Paris that the colony had foundered, things started to unravel quickly for the Compagnie de la France équinoctiale in 1654. Bontemps's Compagnie rouennaise du Cap du Nord succeeded in bringing suit against it before the king's highest council, the Council of State. Cap du nord's petition was signed by Chancellor Séguier—a relative of Brétigny's—and the attorney general Nicholas Fouquet, among others. Both companies had to submit their patent letters. In combination with the Royville scandal, the failure to obtain Vendôme's permission, and rumors of debacle starting to permeate Paris led to a tremendous decline in the company's stock, now worth only 10 percent of face value. Company directors lamely claimed that the crown had no jurisdiction over the Royville murder, because the company had total judicial control over its affairs; and they proffered excuses for the unauthorized departure. The coup de grâce came when the Council of State, absent Fouquet, ruled in favor of Bontemps.

Because he was about to assert great influence over France's maritime affairs, it is germane to speculate about Fouquet's role in these affairs. Unless he was out of town or sick, his absence from the council's decision may indicate his involvement in one or both of the companies. Because he and Bontemps had been involved together in the Compagnie des Isles de l'Amérique and because his father held stock in the Cap du nord company, one might infer that he had a stake in the latter.[46] Other facts, however, point to his possible involvement in the Compagnie de la France équinoctiale, whose chief port was Nantes, on the Loire in Brittany. The Fouquets originated in that province and maintained strong clientage connections there. Next, Abbé Marivaut gave as his permanent address the house of the substitute of the attorney general (i.e., Fouquet). Furthermore, it is known that the bishop of Glandèves was involved with the Compagnie de la France équinoctiale, and he was close to Abbé Fouquet, brother of Nicholas. In the end, the evidence is too ambiguous to draw any firm conclusions, other than the probability of Fouquet's involvement in one or both of these companies.

Contemporary accounts suggest that these events struck a mighty blow against Guiane as a colonial destination and perhaps against French colonization in general. An affidavit in a lawsuit brought against the company by its agent at Nantes—he had lost his life savings—exemplifies the bitterness of those who considered themselves duped.[47] The next two efforts in Guiane would be on a smaller scale and in a lower key, because their authors were aware that only success could overcome public indifference, or even save the promoters from being ridiculed. The contemporary observer of these events and the greatest seventeenth-century historian of the French Caribbean, Father Dutertre, attests to the extraordinary publicity generated by the company, as well as to the depths of public disillusionment. An enormous skepticism, even cynicism, came to characterize public opinion about such enterprises. In the 1660s, memories were fresh and help in part explain public resistance to appeals for investments in companies promoted by Louis XIV and Colbert. Poor Guiane had taken a major step toward its image as a death trap for Frenchmen; an image that the spectacular disaster at Kourou in the 1760s would solidify.

Given these calamities, it is perhaps surprising that Guiane soon attracted another group of adventurers, but not Cayenne. Although confirmed to be in the possession of the Compagnie rouennaise du Cap du Nord, Cayenne was after 1654 actually in the possession of Dutch refugees from Brazil. Instead, the projected site of the new company was to the west, on the Ouarabiche river, a tributary of the Orinoco, and thus much closer to Spanish Trinidad. The initiator of the Compagnie de terre ferme ou l'Amérique méridionale was the Jesuit Pierre Pelleprat, who had gone with a colleague to establish a mission among the main-

land Indians. Pelleprat believed these indigenes to be far more susceptible to conversion than the obstreperous Caribs (who had recently massacred two Jesuits on Saint Vincent).

After the Spanish had lured his colleague in Guiane to their territory
only to imprison him, Pelleprat returned to France,[48] where he published an account of the islands and Guiane in which the latter emerged
as superior in every respect. That old friend of the Jesuits Nicholas Fouquet, now also powerful co-superintendent of French finances, received
the dedication.[49] Simultaneously and probably not coincidentally, the
comte de Pagan dedicated a translation of Spanish writings on the Amazon area to Mazarin and appealed to the cardinal to foster the creation
of a French dominion in northern South America, bounded by the Amazon River, Guiane, and Peru.[50] Then, the famous mapmaker Nicholas
Sanson dedicated a map of northern South America to Fouquet.[51] Concurrently, in 1655, a translation of Thomas Gage's exposé of the vulner-
abilities of Spain's American empire appeared.[52] When one is reminded
that in the same year Oliver Cromwell launched his famous "Western
Design" to dismember the Spanish empire, it may be speculated that
powerful figures in a France still engaged in bitter war with Spain harbored similar dreams. As France was now in alliance with a Portugal in
revolt against Spanish sovereignty, any worries about an Iberian pincer
attack on Guiane settlements had evaporated.[53]

Father Dutertre writes that the public heads of the company, otherwise unknown individuals, were fronts for powerful backers. It is quite
likely that the Compagnie du Saint-Sacrement was involved, because its
registers mention backing a small company to support missions in
"meridional" America. It is possible that Mazarin had a surreptitious part
in this newest Guiane scheme. He invested heavily in the fledgling
Madagascar colony.[54] Fort Anne was the name of the fort at the Ouatinigo River, suggesting the queen mother's patronage.[55] Much more evidence suggests Fouquet's involvement. In a letter to Mazarin in 1655,
Fouquet notes that he is working on a large-scale project with his trusted
client Pierre Chanut to buttress royal finances. Because Chanut often
acted as advisor to Fouquet on maritime affairs, it is not implausible that
Fouquet co-opted Pelleprat's plan to launch his own "Western Design."
Although Dutertre refused to name the powerful backers of the company, it is known that he had access to Fouquet's library and manuscripts.
The fact that the initial reconnaissance expedition of 1656 sailed *prior* to

the registering royal letters of patent with the Paris *parlement* suggests powerful backing (or stupidity); and the all-male composition of the crew argues for a Ribaut-style fortified garrison approach. Finally, the leader of the second follow-up expedition in 1657 was La Grange Fromentau, who was close to Fouquet's father in the 1630s and a veteran of the islands (see Chapter 3).

After a stopover at Martinique, the leader of the reconnaissance established a fort on a promontory on the Ouatinigo River. He sent an optimistic report to the company's directors, who published some promotional materials and its charter under the name of the Compagnie de l'Amérique méridionale. The company sent a follow-up expedition of 150 men in 1657. Upon reaching Martinique, these adventurers were thunderstruck to discover that Spanish besiegers had forced the abandonment of the Ouatinigo. Worse, the leader of the first expedition had simply appropriated all the company's provisions and indentured servants to start a sugar works at Martinique; he would later appear on the first Martinique census as a prominent planter.[56] Du Parquet tried with some success to get the colonists to stay. Some did, some returned to France, and some joined the buccaneers at Hispaniola and Tortuga, a twenty-five-miles-long island off Hispaniola's northwest coast accessible only by a single, easily fortified harbor, making it an ideal haven for pirates. As far as can be determined, there was not much publicity in France about this latest debacle in Guiane.[57]

Among those venturing to Hispaniola and Tortuga was Bertrand d'Ogeron de La Bouëre, the future "father" of the French colony of Saint-Domingue, who lost his inheritance in this Guiane venture. He found the world of the buccaneers in flux. In 1652, the tyrant Le Vasseur had been assassinated by his two closest advisors and heirs because of a dispute over a young woman and other insults, real or imaginary. Meanwhile, Poincy had persuaded a passing naval officer and fellow knight of Malta, the chevalier de Fontenay, to undertake the conquest of the island. Encountering a very different situation than what he had expected, Fontenay persuaded the tyrannicides to surrender the island without a fight in return for their freedom from trial. Fontenay proceeded to wreak havoc on Spanish shipping in the islands and along the Spanish Main, which soon led to a Spanish riposte from Hispaniola. In events more than worthy of a Hollywood spectacular, the Spanish used slaves to haul cannon up a mountain to put the supposedly impregnable fortress of

Tortuga at their mercy. Their maneuver, as described in the chronicles, perhaps surpassed in difficulty the ascent of James Wolfe to the Plains of Abraham at the battle of Québec in 1759.

Disorders and the Struggle for Order, 1656–1664

If there was any truth to Colbert's self-serving thesis of island instability during the proprietary period, then the events of the years 1656–64 provide a veneer of plausibility for it. Even before du Parquet's death in 1658, the population of Martinique may have been in decline due to the terrible hurricane of 1656 and the Carib and maroon challenges of that *annus horribilis*.[58] Small slave upheavals also occurred at Capesterre, Guadeloupe. Du Parquet's demise exacerbated the difficulties, because it left his wife Marie Bonnard (Madame la Générale) as regent for her minor children. Just as in France itself, the regency of a woman meant trouble. Madame ruled the island in conjunction with a faction of fellow Parisians, and the Norman friends of her husband became embittered. These colonists were a hard-driving, hard-fighting independent lot. Calling them "the libertines of the Antilles," one contemporary visitor rightly attributed their independence to their indispensable role as militiamen.[59] In 1658, rowdy rebels briefly imprisoned Madame because she attempted to ensure the quality of tobacco shipped to France. How convenient that they purportedly discovered a copy of Machiavelli's notorious *Prince* in her possession. After her release, she had du Parquet's brother, Adrien Dyel du Parquet, sieur de Vaudroques, come to the island to help her govern in the name of her son, Dyel d'Esnambuc.[60] At the same time, she put out signals about selling the island, and Nicholas Fouquet among others was apparently interested.[61]

On Guadeloupe, Houël and Boisseret squabbled repeatedly over the limits of their share of Guadeloupe, and so did their rival factions of colonists. In 1656, on a visit to Paris, an argument between the two became so verbally violent that Boisseret collapsed and died on the spot. But the sons of Boisseret, Houël's nephews the sieurs d'Herblay and Témericourt, pursued their claims, as did Houël's own brother Robert. Houël's long dispute with the Dominicans over a variety of issues, but especially their land claims proceeding from a contract with Pierre Liénard de l'Olive (1635), had come to the attention of the metropolitan authorities in the 1650s. Although the proprietors controlled justice in their islands, a final appeal was possible to the *parlement* of Paris, and the Dominicans had access to important people. Finally, the land claim disputes were resolved in 1658, but Houël's quarrels with family members were not. These brouhahas and near civil war damaged Guadeloupe and were a major reason why Louis XIV and Colbert decided to change the islands' administration.[62]

Nor was all quiet on Saint-Christophe toward the end of Poincy's rule. The *bailli* had always controlled commercial transactions on the island in conjunction with his chief officers and taxed the colonists,[63] but in 1660, he enraged them when he changed the capitation tax from pounds of tobacco to pounds of sugar. But the man of whom it was said that "few loved him, many hated him, and all feared him" was visibly declining in health, and the colonists were willing to await his death for relief. He had, after all, been their guarantee of safety from the neighboring English and independence from monopoly companies, as well as their means of access to Dutch credit. The sighs of relief at Poincy's death no doubt also emanated from Malta, which had tried to control this colonial Caesar by sending his kinsman and brother knight Charles Huault de Montmagny in 1653 to act as his assistant; but this former governor of New France (died 1657) did not outlive the seasoned Poincy. The latter, a typically enigmatic man of the baroque era, who combined greed and apparently sincere spirituality, a would-be king without a dauphin to succeed him, passed from the scene at the age of seventy-seven. Malta then dispatched Commander de Sales, nephew of the holy man François de Sales, to be governor at Saint-Christophe; he would have a difficult time quieting a turbulent population and dealing with the effects of a devastating hurricane in 1661.[64]

With the aftershocks of the Fronde diminishing in intensity by 1658, and with peace with Spain finally in sight, the sorry state of the French navy and the Dutch monopoly of the French Caribbean engendered calls for change. The young Louis XIV acted vigorously, even if perhaps still directed more toward affairs of the heart than to those of state. Informed opinion was certainly aware of the riches the sugar of Brazil and Barbados produced for Portugal and England, which explains the French enthusiasm for buying Antillean islands. Du Parquet had disposed of Carib-threatened Grenada to Jean de Faudos, comte de Cerillac, for the exorbitant price of 90,000 l.t.[65] That same public opinion chafed at the idea that France's colonies yielded few benefits to the kingdom. Just as the child was the property of the parents who generated him, it was said, so the colonies owed exclusive allegiance to the parent country. This metaphor was, of course, standard among Europe's "mercantilist" thinkers.

As we shall see, however, these colonial children had already reached a stage of adolescent rebelliousness.

The diffusion of authority in the Marine inhibited a coordinated program of maritime renewal. Vendôme still exercised authority as *grand maître et surintendant de la navigation,* and everything had to have his imprimatur as admiral. The fingerprints of the viceroy of America, the duc d'Amville, are detectable in this era; for example, he co-signed the grant of the governorship of Martinique and Sainte-Lucie to du Parquet's son, styled d'Esnambuc, with Vendôme. Secretary of State for Foreign Affairs Lomenie de Brienne involved himself in matters that would fall under the Marine after 1669. The cardinal, far too busy with Spain and with amassing a fortune in cash and objets d'art, could not be expected to supervise these matters closely. So he asked Nicholas Fouquet to take charge of them, or so the latter claimed from his jail cell years later.

Mazarin's valet Colbert thought, and the majority of historians ever since have believed, that Fouquet's claim was an effort to rationalize his plans to launch a maritime Fronde should he be arrested. Nevertheless, a number of his initiatives from 1658 to his arrest in September 1661 attest to his strong interest in overseas affairs. His long-term colonial activities have already been outlined, and he claimed that Cardinal Richelieu had in fact given him principal responsibility for the Marine after Fouquet *père*'s death. The weekly meetings of the Compagnie des Isles de l'Amérique and the Compagnie de l'Orient (founded in Dieppe in 1637 for the exploitation of Madagascar) took place at his Paris *hôtel* (townhouse). Historians credit him with imposing a tax of fifty *sols* per ton on foreign imports into France.[66]

In 1658, Fouquet bought the strategic island of Belle-Île opposite the mouth of the Loire—at the cardinal's insistence, he asserted, to prevent the former Fronde rebel the duc de Brissac from acquiring it—and immediately established a secretive program of fortifications and ship building there. He was now not only attorney general but the sole superintendent of finance, a lucrative post even if the holder were only modestly corrupt. Soon, Fouquet's ships, bought in Holland, were supplying fish for his newly constructed sardine factory, engaging in the Newfoundland cod fisheries, raiding all along the Atlantic coast, and transporting textiles to the Far East for a profit of 350,000 l.t. Simultaneously, he pushed through the *parlement* of Paris registration of patent letters granting the vice-royalty of America to the duc d'Amville, an office that might be useful in reestablishing metropolitan control of the

French islands. Fouquet had similarly used his influence, it may be recalled, to register the patent letters granting his Jesuit friends the right to establish missions in the Americas wherever it pleased them.[67]

The capture of Fouquet's papers after his arrest demonstrated his control of other fortified ports in Brittany and Normandy, and provided evidence that he had systematically acquired clients in the navy and among maritime officials. Particularly damaging was a document apparently composed in panic that Mazarin planned to act against him; in it, Fouquet wildly plotted a riposte, which depended on his maritime strength and powerful people on whom he supposed he could count. In 1660, his money bought the office of viceroy of America for the marquis de Pas de Feuquières; Vice Admiral de Neuchèze was apparently in his pay. Suspicion fell on the comte d'Estrade, hero of the siege of Dunkirk, and the Huguenot Abraham Duquesne, perhaps the best naval captain of his day. These documents also show that the powerful superintendent had secretly bought the island of Sainte-Lucie, had purchased estates in Guadeloupe and Martinique, and had attempted to force the sale of the latter to him. He apparently had significant clients in the islands. All of this and more easily convinced the king and Colbert that Fouquet intended to dominate maritime France for his private benefit and to use this power as a veiled threat against the king. The hand-picked judges who tried Fouquet were not so persuaded, and they convicted him on charges of gross corruption but not of treason.

Fouquet explained his maritime initiatives as a program of maritime renewal for France. He hoped to reduce Dutch dominance of French maritime commerce, and thus his work at Belle-Île to make it a new Amsterdam. The colonies had to be returned to metropolitan control, and trade with Madagascar and the Far East reinvigorated. A memoir of 1663 explains that Fouquet had been in contact with merchants of various port cities to create a company to trade with the Orient. Unlike his successor, Colbert, he apparently believed a modus vivendi could be established with the Dutch, France's traditional friends, on the basis of freedom of commerce in each other's spheres of influence overseas. In a memoir of June 1661, the French ambassador to Holland referred to this "Company of France" as a fait accompli.[68] The navy and merchant marine needed revitalization; although he had no authority over the navy, Fouquet could provide an impulse to the merchant marine.

Fouquet was able to demonstrate his long-term interest in all these matters, and pointed out that upon Mazarin's death, the king had put him

in charge of a council of commerce. This council had started its task by
soliciting memoirs on maritime issues from all over the kingdom. Serving under him was none other than Colbert, now his implacable enemy.
Then just a month before his arrest, and upon the advice of Fouquet's
client Feuquières, the Council of State authorized new companies for
the American trade and ordered possessors of concessions in the Americas to hand them in within ten months. These plans may well have been
to promote the private interests of the superintendent as well as of
France, and in that he would not have been acting differently from his
two cardinal mentors.

If Fouquet had succeeded Mazarin, as he ardently hoped he would,
how would he have dealt with colonial matters? The only safe conclusion is that he would not have paid the detailed attention to these matters that his famous successor, Colbert, did. Fouquet was a very different character indeed. A baroque figure, he managed to reconcile sexual
frivolities with an apparently sincere spirituality.[69] Colbert, who was as
cold in his demeanor as his contemporary René Descartes, exhibited neither pattern of behavior. The would-be *grand seigneur* Fouquet flaunted
his artistic and intellectual interests, and acted the part of a Maecenas
or a French Lorenzo de' Medici. Colbert would have regretted every
livre spent on Versailles had he not recognized the glory it brought his
king.

Whereas Colbert concerned himself only with pleasing Louis XIV,
Fouquet devoted much energy and substantial resources to building immense networks of support—Anne of Austria and other courtiers, the
parlement, the Jesuits, the *dévots*, and intellectual elites. These efforts
were counterproductive, because the future Sun King felt growing resentment at not being the absolute center of attention, especially when
his rival was an individual acting well above his station.[70]

Fouquet would thus never have devoted significant parts of his time
to details of the marine and colonies as his successor did. Fouquet's explicit model was Cardinal Richelieu: "As a great figure, he formed diverse companies for commerce and the establishment of colonies," but
with so many political and diplomatic tasks, he did not handle the petty
details.[71] Already by the 1650s, Fouquet depended on Pierre Chanut to
handle such matters, and on at least one occasion the latter exasperat-
edly asked the superintendent to get a secret royal order to have Vaudroques, the enemy of Fouquet's faction at Martinique, shipped home

for trial. Apparently, the great man was otherwise preoccupied, because this was not done.[72]

Although Fouquet's explanations of his maritime interests most certainly did not convince the king and Colbert, his actions in the years 1658–61 and the information contained in his papers provided an unacknowledged blueprint for Colbert. To be sure, the triumphant new minister already possessed a stock of staple ideas, now sometimes labeled Colbertism.[73] They can be reduced to these: the sinews of war are money; there is a fixed quantity of wealth in the world, as expressed in bullion; short of war, commerce is the best way to increase wealth, as Colbert's nemesis, the Dutch, had demonstrated; the state had to protect the country's merchants by protective tariffs, subsidies, and other privileges, as well as by naval force; colonies were necessary to supply the raw materials that could not be produced in France and to provide outlets for manufactures. However, before an effective colonial program could be implemented, many obstacles had to be overcome. Colbert proceeded with extraordinary energy to overcome these impediments.

Even a Colbert could not act immediately. The early 1660s, especially 1661–62, saw widespread misery in France, the result of famines and disease. "I think the Tupinambá are happier in their barbarism than our peasants are today," one commentator opined.[74] De facto finance minister, but without the title of the abolished office of superintendent of finance, Colbert had a devilish time coming up with the money to purchase Dunkirk from the English in 1662. Revenues for the year 1662–63 declined from 75,568,754 l.t. to 48,053,826 l.t., with corresponding decreases in spending.[75] He had the difficult task of coordinating the prosecution of Fouquet who, after a period of depression and resignation, used all of his considerable talents and friends to make life difficult for "Mazarin's domestic," as he contemptuously labeled Colbert. Trapping the squirrel (Fouquet's emblem on his coat of arms) proved as frustrating to Colbert as homeowners find the task today. The sad state of the navy, which consisted of barely twenty, mostly decrepit ships, and which in 1660 received the derisory annual sum of 300,000 l.t., would have to be overcome before implementing any ambitious colonial or commercial programs. These impediments explain the nearly three-year gap before the launching of the West India and East India Companies; in truth, given the monstrous problems, such a delay appears brief.

In those three years, Colbert prepared for action. Historians sometimes forget that he did not become minister of the Marine until 1669, and especially in the early 1660s, he had difficulty asserting the de facto authority Louis gave him. As secretary of state for foreign affairs, Brienne controlled naval forces in the Mediterranean and asserted authority in a number of colonial and commercial affairs. For example, in 1662, he authorized a concession of the Bahamas to Bertrand d'Ogeron.[76] Colbert's key advisor the comte d'Estrade, recently appointed viceroy of America, complained to Colbert that he had not been consulted about this appointment. It appears that Colbert knew nothing about the Bahamas matter, which may explain his subsequent coldness to d'Ogeron, universally considered a great colonial servant of Louis XIV.[77] The obstreperous Admiral Vendôme still made trouble, and in 1662 would not allow the departure of royal ships for New France. Another key informant and advisor of Colbert's, his cousin Colbert de Terron, intendant of the Marine at La Rochelle, verbally shook his head at such "fantasies." It would take years before Colbert's authority in these matters received unquestioned recognition.[78]

In these same years, Colbert had to assemble a team of advisors and implementers, and almost everywhere he looked, he found men who had had close associations with the redoubtable Fouquet. Some, like Feuquières and Chanut, withdrew from public life, but many others switched horses with more or less alacrity. Those who had unsubstantiated accusations against them, such as d'Estrade and the famed naval captain Duquesne, were immediately employed. The marine engineer Clerville confessed to Colbert that he had taken a 10,000 l.t. gift from Fouquet. Absolved, Clerville soon undertook an important survey of France's ports and naval arsenals.[79] Vice Admiral Neuchèze eventually received rehabilitation. Like Fouquet, Colbert also looked to Holland for ships to start the restoration of the French navy; he found it convenient to employ Fouquet's agent there. Other than trusted intimates such as Terron and d'Estrade, Colbert employed rehabilitated personnel out of necessity. He well recognized the temptations of the patronage of a powerful man.

Obtaining reliable information about the colonies and placing his people in authority was even more difficult than assembling a loyal clientage. The Madagascar and New France companies were not accountable for how they administered their domains. News of the proprietary governments in the Caribbean arrived in Paris only as a result of lawsuits and affidavits. D'Estrade, viceroy of America, admitted that he knew no one in the islands. Terron was not then much better informed. Fortunately, Colbert was able to consult the papers of the incarcerated Fouquet, as well as the seven volumes of memoirs solicited by the 1661 council of commerce, and he borrowed many of the fallen minister's plans for maritime renewal.[80]

Two guiding principles help explain Colbert's selection of naval and colonial personnel. First, whenever possible, he chose kinsmen or clients for key positions on the principle that these were more trustworthy. A historian of New France has shown that nearly all of the intendants appointed there were relatives of Colbert's by blood or marriage.[81] In the Caribbean, the intendant Michel Bégon exemplifies this tendency; like Colbert's relative Jean Talon, the famous intendant of New France, Bégon accepted his overseas promotion with little enthusiasm. The trusted d'Estrade recommended his friend Alexandre Prouville de Tracy to Colbert for the role of proconsul to bring order to the American colonies. Exceptions to the clientage principle sometimes occurred in the case of the office of governor of a colony, because of the overriding importance of military command experience for dangerous frontier areas. The second principle derived from the current belief, fully shared by Colbert, that other than clients, only second-rate men, or men down on their luck, would accept positions overseas. He was explicit on this point, observing that "the difficulty is to find a proper subject for that position, being certain that those who could be effective in it do not want to hazard such a long voyage."[82] To take Tracy as an example, this honorable sexagenarian veteran of innumerable military campaigns importuned Colbert for a position in 1662 because of near bankruptcy. A perennial headache for the minister, and future ones as well, was dealing with colonial officials who acted as if they were doing the king a big favor by relocating overseas, despite the mediocrity or worse of their past performances.[83]

These principles and realities help explain why, in late 1662, Colbert even entertained the proposal of Antoine Le Febvre de La Barre to form a company to establish a French colony at Cayenne. Son of an important official of the *parlement* of Paris, La Barre had risen to be intendant of the Bourbonnais. However, there were such complaints about him that Colbert recommended his dismissal to Mazarin in 1659. Apparently, La Barre's corrupt ties to tax farmers engendered strong provincial antipathy to him.[84] Mazarin for some reason did not act, perhaps because La Barre was a client of the important minister of war, Michel Le Tel-

lier. Things got worse in 1661–62, when revolts broke out in the Bourbonnais. La Barre heard rumors of his impending dismissal and wrote a
sycophantic letter to Colbert begging for his protection. It certainly
seems as though Colbert gambled that the man would perform better
overseas. When Terron reported to him in 1663 about La Barre's incompetence, the minister replied tellingly: "[W]hat we may hope for is
that, knowing that this is his last chance, there is some reason to hope
that if things do not go as well under his command as one might desire,
they will at least not go disastrously. And if we find out that he is attempting to create an establishment independent of the company, it will
be easy enough to remedy that kind of foolishness."[85] Despite repeated
complaints about La Barre's conduct, Colbert stuck with him, perhaps
faute de mieux.

The reader may well wonder how Colbert fell into the "Guiane trap,"
since he was aware of the past debacles. Far from intellectually brilliant,
he was a typical man of action and proceeded full steam ahead, governed
by some simple principles. This trait has fooled some scholars into thinking of him as shackled by dogma. One of his governing ideas in the early
1660s was that a Guiane colony would serve as supplier of horses, cattle,
and provisions to the Windward Islands, as well as develop its potential
in tropical cash crops. La Barre's memoir of 1662 made a very reasonable case that the failures of the past had resulted from the interlocking
problems of poor leadership and shortsighted policies toward the Galibis Indians, who had already been alienated by repeated buccaneer slave
raids.[86] After all, had not the governor of Barbados, Francis Lord Willoughby, sent 300 men to establish a successful settlement at Suriname?
And had not Dutch and Portuguese Jewish exiles from Brazil succeeded
at Cayenne where the French had failed? Colbert can hardly be blamed
for failing to understand that those colonies had possessed two essential
features the French had lacked—seasoned colonists, less susceptible to
disease and more experienced in tropical life, and significant numbers of
African slaves to perform much of the heavy labor. Like all successful
men of action, Colbert would gradually modify his enthusiasm for
Guiane and most other such guiding notions; in short, he was hardly a
slave to dogma.

The minister did not consider the Guiane enterprise in isolation, but
only as a preliminary step to the reestablishment of royal authority
everywhere in the French Atlantic.[87] Other than its reoccupation of
Cayenne, the Compagnie de Guiane was to serve as a stalking horse for

a much larger organization; indeed, its stock would simply be rolled over to form the basis of the 1664 Compagnie des Indes occidentales françaises. Prouville de Tracy accompanied La Barre and his colonists to Cayenne in 1664 with full royal powers to recall the private proprietors and regulate the affairs of the islands and of New France. His visit initiated the beginning of the end of frontier independence in the French Caribbean. Leviathan was slowly awakening from its torpor.

In the first four decades of settlement (1625–64), French colonists, primarily from western France, established themselves more or less securely in the Greater Caribbean without significant assistance or direction from the state. Comparison with English settlement of Barbados, and especially with the Leeward Islands (St. Christopher, Antigua, Nevis, and Montserrat), yields far greater similarities than differences. Neither French chartered colonial companies nor English proprietary lordships were able to exert much control over the lives of the "adventurers" who were risking life and limb to settle in the tropics. In both cases, the island colonies searched for a viable staple, which they found, first, in tobacco, then in alternatives like indigo, cotton, and, finally, sugar. Both tried desperately to secure adequate coerced labor in the form of white indentured servants and enslaved Africans. Both had to learn to live with or fight the Island Caribs. Finally, both French and English settlements in the 1660s had to deal with rising state interest in a greater say in their affairs. Frontier freedom (for free whites, of course) was now to come under serious threat.

CHAPTER FIVE

Frontier-Era Free Society
The 1620s to the 1660s

The early decades of European settlement in the Americas, fraught with struggle, have aroused the imagination of historians and descendants of those pioneers. Today, in our postcolonial era, historians and anthropologists have contested traditional, sometimes romanticized narratives of early struggles. Witness the brouhaha concerning Columbus during the quincentenary in 1992. In my book *Cannibal Encounters: Europeans and Island Caribs*, I contest traditional approaches to the French encounter with the aborigines of the Lesser Antilles. Nevertheless, in Canada, the United States, Europe, and parts of Latin America, it is not difficult to find laudatory appraisals of such as Columbus and Hernán Cortés, John Smith and John Winthrop, Champlain and La Salle, or more broadly of the Western colonial project. A few years ago, the French National Assembly passed a law mandating that the "positive aspects" of France's colonial past be incorporated into school curricula. The Puritan hegira into the "wilderness" and Jesuit exploits in Huronia and Paraguay still are the subjects of histories, novels, and movies, such as *Black Robe* (1991) and *The Mission* (1986). Until recently, French occupation of Caribbean islands in the seventeenth century occasionally generated positive historical treatment, but explicit or implicit condemnation of the settler era has now become the norm; that is, when it is not ignored.

In the first decades of settlement, as depicted in previous chapters, French settlers removed the Island Caribs from various islands, introduced indentured servant labor, and imported African slaves as quickly as they could afford them to work their tobacco habitations (a term that covered land, buildings, and indentured servants and slaves). Concurrently, colonists devastated a fragile environment.

Modern historians view these actions with more or less overt distaste. Unlike the Puritans of Massachusetts or the French in Québec, settlers in the Caribbean did not leave a significant body of descendants who might rise to their defense, or, more properly, put their actions into appropriate historical context. Conversely, the Island Caribs also have so few descendants today that current criticism of European aggression against their ancestors has been marginalized. In 2005, Dominica Caribs attempted to fight Disney's forthcoming sequel to *Pirates of the Caribbean* (2003), in which their ancestors were to be portrayed as cannibals. The film *Pirates of the Caribbean: Dead Man's Chest* appeared in 2006, and after seeing it, I doubt whether more than one in a million viewers would connect the name "Carib" with the farcical "natives" depicted. Furthermore, the tendency to evaluate the society seventeenth-century settlers created in the islands as the original from which the harsh eighteenth-century plantation regime emerged can distort historical interpretations. The burden of this and the subsequent chapter is to place this era in historical context, without, however, seeking to explain away the often unjustifiable conduct of many colonists. The comparative context in which to understand this era is not the classic "plantation complex" of the eighteenth and nineteenth centuries, but other seventeenth-century societies on the Atlantic rim.

The great strength and weakness of many social scientists is their propensity to making grand generalizations without much concern for evidentiary support. In their search to establish social typologies—for example, the structure of the plantation regime—they often take an overly static approach to change over time. On the other hand, the great strength and weakness of most historians is their hesitancy about offering large generalizations, because of the typically insufficient evidence to support such assertions. Many historians' favorite words are a pensive "but," a frowning "except," and—a favorite—"nuance." The dean of modern French Caribbean historians, Gabriel Debien, epitomized this attitude. His classic putdown was: "Il n'est qu'un sociologue" (He's nothing but a sociologist). Debien long resisted writing a general account of the Caribbean plantation regime, arguing that not enough empirical research had been completed. My propensity as a historian is also extreme caution about skyscraper generalizations; however, this chapter on "frontier era" society and a later one on "pre-plantation" society demand some generalizations in the two-story house range (as opposed to historians' preference for bungalows). The brevity of this volume, and the intended audience of upper-level and graduate students, the curious public, and those with a professional interest in the comparative history of the Atlantic World, dictate this approach. What follows is the academic equivalent of seventeenth-century Caribbean colonists setting off on a

Hunting manatees and turning over turtles. From Jean-Baptiste Dutertre, *Histoire générale des isles Antilles*, 2: 246.

journey filled with overt and hidden dangers, albeit that scholarly critics are, of course, far preferable to sharks, mosquitoes, and vipers.

Clearly, the decades before 1660 may be characterized as more "frontier" than those afterwards, with the 1650s as a transition to the pre-plantation era of the 1660s to 1690s. Serious environmental degradation had already occurred by 1660. Where had all the manatees and sea turtles gone? Prized trees such as the mahogany and logwood were becoming relatively rare. Even the number of feral pigs, also responsible for environmental degradation, had dramatically diminished due to colonists' ravenous appetite for them. Practically all of Saint-Christophe was in a state of deforestation, although at least half of Guadeloupe and Martinique still remained untouched by Europeans.

Sugar planting started its very gradual ascent from the 1640s on, but expanded especially after 1654. Some evidence points to a significant growth in the number of African slaves during the 1650s. John McCusker estimates that in 1650, 19 percent of inhabitants of the French islands were black, whereas in 1660, that figure was 36 percent.[1] However, these figures are guesstimates, especially the 1650 number. By 1670, more certainly, some 16,000 slaves toiled in the French islands, representing significant growth from the 1660 figure.[2] By 1660, most Island Caribs had been restricted to the reservation islands of Dominica and Saint Vincent, and their abandoned areas such as Grande-Terre, the eastern island of Guadeloupe, and the eastern half of Martinique became available for habitations. After 1664, the state started to claim greater authority over island affairs, with some limited success. These factors signaled the gradual ending of the frontier era. What I then call a pre-plantation era lasted to about 1700, before the transformation to the plantation complex, the classic planter-slave regime so well known in the historical literature. These are admittedly somewhat arbitrary categories, made necessary by the fact that a chapter on the social history of the era from the 1620s to 1700 would be impossibly long.

This chapter and three subsequent ones (Chapters 6, 9, 10) argue that island society during the frontier and pre-plantation eras was significantly different from the eighteenth-century plantation complex. Furthermore, frontier and pre-plantation societies did not *inevitably* evolve into "mature" plantation regimes, even though they in fact usually did. In the French Caribbean context, I prefer the term "plantation regime" to "sugar and slave regime," because although sugar was the most important crop, others, such as indigo, cotton, and, by the 1730s, coffee played more significant roles than they did in the British Caribbean. My intent is simply to highlight what forces pushed most French colonies out of their frontier and pre-plantation eras into a particular type of "maturity," that of the triumph of plantation monoculture. After all, not all Caribbean islands so evolved; for example, Spanish Hispaniola in this era and some of the smaller French and English islands remained in a pre-plantation or even frontier phase well into the eighteenth century. Sociologists and historians have inadequately recognized the distinct characteristics of society in the French Caribbean prior to the eighteenth-century plantation regime.

As I use it here, the term "frontier era" refers to more than just an initial period of coping with indigenous peoples and the "wilderness," which Native Americans had already significantly altered before Europeans arrived, just as they had elsewhere in the "New World."[3] As with all American frontier eras, the crucial problems for free people in the French Caribbean (habitants) were how to secure laborers to work the (relatively) plentiful land and, once they were secured, how to control unfree workers. Most frontier and then pre-plantation era colonies, especially tropical and semi-tropical ones, solved their labor problems by employing first European indentured servants and then, increasingly, if concurrently, West African slaves. Thus the difference between the earlier periods and the plantation complex regime was not slavery itself but the numbers of slaves vis-à-vis the free population. There is no exact formula here, but when a plantation society such as Barbados in the 1680s had moved toward a three-to-one ratio of slaves to free people, it was in rapid transition to a plantation complex phase.[4] By the mid eighteenth century, many plantation regimes had six, eight, or even ten slaves for every free person. By comparison, in 1700, only the most "advanced" French colonies (Martinique and Saint-Domingue) had even two slaves per European.[5]

The effect of such demographic ratios was felt in all aspects of frontier-era societies. A number of historians have recently asserted that master-slave relations in such societies were less oppressive than the plantation complex regime. Examples of frontier era societies with slaves include seventeenth-century Virginia, the late seventeenth- and early eighteenth-century Carolina Low Country, eighteenth-century Louisiana, Spanish Hispaniola, and the southern section of Saint-Domingue.[6] In such societies, slaves, of course, worked in plantation agriculture—tobacco, rice, cotton, and indigo—but monoculture was far from the norm. Masters employed slaves to perform a large variety of tasks, including plantation agriculture, provision farming, construction, hunting, fishing, logging, and herding, many of which occasioned de facto freedom of movement, the bearing of arms, and decision-making. Colonial insecurities resulting from hostilities with other colonies or with aboriginal populations sometimes led to the use of armed slaves as auxiliaries; in the French case, this was a not infrequent occurrence. Slaves working in agriculture often toiled in proximity to masters, because absentee owners, so typical of the plantation complex phase, were rare during the frontier era. Shortages of European women in the early decades led to "interracial" unions, legitimized or not. It would be extremely naïve to conclude from these facts that master-slave relations were benign—far from it. However, they were marginally less oppressive than those of the mature plantation period.

The slightly provocative subtitle of this book is meant to question whether the seventeenth-century French Caribbean colonies should be described with the same highly negative broad strokes deservedly used for the plantation complex of the eighteenth and early nineteenth centuries. The legitimacy of depicting the seventeenth-century frontier and pre-plantation eras similarly is, at least, debatable. To evaluate the "quality of life" of all island groups during the seventeenth century, the question must be asked: to what or to whom should these islanders—Native Americans, Europeans, Africans, African Americans, and people of color—be compared? The affluent, relatively disease-free middle and upper classes of the early twenty-first-century developed world are obviously not comparable. Such a statement may seem downright silly, but even professional historians have consciously to recall the problem involved. Some historians have fruitfully compared American slave societies to others characterized by forced labor, for example, to tsarist Russia or South Africa.[7] The most obvious comparisons (attempted below) are with other American slave societies at similar stages of development. But it would also be fruitful to compare the lives of African or African American (Creole) slaves with slaves in West Africa, although the state of scholarship makes this difficult. Similarly, why not evaluate the lives of European colonists in comparison to the lives of those of similar social station who stayed in the lands of their birth?

Fortunately, much information is now available about European social conditions in the seventeenth century, when elite comments on the shortage of good white bread in, say, Martinique also described the situation in much of France. That the tropical climate did not support the vine does not mean that every Frenchman had wine with his meals every day in the seventeenth century. The privileged twenty-first century historian enjoying a leisurely drive through lush Normandy or vine-laden Burgundy or the olive groves of Provence may unconsciously filter out academic knowledge about the miseries of most people in seventeenth-century France. Contemporary commentators who described their homeland as the acme of civilization either belonged to or wrote for the elite. Ordinary Frenchmen were not as loathe to emigrate as contemporary and some current writers maintain.[8]

The social misery of the large majority of seventeenth-century Frenchmen is now established beyond doubt. True, historians debate about how bad the times were and the extent of the problem, but it seems certain that conditions worsened after the later sixteenth century. Robert Jütte speaks of the period between 1630 and 1750 as one of "depression" for all Europe.[9] Although France was among the more blessed areas of Europe in terms of its varied resources, its population did not significantly increase in the seventeenth century. The problems were both natural and man-made. In the first category were weather-induced food shortages, usually attributed to a colder climate (the so-called "Little Ice Age"),[10] and related outbursts of epidemic diseases, especially the seemingly decennial bubonic plague. Food deprivation characterized the Paris region in the years 1590–91, 1630–32, 1642–43, 1648–53 (the Fronde era), and 1660–63, and then again in the last decades of Louis XIV's reign, especially the dreadful years of 1693 and 1709. Overall, according to Paul Bondois, eleven major and thirty-three minor famines tormented seventeenth-century Frenchmen.[11]

It is estimated that the French population of some eighteen to nineteen million fell by one to one and a half million in the horrendous years 1660–63.[12] Although France did not suffer the sensational "die-offs" of Italy in the 1630s to 1650s or have an episode equal to the catastrophic London plague of 1665, the kingdom suffered episodically from the disastrous epidemics that pockmarked this century. The mortality rate of Frenchmen at that time has been estimated at thirty-five per thousand per annum, which average includes wildly fluctuating years. When the ravages of malaria and other tropical diseases are discussed below, these should not mentally be compared to hygienic conditions and mortality rates of modern advanced countries.[13] Perhaps the dreadful medical situation in parts of Africa today is a better comparison. When the threadbare condition of indentured servants in tropical climates is discussed below, it must be remembered that poor cousin Jacques in France wore not much more in that exceptionally cold century.

The seemingly incessant wars and internal upheavals of seventeenth-century France both reflected and aggravated the above conditions. In 1652, during the frightening, chaotic Fronde, a contemporary report paints a picture of "villages and hamlets deserted and bereft of clergy, streets infected by stinking carrion and dead bodies lying exposed . . . everything reduced to cesspools . . . and above all the sick and dying, with no bread, meat, medicine, fire, beds . . . or anyone to comfort them."[14] Although foreign invasions did not have as devastating an impact on Frenchmen as they did on contemporary Germans and Poles, to prevent such incursions and to expand French power, royal officials increased significantly the tax burden, almost all of which fell on the poorest 95 percent. And they did so through a mechanism—tax farming—that aggravated the burden substantially. One estimate suggests that the tax burden for a family of four increased from the equivalent of seven days' agricultural output in 1547 to fourteen days' in 1607 to thirty-four by 1675, although estimates vary wildly by region because of vastly differing tax burdens. One estimate is that peasant rents increased by a third to "even a half" between 1600 and 1660, when France's population reached a relatively high plateau after 150 years (ca. 1450–1600) of growth.[15]

The tax burden on French cottages ranged from approximately 20 to 50 percent. It averaged 32 percent in one exceptionally well studied area, the Beauvaisis.[16] Neither social services nor infrastructure construction compensated for this burden, and noble, clerical, and even mercantile elites paid few taxes. Finally, the famous inflation of prices that lasted until the 1640s, during which the cost of bread significantly surpassed any concomitant increase in wages, stirred up social discontent.[17] In the final analysis, only about 10 to 15 percent of peasants possessed enough land to maintain a relatively secure and independent existence.[18] The twenty hectares of land offered to former indentured servants after three years of island service may have seemed attractive given these circumstances.

Social and political protests were to be expected in such conditions. Between 1590 and 1715, 450 tumults erupted in southwestern France alone.[19] Social, political, and religious rebellions had certain characteristics in common, not unrelated to conditions in the Caribbean. With some exceptions, entire communities rebelled against alien, exterior forces, especially outsiders claiming privileges stemming from state authorities (government officials, tax farmers, monopoly companies). Leaders of these revolts were often locally important people, who provided them with some legitimacy.[20] On the whole, these were not class revolts but instead violent outbursts of frustration with the distant royal court. The profession of tax collector was an exceptionally dangerous one. However, outright violence was far from the only means of protest. Much more frequent was tax evasion, especially in the form of extensive smuggling of such highly taxed items as salt (a tax known as the *gabelle*) and, after 1674, tobacco. Just as today, smuggling rings employed children, who usually received lighter sentences when caught. Endemic smuggling was thus not exceptional behavior among the French overseas.

Contemporary privileged groups were certainly aware of, even paranoid about, these upheavals even when they themselves were not involved. Near hysteria about able-bodied and primarily young male "vagabonds" characterizes the era. Elites referred to the underclass as a swarm of locusts ready to descend on the fields of the propertied, and "outside agitators" were always, if often falsely, blamed for riots and rebellions.[21] A veritable crime wave seemed to be engulfing respectable society, and among the responses were massive incarceration in poorhouses (*hôpitaux*), the living death of galley service, and calls to transport the rogues overseas. The brutality of punishments during the era still stuns the modern reader. A soldier who deserted at Saint-Domingue in 1696 was humiliated by having his hair razed, was disfigured by having his nose and ears chopped off and was dispatched to a life-without-parole sentence in the hellish galleys.[22] This desertion did not even occur in battle. To be sure, just as today, desperate, alienated, or unscrupulous people also committed enough crimes and participated in enough threatening gang activities to fuel the fears of more fortunate folk.

Settling Down: From the 1620s to the 1660s

From the 1620s to the 1660s, European settlers arrived, transformed the landscape, and established agricultural habitations. French and other European settlers descended upon islands characterized by extremely alien natural environments and aboriginal inhabitants. Unfortunately, the early settlers were silent about their physical, social, and especially psychological responses to this "New World." Still, enough evidence remains to present impressions of their struggles to cope with new realities, and how such struggles slowly transformed those who survived and decided to stay (a distinct minority) from Europeans into American Creoles. (The term "Creoles" is used here simply to mean those born in the Americas or who had adopted an American lifestyle distinct from that of their European, African, or Native American ancestors.) Their experiences, to be sure, included episodes of regrettable violence toward the native flora and fauna and the aboriginal inhabitants, and these habitants often harshly used indentured servants and slaves. Yet raw courage and adaptability also characterized them. Such contradictions define the human condition during contact and settlement eras.

The passage to the islands took a toll on most passengers, ranging from the mild discomforts of seasickness, temperature swings, and monotonous, overly salty foods to deathly illnesses resulting from contaminated food, putrid water, and the transmission of diseases in crowded, filthy ships. Too often, ship outfitters (*armateurs*) skimped on provisions or used poor-quality goods to maximize profits; the complaints, especially from the mid seventeenth century, are routine and bitter.[23]

The mortality rate could be very high. On his 1627 voyage, Pierre Blain d'Esnambuc, the "founding father" of the French Antilles, lost more than 300 passengers, and 100 others were so weakened that they died soon after disembarking. And of some 600 passengers in 1652 to the island of Cayenne, the chief settlement in Guiane, only ten did not suffer sickness. Such examples could easily be multiplied.

True, many difficulties resulted from uncontrollable natural elements—adverse winds, tempestuous seas, and hurricanes—but many were man-made. Captains made sailing errors. Distances were huge. When our sources refer to *lieues*, or maritime leagues, these were longer than the land equivalent; one French maritime league equaled 5.5 kilometers, or about 3.4 miles. Ships chased by pirates and privateers might be pushed so far off course that supplies ran low or worse.

In his interesting memoir to Colbert in 1669 and in instructions to his ship's captain, Bertrand d'Ogeron pointed out both the myriad problems and how to correct them. He had just transported 225 people in a seventy-ton ship without a single death. His basic message is: treat passengers as human beings, not as cattle, and many more of them will survive; do not treat them as if they were prisoners; keep tight control over the sailors, who, if permitted, will act cruelly and steal the passengers' goods. D'Ogeron instructs his captain to feed the passengers fresh meat and produce as long as possible, because in combination with the salt air, the typical dried biscuit and salt meat fare "terribly heats" the blood and causes such thirst that the ship's water supply cannot possibly satisfy it. He provides a healthy daily menu. At breakfast, he mandates that passengers have oatmeal or barley gruel cooked with "good fat." For midday dinner, the captain should cook a pot of peas, beans, or rice and near the end put in the evening's salt pork to season it and simultaneously preserve water. The sick are to have a special menu, including eggs, butter, mutton, and fowl, and furthermore are to be provided with comfortable places on ship to recuperate. D'Ogeron concludes with a bitter denunciation of the "bourgeois" shipowners and conniving captains who with a "laugh" sent so many passengers to their graves.[24]

The fate of passengers on shore in the Caribbean depended greatly on the stage of the colony's development at their time of arrival. Those debarking during the very first years found their "seasoning" period correspondingly more difficult in almost all ways. Of the first 1,200 or so French emigrants to Saint-Christophe, only 350 still survived in 1629. Such mortality rates will not surprise students of Virginia or Jamaica. Chroniclers described the weakened state of the first colonists at Guadeloupe. Plagued by swellings characteristic of edema (dropsy) and "trembling in the feet and head," these men were commanded to work long hours in a hot climate very different from that of northern France and were fed inadequately. Melancholia quickly overtook them, and many died.[25]

Previous chapters have described French failures in Guiane. One chronicler, Abbé Antoine Biet, laughed bitterly that the 1652 expedition had not even brought fishing equipment.[26] Father Jean-Baptiste Dutertre's story of the first years of the Guadeloupe colony is bone-chilling. On an island from which Island Caribs easily extracted a living, the French starved. The island was not after all a garden of paradise where one simply lived off the fruit. Colonists lacked both the technologies and skills of the indigenes, especially in agriculture and fishing.[27] They could not build or handle the dugout canoes (pirogues) necessary for fishing and turtle and manatee hunting. They could and did slaughter feral pigs and killed sea turtles at proper season (September and October), but these were not the stuff of daily bread. They were not proficient at finding and killing Carib "game" animals such as hutias or iguanas, or shooting fowl. And so they raided Indian gardens, thus touching off a cycle of conflict all too familiar to students of early European–Native American relations.

Without experienced colonists as guides, the earliest settlers had to discover how to build simple palm-thatch huts, how to avoid poisonous fruits (especially the green, apple-like fruit of the Manchineel tree) and, on some islands, aggressive, venomous snakes, especially the viper known as the fer-de-lance. Perhaps most vexing, island vermin, including various kinds of mosquitoes and other biting insects, tormented habitants. Chiggers burrowed into exposed feet. European-imported rats multiplied at an exceedingly fast rate. It is true that as time passed, those colonists who survived acquired experience in coping with the new environment, and the Dutch started to provide cheaper and more abundant supplies. More recent arrivals had mainly to deal with a new climate and disease environment, and from 1653 on, the last stages of the Carib wars. Life became significantly better for the habitant. As militia member, he carried a sword at all times, a symbol of status in Europe.[28] At least, that was the message of contemporary propagandists such as Rochefort and Dutertre. After listing all the "inconveniences" of island life, they concluded that at present (in the 1650s), these had been overcome or attenuated and life had become quite as "civil" as in Europe.[29]

The colonists' attitude to their natural environment was clear-cut—extract whatever could be used and transform the rest into as European an environment as quickly as possible. They had come to America with the sole goal of enrichment in order to return home in a better condition. Sustainability of resources over the longer term was not their concern, for which they deserve far less blame than our far richer and more secure society does for more conscious environmentally destructive behavior. Not surprisingly, often-famished pioneers hunted mammals, birds, and even reptiles anywhere they could be found, and, as they became more skilled with firearms, environmental destruction accelerated. One source claims that no game survived on Saint-Christophe as early as 1650; another, that the same held true for all the French Lesser Antilles soon thereafter.[30] Even on less densely populated and far larger Saint-Domingue, growing concerns could be heard from the 1660s about the declining number of feral cattle and pigs. According to the great popularizer of buccaneer adventures Alexandre Exquemelin, hunters killed a hundred pigs for every ten or twelve they dressed.[31] But such slaughter, akin to the Great Plains buffalo hunts in the nineteenth-century North American West, was rapidly coming to an end.

The astute late seventeenth-century observer Father Labat provides numerous anecdotes about what he considered the foolish depletion of natural resources of the Lesser Antilles. To hunt the few remaining wild pigs in the remotest parts of the islands took planning, time, and much energy.[32] The growth of human population had led to a rapid decline of manatees. By no means had colonists changed their ways. Labat describes their slaughter of birds exhausted by a hurricane and notes the consequences of six decades of indiscriminate forestry practices. The removal of trees for provision farming had caused increasing flooding and thus the spread of sand across the coastal areas. Lumber was in such short supply on Martinique that wood houses had become rare. Logwood for dyes and mahogany for furniture, among other highly useful varieties of wood, were already then found only in areas that were difficult to reach.[33]

Settling down with the Island Caribs proved to be a dangerous affair, despite the precolonial record of benign relationships fostered by common animosity toward the Spaniards. When the French expanded to Guadeloupe and Martinique after 1635, they entered the strategic heart of the Carib world. Not only were there substantial Carib populations there, but aboriginal strongholds at Dominica and Saint Vincent were adjacent. Whereas before colonization, Caribs had often traded amicably with the French and even hosted groups of stranded Frenchmen, these Native Americans did not easily tolerate permanent settlements on what are small bodies of land. Unlike the situation in New France, with its endless acreage and colonists primarily interested in furs, in the Lesser Antilles, settlers planted soil-depleting tobacco. And though Caribs traded such items as hammocks and turtle shell for iron goods, beads, and spirits, their commodities were not colonial staples, as were Canadian beaver pelts. Although we know very little about what French colonists thought of Island Caribs, the social and economic dynamics made war extremely likely. By the end of the 1620s, the Saint-Christophe settlers had eliminated the small Carib presence there.

The sporadic struggles with Caribs between 1635 and 1660 (see Chapters 3 and 4 above) strongly influenced the shaping of island society. As the historian James Axtell asks contrafactually in another geographical context, what would have happened if Caribs had not occupied the Antillean islands?[34] Along with fear of Spanish or English invaders, Carib guerrilla actions led to the development of tough, disciplined French colonial militias under authoritarian governors. Whatever their social background in France, all men, even indentured servants, were required to train, to use firearms, and to fight in units. A special group of men, who in peacetime traded with the Indians and even lived among them, were familiar with Carib territory and available to lead militia forays in wartime.[35] The results were impressive against an enemy whose lack of modern equipment had not previously prevented them from terrorizing other Europeans, and especially the English at Antigua and Nevis. The growing French ascendancy over the Caribs may have been the consequence of the latter's fear of the militia and typical Native American admiration of military valor. The islanders' ability to defend themselves unassisted by France (the importance of Dutch help has been noted in Chapters 3 and 4 above) accounts in part for their resistance to the central government's attempted control of their lives after 1664.

Island governors used a variety of techniques to manage relations with Caribs. Foremost was an eye-for-an-eye response to any provocation (from the European perspective). More pacific policies were also attempted, especially by Governor Charles Houël of Guadeloupe, who had a close relationship with a Carib faction at Dominica under the headman the French called Captain Baron. The latter sent his sons to be raised at Houël's residence, where they served as cross-cultural mediators in training and in effect also as hostages. Houël supported a school for Carib girls, although without much apparent success. In turn, in peacetime, the French supported missionaries among the Caribs, Dominicans appropriately at Dominica and Jesuits at Saint Vincent. Caribs perhaps considered them hostages to French good behavior. At least one governor consented to sending a gunner to accompany a Carib raid on their Arawak enemies at Trinidad.[36]

It has been noted how difficult it is to decipher French attitudes toward their new neighbors. Obviously, the episodic, often brutal conflicts tell their own story. But another side of the story is that a few habitants married aboriginal women and that a surprising number could communicate with Caribs in pidgin. Although the shortage of European women occasioned these alliances and the necessities of trade demanded minimal language acquisition, still these intercultural connections tended to humanize French-Carib relations even under the constraints of recurring hostilities. The number of *métis* resulting from interracial unions cannot be known, as there were no censuses before the 1660s.

A tobacco *habitation*. From Jean-Baptiste Dutertre, *Histoire générale des isles Antilles*, 2: 419.

Peopling: Before the Ascendancy of Sugar

Frenchmen came to the Antilles to attack the Spaniards but also to plant tobacco. The first settlers at Saint-Christophe were very fortunate in that land was still cheap, and they had a decade of high prices for their tobacco. Despite the Spanish destruction of their crop in 1629, hard-working colonists at Saint-Christophe made respectable livings. Assuming that one man could grow between 1,000 and 1,500 pounds of tobacco a year, a conservative estimate, he earned four to six times the average of peasants in France.[37] Habitants' costs in land, tools, and supplies were quite modest. Unfortunately for settlers at Martinique and Guadeloupe after 1635, a decline in prices for tobacco marked the years 1636–40, followed by an era of relatively stagnant prices. Search for another staple led in the direction of cotton and ginger, but these crops were not without difficulties.

The importance of staples, exportable commodities to exchange for European goods, is perhaps too obvious to require explanation. The question of which goods colonists deemed necessary is not so obvious. In these pioneer decades, indentured servants, weapons, tools, and, not least, wine and brandy headed the list. Wheat was desirable, but a habitant could live on manioc flour from the cassava root, local fruit, fish, and game and, if possible, imported salted meat, fish, and dried peas. He did not tolerate manioc beer (*ouicou*), a taste most Europeans never acquired, as a substitute for wine and spirits. A life of subsistence was not the goal for people on the make who wished to return to France for the balance of their lives. Finding fortune depended on profits from a staple crop.

Recognizing the need to replace tobacco, the Compagnie des Isles de l'Amérique put its stock and borrowed capital into promoting sugar at Guadeloupe, considered the best island for it. It sent capital, servants, and slaves to advance its sugar venture under its new governor, Houël. Unfortunately for the company's future, the governor misused company resources to start one of the first sugar works on Guadeloupe. Houël opposed the establishment of other sugar mills, so that habitants would have to bring their cane to him, at a price of course. However, due to his inability to make good white sugar, the greedy governor had to abandon his enterprise by 1648. Also, the impending demise of the company, in part due to pouring money into the governor's sugar works, meant Houël's source of easy capital dried up.[38]

A tobacco shed. From Jean-Baptiste Labat, *Nouveau voyage aux isles de l'Amérique* (Paris, 1722).

In addition to the need for a stockade for defense, the desire for European commodities led to the slow development of tiny towns, or *bourgs*. Writing about the 1640s and 1650s, Dutertre laughs about these so-called *bourgs*, which were, he notes, smaller than most French villages.[39] The company early recognized the need for *bourgs* in which its agents and notaries could control distribution of imported goods and collect and weigh colonial commodities. It mandated that all newcomers pass through an island town as a condition for acquiring land.[40] The most important *bourgs* in these years were Basse-Terre and Pointe du Sable on Saint-Christophe; Basse-Terre, Guadeloupe; and Fort Saint-

Pierre (later Saint-Pierre), Martinique. The chief political figures and dispensers of justice established residences in these chief towns; or in some cases themselves chose the best location for towns, such as Houël's selection of Basse-Terre, Guadeloupe. These governors required all incoming ships to pay fifty to a hundred pounds of gunpowder for the privilege of trading.[41] When missionaries started to arrive after 1640, they received lands in or near these *bourgs*. Towns became the homes of transient sailors and the few skilled artisans.[42] Although settlers resided on their rural habitations, they had to travel to town to market their crops, buy imported goods, and conduct legal transactions.

Potential alternative crops to tobacco were indigo and sugar, but both depended on heavily capitalized and labor-intensive processes before the blue indigo dye or muscavado (sugar with significant molasses content) could be exported. Sugar making cost significantly more than indigo manufacture. Due to political and trade disruptions in the Atlantic World in the early 1640s—Portugal's rebellion against Spain, the decline in Brazil's sugar production due to the fighting between Portuguese settlers and Dutch invaders during the 1630s and early 1640s—the prices of both indigo and sugar shot up on the Amsterdam market. However, after 1642, the indigo price steadily declined for the rest of the decade.

Sugar prices followed downward until 1645, when a Portuguese rebellion in Brazil against Dutch rule eventually led to declines in superior Brazilian sugar exports and a rise in prices. But until the collapse of their production in Brazil in 1654, there was no incentive for the Dutch to take inferior French island sugars. So although English Barbados quickly took advantage of the new conditions, the French islands were too short of capital and cheap labor to match its pace of development.[43] Only Guadeloupe, with heavy assistance from Dutch creditors after 1654, made significant progress toward sugar production; in 1661, according to a contemporary source, seventy-one mills were operating there.[44] However, at Saint-Christophe, there were only six sugar mills in 1658.[45] To talk about a sugar "revolution" in the French Caribbean, or for that matter in the English Leeward Islands, is hyperbole until the last third of the seventeenth century, if then.[46]

To call the Caribbean islands under discussion "French" shades the truth about their demographic composition. True, the majority of colonists were French. Normans departing primarily from Le Havre pre-

Indigo works. From Jean-Baptiste Dutertre, *Histoire générale des isles Antilles*, 2: opposite 107.

A sugar works (*sucrerie*). From Charles de Rochefort, *Histoire naturelle et morale des isles Antilles*, 2d ed. (Rotterdam, 1665), 332.

dominated in Saint-Christophe and Martinique. Rural Normans as well as urban recruits from Paris, Rouen, and Dieppe left from the latter town to people Guadeloupe. Western Atlantic France supplied colonists for Guadeloupe via La Rochelle. From whatever port they left, the recruits came in roughly equal proportions from rural areas and interior towns, whereas the rural portion of the French population was about 85 percent.[47]

Circulating in the dirt streets of the tiny colonial towns, however, were also Catholic Irish, Dutch Calvinists from Europe or those fleeing Brazil, Portuguese Jews from the same area, a growing minority of Africans, and, in peacetime, Caribs on holiday. Island society also diverged significantly from that of the metropole in the earliest decades because a larger percentage of colonists were probably Huguenots than was the case in France itself (about 7 percent).[48] Furthermore, with the authority of the Church and state resting very lightly on their shoulders, many habitants reputedly lived a "libertine" existence.[49]

No reliable population estimates exist for periods before the 1660s. Very likely, the French parts of Saint-Christophe contained more habitants in the 1640s than either Martinique or Guadeloupe, both of which had difficulties with Island Caribs. L.-A. Boiteux estimates 6,000 at French Saint-Christophe, 1,500 at Martinique, and 1,000 at Guadeloupe, and perhaps 1,000 slaves.[50] In 1642, the renewed charter of the Compagnie des Isles de l'Amérique mentions 7,000. It subcontracted with Faulcon and company to provide 2,500 migrants to Guadeloupe in return for a monopoly of that island's commerce, and Guadeloupe's progress was slowed when Faulcon's company failed to fulfill its obligation.[51]

The social composition of the pioneering population also meant far greater freedoms for the habitants. They had been able to pay their passage of some fifty to eighty l.t.,[52] and in the earlier years, they received twenty hectares of land, or close to fifty acres. Habitants, whose status some indentured servants could attain if they survived the three years, were with some few exceptions commoners. But even the handful of nobles, who no doubt thus had a certain prestige, could not replicate their legal separation as in France.[53] Deference did not vanish, because governors and militia captains received it, along with the important privilege of exemption from the capitation tax for themselves and certain numbers of their servants and slaves, but to call this a deferential society would be almost meaningless when compared to France or even New

France. Despite the fact that the Custom of Paris governed legal procedures, some notable customary exceptions to it had force of law in the islands. Most important, no habitant could be pursued for debts contracted outside the islands, and neither land nor servants and slaves could be seized for internal debts.

Before 1660, the white colonial population was primarily male and adult, facts resulting from patterns of emigration. Even males with families often left them in France for what was usually considered a temporary migration. In 1660, some 1,506 men and boys "carrying guns" constituted 58 percent of the total white population of Martinique and a little more than 77 percent of the male population.[54] Nothing suggests that the situation differed on other islands.

Either prior to embarkation or upon return to France for a visit, habitants frequently entered into associations with merchant acquaintances or relatives to acquire capital to hire indentured servants and to procure commodities for sale in the islands. Experienced habitants knew what goods might bring significant profit in the Antilles. The stay-at-home merchant provided some capital to be repaid in colonial produce. When the original loan was paid, the partners split the profits; often the merchant provided further credit to the habitant. The contract usually called for a set period of association. The habitant ventured his life and labor in the tropics as his part of the bargain.[55]

The habitant who could squeeze enough profit out of his hectares to hire indentured servants, purchase African slaves, or both had a chance of success if he survived the tobacco price decline of the later 1630s, the Indian wars and, especially, disease. His twenty hectares, if kept intact, were adequate to attempt a transition to sugar growing (if not to sugar making, an important distinction) in the 1650s and 1660s. By the 1650s, tobacco prices had stabilized, some well-off, politically influential colonists established sugar works, and the Dutch supplied cheap, plentiful goods.[56] Perhaps a significant majority of habitants either died early, returned to France, failed economically due to hurricanes, or were on the wrong side of local political intrigues, like Poincy's and Houël's victims. They moved on, figuratively or literally. (Of some 30,000 migrants to New France, only one-third settled permanently; comparable figures for the Caribbean are not available.) Yet recent work on the tobacco period of early Barbados paints a somewhat brighter picture of ordinary men's fortunes there than has the traditional historiography.[57]

The reputation of the Caribbean islands as a tomb for white immigrants is certainly deserved for the eighteenth and nineteenth centuries. The culprits were primarily *P. falciparum* malaria and yellow fever. There is reason to believe that these notorious killers had less of an impact in the seventeenth century. Although yellow fever appeared on Barbados between 1647 and 1649,[58] there is no certain evidence that it struck the French islands before its devastating appearance in 1691. Yellow fever is dependent on relatively large urban populations as hosts, and tiny French island towns such as Saint-Pierre, Martinique, and Basse-Terre, Guadeloupe hardly qualify. Neither town compared to Bridgetown, Barbados. Unfortunately, *P. falciparum* malaria, the deadliest of four malaria varieties,[59] does not need a dense population to sustain itself. Probably carried to the Americas via the African slave trade, this disease is transmitted by *Anopheles* mosquitoes which breed in any body of water, whereas the carrier of yellow fever, *Aëdes aegypti*, breeds in stagnant mud pools or other standing water and has a very short flight range. Thus *P. falciparum* malaria was a threat to even isolated habitations. The fact that slaves were not as numerous as they would be in a subsequent era, and that most were the property of relatively few owners may well have protected many Europeans from this very dangerous disease. Although it cannot be proven, it seems plausible that the health conditions of Frenchmen in the Caribbean were less dreadful than after 1691, when yellow fever emerged as a great killer.

With the exception of island officials, most notably Lieutenant General Philippe Longvilliers de Poincy, a few merchant-factors, and clergy, habitants in the pioneer era lived very simply, in low-standing cottages (*cases*) made of wood with thatched roofs, and even slept in hammocks fabricated by Carib women.[60] They spent very little in housing themselves and their servants; not only did they wish to return to France as quickly as possible, but the damage done by hurricanes argued against such investment. They were not so parsimonious when it came to food and drink. They were also not willing to devote funds to church buildings. The more prosperous habitants built with bricks and tiles brought by the Dutch as ballast.[61]

Poincy's villa was certainly the most elaborate house in the non-Spanish Caribbean. As early as 1640, Poincy reported to the Compagnie des Isles that his house had three floors and he was working on the fourth. It was at that stage sixty-six feet long, twenty-four wide and thirty-three feet high (thus perhaps 4,500–5,000 sq. feet of space).[62] To arrive at his abode high on a hill overlooking Basse-Terre, Saint-

Christophe, the visitor walked along roads flanked with Old World orange and lemon trees. The château itself boasted red hardwood floors. Water from nearby mountains transported via hollowed palm tree trunks supplied all parts of this Italianate villa. Winds from the east kept residents relatively cool even on the hottest days. The gardens consisted of herbs and exotic flowers. During parties, the oboes and clarions of his musicians could be heard in the town below. According to one of our tour guides, Charles de Rochefort, Poincy's slaves were well housed in wood and brick. Poincy could afford such largesse because in the early 1650s he possessed at least 300 slaves, who among other tasks manned three sugar works. He also employed some 100 "domestics," presumably *engagés*.[63] One contemporary claimed that Poincy made the princely sum of 90,000 l.t. from his sugar works alone, not to mention what he earned supplying rum for Basse-Terre's taverns.[64]

After 1635, the Compagnie des Isles moved to assert some control over island life by sending priests and, from 1639 on, "honorable girls" to settle the colonists and keep them at work on their *habitations*.[65] The first women known to have come to the islands were the wives of l'Olive and Duplessis at Guadeloupe, and l'Olive's niece. In the later 1630s, the company approved of the efforts of Marie Maugendre, wife of a surgeon at Saint-Christophe, to import virtuous young women to marry settlers.[66] A larger group, under Mme. de La Fayolle's supervision, arrived in Martinique in 1643, and most were soon married. On paper, this was a neat solution, providing for impoverished young women in France and slaking the colonial thirst for European marriage partners, and thus children to whom to pass on inheritances. La Fayolle's young women came from St. Joseph's *hôpital* in Paris, and they should not be thought of as forced migrants (*forçats*) or prostitutes (*filles de joie*), although most contemporaries in France regarded all such females as imprisoned sluts. One may presume that the rapidly rising island population in the 1640s and 1650s was in some measure the result of this female migration. What is clear is that habitants desired female servants for domestic service and, if the latter were reasonably attractive, marriage.[67] If married, these pioneer women usually lived on relatively isolated habitations and were participants in all aspects of life. Moreover, a woman could inherit her husband's entire estate regardless of his family's claims, unlike in France.[68]

Knowledge of specific colonial women in this era is rare. The best-known is the beautiful and intelligent Parisian Marie Bonnard, who first

Paysage d'une partie de l'Isle de S. Christofle, avec un Crayon du Chasteau de Mr le General.

Page 53.

1. Le Chasteau. 2. Le Jardin. 3. La Basse cour. 4. La Chapelle et les Offices. 5. Les Escuries. 6. La Tour des munitions. 7. La Ville d'Angole.

The most famous depiction of Poincy's villa. Note the Ville d'Angole slave quarters on the right. From Charles de Rochefort, *Histoire naturelle et morale des Isles Antilles*, 2d ed. (Rotterdam, 1665), opposite 52.

appears in the records in 1645, when, after annulment of her marriage in France to an important company official, she secretly married the presumably infatuated General Jacques Dyel du Parquet. It is not known why the marriage had to be secret, or even that it actually occurred. (Dutertre, to whom we owe our knowledge of it, may be covering here for du Parquet, a man he much admired.) After Poincy imprisoned her husband during the Thoisy affair (see Chapter 3 above), she led a faction in Martinique demanding that Poincy's captured nephews be traded for her husband. According to Dutertre, she suffered much from her husband's enemies in this period.[69] Upon his return, du Parquet publicly acknowledged his marriage to her, and she remained his trusted advisor. She had four children by him, two boys and two girls. After the general's death in 1658, she ruled the island in the name of her oldest son, Dyel d'Esnambuc. But malcontents took the opportunity of her regency to call vociferously for reduced taxes, among other demands. After a brief imprisonment, she died en route to France, where she was going to obtain treatment for chronic illness.

The surviving, moderately successful habitant of the 1650s, who was perhaps married with children, must have been pleased with his status. He hunted and fished unhindered. He paid a capitation, or head tax, for himself and his servants and slaves (usually 100 lbs. of tobacco),[70] but the burden was not onerous. True, he no doubt fumed that company officials, governors, militia officers and clergy were exempt for themselves and for some of their servants and slaves. He paid no degrading hearth tax (*taille*), no iniquitous salt tax (*gabelle*), no remnants of feudal dues (*lods et ventes*) upon sale of his lands, no mandatory tithes (in France, up to 14 percent of gross product).[71] Island customs made it possible to avoid dividing his estate equally among his heirs. Although he contributed little to the Church, he was served by able priests of various clerical orders, which supported themselves on the backs of black slaves and *engagés*. Fortunately for our colonial Jacques, perhaps, disease meant there were too few of these clerics to trouble every waking moment. Our habitant would never end his days in a French jail or the galleys for what moderns deem petty offenses. No lawyers played the parasite in his society, and so there were no lawsuits. Unlike in France, he could not be imprisoned for debt, nor could his slaves and animals be seized.[72]

Although historians debate the extent of the feudal dues that habitants in New France owed the lords (*seigneurs*) and the Church, the lords collected *lods et ventes* and other irritating tributes, and the Church collected tithes on wheat production. In this respect at least, Caribbean habitants were significantly better off.[73] It should, however, be noted that French Canadians had on average a much greater life expectancy.

No matter his previous social background, the successful habitant was now a respectable property owner, a militiaman, and someone who was lord of his small domain. Entitled by militia service, he went about with sword at his side and cane in hand.[74] As a soldier, the honor of military justice was his if he committed a capital offense. It was not long before militiamen, especially officers, assumed the titles of *sieur* and *monsieur*, with their wives demanding to be addressed as *madame*. Despite the efforts of some propagandists, however, these more positive views of island life and society did little to transform metropolitan perceptions of colonists as all emanating from the dregs of society. Of course, successful habitants were a minority in the European population.

These advantages may well explain why some habitants were able to make the switch to sugar, or at least switch to growing sugarcane to send to other men's mills. Many other factors of course were involved—Dutch supply of slaves and manufactured goods on credit, and government support both during the proprietary period and that of the Compagnie des Indes occidentales—but the ability of some hardy survivors to slowly accrue capital over time should not be discounted. The capitation tax and those for weights and measures constituted relatively light burdens. Governors such as du Parquet granted three-year exemptions from the capitation tax to encourage potential sugar growers.[75]

Dutertre notes that money and military rank dictated social position in this new society, not one's birth as noble or commoner, as in France. Already by the 1650s, the wealthier element displayed a desire to acquire the finest clothing available. They loved Dutch shirts, worn with a cravat. They favored breeches made of serge embroidered with gold and silver. Officers among them spared no expense to buy plumed hats, and their very socially conscious wives sported taffeta and satin dresses. Ribbons and Genoese lace were becoming de rigueur for an emerging nouveau riche island elite.

Royal Efforts to Impose Order in the Frontier Era

Historians of seventeenth-century France have delineated the attempts of state and Church to impose order on a fractious society. These institutions had a difficult task when one recalls the social and political upheavals of the hundred years after 1560. Rebellions by powerful nobles and judges, stern Huguenot resistance to Catholic hegemony, and popular revolts made the slogan "one king, one faith, and one law" more wishful thinking than reality. Yet through it all kings and prelates continued the struggle for "order," and ultimately they held the winning cards, because people tire of disorder. The situation was somewhat similar in tropical America, but with an important difference. Prior to 1664, neither French political nor ecclesiastical authorities were able to impose their will. They could not project adequate power over such distances, especially in an era when they could but barely cope with problems at home. Yet preliminary, halting steps were taken.

If we are to believe elite political writings, seventeenth-century men accepted as core values the proper ordering of their spiritual and material lives and the subordination of individual, "selfish" needs to the interests of larger social organizations—family, kinship group, corporate bodies (e.g., noble and clerical "estates," guilds, confraternities). King, bishop, nobleman, parish priest, and paterfamilias all promoted deference to authority and submission to law, at least rhetorically. Presumably, most colonists had had this message inculcated into them. We can reject the typical, biased metropolitan view of colonists as scum of the earth, while at the same time acknowledging the atypical status of these primarily young and male individuals willing to undertake such a fearsome, perhaps permanent voyage to an alien environment. Adventurers of maritime ports, journeymen artisans extending overseas the traditional *tour de France*, and young runaways from difficult situations in villages and small towns did not constitute soft clay for the would-be potters. Living hard and threatened by death in a hostile environment among a mix of ethnic and religious groups, these tough habitants usually followed the commands of their governors and militia captains, but they did not easily tolerate the efforts of faraway authorities to tax and control them.

Louis XIII, the young Louis XIV, and their cardinal ministers attempted to assert sovereignty over the Caribbean islands through the medium of colonial companies. The king granted the letters patent authorizing the companies and he named a lieutenant general for the region, which he first did in 1638 (Poincy). The king retained ultimate control over justice (in theory) by virtue of the right of colonists to appeal their cases to a *parlement;* during the tenure of the Compagnie des Isles (1635–51), the *parlement* of Brittany served as that penultimate court.[76] As *grand maître et surintendant de la navigation*, Cardinal Richelieu and his successors controlled travel to and from the American Tropics, which would have been a crucial weapon of state authority had not the Dutch gained a near monopoly on the trade. The offices of the Admiralty and the viceroyalty of America might have been a source of control but were not because of flows of commerce and the incompetence or indifference of the officeholders.

Among its other powers, the Compagnie des Isles controlled justice in the islands, and in 1636, it sent a judge to Saint-Christophe, accompanied by a fiscal agent, a notary, and a sergeant. As normal in France, these were to receive salaries supplemented by "presents" (bribes, called *pôts de vin*) from supplicants. When the company attempted to do likewise at Martinique, du Parquet categorically refused.[77] His colonists preferred his swift, free justice (as *sénéchal*, a feudal judicial office).[78] Just prior to Richelieu's death, the Compagnie des Isles received a new charter and took actions intended to reinvigorate it. Quite clearly, company directors recognized that the governors ruled in their own interests, and that the Dutch dominated commerce. One Clerselier de Leumont was named as the first intendant for the company's island affairs.[79] Not long afterwards, the Compagnie des Isles persuaded the regent, Anne of Austria, to replace Poincy as lieutenant general with Thoisy (see Chapter 3 above). In the same year, 1645, the first sovereign councils in the islands were sanctioned.[80] Their role was dual: to serve as court of last resort (except for cases prorogued by the king) and to serve as a privy council to the governors. All of these company initiatives ceased with the Thoisy debacle, and the company soon sold its concessions to the private proprietors. The center did not hold.

At the local level, the company governors, then the private proprietors, created relatively efficient government. Each island was divided into districts (*quartiers*), which in that era were coterminous with the church parishes. There were two *quartiers* at tiny Saint-Christophe, one at each end of the island, and four at much larger Martinique. The crucial figure in each *quartier* was the militia captain, a veritable boss in charge of most aspects of local life. If laws were to be implemented, churches built and cared for, and roads maintained, then the captain and his lieutenant had to oversee these functions. Governors who could control their militia captains and maintain the militia's confidence were the supreme authorities. Poincy proved that in the Thoisy crisis of 1645–46. No wonder he entertained his officers (including five nephews) every

Sunday morning at his splendid villa.[81] Governors, their militia captains, and one or two prominent habitants constituted the sovereign councils.[82] Not only did this simple form of government make sense for a frontier colony, but it worked quite well as long as there was a strongman at the top; and as long as that individual recognized that commanding habitants "is altogether different in this region than in the armies of France."[83]

It was extremely difficult for the Catholic clergy to impose spiritual order on the rough, diverse island population. Priests complained of constant difficulties with Huguenots and Jews, as well as with anticlerical colonists. Students today of a Catholic background have a difficult time understanding the antipathy toward the Church, although it is true that the regular clergy (Jesuits, Dominicans, Capuchins, and Carmelites) received greater respect due to their vows and their education. The missionaries did not have the benefit of an *established* Church, as in France or New France. There were no bishops, no monasteries, no assemblies of the clergy, and, mercifully, no tithes! The regular clergy that serviced parishes received an allotment of land from the Compagnie des Isles for their subsistence. In 1645, the Dominicans at Guadeloupe asked the company for twelve slaves; they received four and the right to buy others on the same conditions as any habitant.[84] There would be no replication of the metropolitan Church in the French Caribbean colonies, as was more the case in the Spanish American empire.

Other problems inhibited clerical regulation of colonists' lives. Technically, French missionaries were under the jurisdiction of the Roman Holy Congregation of Propaganda Fide, created in 1622 to supervise missions overseas not ceded to the authority of a king. In truth, the Propaganda's jurisdiction was more an irritant than an obstacle to the king's direction of missions, but delays and other problems resulted. Take, for example, the Propaganda's grant of the title of apostolic prefect of the American missions to the self-important Capuchin Pacifique de Provins. The other established orders refused to accept his "pretensions" to authority over them. They answered first and foremost to the company and the king, although to be sure they corresponded with Rome on relevant jurisdictional matters.

The physical toll on missionaries also limited their authority. Of forty-three missionaries at Guadeloupe between 1635 and 1654, thirteen died. The average length of stay was just two years. Only Father Breton, with nineteen years there, managed to reach double digits.[85]

The missionary orders brought trouble upon themselves with intra-mural squabbling, a practice hardly unknown in France. Each order wished to have monopoly authority on "its" island, and at first that oc-curred. It may be recalled that the Capuchins serviced Saint-Christophe, the Dominicans Guadeloupe, and the Jesuits Martinique. However, the Capuchins became embroiled with Poincy and the Dominicans with Houël. When Poincy forced the Capuchins to leave, Carmelites and then Jesuits replaced them. The Dominicans hung on at Guadeloupe, but Houël invited the Jesuits, who came only on an ad hoc basis as long as the Dominicans still claimed jurisdiction there. Given this disunity and the fact that illness or exile kept their numbers low,[86] the priests could only dream of the authority their brethren asserted at home.

The religious situation improved somewhat in the 1650s as a result of the expansion of the Jesuits. By the end of the 1650s, there were twenty-nine missionaries, despite the loss of the two martyred at Saint Vincent. In 1658, they finally had registered in the Paris *parlement* the measure allowing them to establish anywhere in the Americas. Perhaps related to this expansion was the campaign by the Compagnie du Saint-Sacrement to promote missions in Guiane and the islands. The close ties between it and the Jesuits are well known. Even Houël and the Do-minicans ceased their perennial warfare by 1658 when powerful inter-mediaries in Paris persuaded the recalcitrant proprietor to confirm the original land grant of 1635. Despite these positive signs, there were nev-ertheless only thirty to thirty-five clerics to serve a widely scattered pop-ulation of perhaps 25,000.[87] Missionary authors testify to the terrible fa-tigue and dangers of their constant circuit in order to supply the most basic services. There was little time for daily censorship of parishioners' morals, as was the case in France.

What may be concluded from the scanty record of the first three to four decades of French colonization? Did the new environment—trop-ical climate and disease, strange flora and fauna, life amongst Caribs and Africans—"pulverize the cultural attributes" of the French? Were the French island communities thus more similar to English Barbados or Antigua than to the nascent French settlements in the Saint Lawrence Valley? Or did much of the colonists' Old World cultural baggage sur-vive in the strange environment? Neither extreme position would hold for any European transplant to the Americas, of course. The above sketch suggests that Frenchmen in tropical America were more similar to their cousins on the Saint Lawrence River in their lack of commitment to building communities. The *esprit de retour* was notable in both populations. Younger males, especially those in dangerous and desperate circumstances, are hardly the human material to insist on old ways. At the same time, faced with a hostile and exotic environment, it was natural to preserve as much of the old ways—custom, food, drink—as possible; although certainly not as much the governmental and religious institutions of repression. When possible and advantageous, colonists made conscious cultural selections from a "European menu,"[88] but simplified rather than replicated old ways. The social collectivities dominating ancien régime France—titled aristocracy, institutional Church, legal apparatus, guilds, confraternities—were only palely reflected in the American Tropics.

Tempting though it is to paint an overly rosy picture of island life for free habitants in this frontier era, the high incidence of natural, medical, and political difficulties stays one's hand. Aside from coping with hurricanes, snakes and insects, bouts of malaria, and Carib attacks, the successful habitant had to control, discipline, and live among whites and blacks on whose coerced labor his fortunes depended. It is the lives of these laborers that the next chapter addresses.

CHAPTER SIX

Frontier-Era Society
The World of Coerced Labor

It is highly likely that a majority of people in the French Caribbean during what I have called the Frontier era were unfree laborers. European
indentured servants and enslaved West Africans did most of the difficult
work on tobacco habitations and provision farms, although often alongside their masters. Chroniclers expressed astonishment at the severe
treatment of these workers, especially that of fellow European Christians. If their reports are accurate, then a number of interrelated economic, political, and psychological factors perhaps explains the masters'
behavior: the desire to make a fortune and return in triumph to Europe
before medical difficulties or conflicts with Caribs took their grim toll;
the remoteness of legal, political, and customary impediments to unre-
stricted labor use; the habitants' youthfulness and predominantly bachelor status; and, perhaps related to social isolation, the possibly high incidence of alcohol consumption. However, it should be remembered that
most chroniclers were members of highly educated, elite religious orders, especially Dominicans and Jesuits, who probably had little direct
experience with the nitty-gritty world of lower-class working conditions
at home, as opposed to Capuchins and other Franciscans, whose mission
was primarily to serve the downtrodden.

Less is known about the free colonists than about indentured servants, because the latter signed contracts in France, some of which have
survived in provincial archives.[1] The habitants were plain men who did
not write diaries, journals, or letters.[2] Many of the earliest settlers came
as *engagés*, as a result of their acquaintance with the d'Esnambucs or the
l'Olives, whose success in recruiting servants testifies to the lure of tobacco and the possibility of fighting the rich and hated Spaniards. Some
former indentured servants developed partnerships. Two men would
build and share a primitive *case* and split the profits, and upon the death
of one partner, the other inherited his property. This practice had the
wonderful sailor name of *matelotage*, a relationship in which two sailors
shared one hammock, sleeping in it in alternating shifts. One can imag-

ine hearing the equivalent of "hey, matey" as the partners struggled to create a tobacco farm. (Seventeenth-century missionaries, not slow to condemn immorality wherever they saw it, do not even hint that such partnerships involved homosexual relations.)

Although indentured servants probably constituted a majority of French migrants to the Caribbean, it is not possible to estimate their numbers accurately.[3] The fare for passengers to New France varied between sixty and eighty l.t., equivalent to the gross annual artisan wage at that time.[4] Boatloads of free passengers such as the *Arabella* (the Puritan "mother ship" of 1630 fame) never made their way to French America. Far fewer bonded servants went from France to the Americas than those from the British islands. However, the contrast is far less startling for the Caribbean than for continental North America, where in 1660 the roughly 3,000 people of New France paled in contrast to at least twelve times as many New Englanders. In the Caribbean, the English outnumbered the French by just a little over two to one.[5] Surely, the misery index of English lower-class people was not less than that of their French counterparts, although recent studies of the French indentured servant system argue that they came from a social niche slightly above the lowest.

Of an estimated 12,000 emigrants leaving France annually, only 2,500 went to the American colonies, compared to 60 to 72 percent of British migrants who chose America.[6] Most outward-bound Frenchmen probably chose to cross the Pyrenees to labor-starved Spain. One apparent difference between the English and French pushes to migrate is that the English gentry, enclosing common lands, gave strong and effective support to programs relieving English "overpopulation." To keep French projects in the Caribbean secret from Spain, there was no official propaganda in support of them prior to 1638. The English economic recession of the 1620s and 1630s, the continuing pace of enclosures, and the hounding of Puritans, none of which applied as much in the French situation, also are part of any comparative analysis.[7] This contrast in numbers partially explains the much more favorable terms given to French servants willing to cross the Atlantic.

French scholars have exploited notary archives to gauge the number of contracts in various western French port cities: 3,600 indentured contracts exist for Le Havre in the years 1627–52; 600 in Honfleur from just one notary in the years 1637–39; 319 at Dieppe in 1654–60; 5,918 at Nantes between 1636 and 1732; and 7,300 at La Rochelle between 1638 and 1772. As notary records are far from complete, and none exist in some other ports of embarkation, one scholar estimates that between 30,000 and 40,000 indentured servants left for the islands in the seventeenth and eighteenth centuries. At least half that number crossed the Atlantic from the 1620s to the 1660s.[8]

The comparative lag in the transport of French servants occurred despite three-year contracts as opposed to longer English ones (four or five years usually, and up to seven, especially for the Irish). This discrepancy between the French and English figures can be explained by the following factors: Frenchmen looking for alternatives to their current situation could choose enlistment in the monstrously growing French army; the inferior propaganda and recruitment system in France;[9] the awful reputation of New France; the refusal of most, especially elite Frenchmen, to believe that colonies were anything but last resorts for social scum. Three out of four, or even four out of five, French indentured servants opted for "the islands" in large part because of the strongly negative reputation of New France.[10]

At first glance, the indentured servant system resembled apprenticeship in France. However, a deeper analysis demonstrates at least two profound differences. First, the Caribbean master had the right to sell a contract to another master or to exchange servants. Some contemporary observers likened the system to slavery, if of a temporary character. Second, the Caribbean master had no obligation to teach a skill to the servant; indeed, the basic work of tobacco production required few skills.

Although Gabriel Debien identifies eight types of contracts, only the two most important merit discussion here. The contract of association was a privileged one given to skilled artisans in high demand in the islands. Among others, coopers, carpenters, surgeons, and stonemasons were able to bargain concerning length of service, and they received specified wages, as well as the right to live and eat with their masters. After about 1670, when slave labor dominated the humblest work in the tropics, skilled French laborers came to constitute a high percentage of the precipitously declining numbers of indentured servants; however, in the "frontier" decades, these privileged workers were a small minority.

A rare document provides an example of a servant who parlayed such skills to become a habitant. In 1636, at Nantes, one Nicola Touzeau, a sixteen-year-old surgeon/barber, became an *engagé* bound for Saint-Christophe. He promised to work in tobacco but also to attend to his master and other servants. Not only was he granted the right to practice his surgeon's skills, splitting the wages fifty-fifty with his master, but he also received the unusual wage of 200 pounds of tobacco a year. Within eighteen months, not only had he acquired his freedom, but he had returned to Nantes to sign another surgeon to an indentured servant contract. Touzeau granted many of the same terms he had received to his new servant, but he promised his *engagé* only one-third of the profits the latter made in after-hours surgical services.[11]

The second type, which may be called the contract of thirty-six months, was that of the majority of *engagés*. To smooth tensions among these servants, who complained in the 1630s that masters were emulating the more "flexible" custom at English Saint Christopher, the first French governor, d'Esnambuc, mandated a limit of three years' service. These servants signed contracts directly with masters. They possessed few skills, and they labored primarily in tobacco and provisions production. After three years, in principle, they usually received between 200 and 400 pounds of tobacco, if they had not borrowed from their masters against that sum. Until the price collapse of the late 1630s, that wage was adequate to pay one's return passage or to start a tobacco farm.

Almost certainly, a majority of servants either died during passage or during the three years of "service," ran off on passing ships heading west, or returned to France. Some, probably a distinct minority, stayed on as tobacco farmers and others, who had learned skills such as tobacco rolling or spinning, carved out a place in the island labor force for themselves.[12]

Disproportionately, *engagés* came from more urban areas and tended to be artisans or urban day laborers, rather than common peasants or farm laborers.[13] For example, of those servants signing contracts at Nantes before 1660, 54 percent were from urban areas; the percentage of urban recruits signing contracts at Dieppe in the same period was 43.[14] Some 85 percent of French people by contrast lived in rural areas. Servants were overwhelmingly male, in part because of the traditional mobility of young men and the cultural reluctance of masters to employ white female labor in harsh agricultural tasks.[15] Skilled men in urban areas no doubt found the extraordinary wages obtainable in the islands attractive; less well known or publicized were the very high prices of all commodities there. Of recruits leaving Nantes before 1660, about a fifth are identified as possessing specific skills, such as carpentry, metal- and leatherwork, cloth preparation, and medical healing. Such servants hoped to work in their craft at least part time. Only fourteen received written guarantees that their sole labor would be in their expertise. Some identified skills, such as bookseller and pastry chef, were not suitable to island conditions.[16]

Of servants who did not have a skill listed, the vast majority of rural recruits, only a tiny minority signed contracts in the July–October period when the heavy labor in agriculture took place.[17] Rural agricultural laborers outpaced all other occupations, followed by textile workers, who might also live in rural villages.[18] Unskilled laborers living in town often hired themselves out to rural employers during that time of the year. Another factor to consider, of course, was that departure for the islands at the zenith of the hurricane season was not prudent.

Gabriel Debien examined some 6,100 contracts of servants leaving La Rochelle for the Caribbean between 1634 and 1715. As has already been noted above, three out of four, or even four out of five, indentured servants opted for the islands.[19] A warm climate, perceived greater opportunities in tobacco, and the possibility of privateer jaunts made the Caribbean preferable to frozen, Iroquois-plagued New France. However, miseries at home as much as the pull of adventure overseas motivated some young men to sign contracts.[20]

Debien examines in detail the many pushes that explain the willingness of servants to undertake a frightening voyage overseas. The pushes may be divided into a macro category that includes seventeenth-century social miseries—famine, disease, insecurity—and a micro category emphasizing individual indebtedness or the need to escape from some no exit situation. He does not argue that an index of social misery alone explains the pattern of migration. For example, few left La Rochelle in the terrible years of the Fronde, 1648–53. Yet, according to Debien's own statistics, the miserable years between 1640 and 1646 saw the second largest recruitment in the seventeenth century.[21] Young men, even in more affluent times and societies, often have "issues" making escape attractive. The lure of adventure and quick wealth in the fabled tropics no doubt was part of the mix of motivations.[22]

The large majority (77 percent) leaving Nantes before 1660 received 300 pounds of tobacco at the end of three years. The price of tobacco at Nantes in 1639 was 16 l.t. the hundredweight, and so the servant completing his contract then received about 48 l.t. if he had not borrowed from his master. That was barely enough to pay his passage home. In 1645, the price of tobacco dropped to 10 l.t. the hundredweight, and the resulting 30 l.t. did not suffice for a return passage. Such yearly salaries were similar to what was paid simple farm laborers, who, like the indentured servants, received "room and board."[23] It is difficult not to conclude that servants signing contracts after 1640 were most likely desperate people.[24]

Indentured servants came from a variety of regions and "walks of life."[25] Young males usually between the ages of fifteen and thirty, accustomed to taking to the road in search of employment and adventure within France, formed the large majority of recruits.[26] Although most who signed a contract were in difficult straits, whether economic or as a result of personal problems, they did not belong to the structurally poor (the handicapped, very young, or very old). The typical grant of a set of clothing to servants may have been due to pure necessity.[27] An uncertain relationship existed between conditions in France and the willingness of people to leave. From the 1630s to 1665, seasons of famine were far more frequent than those of feast, and the burdens of royal taxation made the people groan in despair. Thanks to the studies of Debien and others, we know that 500 servants left the Norman port of Honfleur alone in 1637–39, a time of local revolts.[28] The peak periods of servant transports in this era were 1642–47 and 1660–64, times of catastrophic difficulty.[29] However, recent scholars have questioned the "bad times" thesis, arguing that it was not the most impoverished who signed contracts.

When addressing the difficult question of motivation, it is crucial to understand that most servants assumed that they would be returning to France after the term of contract. They thus did not intend to migrate permanently. Some contracts even stipulated that payment would take place in France.[30] No doubt bad family situations, petty crime, "girl problems," underemployment or temporary unemployment, escape from the recruiting sergeant, and a myriad other difficulties contributed to the urge to explore new horizons.[31] The persuasiveness of a master may have played a significant role in what must often have been on-the-spot decisions. Some children were apparently "sold" to masters, as was the recorded case of a Paris coal man's daughter, whose father received up front one half of the 100 l.t. promised the daughter at the end of three years' work.[32]

Upon arrival in the American Tropics, the indentured servant came face to face with what was literally a new world. Not only were climate, flora, fauna, and the disease environment dramatically different, so too were the social, political, and psychological contexts of life. The primarily male and young migrants sought to make a fortune as rapidly as possible, thus psychologically vindicating their decision to leave. Given that the thirty-six months of harsh, hot work left those who survived no closer to that goal, many of the newly freed must have sought to escape, especially since less and less good land was available for freed servants as the decades of the frontier era passed. In the more intensely studied case of New France, it is estimated that two-thirds of servants migrating after 1660 did not stay on as colonists.[33] All island chroniclers agree that few, if any migrants, *intended* to stay in the Caribbean, although some did. In the first two decades of recruitment, lesser nobles from Normandy such as d'Esnambuc recruited people who knew and trusted them.[34] Nothing in the early demography of the French islands resembles Massachusetts Bay of the same era with its families and integrated communities—that is, with women.

From the 1640s on, as the system moved increasingly from a paternalistic to a colder business arrangement, the term "indentured servitude," as opposed to apprenticeship servitude, should be used. Even during a more benign era, mortality during passage could be frightening. During d'Esnambuc's 1627 passage and in the immediate aftermath, probably one-third to one-half perished.[35] By mid-century, merchant *armateurs* and ship captains increasingly made a business of contract labor for the islands. In some cases, the results were not dissimilar to the contracting of Indian labor for the Caribbean in the nineteenth century or Mexican labor by farmers in the western United States today. Seventeenth-century entrepreneurs sometimes engaged in disreputable practices, such as tricking unsuspecting people on board.[36] According to Dutertre, one rascally entrepreneur tricked 200 young French to contract for English Barbados, where they had to serve up to seven years.[37] As d'Ogeron complained to Colbert, shippers effectively imprisoned servants on board ship after they signed contracts, and if paid up front per head, they fed the *engagés* nasty, inadequate food and water and cared little about their survival. D'Ogeron himself gave extraordinarily generous conditions to his recruits, which is why he was so successful. Angry denunciations of forcible departures did not, however, depict the ordinary experience of indentured servants who signed proper contracts.

Those servants who perished en route may have been the lucky ones, if we can believe the chroniclers, who launched jeremiads against the inhumane way Christian masters treated bonded servants. The crueler masters worked their people incessantly, fed them inadequately, did not

care for them when they were sick, and beat them mercilessly for insubordination or merely because it amused them to do so. If they worked
them to death, so be it. Chroniclers exclaimed, almost unanimously, that
because indentured servants labored for only three years, they were
treated more brutally than African slaves.[38] If these sources are credible,
the situation does not seem much different from the abominable way English masters treated their indentured servants, especially the Irish, except that the pitiful French bondsmen had to survive only thirty-six
months, compared to five to seven years for the Irish.

How many of those who signed contracts survived the voyage and
three often miserable years of contract labor in a strange, disease-ridden
environment? We do not know, but well fewer than half seems a probable answer. According to Dutertre's guess, "stomach problems and
dropsy [edema]" killed two-thirds of those who died.[39] Charles de
Rochefort refers to the killing fevers "from the coast of Africa" that had
recently attacked all the islands. Were these fevers the same as the yellow fever that attacked Barbados in the 1640s?[40] What is truly ironic is
that servants in despised Canada no doubt had almost as long a life expectancy as did the free colonists. How many of the island servant survivors returned home? We do not know, except by extrapolation from
data on New France, where return was the norm. How many stayed in
the islands? We do not know, but conditions in the Lesser Antilles became less attractive as governors, their relatives, company directors, and
missionary orders increasingly monopolized the best lands. In most islands, officials had reduced grants of land to ex-servants from twenty to
ten hectares by mid-century. With the dramatic fall of tobacco prices
from the late 1630s on, the 200–400 pounds of tobacco payment at contract's termination was insufficient for its original purposes. A few survivors "made it" as corsairs or as owners of habitations employing relatively large number of servants and slaves, although they could not easily
overcome the social stigma of being former indentured servants. Soon
enough, this mainly bleak picture became more publicized in French
ports by the 1650s and thus made it increasingly difficult to attract European labor.

The fact that an unknown but significant percentage of French island colonists died of various diseases and other causes (Carib reprisals,
snakebites, drowning, hurricanes, earthquakes, brutal masters) must
only have fueled the urge to get out. For example, very few *engagés* who
embarked for Martinique in 1655 appear in the 1660 census.[41] Especially

debilitating to Europeans was *P. falciparum* malaria, spread by the *Anopheles* mosquito, which thrives in warm and humid climates, exactly that of the leeward coastal areas the colonists first settled. Servants in towns were most susceptible to this disease, especially new arrivals. The worst months were apparently August and September, also the height of hurricane season.

Except for militia obligations, the governors' peremptory justice, and environmental restraints, island life in the frontier period imposed relatively few constraints on conduct or on opportunity. If they survived the grueling three years, freed servants might obtain land to start a habitation. Governors desiring to enhance militia roles and profit from capitation taxes had every reason to distribute land, that is, until the best land was gone. Some former indentured servants became landowning habitants and prospered. Others made adequate livings as artisans such as surgeons and tobacco rollers, or in the "service" sector (tavern owners, canoe men, petty traders).[42] Former indentured servants could move from island to island and to non-French islands. They could become *coureurs des îles* and live among the Indians. They might even sail away to the buccaneer haven of Tortuga in the heart of the Spanish Caribbean and join the freebooters. One such was Jean Roy, who went from tobacco spinner to freebooter and then prosperous sugar planter, eventually owning six sugar habitations and more than 800 slaves.[43] Guillaume Pinel used theft to finance a habitation employing thirty-five servants.[44] However, the few success stories should not mask the negative outcomes for most *engagés*.

Those chroniclers not committed to promoting the islands professed utter horror at what they considered the anarchic freedom (*libertinage*) of early settlers. The relative lack of secular, clerical and customary authority meant that there were few restraints on conduct. The youthful and male character of the indentured servants was, of course, a recipe for rowdy, sometimes violent behavior. To be sure, what they witnessed in the Caribbean islands shocked seventeenth-century clerics, accustomed to the various webs of authority keeping people in their appropriate place.[45] The countervailing force to this "licentious" atmosphere were the physical insecurities of life among many potential enemies—Island Caribs, Spaniards, and Englishmen. Governors and militia captains easily justified strong disciplinary measures without excessive need of coercion. Martial law governed misconduct of militia on active duty.[46]

Economic historians have questioned why European colonial powers did not enslave large numbers of their "useless" people—criminals, vagabonds, and the unemployed or underemployed—for forced transportation to the colonies. Hypothetically, these people would have served for life, thus eliminating the chief drawback of the indentured servant system. These economists are certain that this solution to the endemic labor problem in America would have been more rational—in their bleak world, meaning cheaper—than the costly Atlantic slave trade from West Africa. They assume that Europeans could have worked reasonably efficiently in tropical climates. French kings did not hesitate to condemn some criminals to the galleys, and occasionally imprisoned Native Americans and West African slaves to row alongside them. Since such a penalty was usually a death sentence, why would the king shy away from transporting undesirables to labor-starved Caribbean colonies? Among other practical problems, the issue of whether authorities could have controlled European Christian slaves in faraway places perhaps occurred to some officials.[47] And what would have been the status of children of such *forçats*?

In the final analysis, however, the outrage of missionaries and visitors that the habitants treated fellow Christian indentured servants so brutally helps explain why outright slavery was an unthinkable alternative. One chronicler counsels patience to "so many honest young people, surprised in the ports of France; who then are transported to the islands, sold, that is, inhumanly indentured; who see themselves reduced to despair when they contemplate the awful state to which their criminal masters have brought them; weakened by their excessive labors and their meager food rations; horribly beaten and most of them ending their lives as a result of their miseries in this terribly hot climate."[48] This description is far from unique. French officials and elites never seriously entertained the concept of permanent servitude for those who had not committed grave crimes.

If death came early to many *engagés*, then perhaps the ministrations of the Church played a comforting role in their lives. This statement may be true of those residing close to the islands' *bourgs* where the Dominicans and later Jesuits received large tracts of land. Du Parquet was lavish in his gifts of land and slaves to the Jesuits.[49] Unlike in France, in these early decades the familiar parish structure did not exist, and there were insufficient numbers of priests to cater to isolated habitations. For major religious rites such as baptism, Mass, and marriage, habitants and their servants usually had to travel to the *bourgs*. Disease and climate led to early deaths for some priests and an early return to France for others. Also, clerics had to tolerate the presence of Protestants, Jews, and rowdy libertines in the island. In short, island clergy faced many obstacles and played a less dynamic role than they did in New France.[50] Their ability to console the poor indentured servants must have been very limited. How many masters simply disposed of dying servants without any religious or other formalities is unknowable.

When d'Esnambuc put into Saint-Christophe in 1625 for recuperation of his battered vessel, he found a few African bondsmen among the French and English settlers. Unlike the ambiguous status of Africans in contemporary Virginia, those of Saint-Christophe were apparently slaves. When d'Esnambuc and Thomas Warner signed the first treaty of amity in 1627, they agreed not to steal each other's slaves.[51] The initial contract between d'Esnambuc, Roissey, and the Compagnie de Saint-Christophe granted the expedition leaders one half the profits of the labor of company "negroes, savages, or slaves," though for the first year only.[52] The origin of these slaves is unknown, but they were presumably booty from raids on Spanish and Portuguese ships and settlements. Since 1571, French courts had declared definitively: "There are no slaves in France."[53] According to a legal scholar in 1608, "all persons are free in this kingdom and, as soon as a slave reaches our borders, and is baptized, he must be considered free."[54] Father Dutertre, writing a few decades later, wondered how to explain African slavery to a French populace "which abhors slavery more than any other nation and where all slaves happily recover their lost liberty as soon as they land and touch its soil."[55] What explains this disjunction between abhorrence in France and the "unthinking decision" of Frenchmen in the Caribbean to enslave fellow humans is some mixture of greed, ample colonial precedents, and the Africans' alien culture and physiognomy.[56] Few seventeenth-century people would have agreed with the sociologist Orlando Patterson that slavery is "a monstrous distortion of human society"; in truth, unfortunately, slavery has been more the norm than a distortion of it in human civilizations.[57] Seventeenth-century Frenchmen might not countenance enslaving other Christians, but had no problem with enslaving North African Muslims, for example.

Before the 1660s, the number of African slaves grew slowly if steadily, in what the historian Dan Usner calls a "frontier exchange" economy of small-scale agriculture, trading, raiding, and pillaging.[58] One source estimates 500–600 slaves at Saint-Christophe in 1635, no doubt the result of more regular arrival of Dutch ships after 1629.[59] The founding of the Compagnie du Cap Vert et du Sénégal for trade with Senegal in 1633 slowly developed an infrastructure to support French trade with Africa. The head of the 1635 expedition to Guadeloupe, Pierre Liénard de l'Olive, stopped in Africa, and later, in 1638, he applied for permission from the Compagnie des Isles to send a ship there for slaves. Before the mid 1640s, slaves arrived in the islands only sporadically, usually via captures of foreign slave ships or because of foreigners trading with French islanders.[60]

From the mid 1640s to the early 1660s, the Dutch became the steadiest suppliers of slaves to the French Antilles. Broad geopolitical factors explain this Dutch initiative. In the 1630s, they overran the Portuguese slaving factories in the Gold Coast and Angola, which they exploited to service their recently conquered sugar lands in Brazil. However, from the mid 1640s on, a Portuguese rebellion lasting a decade first disrupted and then ended Dutch sugar operations in Brazil, so that assisting French planters to develop sugar works became less threatening to Dutch interests. Subsequently, when the first Anglo-Dutch War (1652–54) largely lost Dutch slavers access to booming Barbados, the French Caribbean market became ever more attractive to them. Because about 65 percent of Africans transported across the Atlantic in this era came from Angola, one may assume that the majority of French slaves came from that region in Dutch ships.[61] Dutertre claims that the colonists preferred Angolans to slaves from Cape Verde (Senegambia), because of strength and skills of the former; to be sure, the habitants had to accept whatever slaves arrived in their ports.[62] In 1664, Lieutenant General Alexandre Prouville de Tracy estimated that Dutch slavers annually supplied 1,200 to 1,300 slaves to the French islands.[63]

Apparently, the issue of slavery in the French islands finally bubbled up to the highest level of the French government. According to one obscure tradition, Louis XIII had serious qualms of conscience about enslaving Africans. He supposedly acquiesced after exposure to the argument that Africans gained by the sacrifice of their temporal bodies in return for salvation of their eternal souls.[64] The francophile Pope Urban VIII is said to have given France permission to engage in slaving operations in West Africa.[65] No more questions needed asking, save what would happen to the baptized children of slaves. Iberian precedent, Roman law, and the practical interests of owners all led to the same conclusion.

The price of tobacco remained low during the 1640s, and as some settlers attempted to plant more labor-intensive indigo and sugar, a shift in colonial ideas about the most efficient type of labor occurred.[66] Too many indentured servants ran away, resisted "excessive" exploitation, or died before the end of their terms, for which some writers, such as the Capuchin Father Pacifique de Provins, blamed the climate instead of disease and brutal workloads.[67] Despite the high initial cost of transporting Africans, habitants and their counterparts in other plantation colonies came to view Africans as more dependable and cost efficient units of labor than indentured servants. In about 1650, according to one source, male slaves cost 15,000 to 16,000 pounds of tobacco, as compared to about 300 pounds for three years of indentured service.[68] The Dutch were willing to provide slaves to the French on credit, especially after their expulsion from Brazil.

Governors such as Poincy, Houël, and du Parquet, militia captains, and the clerical orders were most able to take advantage of slaves because of the extent of their land concessions and exemptions from the capitation tax for a number of indentured servants and slaves. Poincy's estate, as documented and illustrated in Rochefort's *Histoire naturelle et morale des isles* . . . (as well as in the writings of Dutertre and Maurile de Saint Michel), is relatively well known. His various plantation crops in the 1650s drew upon the labor of more than 300 African slaves and about half that number of "servants."[69] A 1660 inventory of Poincy's holdings listed 246 slaves at his main plantation on the mountain, of whom 131 were men, 82 women, and 33 children. Not included in this number were five runaways and four mulattoes, aged nine, ten, eighteen, and twenty. In addition, Poincy's smaller habitation at nearby Cayonne employed 74 slaves, of whom 31 were men, 25 women, and 18 children. A third estate depended on 54 slaves, of whom 21 were men, 13 women, and 20 children.[70] Poincy thus owned 374 slaves in all, as well as more than 130 cattle, horses, and other large work animals.[71] In comparison, Thomas Modyford and Colonel Hiliard, the largest planters on booming Barbados in the late 1640s, owned about 100 slaves each.[72]

During the governorship of Houël, Guadeloupe became "one of the most considerable and flourishing" settlements of the Antilles.[73] Governors had first pick of the arriving Africans, just as African headmen had first right to European slave traders' goods at bargain prices. Du Parquet at Martinique owned 133 slaves. The governors determined who could get into the sugar business by their control of land concessions and their power to grant the "right to make sugar."[74] Other than these governors, their relatives and cronies, some exiled Dutch and Portuguese Jewish planters and the missionary orders, few habitants grew sugar before the 1660s.[75]

Larger-scale agriculture and African slavery became more significant in the later 1650s. Simultaneously, the availability of indentured servants stagnated as the island demand for cheap, exploitable labor grew. The economic advantages of slave labor became more manifest to wealthier colonists. Though islanders had been experimenting with cotton, indigo, and sugar in the 1640s, the Dutch loss of Pernambuco in northeastern Brazil by 1654 and thus their lucrative sugar plantations provided the catalyst. A number of Dutch, then Portuguese Jewish planters transferred their operations—slaves, stocks, and barrels—to the French islands. Governors gave them land and tax concessions in return for their tutelage and the tax revenues they generated.[76] Sugar production demanded capital in the form of adequate acreage, industrial infrastructure of sugar works, animal power to drive the mills, and intense human labor.[77] Dutch traders, now unconcerned about competition from French sugar, steadily brought in slaves and supplies, especially to Guadeloupe. On average, Dutch-carried slaves cost islanders 250 l.t. in 1660, one-third due immediately and the rest after ten months.[78] Dutch artisans taught the French how to make the molds in which the sugar syrup crystallized and how to make white sugar from muscavado.[79]

By 1660, it is likely that Africans constituted more than one-third and up to half of the population, although we have mainly impressionistic evidence. At Martinique, a 1660 estimate said that 3,000 of 6,000 thousand inhabitants were African.[80] In the more rigorous 1664 census, there were 3,052 slaves compared to 2,790 Europeans.[81] In global terms, by 1660, between 10,000 and 12,000 Africans and 13,000 to 15,000 Europeans in the French islands is perhaps not an unreasonable estimate; but all such figures are approximations.[82]

Jacques Petitjean Roget's observation that slavery in the French Caribbean islands was "a practice long before [it was] an institution" will little surprise students of embryonic plantation societies.[83] Legal theorists in France notwithstanding, no serious colonial debate about slavery's legitimacy took place. No legal contradiction existed between not enslaving Frenchmen and enslaving Africans. The Iberians had long practiced slavery in the Atlantic islands and very profitably in Brazil, Mexico, and Peru. Popes had sanctioned Iberian enslavement of West Africans since the mid fifteenth century. So, when idealistic Capuchin fathers preached against the enslavement of children of converted slaves on Saint-Christophe, it was the priests who were taking a novel position. Poincy, a servant of Christ but also largest slaveholder in the Caribbean, strongly opposed their stand (although there were certainly other grounds for dispute between them—the Capuchins had, for example, sided with Thoisy and du Parquet in the 1646 conflict). Other missionary orders, dependant on land and slaves to provide for their subsistence, demonstrated their acquiescence by prospering in plantation-style agriculture, with the Jesuits running the largest or second-largest sugar works on Martinique in 1660.[84]

Not much hard evidence is available to characterize master-slave relations in the French Caribbean before 1660. My conclusions here are very tentative and largely deduced from better-known later conditions in the French islands, from comparisons with practices of slavery in frontier era conditions elsewhere, and from the comments of chroniclers. Many variables have to be evaluated to grasp the evolution of master-slave relations. Time and place matter a great deal, as do disease environments. Frontier conditions differed from later, more settled ones. Geography and topography influenced the type of crop worked, or whether slaves worked on a plantation crop at all. Slaves engaged in many types of manual labor, not just agriculture. The ethnic and religious backgrounds of both masters and slaves counted, although these cultural factors are especially difficult to analyze. The variables are so many that even in the later, better-documented classic plantation regimes, strong disagreements of interpretation continue among the system's most sophisticated students.

Societies in which there are slaves are ranked by scholars according to the importance of forced labor to the overall economy. A "society with slaves" is one in which their importance is only marginal. The French Caribbean before the 1650s belong in this category, as does eighteenth-century New England (although the latter's wealth derived from the triangular trade that depended on slavery). A "mixed slave and free society" is one in which slave labor is crucial but not to the extent of excluding free labor. The ratio of free to slave laborers in such societies may range from 2:1 to 1:2. Virginia in the eighteenth century or the

French Caribbean in the pre-plantation era (1660s to 1690s) are examples. The mature plantation society, or the plantation complex, belongs in the category of "slave society." The main eighteenth-century English and French Caribbean colonies (small islands such as Saint-Barthélemy, Saint-Martin, and the Saints had few plantations) and perhaps the eighteenth-century North American Low Country settlements were true slave societies. The ratio of slave to free labor became ever greater, even attaining ten or twelve to one. The master class, where present and not absentee owners, increasingly dominated these societies' social and political structures.

Obviously, these categories are somewhat arbitrary. Slaves everywhere were legally powerless, but social and cultural realities shaped their everyday lives, and hard-won customary "rights" often trumped legalities. Perhaps most important, despite the legal impossibility of slaves owning property and passing it on to their children, everywhere in the Americas they did.

Although practically nothing is known about the individual West Africans who arrived in the French islands, some generalizations are possible about their ages, gender, and genetic characteristics. European slave traders preferred young adult males, followed by young females. In a later era of a more organized slave trade, after around 1700, over 60 percent of arrivals were males. As we have seen, before 1700 the French acquired slaves in a variety of ways. Inasmuch as the Dutch were apparently the largest suppliers, a significant percentage of those slaves were "Angolans," at least until the Portuguese regained control of Angola in the 1650s. This does not mean that they belonged to the same tribes, but their Bantu languages were mutually intelligible.

In the seventeenth century, the average rate of mortality on the middle passage was around 20 percent.[85] The death rate on Spanish ships was nearly 30 percent, on English ones, it was about 21 percent, and Dutch slavers lost a little more than 14 percent. No figures are available for mortality rates on the few seventeenth-century French slave ships.

The survivors arrived on ships also transporting the mosquitoes that were the vectors of malaria and yellow fever. West Africans had some genetic resistance to these diseases, but they were disastrous to European newcomers and, probably, to Island Caribs. Through long contact, Africans had developed some immunological resistance to great Eurasian killers such as smallpox, measles, diphtheria, and whooping cough, diseases lethal to Native Americans. Some resistance does not mean that they, or the Europeans themselves, did not suffer from outbreaks of these killers. However, West African victims of enslavement had as infants and adolescents survived perhaps the world's most lethal disease environment. External diseases such as leprosy and yaws, internal parasites such as guinea worm and hookworm, nutritional deficiency diseases such as scurvy and dirt eating (geophagy), and airborne diseases such as sleeping sickness, tuberculosis, and bacterial pneumonia meant that at least half of West African children did not survive to adulthood. Endemic malnutrition, occurring almost everywhere in West Africa, was both contributory to and an effect of these disastrous medical conditions.[86]

Some students of slavery, such as Orlando Patterson, believe that initial or "frontier" eras allowed for the most unrestrained exertion of power over bondsmen.[87] That view might be more persuasive if later laws intended to limit masters' powers had been enforced. In later chapters, an evaluation of the enforcement of the famous 1685 French *Code noir* (Black code) will conclude that it was selectively enforced to the benefit of masters not slaves.

More recently, some scholars view frontier eras as ones of *relative*, de facto freedoms before the all-encompassing shackles of plantation agriculture were closed. For the most part unable to choose their living or laboring conditions, slaves in these societies were more likely to be employed in agriculture, construction, herding, fishing, hunting, and petty trading as "jacks of all trades."[88] Early French slaves labored on tobacco, of course, alongside masters and indentured servants, but also worked in provision farming, in logging, and in that era's primitive construction. Of necessity, on occasion, they carried firearms and other weapons. How could it be otherwise, especially on Carib and snake-infested islands such as Martinique and Sainte-Lucie? To be sure, as Patterson emphasizes, they also had to fell forests and prepare the land for cultivation, onerous tasks indeed.

It was also a time when Africans did not outnumber the European population. Relations among masters and slaves may have been relatively relaxed. At this time, masters tolerated slaves going off into the woods on Sundays and feast days for long sessions of song and dance featuring drums; they exhibited little of the paranoia of some eighteenth-century masters.[89] Because of the shortage of European women, African females performed both domestic chores and field tasks. If clerics' complaints are to be believed, some, willingly or not, became companions to European masters; others, a few, married Frenchmen.[90]

However, all conclusions about master-slave relations in the frontier era and beyond are tentative. As we do not know either the number of slave arrivals or their numbers prior to the 1660s, not even a guess at their mortality rates can be ventured. Thus, a major if crude tool for evaluating the physical, not to mention psychological, conditions of slaves is unavailable. The chief chroniclers (notably Rochefort and Dutertre) assign little space to African slaves, while devoting hundreds of pages to Island Caribs. (Some of the relatively numerous seventeenth-century depictions of Island Caribs are reproduced in this book; illustrations depicting seventeenth-century African slaves are exceedingly rare.) It is true that Dutertre's more voluminous edition of 1667–71 is more informative. However, not until Father Labat's great work (1722) did French readers have extensive information on the subject, however biased. For the pre-plantation period, the existence of island censuses and official correspondence allows for more empirically based analyses of master-slave relations. Chapter 10 examines this later period.

None of the above is intended to assign a benign character to the early French practice of slavery. The chroniclers, most of whom reflected what were no doubt negative settler views of Africans, unanimously attested to the harshness of treatment, especially by "bad" masters. "They are sold as slaves, they are fed haphazardly; they are forced to work like beasts and their owners get from them by force or otherwise all their services until their death," Dutertre writes.[91] Some missionaries hinted at their unease about these conditions,[92] but they were much more likely to express outrage that *engagés*, fellow Christians, supposedly received treatment as bad or worse. Indeed, one modern authority claims that Africans received identical treatment to indentured servants, down to their clothes ration.[93] Clerical authors all too easily accepted the traditional rationalization that slaves exchanged temporary labor on earth in exchange for the possibility of eternal salvation.

Among the unknown factors about the condition of frontier-era slaves is their adjustment to a relatively new disease environment, a precarious situation for all island pioneers. The sources have little to say about the issue, and what they do say is very difficult to pin down. For later periods, the situation is a little clearer. According to Patterson, slave mortality at Jamaica was the result of "smallpox, fevers of all kinds, inflammations, venereal disease, guinea worms, dropsy, and above all, yaws and dietary diseases, especially dysentery."[94] This describes a mixture of West African and Eurasian maladies, as well as some whose descriptions are too general ("fevers of all kinds," which could be influenza or malaria, among other possibilities) for their nature to be determined.

Based on evidence from the eighteenth- and nineteenth-century British and Spanish Caribbean, Ken Kiple attributes the horrible mortality rates of *mature* sugar and slave systems largely to nutritional deficiencies, especially to shortages of protein, fat, and calcium in slaves' diets. These deficiencies, compounded by a notorious work regime and ineffective medical practices, meant that well over half of newborns did not achieve adulthood, which in Kiple's view is the best explanation for the 4–6 percent annual decline in the number of slaves on West Indian sugar islands in the mid eighteenth century. Slave women, in his analysis, had an adequate number of pregnancies to maintain the population but malnutrition-induced stillbirths, as well as thiamine, calcium, and iron deficiencies, meant that infants under the age of four, in particular, ran a gauntlet of killing diseases, perhaps most especially wet and dry beriberi.[95] The question of whether such nutritional deficiencies had as severe an impact in the frontier era is pursued in greater detail below. However, there is anecdotal evidence that the clay eating (geophagy) habitual in West Africa, which is caused by iron deficiency, was also found among slave women and children in the Caribbean.[96]

What may be hypothesized is that conditions for frontier-era slaves were marginally better than in eighteenth-century slave society. There are several layers to the argument. First, during the frontier era, masters seem to have had little fear of the slaves in their midst. If they are accurate, demographic ratios of roughly equal numbers of slaves and free people may be the key here, but other factors should also be considered. Emanating from different physical and cultural locations in West Africa, and without much of a lingua franca yet, "saltwater" slaves (in French, *bossales*, from the Spanish *bozales*, "muzzled") found it difficult to unite in opposition to masters. True, perhaps a majority of early French slaves were "Angolans" brought by Dutch slavers from Africa or by planters from Brazil.[97] Poincy's hundreds of slaves lived in what was called a *ville d'Angole*, or Angolan village.[98] If so, many of these may have been what Ira Berlin has recently called Atlantic Creoles, people familiar with European and coastal African ways and exposed to Christianity.[99] Slave maroons (*marrons*) had little chance of permanent escape in an alien terrain. Before the wars of the 1650s, Island Caribs made a practice of capturing such refugees for resale or for their own use. In at least one case, Portuguese-baptized slaves (presumably Angolans) fled their Carib captors at Grenada to return to French masters so as "not to live among beasts."[100] The one serious upheaval in the frontier era seems to have involved Angolans uprooted from Dutch Brazil.

In these early decades, skirmishes against Caribs had toughened French colonists, and those who survived that and the "seasoning" process would have been little fearful of disorganized and mostly disarmed slaves. Dutertre asserts that colonists armed some 500 to 600 slaves with torches and knives under French officers to threaten the English at one particularly difficult period.[101] It seems reasonable to assume that psychological security would have rendered the islanders less likely to perpetrate the kind of random terror some of their descendants believed necessary to keep a majority slave population under control.

Habitants may have viewed their few slaves as valuable beasts of burden to be exploited but preserved. Unlike eighteenth-century planters with a seemingly endless supply of slave labor, frontier era owners were uncertain about when new slaves might be available, and whether they could afford them. As indicated earlier, male slaves in the 1640s may have cost as much as 4,000 pounds of tobacco, with females bringing 3,000. Also, when the price of the staple crop was weak, as the tobacco price was in the 1640s and 1650s, masters likely used some slaves for less monotonous tasks such as truck farming, herding, hunting, and fishing; of course, some habitants attempted to switch to indigo or cotton or sugar production.

If nutritional deficiencies were the ultimate cause of high slave mortality rates in the eighteenth-century mature plantation era, as seems very likely, it seems not unreasonable to hypothesize that the frontier-era slave diet was more varied and less monotonous. True, the staple cassava flour is notorious as a starch containing little protein and few vital nutrients. Even if supplemented by dried beef and/or fish, the resulting deficiencies of protein and fat would have had deleterious, even life-threatening, consequences. If, however, slaves had access to adequate amounts of fat, then they would have avoided such deficiencies. With land relatively plentiful, habitants could sow provision grounds rather easily with yucca root, sweet potatoes, and the Africans' preferred yams. The striking ability of Africans and African Americans in the eighteenth- and nineteenth-century United States to grow their population was probably due to the availability of sweet potatoes and fatty pork, which provided an adequate fat, protein, and vitamin base for good health.[102] Slaves in this era, who were often employed as fishermen and hunters, were better able to supplement these starches with still relatively readily available fish, crabs, turtles, manatees, and small game, as well as feral pigs, snakes, birds, and hutias. Turtles and manatees were not available on all islands, however, and the former were only a seasonal food source. Insofar as guavas, avocados, and papayas were available, the vitamin C deficiency causing scurvy would have been alleviated. Where coconuts were available, fat deficiency was perhaps less of a problem. Authoritarian governors, when necessary, enforced the rational policy of cultivating adequate food gardens as opposed to the "Brazilian" practice of allowing free Saturdays for slaves to nourish themselves.[103] In the later seventeenth century and then in the eighteenth, big planters transformed food gardens into staple crop cultivation, leading to occasionally severe food shortages. They did not take seriously Versailles's repeated admonitions to plant so many acres of food per slave. Environmental degradation by 1700 and the more intense regime of emerging sugar meant fewer opportunities for slaves to get fresh provisions. To reiterate, lack of strong evidence means that the above argument is only hypothetical, but it is not implausible.

Although it may have been a mixed blessing, frontier-era masters and slaves had frequent face-to-face contacts, unlike the eighteenth-century situation, when masters were often actual or psychological absentees. Habitants were utterly unfamiliar with Africans prior to their arrival in the islands and presumably had negative reactions to their alien physical and cultural features. Certainly, the chroniclers did. Recall, however, that the Island Caribs were almost equally alien, which did not always prevent interactions of a benign character. The increasingly harsh racism of the eighteenth century certainly had very negative consequences for the enslaved.

Simultaneous with the arrival of more Africans from the later 1630s on was that of the missionary orders. In conjunction with the Compagnie des Isles, the priests insisted on the baptism and instruction of all slaves, although it is not known to what extent practice followed intent. Dutertre's estimate of 15,000 baptized Africans by the 1660s should not be taken as fact.[104] Certainly, a governor like Poincy set the example by having his slaves marched off to catechism every day.[105] The sovereign council of Martinique in 1652 passed an ordinance reaffirming that masters must not work slaves on Sundays and holy days, a substantial number in the Catholic calendar.[106] Du Parquet mandated 6 P.M. prayer sessions for slaves in all households.[107] Who can say what the impact was of measures intended perhaps more for social control than social integration. Slaves perhaps appreciated the symbolism and ceremony of baptism in addition to the little presents distributed. No doubt, they also valued whatever time off from the fields these activities consumed, although they may have occurred during the slaves' "leisure time." According to Dutertre, masters pushed their slaves to "marry" as soon as possible to obtain the fruit of these unions, and they attempted to accommodate slaves' preferences for partners.[108] It is uncertain whether the formal Christianizing of many slaves in any way humanized their treatment, especially if one remembers the treatment of Christian *engagés*.

What did the enslaved think of their new condition? Gabriel Debien calls this question a "great paradox," in that when slaves "spoke" it was through the medium of clerics.[109] Scholars debate the extent of the cultural destruction visited on the slaves. Some assume that baptism, the changing of names, clothing and diet, and servile work, accompanied by occasionally brutal punishments, virtually annihilated African cultural traits. Other scholars argue that despite these cataclysmic changes, Africans maintained some level of cultural integrity. If, in these early decades, more than half came from "Angola," then perhaps they possessed greater linguistic and cultural commonalities than would be the case in the subsequent century, when English and French slavers found their human product all along the African coast from Senegal to Angola.[110] Angola was the least linguistically diverse zone in sub-Saharan West Africa, and the large majority of slaves spoke closely related Bantu languages.[111] Some chroniclers noted that slaves from different areas on a habitation quickly forgot past wounds and helped each other out. Rochefort comments: "They love one another passionately and despite having been born in different countries and sometimes enemies, they support and help each other in need as if brothers."[112]

Some missionaries claimed that after baptism, some slaves became willing and faithful Christians, even if having only an elementary understanding of central doctrines and mysteries. These clerics were well aware that many French commoners also had only the barest knowledge of central Christian tenets. At this early date, the development of Creole language was in its infancy.[113] Was the claim that some slaves became faithful Christians just propaganda, or was it possibly a case of slaves seeking community in an alien world? Why were island leaders willing to arm slaves, although always under French officers, and why would those slaves not refuse to fight? Other than perhaps coastal Africans, those setting foot in the American Tropics in this first generation must have been more adrift in every way than later generations, who at least had Creole African Americans as guides and tutors to a new and brutal world. However, by the 1640s, a few slaves had already acquired enough French to serve as interpreters for priests.[114]

In these circumstances, it is hardly surprising that organized, overt protest happened rarely among what must have been severely disoriented people. True, Dutertre mentions that in 1639 about sixty maroons, including men, women, and children, marauded on Saint-Christophe before Poincy suppressed them.[115] Some observers blamed the phenomenon of *marronage* on masters' poor treatment of slaves.[116] More serious eruptions flared up in the 1650s in the midst of the Carib wars, but probably the participants were slaves of the Dutch and Portuguese troubled by their uprooting from a more familiar Brazilian environment. At Guadeloupe in 1656, an upheaval of "Angolan" slaves led by Pedro and Jean Le Blanc briefly troubled the island; according to sources, the failure of Cape Verde slaves to assemble at the agreed time undermined the revolt. Slaves from the Cape Verde area in fact warned the French about the Angolans' intentions.[117] In the same year, armed maroons, some fleeing from Guadeloupe, joined the Caribs in their struggle at Martinique. This no doubt explains the 1658 Martinique Council's order requiring that all slaves out at night have their master's written permission.[118] On the other hand, slaves loyal to "kind" masters such as the sieur Dorange fought furiously in the mountains against the Caribs and their maroon allies, according to Father Dutertre.[119] Otherwise, the record of slave responses is unfortunately bare.[120]

No doubt the enslaved expressed discontent in a variety of ways, from "laziness" on the job to theft of necessities. All observers comment on their "natural" indolence, although the more astute seem to have recognized that slaves had no reason to work diligently for owners to reap the profit.[121] Dutertre attests to this last "vice," but claims that he heard from the slaves themselves that stealing was a "natural" flaw in their character and not entirely explained by shortages of food and goods.[122]

Although the number of mulatto children was not large in these decades, that interracial relationships occurred cannot be doubted. Some Frenchmen married their female slaves.[123] The extent of coercion in such relationships is impossible to decipher, although the gross imbalance of power relations certainly implies some measure. The white father paid for the infant's care until the age of twelve, and furthermore paid a fine. Authorities handled each case depending on circumstances, especially whether the father was also the owner of the slave mother. Dutertre engages in clerical hyperbole when he avers that the problem was "horrendous and without any remedy," at least at the colonies' beginnings. However, he claims that this "detestable abuse is not as common as it used to be."[124]

There are, then, many unanswered questions about the conditions of coerced labor. To be sure, our ignorance applies even more to the condition of enslaved Africans, whose numbers increased slowly before around 1650, and then much more rapidly in the 1650s. However, there are reasons to believe that conditions of those forced to work in the American Tropics would only deteriorate in subsequent generations.

The frontier era of the French Caribbean drew to a gradual close by about 1660. In France, the Treaty of the Pyrenees (1659) with the ancient Spanish foe had finally brought peace. In the following year, the young and vigorous Louis XIV asserted that he would rule France without intermediaries. Many problems had to be resolved before Louis could undertake the aggressive policies that would bring him *gloire* (glory, reputation, prestige), such as coping with famine conditions throughout the kingdom, dealing with corrupt financiers, and refilling an exhausted treasury. Meanwhile, in the islands, the Carib wars came to an end by 1660, with the effect of opening fresh lands for would-be sugar barons. By 1661, two of the titans of island life, the proprietor-governors Poincy and du Parquet, had passed from the scene, leaving only the irascible Houël still in charge. However, offsetting political uncertainties, the Dutch still swarmed in the French Caribbean, the essential midwives to the transformation to a plantation economy. Overall, conditions seemed to indicate continued, steady growth of the French islands as annexes to the Dutch commercial empire. Soon the Sun King would challenge this complacent status quo. The frontier era of French tropical America was coming to an end.

CHAPTER SEVEN

The Transformation from Settlements to Colonies Begins

The 1660s to the 1670s

There are probably no areas of the world where there are more laws than in colonies. Kings send laws, ministerial directives have force of law, governors issue new laws and discard those of their predecessors, sovereign councils contribute to the chaos.

Pierre-François-Régis Dessalles, *Les Annales du Conseil souverain de la Martinique*

In early 1664, a flotilla consisting of two royal warships and four merchantmen belonging to the new Compagnie de Guiane (1663), weighed anchor at La Rochelle and set out for the Caribbean. The fleet carried some 1,200 passengers, including Lieutenant General Alexandre Prouville de Tracy, commanding some 200 soldiers. Tracy's instructions were to survey the French settlements, confirm allegiance to the king, and restore order. Second in command was Joseph-Antoine Le Febvre de La Barre, who led a contingent of colonists to reestablish the French at Cayenne. This was the largest French convoy that had ever crossed to the Americas. Arriving at Cayenne in May, this large force persuaded the few dozen Dutch and Portuguese Jewish planters there to capitulate. La Barre's colonists settled down to the hard work of sowing provision crops and then planting tobacco and sugarcane. Acutely aware of past Guiane disasters, La Barre insisted on fair treatment of the Galibis, thus practicing what he had preached in his 1662 memoir.[1]

La Barre agreed on a pact in which the Galibis promised to abandon Cayenne and to assist in the capture of runaway slaves and indentured servants. The terms accorded the defeated Dutch were generous, and some with their slaves accompanied Tracy to Martinique. Uncertain of French treatment, most Jews headed for English Surinam. La Barre's settlement of Cayenne established a French presence that has lasted to the present. Satisfied, Tracy sailed for the Windward Islands.[2] Leviathan was stirring.

This chapter examines how Louis XIV and Colbert slowly imposed royal authority on the tropical colonies. It also depicts the degree to which habitants accepted or resisted state direction. Except in rhetoric, the court could not dictate to the habitants. In time, colonists came to accept the principle of royal authority, although they often resisted its implementation in particulars. A similar rough progress of "absolutism" occurred in France. The absence of long-established French institutions in the islands capable of tempering royal authority—the Catholic Church, *parlements*, provincial estates—ought to have facilitated the implementation of royal mandates. For a variety of reasons, that was not the case.

The first half of Louis XIV's reign, characterized by military victories, territorial expansion, the building of Versailles, the patronage of artists, scientists, and *littérateurs*, is regarded as successful.[3] Colbert likewise receives praise in many quarters for his economic policies and his codification of laws. His mercantilist policies involved infrastructure development, the building of a navy and merchant marine, and support of industries ranging from silks and tapestries to mining and forestry. Between 1661 and 1677, Louis and Colbert brought into service ninety-eight ships of the line.[4] In 1661, Louis had nine ships of the line, none of them the large first or second raters. By 1671, he had 119, with thirty-two first or second raters. Construction of great naval arsenals at Brest, Toulon, and Rochefort was begun.[5] The king maintained from 109 to 137 ships of the line between 1671 and 1710. An avalanche of regulations governing every aspect of the royal navy emanated from the minister's bureaus.[6] Newly appointed intendants of the Marine, almost all relatives of the Colberts, had the Herculean task of implementing these.

Below the surface of these royal successes is the fact that between the 1660s and the 1690s France was "suffering from a deepening recession."[7] How to reconcile these apparent contradictions? According to Jan de Vries, France's economy was in fact three separate ones. Northern France's economy had been in contraction since the 1620s, while Mediterranean France suffered hard times from the 1670s on. In contrast, the economy of the major ports and their hinterlands, de Vries's third economic zone, was relatively healthy. "The maritime fringes were more prosperous than the interior," Hubert Méthivier observes.[8] Mercantilist policies privileging manufactures and commerce in part accounted for coastal prosperity, but to the detriment of rural France. Peasants paid the bulk of taxes, which the king used to promote the mercantile and manufacturing sectors.

Within these broader economic contexts, two developments were crucial for the French Caribbean. Louis's wars were the first of these. French colonists fought the English in 1666–67, and the Dutch in 1672–78. Significant French royal naval forces now for the first time fought in Caribbean waters, although not frequently. For the first time, too, planned colonial towns or the fortification of existing ones became a French royal priority. At the best harbor in the Lesser Antilles, Fort Royal, Martinique, an ambitious fortification took shape. From the 1670s to 1713, it served as the administrative capital of the French West Indies. Louis recruited the best military engineer of the age, Sébastien Le Prestre de Vauban, to design Cayenne's fortifications.

While participation in his wars increased loyalty to the king, it also allowed reprieves from implementation of mercantilist regulations that often harmed colonial interests. Conversely, the surprising martial valor of the colonial militias gained the king's attention; it was surprising because these habitants were commonly assumed to be the social detritus of France.

The second development was the gradual evolution of French Caribbean economies toward a sugar plantation regime. The state assisted this process through tariff reductions, support of an embryonic slave trade by removal of duties on slaves landed in the Americas (1670), tax breaks for French sugar planters and refiners, and drastic increases in the tax on imported refined sugars, as well as by measures that damaged the small farmer's crop, tobacco. However, the state simultaneously slowed the transition to a sugar plantation regime by only impeding, not halting, importation of cheaper Dutch and English slaves and provisions. Louis XIV also erected barriers against the more efficient, less expensive shipping of French colonial staples by the Dutch. The French West India Company did not start to replace the Dutch in supplying credit, the industrial components necessary for sugar milling, and, perhaps most important, the slaves to operate sugar plantations. At the very same time, prices for sugar in Europe plummeted.[9] Louis and Colbert also delayed the transition to sugar by banning the reexportation of colonial muscavado, a trade that in the eighteenth century allowed France to dominate the continental sugar trade. Finally, after initially encouraging an island refining industry, the king and Colbert did everything possible to prevent it in favor of metropolitan refineries.[10]

The transition to sugar was thus far less rapid in the French Caribbean than on Barbados between 1640 and 1680.[11] The pace of change in the French islands resembled that of the English Leeward Islands (Antigua, St. Kitts, Montserrat, and Nevis) where the shift was much less rapid than at Barbados. In fact, if one excludes Barbados, the growth of the French Windward Islands was faster than that of the neighboring English Leewards, which were occupied by about 7,000 whites in 1660, as against from 10,000 to 15,000 on the French islands.[12] By 1680, the French colonies were no longer annexes of the Dutch commercial empire and were emerging from a frontier stage of development.

Struggles over Authority, 1664 to 1667

The debarkation of Tracy at Saint-Pierre, Martinique, with his soldiers' drums beating, no doubt evoked ambivalent feelings among the assembled habitants. His arrival proved that Louis had not forgotten his people across the ocean. Some habitants, especially the wealthier sort, would have been glad to think that Tracy might restore peace and stability to their society, which had been in turmoil ever since the death of Jacques Dyel du Parquet in 1658. A man of presence and authority had come to represent the young monarch. Elderly but vigorous, stern but fair, Tracy boldly signaled by refusing to accept gifts that he would not play favorites—a striking gesture in an age of bribes.[13] The savvy colonists suspected that a price would be paid for this royal attention. They soon learned about creation of the monopoly Compagnie des Indes occidentales françaises (French West India Company). At Martinique, the Dyel du Parquet family paid the highest price, the loss of its proprietorship.[14]

After an extensive survey of island affairs, the lieutenant general issued an ordinance that corrected abuses and addressed problems he detected. He resolved all disputes and lawsuits fairly and efficiently, at least according to Father Jean-Baptiste Dutertre's adulatory account. Colonists must have been pleased that the excessive taxes imposed by Adrien Dyel du Parquet, sieur de Vaudroques, were declared null and void; or that Tracy ended restrictions on habitants removing to other islands. Not so pleasing were measures allowing habitants' creditors to seize their slaves, a statute contrary to island custom, or those protecting *engagés* and slaves against brutal masters. To his credit, Tracy insisted that colonists treat the remaining Island Caribs fairly.

A disciplined, lifelong soldier, Tracy aimed to curb the frontier tenor of island life by restricting taverns, returning renegade priests to France, enforcing observation of the Sabbath, encouraging marriage, penalizing concubinage, and a host of other measures.[15] He settled land claims disputes, especially the long-standing one related to the Dominicans, and he complained there were too few priests to fulfill their duties.

Louis and Colbert had chosen well. Whether on the Rhine or in the American Tropics, Tracy reacted swiftly to what he perceived as insults to his king. Although his instructions were to promote peace with the English, he reacted angrily when the governor of Barbados, Lord Francis Willoughby, maneuvered to gain control of Sainte-Lucie and indirectly of Dominica. Tracy recognized the strategic threat and responded vigorously. He imprisoned the commander of the French fort at Sainte-Lucie for cowardice and sent Frenchmen friendly with a faction of Dominica Caribs to undermine the pro-English Caribs there under the enigmatic headman "Indian" Warner.[16]

After his stint at Martinique, Tracy proceeded to Guadeloupe, where he ended the endless quarrels between the sons of Charles Houël and those of the latter's brother-in-law Jean de Boisseret d'Herblay by shipping them home. He reduced the excessive taxes these co-governors had imposed.

Tracy repeated his Martinique formula on the other French islands prior to sailing northward for New France, where his work would become equally celebrated. (It may be wondered why Tracy went to the Caribbean first, when French Canadians were desperate for assistance against the Iroquois. Sailing routes and times may be a partial explanation, but more important was the greater value placed on France's tropical settlements.)

By then, the Compagnie des Indes occidentales had sent out new governors, Robert de Clodoré for Martinique and Claude François du Lion for Guadeloupe. Since the Knights of Malta did not sell Saint-Christophe to the company until 1666, Charles de Sales remained in command there. On the way to Canada, Tracy had extensive conversations with Bertrand d'Ogeron at Saint-Domingue on ways to strengthen that embryonic settlement.[17]

Meanwhile, Colbert was far too impatient to await the completion of Tracy's tour before implementing maritime reform. In 1664, the king imposed far higher tariffs on Dutch imports, despite a 1662 treaty of alliance. In fall 1664, Paris announced that Dutch ships could not visit the islands, on the pretext that they might carry plague, which had ravaged Amsterdam the previous year. However, the Dutch predominance in overseas trade had to be met directly; even Colbert admitted that French ships required twice as many sailors and provisions per ton, a disastrous disadvantage.[18]

The minister planned to imitate the giant Dutch East and West India Companies as one means of countering Dutch advantages. Colbert's analysis of the problems facing French commerce was one-sided but not entirely inaccurate. He believed previous commercial and colonial organizations had been too small, too undercapitalized, and impotent in face of the Netherlanders' octopus reach. France's bourgeois merchants, in Colbert's view, preferred short-term, limited profits to riskier investments that might pay big dividends. This flaw explained why they resisted investing in colonies that might produce profits but only after inevitable losses. French merchants, Colbert complained, preferred profits to service to the king. The "bourgeois" temperament of French merchants was, however, simply a rational response to the dangers of overseas commerce, not a national characteristic, as Colbert believed.

Colbert did not allow the annoyance of not wielding all authority in maritime matters to deter him. First, he organized the Compagnie des Indes occidentales by enlarging the Compagnie de Guiane, whose directors he appointed to run the new company.[19] The year 1664 thus witnessed a flurry of activity to jump-start the renewal of overseas France. Among many other such measures, the king launched surveys of ships and sailors in France's maritime ports, and issued edicts to better regulate marine affairs.[20]

Given Colbert's lack of faith in French merchants, it is not surprising that only a few appear on the subscription list of the Compagnie des Indes occidentales.[21] Fewer served as directors. Colbert enlisted royal assistance to enroll court grandees, on the assumption that lesser folk would be delighted to join such a prestigious organization. Louis guaranteed that such investments would not entail a loss of nobility. Colbert contributed 30,000 l.t. and pressured every official over whom he had some control to contribute as well. If officials enrolled for 20,000 l.t., they could avoid residing in the district of their office. After much pressure, individuals, largely officials and tax farmers, invested 1,297,000 l.t. in the years 1664–68.[22] In 1664, 2,000,000 l.t. in fines, which found its way into company coffers, was yielded by the special chamber to try Fouquet and corrupt financiers (i.e., those not tied to Colbert).[23] Tax farmers beholden to Colbert coughed up 700,000 in the form of investments and loans. Colbert enlisted provincial intendants to press for investments, and he made it clear that policies toward municipalities would re-

flect their contributions. Paris ponied up 350,000 l.t., and the seaport of
Nantes pledged 200,000. The king made a substantial original contribution and made it plain he would be constant in support. Over time,
royal funds of 3,026,545 l.t. were invested in the Compagnie des Indes
occidentales, more than half an estimated 5,522,345 l.t. raised.[24] Louis
furthermore ordered all bishops to have their parish priests promote it.[25]

While impressive on paper, the sum raised was more than offset by
the new company's debts. The purchase of colonial properties at a pre-
mium, the expense of outfitting expeditions that too often came to grief,
the creation of an infrastructure, and the spendthrift provision of credit
to colonists unhappy about losing their Dutch friends all drained the
company purse.

Some historians have criticized Colbert for his strong-arm tactics in
procuring funds. They are correct in that such methods tend to work
only once. However, given the situation of the 1660s, when so many previous companies had failed, financing such a large, multipurpose organization by truly private, voluntary means appeared fruitless. The Dutch
had too great an advantage. The structural costs of strategic responsibilities (arming of ships, building forts and trade factories) and of
strengthening colonies (building infrastructure, supporting missionaries, etc.) frightened merchants comfortable with their traditional, less
risky commerce. Thus, a state-supported enterprise in combination with
private capital may have been the only recourse.

The Compagnie des Indes occidentales offered exceptionally generous—and costly—terms for those migrating to its domains.[26] Volunteers for increasingly ill-reputed Guiane received free passage and free
food, as well as advances of slaves and tools. Those going to the more established islands paid only fifty l.t. passage. Indentured servants received
promises of free land after their three-year contracts were up. Company
posters containing these promises may have been somewhat successful
in drawing new recruits.[27]

Colbert promoted the company by supporting propaganda, but not
of the chimerical type of previous companies. Too many failures, too
many disappointments, meant that a new approach, that of a frank realism, was needed. "I am persuaded that all great endeavors cannot be successful without great difficulties and great losses in their beginnings; but
the powerful protection and assistance accorded by the king will overcome all obstacles," Colbert declared.[28] The message of Abbé Biet and
La Barre for those interested in Guiane was that only time, patience, and

hard work would realize the enormous potential of that tropical region. This approach was one approved by a minister famed for his work ethic. If Frenchmen could avoid past mistakes—incompetent leadership and disastrous policies toward the aborigines—then success was likely. Biet wrote his book in 1664, when the Compagnie de Cayenne launched its expedition; La Barre published his account the next year when he returned to France.[29] Both provided would-be colonists with lists of do's and don't's for success and necessary supplies to carry overseas. In addition, probably in 1664–65, Dutertre undertook the writing of his major history. He shared the new realism—he did not hesitate to discuss the early colonial difficulties and disappointments—and he had access to official naval papers. It seems quite likely that he received Colbert's encouragement.[30]

Colbert's decision to give the Compagnie des Indes occidentales control over all French Atlantic activities has received much criticism. He forced earlier companies to relinquish their charters and coerced the Caribbean proprietors into selling their properties. Jéremie Deschamps du Rausset spent time in the Bastille when he resisted selling Tortuga.[31] Du Parquet's heirs settled quickly for 240,000 l.t., a tidy profit on the 60,000 du Parquet had paid the Compagnie des Isles in 1649. The Compagnie des Indes occidentales paid the Knights of Malta 500,000 l.t. for Saint-Christophe, a neat profit considering the 120,000 l.t. purchase price in 1651; obviously, it was the most valuable island. In the end, all proprietors except the stubborn Charles Houël sold in the face of royal pressure. Champigny received 120,000 l.t. for his share of Guadeloupe; in 1649, all of Guadeloupe had been sold for 60,000 l.t.[32] The company eventually spent 1,110,000 l.t. for these islands and the African possessions of the Compagnie du Cap Vert et du Sénégal, one cause of its failure.[33]

In fifteen years, the islands' worth had apparently increased dramatically. Did the Compagnie des Isles sell its islands at bargain-basement prices because of financial difficulties, or because it did not understand their true value? Or did the Compagnie des Indes occidentales pay an inflated price to expedite the consolidation of its properties? Another explanation focuses on the growing value of island properties during the era of private proprietorship, primarily due to an expanding population and the promise of the sugar industry. The latter explanation subverts Colbert's dim view of proprietary rule.

Some critics claim that the Compagnie des Indes occidentales had too many responsibilities. Slaving stations in West Africa, an embryonic settlement in Guiane, established colonies in the Windward Islands, a buccaneer haven on Saint-Domingue, fur-trading posts in Acadia, and the struggling settlements along the Saint Lawrence were all run by an organization that lacked experienced directors. The company did not possess the know-how to manage or the capital to develop such diverse possessions, and one policy could not fit them all. Company ships could not service all these establishments, and if war came, the company could not protect them. Even though its charter guaranteed royal protection, in 1665–66, that assertion was largely rhetorical, considering the early stage of naval rebuilding. The expense of outfitting ships and of maintaining officials who acted as if the company owed them a living weakened its financial position. Furthermore, to gain the loyalty of the colonists, "who love the Dutch," the company provided merchandise valued at some 19,000,000 pounds of muscavado on credit.[34] Most of this debt, worth about 2,280,000 l.t. in 1666, remained unrepaid. In any case, since the price of sugar soon declined from twelve to six l.t. the hundredweight, the company lost money on whatever debts habitants repaid in kind. Finally, though somewhat offset by further royal subsidies, the company's losses in the war of 1666–67—for which it armed thirty ships, at a cost of some 4,000,000 l.t.—were devastating.[35] The company continued in operation, but even royal nursing could not heal its early wounds.

Yet the company persisted. Like its twin, the Compagnie des Indes orientales, it was very different from its predecessors. Colbert kept a tight grip on company administration, and harried its directors for more and more information, more and more progress on very specific goals. For example, he wanted the directors to specify monthly the number of cattle shipped to the islands. With royal prestige at stake, the company could not fail like its predecessors. Royal funds and Colbert's supervision made the company a semi-official government agency. Colbert was passionately determined to make it the instrument to forge a powerful overseas France.

Experienced foreign entrepreneurs such as the German slave trader Henry de Carolof, who had decades of experience in Brazil and West Africa with the Dutch West India Company, received strong encouragement to jump-start the operations of the Compagnie des Indes occidentales in West Africa. In return for the company receiving 7 percent of slaves brought to the islands and of sugar and other merchandise returned to France, Carolof was given carte blanche to supply the French Caribbean.[36] When the results were less than hoped for, the king encouraged the powerful financier Pierre Formont to enter the slave trade in 1668, but the latter's initiative also sputtered.[37]

Colbert recognized the importance of the slave trade to colonial growth in the tropics, given the unwillingness of Europeans to work there at low wages. In 1669, he ordered the Compagnie des Indes occidentales to focus its activities to establishing posts in "Guinée" and Senegal. Despite the complaints of the governor-general of the French Antilles, Jean-Charles de Baas, that inexperienced French traders lost half of their slaves during the middle passage, and that the survivors were "skeletons" whom no one would buy, Colbert pushed ahead. The first company slaver to reach the Antilles, the d'Elbée expedition, in fact lost 100 out of 410 slaves, and the rest, according to de Baas, arrived in very bad shape.[38]

Undeterred, Colbert persuaded the king to issue an edict in 1670 removing the company's right to levy a tax of 5 percent on all "Guinée" slaves private French traders transported. Early in 1672, an edict ordered that traders were to receive ten l.t. per slave landed in America. Although a few such traders did launch expeditions to "Guinée," the results must have been discouraging to Colbert. Then, when war broke out with the Dutch in 1672, such initiatives fizzled out.[39]

Colbert understood the importance of sugar, but also the need to maintain a large European population in the islands for the sake of external and internal security; as it turned out, these economic and political desiderata proved contradictory, because sugar production gradually drove the poor habitant's crop of tobacco from the marketplace. As early as 1663, Colbert explored how sugar and tobacco from French Caribbean islands could be reexported to the Baltic in exchange for naval supplies. On the other hand, he overreached himself with designs born of what proved to be wishful thinking. As noted above, the notion of Guiane as provisionary of the Antilles exemplifies that thinking. Colbert did not understand how difficult it is to sail from the islands against the wind to Cayenne, a trip of a month or more. In addition, Cayenne had anchorages safe from the fort's cannon and was thus especially vulnerable to enemy attack.[40]

Another fond notion of Colbert's was the development of trade between New France and the French Caribbean. However, the distance between the two was enormous, there were few Canadian ships, and the

Saint Lawrence was inaccessible in winter. Moreover, other than fish, what New France had a surplus of was fur, and not even the most dandified tropical colonists wanted fur hats and coats. Because New France did not possess sources of salt, sale of surplus cod and other stockfish to the Caribbean was impracticable.[41] The islands needed flour and biscuit, staves for barrels, beasts to power sugar mills, and salted meat and fish for settlers and slaves. Eventually, in the eighteenth century, some fruit would mature from the seeds nurtured by Colbert; by then, however, British North American smuggling fulfilled these needs.[42] The dream of an autarchic imperial economy turned out to be a fantasy.

In 1665, the habitants' resentment burgeoned. An edict of 1664 preventing the Dutch from playing their old role as trade partners, in combination with disappointingly few company ships, fueled bitterness that the colonies could trade only with France and on the latter's terms. The Dutch were unwilling to abandon a trade that annually occupied about a hundred ships. For example, in a 1663 fire that consumed sixty warehouses at Basseterre, Saint-Christophe, Dutch merchants lost more than 2 million l.t. worth of goods. Until new supplies arrived some five months later, both French and English colonists suffered.[43]

Not only did the company charge more than the Dutch, and for inferior goods, but many colonists must also have felt friendly toward the Hollanders, who had served them well for a fair profit and fought alongside them against Caribs and maroons. For some, furthermore, the Dutch were fellow Calvinist Protestants. However, the company's inadequate imports and the arrogant behavior of its agents were what most damaged relations—although, according to Tracy, the settlers themselves were to blame for food shortages, which, he said, had resulted from too rapid transformation of provision grounds to sugar growing.[44]

Finally, as the young company could not immediately enter the difficult and costly slave trade, colonists greedy for African labor had no sources other than nearby Dutch (St. Eustatius, Curaçao) or English islands. In 1661, various French captains responded to official queries about how to introduce slaves into the French islands by recommending that they be bought from the Dutch.[45] Given the circumstances, one may assume that habitants who ventured their lives in exotic and dangerous milieus traded smuggled goods and slaves with clear consciences; and indeed they would do so for the rest of the colonial era.

Once the Solomon-like Tracy had sailed northward, some colonists on Martinique challenged company authority directly. After all, had they not colonized the island without effective assistance from France? Had they not endured exile from the homeland to the benefit not only of themselves but also of their kingdom? Had they not dealt with the ferocious Caribs by their own arms? Why should they now stand by and see the company ruin what they had worked for so diligently? Given food shortages that resulted from a premature ban on Dutch shipping before the company's ships could arrive and an emerging colonial mentality emphasizing defiant self-reliance, it is not surprising that settler tumults erupted in 1665 and 1666.

The appearance of the companies' first ships aggravated the situation, because their inadequate goods could not begin to replace what the Dutch had supplied.[46] Some mutinous types saw a conspiracy when the company brought peasant-type shoes (*sabots*) for colonial footwear.[47] They were habitants and emphatically not peasants (*paysans*). To appease their anger, company agents distributed what goods they had on incredibly liberal terms without regard to settlers' debtworthiness. Inability to collect these debts gravely harmed the company.

In 1666, the newly appointed lieutenant general, La Barre, temporarily quieted the habitants with a variety of measures. Habitants could bring servants and supplies from France on company ships without paying duties, only freight charges. Furthermore, they could import and export goods paying only a 2½ percent duty. Foreigners not enemies of France could do the same paying 5 percent.[48] However, La Barre's relationship with the Martinique council deteriorated quickly. Further tumults and disorders erupted.

Dutertre chronicles these troubles from the perspective that, although the habitants involved had understandable motives, they were nevertheless rebels against the king's just authority.[49] Fortunately for the king and the company, the new governor, Clodoré, had had a long and distinguished military career, which enabled him to control the outbreaks, despite great personal danger.[50] The governor successfully appealed to more substantial habitants by warning them against allowing the "rabble" to have their way.[51] Perhaps Clodoré would have been consoled had he known that his friend Bertrand d'Ogeron was facing similar or perhaps more grievous difficulties at Saint-Domingue.[52]

Unlike Clodoré, d'Ogeron had had substantial experience in the Caribbean. A major French colonial figure, d'Ogeron was born in western France into a merchant family. An uncle, however, became apothecary to both Cardinals Richelieu and Mazarin prior to obtaining other offices, and his patronage gained Bertrand a marine commission. He fought at the famous battle of Rocroi in 1643, then in support of the Catalonian rebellion against Madrid in the later 1640s, and elsewhere, until his father's death at Anjou in 1653. Soon Bertrand resigned his commission and became involved in the 1656–67 Compagnie de l'Amérique méridionale. After its failure, and his dissatisfaction with an offer to stay in Martinique, d'Ogeron took his *engagés* to Saint-Domingue. However, his rickety ship was wrecked off Saint-Domingue, with destruction of his supplies, although there was no human loss. Thus he had to live the rude life of a buccaneer, hunting wild cattle for their hides and feral pigs for their flesh. This experience prepared him for his later career as governor of the buccaneers.

In 1660, d'Ogeron returned to France, where, with his sister's financial assistance, he hired more indentured servants to grow tobacco. He treated them so well that he had no difficulty recruiting more on annual visits home. In 1662, to fulfill his long-term ambition of establishing a colony in Florida, he secured the governorship of the Bahamas through the comte de Brienne, secretary for foreign affairs.[53] Meanwhile, his habitations in Saint-Domingue and Tortuga were doing well. So it was that in 1664 on the advice of Clodoré, the Compagnie des Indes occidentales wisely appointed d'Ogeron governor of Tortuga and Saint-Domingue.

If Martinique's colonists believed that they had developed their settlements with little metropolitan assistance, then those of Saint-Domingue felt so a fortiori. These "brothers of the coast" were desperadoes—shipwrecked men, escaped indentured servants, mutinous sailors, pirates, and adventurers like d'Ogeron. Living as hunting and hunted men, they taunted the Spanish who came to burn their ramshackle huts, because a new one could be quickly thrown together. Some lived as true buccaneers, that is, selling hides to passing ships and exchanging their seared, smoked, preserved viands with Tortuga pirates. Sometimes they joined freebooters (*flibustiers*) filibustering on the Spanish Main. Any man attempting to govern this lot was in for violent headaches.

In the long run, d'Ogeron had some advantages. The number of wild animals had decreased due to the buccaneers' hunting efficiency, the Spanish policy of employing mulatto and slave hunters to deprive the buccaneers of a livelihood, and, not least, packs of wild dogs. The new governor had also demonstrated that profits could be made from tobacco if a man could acquire indentured or slave labor. His ship brought many servants, and he treated them humanely and fairly. Most servants and friends and relatives he enticed to Saint-Domingue were from his native Anjou. He brought young women from France and encouraged the better-established colonists to marry. He could rely on the support of his nephew Jacques Nepveu, sieur de Pouançay, and friends such as Pierre-Paul Tarin de Cussy, who would be his successor as governor.

In the short run, however, d'Ogeron faced mutinies when in 1665 he tried to force freebooters to bring their prizes to Tortuga to regulate the distribution of prize money, with d'Ogeron getting a 10 percent commission. In 1666, he attempted to institute a militia system requiring training for all men. Fortunately, the governor was a supple man and aware that it would take time and patience for these wanderers to settle down. D'Ogeron did not attempt to enforce the putative company monopoly at this time, because its ships were not visiting Saint-Domingue in any case.[54]

The flames of revolt died down to a flicker of embers in 1666, but the island colonies then became engulfed in the brush fires of European wars. The second Anglo-Dutch War started in 1665, and the Dutch pressed Louis XIV to honor his treaty commitments. Grudgingly, the king did so in 1666. Louis and Colbert were ill pleased to be assisting Dutch republicans. A measure of October 1666 allowed the Dutch to trade in the French islands in return for a 5 percent duty.[55] In turn, the Dutch were uncomfortable with Louis's growing military might. Receiving warnings of forthcoming hostilities, the English at Saint Christopher planned a preemptive assault on their French neighbors; so, without declaration, war commenced in the Caribbean.

At first, just as in the Seven Years' War a century later, the French were victorious everywhere. On Saint-Christophe, the French armed their slaves with torches to devastate the plantations of the English, and the latter, led by Governor William Watts, and including hundreds of Henry Morgan's Jamaican buccaneers, were routed by the French militia under Commander de Sales. Watts, Sales, and Robert Longvilliers de Poincy all perished in the fighting. Much ado was made at the French court of this triumph, and Louis had medals of celebration struck. Glorious victories secured the place of even remote, reputedly déclassé sites in the Sun King's proud heart.[56] Saint-Christophe, where the English and French had maintained a precarious condominium for forty years,

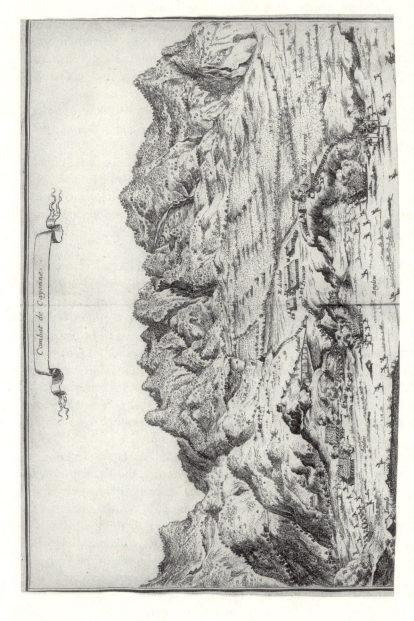

The Battle of Cayonne on Saint-Christophe, 1666. From Jean-Baptiste Dutertre, *Histoire générale des isles Antilles,* 3: opposite 25.

thus erupted in bloodshed; tensions and conflict there would not end until the English removed the French permanently during the War of the Spanish Succession (1702–13).[57]

The English did have one victory in 1666, when Francis Willoughby sacked Cayenne. But later in 1666, things again soured for the English in the Antilles. The new lieutenant general, La Barre, arrived with a fleet and 400 regular troops.[58] He and island governors formed a council of war to attack the remaining English Leeward Islands. Reflecting continued distrust, the king had given La Barre authority only at sea. The head of the regular troops and the governors at the head of the militias were to command on land. Making matters even more confused, Governors Clodoré and du Lion disliked each other and bitterly disagreed about the propriety of using Caribs as auxiliaries. Clodoré not only deployed Carib auxiliaries but also armed a unit of black slaves under the "general" Francisque Fabulé, former leader of a maroon band.[59] Despite this divided command, the French easily conquered Antigua, defended by planters much more worried about Carib depredations than the French; and rightly so, because the Caribs captured eighty English including the governor's wife.[60] But French commanders also allowed the troops to ride roughshod over capitulated English plantations. The next target was Montserrat, where disgruntled Irish Catholic indentured servants assisted in the French victory. Nevis was ripe for plucking, but disagreements among the French leaders meant a lost opportunity.[61]

Lord Willoughby brought reinforcements from Barbados to the Leeward Islands, but a hurricane devastated his fleet in the Saints, the site of Rodney's enormous English victory over Grasse's French fleet in 1782. Willoughby himself was a victim. Excluding Barbados, the French islands, with roughly double the European population of the English Leewards, Saint-Christophe in French hands, Carib allies, and a French fleet on hand, were poised to dominate the eastern Caribbean.

Charles II, who had previously been complacent because the Barbadians had repulsed Admiral Michiel Adriaenszoon de Ruyter's powerful Dutch fleet in 1664, was shocked by these losses and sent Sir Henry Willoughby with a relief force, while preparing a more powerful armada under Sir John Harmand. Sir Henry, nephew of Lord Francis Willoughby, defeated French ships off Nevis, thereby relieving that threat. Subsequently, Harmand first defeated a small French naval force off Martinique and then destroyed nineteen ships and fourteen barques in the roadstead of Saint-Pierre, with the loss of a million pounds of

The French foil an English attempt to retake Saint-Christophe, 1667. From Jean-Baptiste Dutertre, *Histoire générale des isles Antilles*, 4: opposite 261.

sugar.[62] His fleet then appeared at Cayenne. The temporary commander, the chevalier Le Febvre de Lézy, brother of La Barre, panicked and
fled with 200 colonists to Dutch Suriname. There they showed more
gumption and helped the Dutch beat off Harmand's attack.

Aware that peace would probably return Cayenne to the French,
Harmand destroyed everything he could. News soon arrived of the
Treaty of Breda, which restored the status quo ante, although it awarded
Tobago to the French. But not so easily restored were Cayenne's burnt
plantations, the tremendous losses in commercial vessels, or the destroyed English estates at Antigua, Nevis, and Saint Christopher.[63] In
the latter case, the French delayed restitution because of similar English
obstructionism in recognizing French damage claims in Acadia. Increasingly bitter Anglo-French colonial wars, which would continue off
and on to 1815, were thus precipitated. These wars played an important
role in shaping the contest for authority in the French Caribbean islands.

Trials and Errors, and Further Trials, 1667 to 1672

The losses of the Compagnie des Indes occidentales as a result both of
the war and of overly liberal credit policies clearly discouraged many
stockholders. The English captured five company vessels and sank seven
more, a disastrous blow.[64] A company official told Colbert that "our
company can give no help to the colonies, neither foodstuffs, nor all the
other things necessary."[65] Nevertheless, Colbert and his master persisted. The royal treasury bailed out the company with a million l.t.[66]
Colbert initiated changes to revitalize the colonies. A new, ferociously
protective tariff targeted the Dutch, France's former ally. Colbert opened
the colonies to all French merchants, reserving the company monopoly
to the slave trade, which he deemed "the trade that more than others
brings great advantages."[67]

With Colbert's encouragement, the banker Formont sent two ships
to Ardres on the Gold Coast in the name of the Compagnie des Indes
occidentales. After lengthy bargaining, the company's veteran agent
Carolof managed to accumulate 997 slaves. Because of delays along the
coast and probably overcrowded ship conditions, only 753 slaves reached
Martinique. Still, a profit was made. and the returning vessels transported Mattheo Lopez, the ambassador to Louis XIV from the king of
Ardres. Apparently, Lopez and his entourage of wives, children, and
slaves made a splash at court. Colbert dreamed of a lucrative slave trade

that would not only supply the French islands but also Spaniards in America, always hungry for slaves.[68]

The former French and Dutch allies came to view their connection as unnatural. The Dutch moved quickly in 1667–68 to form the Triple Alliance with England and Sweden, much to Louis's irritation. He began diplomatic talks with England's Charles II, a Bourbon manqué, which in 1670 resulted in the Treaty of Dover. The French proposed formal worldwide commercial and colonial cooperation, an interesting twist on these negotiations, but the suspicious English did not take the bait. The Dutch received the shockingly prohibitive tariff of 1667 as a virtual declaration of war. Colbert finally had his wish, economic battle *à l'outrance* (to the end). He was determined to end the temporary, war-related access of Dutch ships to French colonies. Accordingly, in September 1668, a royal ordinance excluded Dutch ships.[69] French cruisers had some success in enforcing the edict in 1670 and 1671.

In Paris, Colbert finally received official authority over all maritime affairs as secretary of state for the Marine in 1669 (although it was possible to hold that office without being designated a minister, Colbert was also a minister, so historians call him "minister of the Marine"). He established the embryo of a Colonial Office and started the centralization of records, which ever since has had historians singing his praises. He accelerated his efforts to build a competitive navy, which required the crown to support shipyards, maintain or create harbors, develop royal naval arsenals, maintain lists of sailors, and establish schools for engineers and mapmakers. He issued a flood of directives and requests for information to colonial officials. He started to train his designated successor, his son, the marquis de Seignelay. In 1669, at fifty, Colbert reached the pinnacle of his powers.

The king eliminated the divisions in island command that had botched the war effort and created the new office of governor-general of all France's Caribbean possessions, to whom all the other governors would be subordinate. (The English took a different tack: in 1672, the administration of the Leeward Islands was detached from Barbados, and they received their own governor.) Along with the nomination of Jean-Charles de Baas as governor-general, the administrative center of the French Caribbean was moved from vulnerable Saint-Christophe to Martinique, the commercial and geographical center. It is unsurprising that a hard-nosed military man like de Baas received the post, although as a cautious Protestant with a name of Dutch origin, he may seem a strange choice to enforce a heavy-handed anti-Dutch policy.

He arrived in the islands in early 1669, with an independent attitude. Colbert had a different view. He wanted a dynamic military commander combined with an obedient paper pusher in his own mold. The minister soon expressed amazement that de Baas pretended not to understand who was *really* in charge of the Compagnie des Indes occidentales; and that the governor-general did not write voluminous memoirs except when repeatedly prodded. (Luckily for de Baas, e-mail was not available.)

De Baas possessed other characteristics that annoyed Colbert. Of an old-fashioned noblesse oblige temperament, the governor-general hesitated to implement orders to exclude Dutch commerce under any and all "pretexts," even severe misery for colonists and their slaves. Inasmuch as he profited from contacts with Dutch merchants, his humane sentiments were perhaps not unalloyed. That the Dutch in 1670 marketed 100,000 lbs. of French West Indian tobacco at the Baltic port of Königsberg (today's Kaliningrad) alone demonstrates the very gradual impact of Colbert's measures.[70]

Colbert and Louis XIV grudgingly put up with de Baas, as they did with a similar personage in New France, Louis de Buade, comte de Frontenac, because these men were proven commanders and tough guys. De Baas almost immediately quarreled with island officials, including the chief company agents, the governor of Guadeloupe, Claude François du Lion, the governor of Martinique, Antoine-André de Ste-Marthe, and royal naval officers. Lines of authority were unclear, but de Baas believed that all military matters were in his purview, including the important task of naming militia officers. Frustrated by insubordination, de Baas often resorted to severe measures that in turn brought reprimands from Paris. The king and Colbert continually advised him to act as a beneficent paterfamilias, firm but kind toward colonists and subordinates. The king advised him "to treat them with *douceur*, as the principal goal must be to maintain and augment these colonies by attracting people, which cannot be done without treating them well, excusing their small errors and only punishing major ones that could cause the ruin of the colonies." Louis added that de Baas should be aware that "anyone well established in my kingdom would never resolve to go to live in the islands; so you should not expect colonists to demonstrate the same conduct and good morals as someone in my kingdom."[71]

Paris backed its anti-Dutch policy by dispatching a formidable fleet under an old-fashioned seadog, Louis de Gabaret, in 1669, which patrolled into 1670. However, because teredos, or shipworms, ate away at wooden hulls, such fleets could stay in tropical waters for only a limited time in the absence of extensive infrastructure and repair facilities in the islands, which the French never created. The English did create such facilities, which gave them a substantial advantage in the struggles to come. Muscle now matched rhetoric, although, fortunately for most colonists, only temporarily. But Colbert sought other means to promote the islands' economies, by favoring sugar, slaves, and supplies. In 1669, he opened island commerce to private French traders. He now touted the idea that "liberty is the soul of commerce"—liberty, of course, for French subjects. In the early 1670s, Colbert complained to de Baas on the subject of free trade "that we should not be surprised that company officials want to maintain their monopoly because they think only of their selfish interests and not of the general good of the state and the islands."[72]

The company was now given the slave trade as its chief operation, but private traders could purchase licenses and receive from the treasury ten l.t. "per head" delivered, following the Iberian practice of pricing all others in relation to the value assigned a prime slave, the so-called *pieza de Indias* (*pièce d'Inde* in French). In the years 1670–72, duties payable to the company on slaves that private traders brought to the islands ceased, as did duties on French goods used to purchase slaves. A six l.t. bonus "per head of blacks" taken from the "Guinée" coast went to the shipowner, and three l.t. to the captain. Edicts of 1671 and 1673 exempted the company from all duties on exports used to pay for slaves in West Africa.[73]

These measures in the years 1668–73 all point to state support of private French merchants at the expense of the Dutch and, in effect, of the moribund Compagnie des Indes occidentales. The high tariffs against the Dutch increased the price and availability of Dutch and northern European goods essential to the purchase of slaves in West Africa. In 1671, Madeira wine was the only foreign product that could be transported to the French islands.[74] By 1673, the now bankrupt company had not supplied anywhere near enough slaves, and its trade concession in Senegal was granted to another monopoly company, the Compagnie du Sénégal. Although the Compagnie des Indes occidentales had paid the Rouen Compagnie du Cap Vert et du Sénégal 150,000 l.t. for Senegal (which included the Cape Verde Islands, as well as the Senegal and Gambia River basins) in 1674, the new Senegal company reimbursed it only 75,000, which says a good deal about its record in West Africa.[75] The Gold and Slave Coasts remained open to private traders.

In 1675, the new Senegal company, which exhibited little energy, contracted with the financier Jean Oudiette and the directors of the Domaine d'Occident (Western Domain) tax farm to transport 800 slaves a year to the French Caribbean. Little came of their efforts. Oudiette's ships transported only 500 slaves in a four-year period.[76] Louis must have been disappointed, given his belief that "nothing contributes more to the augmentation of colonies and the cultivation of their lands than the heavy labor of Negroes."[77]

Throughout the 1670s, Colbert urged island officials to promote colonial refining of sugar, and five small refineries were in fact established. Colbert promoted this trend by keeping duties on refined island sugar the same as for raw sugar. Refined sugar reexported from France received even more favorable treatment; simultaneously, higher duties targeted Brazilian and other foreign sugar. These measures were taken against a background of slumping sugar prices after 1670. The price for muscavado in France was so low as to devastate planters if a solution were not found. Refined sugar fetched up to five times as much as muscavado, and cost much less to transport. Thanks to these colonial refineries, sugar prices increased by a third. In 1679, the first island intendant, Jean-Baptiste Patoulet, promoted the establishment of larger refineries, which Colbert strongly supported in 1680. Patoulet was a partner in one of the new refineries. The former freebooter Charles-François d'Angennes, marquis de Maintenon, by 1680 the largest sugar magnate in Martinique, built two more refineries at Saint-Pierre in the early 1680s. Colbert gave him permission to export half a million pounds of sugar in secret to Spanish America. Before coming to the islands, Maintenon had sold his estate to Louis XIV, who bestowed it on Françoise d'Aubigné (the widow Scarron), his future morganatic wife, Mme. de Maintenon.[78]

Increasingly, metropolitan refiners, some thirty to forty entrepreneurs, protested these developments. Colbert had also encouraged their industry, and they were outraged at his support of colonial competitors. To promote some thirty refineries at Nantes, Orléans, and Bordeaux, and to increase Oudiette's revenues, exporters of Antillean refined sugar had to pay eight l.t. the hundredweight to the Domaine d'Occident in 1681.[79] Five island refineries were producing 3,000,000 pounds of sugar

a year in 1684, when Versailles summarily decreed that no new island refineries could be established, subject to a penalty of 3,000 l.t. By then,
refineries in France were milling some 17,700,000 pounds of sugar.[80] Islanders were restricted to muscavado or semi-refined "clayed" sugars.
The larger planters responded by shifting almost exclusively to clayed
sugars, which significantly reduced the molasses content of muscavado.
Clayed sugars even competed with refined white sugar in French markets, and despite the government's increase of duties, triumphed in the
Lesser Antilles.[81] Despite inconsistent policies emanating from Paris,
and continuing price pressures, sugar production increased significantly
in the later 1670s and 1680s.[82]

By 1668, when an *arrêt* reestablished all colonial laws unenforced
during the war years, provisions in the French islands were in short supply. In 1671, duties ended on goods sent to the islands, and those on colonial staples to France were reduced from 5 to 3 percent.[83] Unfortunately,
before these measures might have yielded significant benefits, war with
the Dutch delayed their intended impact. The first war casualty was the
Compagnie des Indes occidentales, which went into receivership in 1672
and termination in 1674, with the king paying off its debts in return for
its assets and projected revenues.

By the early 1670s, Colbert's thinking about colonies had matured
beyond the mercantilist formulas to which his name is often attached
(Colbertism). Although continuing to view colonies as dependent on the
mother country, he developed sophisticated ideas about stimulating their
growth. Rejecting the idea of sending convicts (*forçats*)—"it is not in the
king's power, no matter how powerful he is, to populate the islands by
force"[84]—Colbert insisted that only favorable conditions would foster
growth, by attracting Frenchmen understandably reluctant to undertake
a dangerous adventure. He promoted policies supporting reproduction
of existing colonists. They should be granted all manner of economic
privileges, promised swift and sure justice without the lawyers or legal
shenanigans that plagued France, and taxed lightly. To implement these
notions, beyond what has already been discussed, Colbert reduced the
term of indentured servants in half, to eighteen months. Shorter terms
might tempt more of them to stay and thus maintain a "reasonable" balance of European and African populations, as well as supply men for
colonial militias.

Colbert constantly informed the governors that they should rule
with as much leniency (*douceur*) as possible; for example, they should not

allow overzealous priests to annoy Jews and Protestants. Officials were to try to prohibit colonists from returning permanently to France, but to do so subtly. Colbert did not accept d'Ogeron's advice to encourage colonists to return periodically to the motherland because such visits would fire their love for France. Although his policy of effective toleration rested on pragmatic grounds, its reversal in the 1680s after Colbert died is not sufficiently acknowledged by his detractors.[85] If colonists did not understand the need to make sacrifices, "reason, justice and, if necessary, force should be employed to make them submit." In the end, however, the king did not have the "funds to buy obedience or force to command it."[86]

The slump in sugar prices and the low demand in France for it prompted Colbert to promote other island products such as cotton, indigo, and ginger. He encouraged the planting of spices, flax for linen, mulberry trees for silk production, and much more. He and his successor, his son, Seignelay, beseeched island officials to send home choice products of the islands, from succulent oranges to exotic flowers. Colbert's cousin and island intendant Michel de Bégon used his two years of "exile" at Martinique collecting curiosities and promoting the work of naturalists. One of them, Father Charles Plumier, later named an exotic and beautiful tropical flower "begonia" after his patron.[87]

Despite all such measures, a significant rebellion erupted at Saint-Domingue against the "pretensions" of the Compagnie des Indes occidentales. Any serious effort to force tobacco growers of that isolated colony into the company's orbit had to face the fact that the leaf paid half the duties in Dutch ports, and that company ships rarely appeared. A significant number of immigrants had increased the population by about a thousand.[88] The 1670 upheaval proved more serious than that of 1665–66, no doubt because the previously respected d'Ogeron had in 1669 "betrayed" the colonists by becoming the company's agent. He attempted to prevent widespread fraud among tobacco producers by ending the use of tobacco as payment. Growers would have to sell their crop in France or in Spanish America to obtain hard money, ending their habit of hiding inferior leaf.[89]

When the habitants of Saint-Domingue heard that d'Ogeron intended to enforce the monopoly of the Compagnie des Indes occidentales, and that privateer commissions were to be revoked, they exploded into rebellion. That Louis XIV wished to pursue peaceful relations with Spain to isolate the Dutch carried little weight with the islanders. Feral

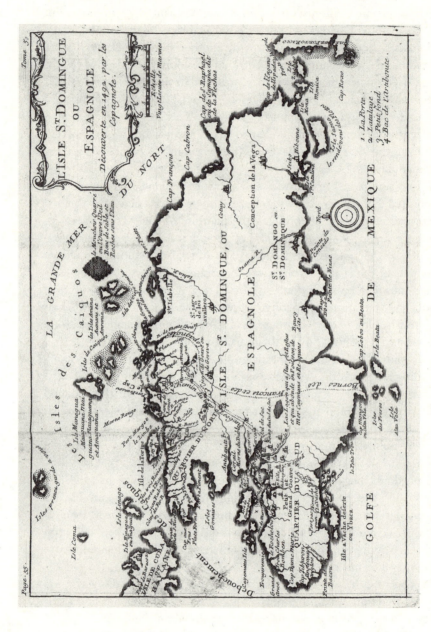

Hispaniola, or Saint-Domingue. From Jean-Baptiste Labat, *Nouveau voyage aux isles de l'Amérique* (Paris, 1722), 5: opposite 55.

cattle and pigs were becoming so depleted as to leave those who refused to settle down few options. Desperate colonists preferred, as they said, a quick death to a slow one, and they were in d'Ogeron's words "ferocious men."[90] They burned his habitations. Rebel affidavits claimed d'Ogeron monopolized island commerce, giving them too low a price for their tobacco and charging them too dearly for supplies. For example, they paid 750 l.t. for a barrel of beef, while the Dutch charged 200. They called their condition "white slavery." They also asserted that he still issued privateer commissions to favorites and armed ships himself. In turn, d'Ogeron blamed Dutch captains for egging on the "mutineers." The rebellion finally calmed with the appearance of a French fleet and with d'Ogeron's promise of general amnesty, "among other things."[91] Many rebels retreated to the central western end of the island, the Cul de Sac.

Considering that Saint-Domingue would one day become by far the richest French colony, the "Pearl of the Indies," Colbert's apparent indifference to it may surprise. He seems to have viewed it similarly to the frontier outposts of New France, which undermined his "compact colony" philosophy. Colbert hated disorder of any sort, and he may have lumped together Canadian fur traders and hunters and Saint-Domingue buccaneers. He opposed d'Ogeron's project to transfer his colony to Florida. In 1674 and 1675, d'Ogeron issued commissions to Jamaican buccaneers to attack Spanish shipping, with the connivance of Sir Henry Morgan. (Since the English and Spanish were then at peace, Jamaican officials could not issue such commissions.) Colbert was outraged by evidence that d'Ogeron's own ship had participated in privateer activities after the king's prohibition, and he was satisfied only after the governor had returned what remained of the booty.[92] In 1670, d'Ogeron established a new settlement, Le Cap François (commonly called Le Cap; today's Cap Haïtien), although Colbert constantly lectured him about grouping the settlers together for protection, despite d'Ogeron's insistence that such concentration made them inviting targets. The king no doubt concurred. Louis instructed Frontenac at Quebec: "You must hold to the maxim that it is far more worthwhile to occupy a smaller area, and have it well populated, than to spread out and have several feeble colonies which could be destroyed in all manner of accidents."[93] Colbert also encouraged d'Ogeron to recruit young women to marry his wayward subjects. That d'Ogeron was a champion recruiter of indentured servants did not save him from Colbert's harping on the subject.

Despite rebellions and the pessimistic correspondence between Paris and Saint-Domingue, the colonists produced some 3,000,000 pounds of tobacco annually by 1674. Their anguish about the inadequate supply of slaves suggests a growing economy.[94] When a dysentery-weakened d'Ogeron returned to Paris in 1675 for the last time (he died in 1676), he left behind some 4,000 to 5,000 colonists of tenuous loyalty to the crown.[95] Unable to get an audience with the king or Colbert to promote a project to conquer Spanish Hispaniola, d'Ogeron passed from the scene unappreciated and heavily in debt. Twenty years more passed before Spain recognized French sovereignty over Saint-Domingue.

The Tribulations of the Dutch War, 1672 to 1679

From 1668 on, the French government plotted to isolate the Dutch, and when Louis's large army invaded the Netherlands in 1672, success seemed certain. However, the Dutch opened their dikes to halt the French, and God was evidently on their side, because the water did not freeze in the first winter of war, aborting the projected French cavalry gallop to Amsterdam. As the war dragged on, the Dutch gained confidence, and the French position weakened. Under William III of the House of Orange, elected Stadtholder (*stadhouder*) of Holland, Zeeland, and Utrecht in 1672, the Dutch took the offensive against France overseas. The same year saw the beginning of the Third Anglo-Dutch War (1672–74).

These were difficult years both for France's Caribbean colonies and for Colbert. Harried with the endless search for money to support the war, he had less time to devote to colonial oversight. A dramatic decline in correspondence across the Atlantic and a sharp reduction in laws emanating from Paris reflect that.[96] The war so frustrated the minister's plans that some historians have claimed falsely that he must have been covertly opposed to it.

France moved against its erstwhile ally immediately after the Treaty of Breda ended the Second Anglo-Dutch War. The exclusion of Dutch traders from the Caribbean was reaffirmed. De Baas's instructions were clear on this point. Nevertheless, it became apparent in 1668 and 1669 that, despite the passage of French fleets, the Dutch still infested Caribbean waters. Du Lion and others informed Colbert about de Baas's permissiveness toward the Dutch; indeed, the governor-general took few pains to cover the "exceptions" he granted in "times of necessity." In 1670, when the Treaty of Dover solidified French-English relations, Colbert prepared for war with the Dutch. Gabaret's squadron sailed to the islands with instructions to sink any Dutch ships there. His instructions made him independent of de Baas, and when the governor-general demanded that Gabaret go to Saint-Domingue to put down the rebellion, the latter refused. Presumably, Gabaret believed that this was a ploy to get rid of him, because of the difficulty of returning to Martinique. Only a royal order persuaded Gabaret to assist d'Ogeron.[97]

Colbert meant to use war with the Dutch to destroy their control of the slave trade and to replace them as chief interlopers in the Spanish colonies. Just before the war, he encouraged de Baas to conduct a proxy war against the Dutch entrepôts at Saint Eustatius and Curaçao by assisting the Caribs of Saint Vincent, currently hostile to them. De Baas refused a formal Dutch plea for support against the "savages."[98] Such considerations explain Colbert's fixation on the colonization of Grenada, southernmost of the Lesser Antilles and strategically placed not only for an assault on Curaçao, but also as a stopover for French ships sailing to the Spanish Main. During 1670, Colbert reiterated his order to de Baas to confiscate or sink any foreign ships. Not even maritime emergencies constituted an excuse for Dutch landings in French ports. The governor-general was promised 10 percent of the value of confiscated cargos.[99]

In contrast, island officials were to pursue amicable relations with the English, despite lingering resentments from the previous war. And despite the prohibition of foreign commerce, Colbert gave carte blanche to de Baas to promote clandestine commerce with Spanish America. During the difficult 1670s, when sugar prices slumped because of overproduction, and when few French merchants brought goods to the islands, some habitants survived selling cattle and fowl to neighboring Spaniards.[100]

Perhaps Colbert believed that Louis's armies would triumph quickly in the Netherlands, and that the fruits of victory could then easily be plucked in the Caribbean. With the failure of the Compagnie des Indes occidentales by 1672, prosecution of the war rested with the navy. Yet naval rebuilding, impressive as it was,[101] had not reached a level both to protect France's coasts and support aggressive actions overseas. Thus in the early war years, small naval forces sent to the Caribbean played a purely defensive role, and instructions to colonial governors also promoted a cautious posture. Meanwhile, the English, under Lord William Willoughby, took Saint Eustatius and Tobago from the Dutch in 1672 and, ominously for France, also attempted to occupy Dominica. In 1673, de Baas organized a colonial force to attack Curaçao, which he thought was weakly defended, but he withdrew when he recognized the need for a siege with heavy cannon, which he did not possess. De Baas's prudent saving of his militia would pay off the following year.

More bad news accompanied this failure. D'Ogeron had intended to join de Baas with 400 men, but they were shipwrecked off Puerto Rico. Many survivors became prisoners of the Spanish, including d'Ogeron and his nephew Pouançay. After escaping, d'Ogeron returned with reinforcements to liberate the imprisoned, but ran into storms and then a Spanish ambush. Very few French made it out alive. One who did was the future governor Pouançay, who was being shipped to the mines of Peru and oblivion when an English privateer captured the Spanish transport carrying him.[102]

Louis XIV's isolation of the Dutch proved temporary. Spain, the Hollanders' ancient enemy, recognized that a French victory would make Madrid's control of the Spanish Netherlands untenable. Spain's Charles II formed a coalition in support of the Dutch Republic. Across the Channel, growing anger in Parliament about the Treaty of Dover augured ill for France. Worse, the planned victory march to Amsterdam had turned into a sluggish campaign of endless sieges.

In 1673, Dutch squadrons menaced the French islands, and in 1674, the great admiral de Ruyter threatened to end the French presence altogether. An ill de Baas had recently heard from Colbert assuring him the Dutch were too occupied with the king's armies to threaten the islands.[103] A large Dutch fleet of forty-six ships, 1,100 cannon, and some 4,000 soldiers among 7,500 men attacked French positions at Fort Royal, Martinique.[104] Only one decrepit ship and 161 men defended against the 1,000 Dutch troops put ashore.[105] Fortunately for the defenders, a Captain Aycard sank his richly laden forty-gun frigate to block entry of the Dutch fleet into the inner harbor, and the Dutch troops thus did not have the protection of the fleet's heavy cannon. (A grateful Louis XIV gave perpetual tax exemption to Aycard and his descendants.) The French used their superior position to pour fire into advancing Dutch columns, causing many casualties, especially among the officers. After the Dutch captured the wine stores, drunken soldiers without adequate officer control spelled defeat. In spite of the odds, therefore, the French under Governor Sainte-Marthe won an extraordinary victory. The venerable and much beloved Sieur Guillaume Dorange was among twenty French dead; the Dutch lost 143 dead and 318 wounded.[106] With de Ruyter's decision to withdraw rather than risk another debacle, the last serious Dutch threat to the French Caribbean colonies dissipated.

Along with the dramatic news of de Ruyter's rebuff, de Baas reported to Colbert that Caribs of Saint Vincent had killed some French traders there and were harassing Grenada settlers. De Baas begged for a few ships and 200 soldiers; the minister advised him to dissimulate his anger.[107] The situation was grave in Europe, with defeats near the Rhine. The English made peace with the Dutch in 1674 at the Treaty of Westminster and restored Tobago. The Dutch there soon made peace with the Caribs and supplied them with guns to attack exposed French habitants at Grenada. Colbert had to inform de Baas and the island governors that "the king's intention is to halt all naval expenses, and to allow only those which are indispensably necessary."[108]

Colbert's dreams were turning into nightmares, and worse was to come. He had previously brought the royal budget into rough balance, but the war shattered those efforts.[109] Now, the royal treasury had to pay the huge debts (over 3,000,000 l.t.) of the Compagnie des Indes occidentales in 1674; company assets became part of the royal domain in return for another 1,300,000 l.t., slightly more than the company had paid the former concessionaries in 1664–66.[110] Meanwhile, the minister of war, marquis de Louvois, was pressing hard for more money. Colbert's pain is evident in letters to island governors demanding that they collect the millions owed the company, albeit do so discretely so as not to alert habitants to its demise. One estimate is that they owed the company some 13,740,000 pounds of sugar.[111]

This desperate search for cash explains the granting of a "farm" on revenues from island produce to Jean Oudiette and the Domaine d'Occident in return for 350,000 l.t., 150,000 of which was to pay the company's debts. Oudiette collected the 3 percent duty on colonial produce formerly paid the company and also received all revenues that had previously gone to it.[112] Royal duties on muscavado were raised two l.t. the hundredweight, an increase that the king explained was made necessary by the "great expenses" needed to conserve the islands.[113] Island refined sugar continued to pay only the same duty, once again demonstrating Colbert's promotion of local refineries at that time.

Also the result of government penury was the establishment of the tobacco *ferme*, or monopoly. This was not Colbert's idea. Louis agreed to give the governess of his illegitimate children the monopoly of tobacco sales in France. Françoise d'Aubigné could now buy the property of Maintenon. In time, this American-born woman, known in her youth as "la Belle Indienne," would become the Sun King's second wife. Horrified at these machinations, Colbert persuaded the king to create a state tobacco monopoly, which would yield the state a good return. The auction proceeded, and a six-year monopoly brought in 3,400,000 l.t. In fact, the tobacco *ferme* failed and provided relatively little cash. In the Lesser Antilles, tobacco, which was already declining, received its coup de grâce. The difficulties were far more severe at Saint-Domingue.

In the Caribbean in 1675 and 1676, the few French warships suffered from teredos that bored into and ate their wooden hulls required careening facilities to scorch them off or replace the infested timbers, but these were unavailable. Naval officers quarreled constantly with de Baas over precedence and authority. Also, they seemed more interested in selling merchandise illicitly brought in royal ships, and in acquiring colonial commodities for the return voyage. Illnesses wracked the sailors, made worse by inadequate provisions, because officers were intent on transporting trade goods for profit. So few merchantmen reached the islands that provisions and munitions became scarce; so much so that de Baas openly allowed English commerce. The shortage of dried beef to feed slaves was a serious problem.[114]

Naval weakness made the French impotent in face of Jacob Binckes's 1676 Dutch incursion. Starting with Cayenne, where Lézy once again surrendered without a fight, Binckes also captured Marie-Galante and Saint-Martin.[115] He transported confiscated slaves, beasts of burden, and even a few willing French planters to strengthen Dutch Tobago. Binckes then sailed to Saint-Domingue to try to raise the settlers in revolt. Somewhat surprisingly, they did not bite, which attests to d'Ogeron's success. However, Binckes captured a huge amount of tobacco there.

These disasters finally galvanized Louis XIV into action. He and Colbert were aware of the danger that a solid Dutch colony at Tobago posed. Strategic vulnerability aside, Bincke's insult to Louis's *gloire* largely explains the vigorous response. Fortunately for the court, Jean, comte d'Estrées, a nephew of Henry IV's mistress Gabrielle d'Estrées, had been promoting a plan whereby he would arm a privateer fleet for the Caribbean in return for a percentage of the expected prizes. Approval came quickly now, and he sailed accompanied by a few royal vessels.

D'Estrées's career was fraught with controversy.[116] He switched from the army to the navy in 1668 after a spat with Minister of War de Louvois. Colbert was delighted to have a grandee of royal blood in the reviving navy, which explains his immediate rank of *chef d'escadre* (head of a squadron) and then vice admiral of the *Ponant* (the Atlantic). He has traditionally been viewed as a rank amateur and incompetent to boot, but his reputation has recently revived. Fortunately, his second in command was Gabaret, a captain with extensive experience in the American Tropics. Commanding another ship was Charles de Courbon, comte de Blénac, the future island governor-general.[117]

Sailing first to Cayenne, d'Estrées's fleet retook the fort in an attack led by the vice admiral himself.[118] Moving on to Martinique, where he learned of de Baas's death, d'Estrées enlisted more than 600 militia for an assault on Tobago. His fifteen ships faced fourteen Dutch vessels, making it the biggest naval battle yet in American history. The French attempted a frontal attack, which destroyed the Dutch squadron but also bloodied the French. D'Estrées lost the four biggest royal ships and some 800 killed or wounded.[119] The Dutch retained the island.

With the "victory" much ballyhooed in Paris, the king outfitted d'Estrées with an even more powerful fleet, including three ships larger than any in the previous expedition. Blénac, now carrying a commission as governor-general, once again commanded a ship. D'Estrées sailed to Gorée in Senegal, an important Dutch island slaving station (and now a UNESCO heritage site), and destroyed it. His victories significantly tilted the balance of force in Senegal toward the French. The Domaine d'Occident agent there, Jean du Casse, aggressively acted to remove Dutch trading influence and to subordinate local headmen. With these successes, the company launched a burst of commercial activity in 1678–79.[120]

D'Estrées proceeded to Tobago and, now better prepared with siege artillery, reduced the fort to ruins. In the land assault, led by Blénac, the Dutch fort suffered massive damage; Binckes and 266 men died, and another 600 became prisoners. From that time on, the Dutch never again presented a serious threat to the French islands. The fleet then sailed through the French islands recruiting volunteers for an assault on Dutch Curaçao. Fifteen buccaneer ships led by Pouançay joined the campaign. After all the frustrations of the previous fifteen years, the opportunity to remove the Dutch forever from the Caribbean and acquire their lucrative trade with the Spanish empire presented itself.

Alas, the aging Colbert's hatred of the Dutch was not to be satiated. Rejecting pleas not to set out without an experienced pilot, d'Estrées ordered the fleet to sail. Unlike many naval officers, he favored daring initiatives. Lured into a chase after three Dutch vessels, the fleet of thirty-five ships ran aground on the night of May 11, 1678, on the low-lying Las Aves islands, sixty miles away from the target. Intensive subsequent investigation demonstrated that the vice admiral and his captains were uncertain of their location.[121] Fourteen vessels, including seven precious ships of the line and up to 500 men went down, the greatest French naval disaster up to that time. The flagship, the *Terrible*, a seventy-gun first rater, sank to the bottom.[122] Up to 1,000 men died of starvation or disease before a relief expedition rescued 1,500 survivors three months later. The only winners were hundreds of buccaneers dispatched to protect the wrecks. Apparently, casks of brandy and wine were washed up on shore, making guard duty pleasant for these notorious imbibers.[123] Using slave divers, the relief expedition did raise a significant number of cannon.

Colbert never entirely recovered from this blow to Louis's prestige. Royal confidence in the navy sagged.[124] Three years later, after an investigation failed to blame his conduct, d'Estrées received promotion to marshal of France.[125] In 1687, he became viceroy of America, and his plan for an attack on Cartagena, in what is now Colombia, inspired his cousin the baron de Pointis to promote that project in the 1690s.[126]

Not long after the disaster, the exhausted parties signed the Treaty of Nijmegen. The Dutch ceded Gorée and Tobago and gave up claims to Cayenne, but retained Saint Eustatius, along with Curaçao. No military threat to the French, these Dutch entrepôts illicitly supplied French colonies with the slaves and materials that French merchants could not come up with. For the habitants, these were very satisfactory results. Colbert had to relinquish his beloved tariff of 1667. Louis's gains in Flanders and the conquest of Franche-Comté in what is now southeastern France only increased his focus on land wars. Only in 1680, after repeated badgering by Colbert, did the Sun King visit one of the new French naval arsenals, that of Dunkirk.

Although Louis XIV's standing in Europe had reached its zenith, the successes of French arms in tropical America were ambiguous. Largely abandoned to their own devices, French colonists had held their own on the military front, but the war had hindered demographic and economic development. True, the Sun King's challenge to Dutch power led to a surge of French commercial interest in the Caribbean in the 1680s. However, the disaster off Curaçao torpedoed the hope of a decisive French advantage. Nevertheless, Louis and Colbert had established the foundations of royal rule in the Caribbean.

CHAPTER EIGHT

The Sun King Asserts Control
The 1680s to the 1690s

Royal efforts to assume greater control of France's tropical American colonies led to two important developments in the later 1670s. First, the king reconstituted the sovereign councils to administer civil justice and to assist in colonial administration (1675). Henceforth, Paris insisted that the practice of handling some judicial matters according to military justice cease. Because councilors were usually wealthy planters and militia captains, changes were gradual. As governor-general, Jean-Charles de Baas continued the traditional ban on lawyers in the islands, which was not lifted until 1710. The custom of militia officers dispensing justice in the *quartiers* was also prohibited, although the practice by no means ceased overnight.

Second, the first royal intendant, Jean-Baptiste Patoulet, arrived in 1679. Among his many functions was heading the sovereign councils in all matters civil and political. While the governor-general still retained the highest place of honor should he attend the meetings, the king and Colbert attempted to control his interventions in affairs not in his purview. Given that the governor-general for most years down to 1696 was the headstrong comte de Blénac, there was a constant need for such surveillance. For example, the king strongly cautioned Blénac that he could arrest individuals on his authority only in cases of treason or some "grave emergency"; however, he must immediately explain the reasoning. Because Blénac took such an expansive view of his powers, he and successive intendants battled over each other's prerogatives.[1]

Colbert's intentions to provide colonists with the most favorable conditions melted away in the cauldron of war, as in the example of the state tobacco monopoly in France and the increase of duties on sugar exports. Unfortunately, with the return of peace in 1679, he did not push for the abolition of the tobacco monopoly, despite howls of colonial protest, especially from Saint-Domingue. His emerging rival Louvois made the most of these embarrassments then, and after Jean-Baptiste's death launched a purge of Colbertistes based on financial corruption relating in part to the tobacco monopoly. It was shown that Colbert's nephew and two other close associates had received gratuities of some 40,000 l.t. per annum from the monopoly.[2] The new minister of the Marine, Seignelay, Colbert's son, thus came into office in a weakened position, although he emerged personally unscathed from corruption accusations. An energetic man, and one with better technical knowledge of maritime affairs than his celebrated father, Seignelay surrounded himself with a talented cadre of marine administrators.[3]

Much official soul-searching after 1678 followed d'Estrées's disastrous thrust at Dutch Curaçao. Patoulet authored two extraordinary memoirs for Seignelay pinpointing the naval weaknesses made evident by d'Estrées's campaign. Naval expeditions to tropical waters consumed men and ships. Teredos, or shipworms, gorged on wooden hulls, while scurvy, dysentery, and malaria incapacitated sailors. Ships' officers starved crews to make space for goods they planned to barter once ashore. To address these problems, Patoulet advocated the construction of a major naval station at Fort Royal, Martinique, equipped with careening and repair facilities, a hospital for sick sailors, and stores to guarantee supplies for royal ships. Little came of his suggestions, because ancien régime France never established a base allowing ships to cruise for any substantial time in Caribbean waters. However, the perceptive Patoulet received a commission in 1679 as the first Caribbean intendant.[4]

In his first years, Blénac moved quickly to remedy weaknesses in military preparation. Finding island fortresses in a miserable state, he worked diligently to strengthen these. He mandated that habitants furnish Negroes to do the heavy work (*corvée*), and despite the grumbling continued the policy. Taxes on the islands' many taverns were channeled into the work. Despite some notable victories of the islands' militias in the last war, Blénac found their officers negligent in enforcing regular maneuvers, and that particular governors, royal lieutenants, and majors did not compel them. Blénac expressed concern to the minister that the new royal prohibition against governors and royal officers arresting habitants removed a major tool in enforcing compliance with militia duty. Perhaps because of his long tenure and commitment, he solved or mitigated many of these problems. At his death in 1696, he received praise for making Fort Royal impregnable.[5]

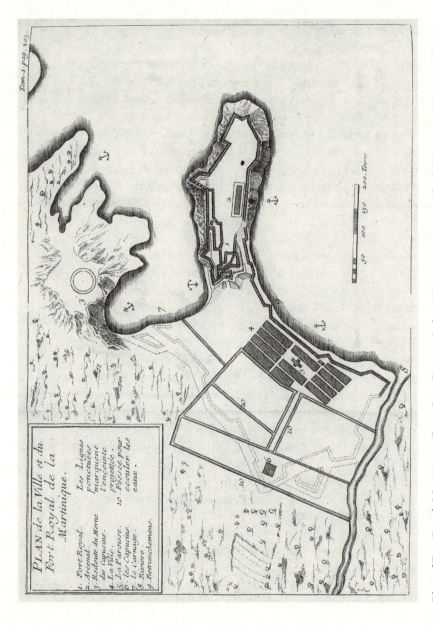

PLAN de la Ville et du
Fort Royal de la
Martinique.

1. Fort-Royal.
2. Arcenal.
3. Redoute du Morne
des Capucins.
4. La Ville.
5. La Paroisse.
6. les Capucins.
7. le Carnage.
8. Rivière.
9. Retranchemens.

Les Lignes
ponctuées
marquent
l'enceinte
projettée.
10 Fossés pour
écouler les
eaux.

50   100   150   200. Toises

Plan of Fort Royal, Martinique. From Jean-Baptiste Labat, *Nouveau voyage aux isles de l'Amérique* (Paris, 1722), 1:
opposite 204.

A Decade of Cold Peace, 1679 to 1689

Despite disappointments, Louis XIV emerged from the Dutch Wars in an enviable position. He was the most powerful European leader between Philip II and Napoleon, and he acted as the arbiter of Europe in these years. France's ancient Hapsburg enemies were down on their luck. The invalid Charles II (r. 1665–1702) feebly occupied the throne at Madrid; at Vienna, the stolid, steady Leopold I (r. 1657–1705) was preparing to face an Ottoman siege. Sweden depended on French gold, and Charles II of England was equally happy to receive silver *écus*. His Catholic brother, James, duke of York (later James II, r. 1685–88), was surviving challenges to his claims to the succession. In the Dutch Netherlands, William III of Orange remained hostile to Louis's designs, but his prospects were bleak in the 1680s. His marriage to James's Protestant daughter Mary (1677) seemed less promising in dynastic terms than it had at the honeymoon. Those French colonists who knew about Louis's brilliant standing must have felt some pride as his subjects.

Pride goeth before the fall—"L'orgueil précède les chutes"—was no doubt a maxim familiar to Louis. But humility, never a virtue of the Sun King, was a stranger to him in these heady years. Not about to rest in such a favorable situation and devote himself full-time to the pleasures of his new palace at Versailles, and of his new wife Mme. de Maintenon (1683), Louis aggressively sought to expand his territory, power, and prestige. His bold seizure of the strategic city of Strasbourg on the Rhine sent shock waves throughout Europe. It was the seventeenth-century equivalent of Hitler's brazen occupation of Czechoslovakia in 1938–39, a gambit that erased all doubts about its perpetrator's intentions. Louis's encroachments in northern Italy, his deafening silence to appeals for help against the Turks besieging Vienna (1683), his extensive building of frontier fortresses, and much else threatened Europe.

The Sun King's growing repression of the Huguenots from the 1670s on led to the Revocation of the Edict of Nantes (1685). This measure, and the accelerating religious oppression used to implement it, promoted justifiable anxieties, even paranoia, among European Protestants, without mollifying the Hapsburgs or the pope. So this period of "peace" generated diplomatic tensions that led to another series of wars; unfortunately, these conflicts would demonstrate that Louis's greed for *gloire* exceeded France's ability to gratify it.

The king's designs in Europe had their counterpart in the Americas. True, a remarkable quiet prevailed in the eastern Caribbean, in part because of Dutch passivity and good relations between Versailles and the Palace of Whitehall (the English equivalent). Blénac and the English Leewards' Governor Colonel William Stapleton had discussed the terms of a projected treaty of neutrality as early as 1678; the size of the fleet with which d'Estrées had sailed for Curaçao had impressed the English. By the early 1680s, neither side was encouraging Island Caribs to torment the other. When James II mounted the throne in 1685, negotiations started that resulted in the Treaty of Neutrality for the Americas (1686), which promised an end to brigandage, the return of runaway slaves, and peace in America even if war broke out in Europe. Only minor irritants disturbed this peace over the next few years.[6]

Settled conditions in the Lesser Antilles focused attention on the supposedly ramshackle Spanish American empire. Spain's King Charles II was physically and mentally incapacitated, the imperial administration was corrupt, and Hispanic Creole settlers were notorious for their habit of least resistance. As early as 1675, a confidant of Colbert's advised him that 10,000 men sent to Saint-Domingue would permit French conquest of Spanish America. French archives abound with memoirs of the 1680s about the best means to appropriate the wealth of Spanish America, and a spate of translations into French of Spanish accounts of it also attests to this zeal.[7]

Louis and Colbert attempted to encourage contraband trade with a Spanish America flush with silver and thirsty for all kind of goods. In 1680, they awarded the marquis de Maintenon the exclusive privilege of trading with Spanish America, or the authority to provide others with passports for such trade, at a price naturally.[8] Complementary was a policy restricting buccaneering out of Saint-Domingue.

Given the dramatic decline of tobacco production at Saint-Domingue and the decimation of feral cattle and pigs, a surplus of fighting toughs prowled the waters of the Spanish Caribbean ever more incessantly. The 1678–79 Nijmegen peace treaties did little to change the tradition of no peace beyond the line. The catastrophic naval destruction off Curaçao meant that Louis could not or would not dispatch enough royal ships to rein in the buccaneers. Despite Colbert's orders to turn these freebooters into colonists, Pouançay continued to issue letters of marque and even returned to Paris to argue unsuccessfully against terminating those letters. The traditional freebooter base at Tortuga increasingly gave way to various ports along the coasts of Saint-Domingue.

The years after 1678 were the "golden age" of the French buccaneers. Led by such notorious figures as Michel de Grammont and Laurent de Graffe, they raided sites such as Trinidad, Margarita, and ports
along the Spanish Main.[9] Because of Dutch and English crackdowns on
freebooters in the 1680s, those ruffians gravitated to Saint-Domingue
ports, such as Petit-Goâve in the western part of the island. Graffe—who
may have been three-quarters African by descent—had an extraordinarily interesting career, although he is not as well known as Grammont,
Henry Morgan, or William Kidd. According to one of many versions of
his early life, the Spanish captured him in the Netherlands and transported him to the Canaries. Sent to the West Indies with a Spanish fleet
designed to exterminate pirates, Graffe escaped and joined the intended
victims. He soon rose to the rank of freebooter captain and as such participated in d'Estrées's disastrous encounter with the Aves Islands. In
1683, Graffe's successes drew about 1,000 freebooters to his base at Petit-Goâve for an attack, legitimized by Pouançay's letters of marque, on
the crucial Mexican port of Vera Cruz, which they succeeded in taking.
Graffe reputedly possessed a humane and refined temperament, highly
unusual among buccaneer leaders. He reportedly refused to sanction the
usual barbaric torture of prisoners to gain knowledge of the town's hidden treasures. Along with a modest haul of gold and gems, the raiders
carried away about 1,500 slaves from Vera Cruz to compensate them for
their efforts.[10]

The buccaneers' bellicose urges, however, conflicted with France's
policy of trying to control the Hispanic empire by dominating its trade.
The sacking of Vera Cruz had been one of the causes of a brief Spanish-
French conflict starting at the end of 1683. At the negotiations leading
to the Truce of Ratisbon in 1684, Louis XIV agreed to crack down on
the buccaneers. Seignelay wrote to Blénac in 1684 ordering him to rein
in the freebooters because they damaged the flourishing illegal trade
with the Spanish possessions.[11] The new governor, Cussy, was not, however, able to prevent a large force under Graffe from raiding Campeche
along the Central American coast, a center of the logwood trade that attracted mainly English ships.

Crown policy made Cussy's rule very difficult. Pursuant to royal instructions, and despite his strong protests, he outlawed freebooting and
threatened anyone who disobeyed with corporal punishment and loss of
goods. He prohibited the departure of any boat manned by more than
eight men. To settle the buccaneers after the sack of Campeche, Cussy

gave commissions as royal officials to Grammont and Graffe.[12] The latter first served as major at the Ile de vaches (island of cows), and in 1690 as king's lieutenant at the Cap, where he married a rich heiress.[13] Two years later, the king ordered Cussy to hunt down those freebooters who refused to accept letters of amnesty and settle down. With the resumption of war in 1689, Cussy complained that his successes in this endeavor had deprived the colony of important military support. In fact, in a decade, the number of militiamen at Saint-Domingue declined by a third, from about 3,000 to 2,000.[14]

The conclusion of the Dutch War allowed Colbert and Seignelay to continue to strengthen the navy and to implement reforms in the islands. By 1685, the navy boasted 150 ships with more than fifty cannon and was bigger than the English fleet.[15] Although the cherished 1667 tariff against the Dutch had been abandoned, the war itself had seriously diminished their presence in the French Caribbean, except perhaps at Saint-Domingue, with its long, irregular coastline. Over 200 French merchantmen serviced the French islands by the time of Colbert's death in 1683.[16]

The chief complaint of the Caribbean colonists remained the shortage of slaves, but the capture of Gorée had strengthened the French presence in West Africa, and in 1679, Colbert reorganized the Compagnie du Sénégal, granting it extensive monopoly privileges and extending its geographical scope to all of the region.[17] Moreover, the French crown corporation known as the Domaine d'Occident paid the Senegal company a subsidy of thirteen l.t. per slave landed in the Americas.

At first, the new Senegal company showed remarkable energy, probably encouraged by the much-strengthened position of the French from Cape Blanco to the Senegal River and beyond to Gorée. The energetic company agent Jean du Casse prevented the Dutch from reoccupying Arguin, north of Saint Louis, and he harassed Dutch trade throughout the area the company claimed, forcing local headmen to sign treaties acknowledging French suzerainty.[18]

Meanwhile, the company had assembled a fleet of twenty-one ships to trade for slaves and a variety of other products, such as gold dust, gum, wax, ambergris, and ivory. Four ships traded successfully with Spain, and five were involved in trade with Senegal. However, the company was effectively bankrupt by 1680. Two ships transporting sugar and tobacco to France from the islands sank, as did two ships en route from Senegal to France. Eight of company ships carried some 2,000 of the Africans to the

Caribbean, but half or more seem to have died during the Middle Passage. Of the slaves delivered to the king's galleys at Marseille by four of the ships, half or more were found unfit for use. Of seventy-three slaves intended for the Marseille galleys, sixty-seven were somewhat illogically landed in Normandy, and eleven died or became unfit for service en route overland.[19]

Ambitious though it was, the new Compagnie du Sénégal was thus no more successful than its predecessors, the 1673 Senegal company and the slave trade concession of the farmer-general Oudiette of 1675. In its short two-year history, the company provided between 600 and 1,000 slaves to the islands and ended with a debt of more than 1,000,000 l.t.[20] Island planters owed about 175,000 l.t. for slaves purchased on credit, but these funds and any insurance money took a long time coming. Despite royal assistance in proceeding against its debtors, the company had to declare bankruptcy in 1681.[21]

Immediately, a new group of associates, almost all high officials and financiers except for du Casse, formed a new Senegal and Africa company. Meanwhile, contraband slaves, primarily conveyed by the Dutch but also obtained through the auspices of the English, the Danes, and the Caribs, remained an important alternative to the deficient French slave trade. Buccaneer operations provided others. For example, a raid on Jamaica in the early 1690s netted 1,900 slaves.[22] The new company soon discovered it had overestimated the value of the older company and found it difficult to cover the debts it had incurred. Thus, between 1681 and 1684, its trading and slaving enterprises were very modest. Though it supplied few slaves to the Caribbean colonies, company agents there attempted to enforce its monopoly, which unsurprisingly irritated islanders. Island administrators estimated the needs of the islands at 2,000 slaves annually, whereas the company provided only a few hundred in good years.[23]

Colbert and Seignelay continued to tinker with colonial administrative forms and practices. Most important, they inaugurated the office of intendant, and in 1679, the capable Patoulet assumed the post. Given his experiences with the headstrong de Baas (1667–76) and his successor Blénac (1677–90 and 1692–96), Colbert's resort to the metropolitan means of restraining provincial governors does not surprise one. The intendant presided over the islands' sovereign councils and had responsibility for finances and civil and judicial affairs.[24] Although second to the governor-general, in his areas of responsibility, he answered only to the minister. Both men wrote individual reports to Versailles, as well as joint memoranda.

Although the court could thus obtain different perspectives on island affairs, this system in effect promoted disharmony. In the distant and exposed Caribbean colonies, the governor-generals wielded more power than provincial governors in a relatively secure France, because the latter were within the royal army's corrective reach. Island governors were military officers of noble origins. Often contemptuous of the social and professional background of intendants, island governor-generals frequently were intolerant of the paper pushers. The king had to remind councils more than once that they functioned under the intendant's authority. Blénac and Patoulet (1679–82) initiated this tradition of unfriendly relations, and only a minority of such teams acted with anything more than cold civility. When Gabriel Du Maitz de Goimpy, Patoulet's successor became a leader of islanders disgruntled with the rule of the hot-tempered Blénac in 1684–85, the two stopped speaking. The king, having pled with his administrators to get along, eventually recalled the intendant.[25]

Other sources of internal turmoil were conflicts between planter-dominated sovereign councils and the local and French merchants who supplied imports and shipped planter produce to Europe. Merchants constantly complained about the quality of the produce and planters complained about the high price of imports and the low prices offered for sugar, cotton, tobacco, and other products. Both sides squabbled over the value of the Spanish coins in circulation at Saint-Domingue.[26] In one case, Blénac sided with the merchants and even suspended the operations of the Martinique sovereign council until the king adjudicated the dispute. The king reprimanded the governor-general for undermining the council's authority.[27] Councils, representative of the richer habitants, attempted to regulate prices for basic goods—wine, spirits, bread, and biscuit—and to ensure reasonable quality.[28]

Patoulet's voluminous reports on island conditions stimulated a flurry of measures to address perceived problems. Many administrative actions responded to islanders' complaints, showing that Colbert's philosophy of making life there attractive was pursued until his demise. He counseled Blénac that his most important goal was the "augmentation of the population," which would result from even dispensing of justice and good treatment of all. When Blénac complained about the pretensions of the Martinique council, the minister advised him to practice restraint, because "it is good that the principal inhabitants believe themselves to be held in honor."[29] Colbert's reputation for coldness, based on anecdotes perpetuated by privileged and pampered nobles, does not harmonize easily with the sentiments he expressed vis-à-vis the colonists and the Island Caribs.

A few examples of Colbert's policy of *douceur* (using only gentle means) will suffice.[30] In 1679, an edict reaffirmed the island custom that slaves, sugar works (i.e., copper utensils, earthenware jars, the mills even), and beasts of burden could not be seized to satisfy debts.[31] Another order prohibited governors from arbitrarily arresting habitants. Colonial officials imitating old-fashioned feudal lords were thus not to be tolerated, Other measures reflected the state's impulse to control irregular behavior so that, in the terminology of the day, society would be *bien policé* or well policed, but with the meaning of promoting the social good and not just defending against criminals. The king subsidized a few convoys of marriageable, impoverished young women of good morals to stabilize the primarily male colonists. Unfortunately for the islands' reputation, critics assumed that these *filles du roi* (king's girls) were *filles de joie* (prostitutes).[32]

Government pursued its self-perceived duty to force individuals to recognize that their private desires often had to give way to the public good. Thus, in 1682, strong measures (on paper) forced islanders to perform their mandatory militia exercises. The next year an annual tax of 3,000 lbs. of sugar was imposed on taverns to limit their numbers and thus opportunities for debauchery and indolence. To put this in perspective, the price of a slave averaged between 5,000 and 6,000 pounds of sugar.[33]

The king's drive for religious unity at home had significant consequences in the islands. Although not numerous anywhere else in the islands, Jews of French and foreign background played a significant role as factors at Saint-Pierre, Martinique. Jews were to be found on Martinique from the 1630s on, and they had received remarkably humane treatment during the proprietorship of du Parquet and the tenure of the Compagnie des Indes occidentales, which even allowed some Jews to buy habitations, something not possible in France itself. Jacob Luis, for example, owned a sugar works, as well as two other habitations. In 1664, Tracy issued regulations preventing Protestants from holding public services and forcing them to bring their servants and slaves to Catholic services. However, when de Baas, subjected to clerics' badgering, tried to restrict Jews from honoring their Sabbath, the king told him to leave them in peace unless their actions scandalized Catholics. However, in the early 1680s, Jesuit critics of tolerance for Jews found a strong ally in the devout Blénac. The Jesuits' vitriolic denunciations of supposed Jewish dominance of local commerce and of Jewish slaveholders accused of refusing Christianity to their bondsmen led to a royal order expelling them in 1683. Jews were given one month to leave.[34]

Louis XIV's Revocation of the Edict of Nantes in 1685 had an impact in the islands. Previously, zealous priests could not overcome Colbert's worry about needlessly losing valuable subjects. But with the minister declining rapidly, and with a governor-general hostile to religious tolerance in any form, island Huguenots were in for a difficult time. By 1683, Huguenots could no longer purchase land. In 1685, increasingly repressive measures prevented their marriages and the right of their children to inherit (article 8 of the *Code noir*). Although forcible conversion of some Huguenots in France did not have an immediate impact in the islands, oppression increased after 1687. Huguenots willing to convert received a one-year exemption from capitation taxes.[35]

This attitude of state paternalism explains the content and tone of the 1685 *Code noir*, which regulated master-slave relationships. The Custom of Paris, the law code used in the islands, contained no provisions on master-slave issues. For that reason and because he usually sought guidance from local officials, Colbert designated Blénac and Patoulet to lead an examination of the question. The local sovereign councils and prominent habitants were consulted, as well as island laws and customs. The finished code, to be examined in more detail later, thus reflected planters' concerns; in some cases not covered by island customs, resort to Roman law probably occurred. Some articles demonstrate a close correspondence to Roman law precedents, especially concerning slave emancipation.[36] Vernon Palmer estimates that 90–95 percent of the articles recommended by island officials appeared in substance or even verbatim in the final code. All in all, the compendium of 1685 appears to be more the codification of existing island laws and customs than a product of Roman law precedent.[37]

Intendant Michel Bégon cautioned in 1683 that nowhere else in the world were ordinances "so quickly forgotten" as in the islands.[38] This observation certainly applied to the selective enforcement of the *Code noir*. Although it strongly reflected planter interests, the code also reflected the official view of the planters' obligation to ensure that their slave property was protected and well maintained, contrary to some masters' shortsighted urge to extract as much labor from slaves as possible. After the code had been promulgated in the islands, the king was willing to listen to his subjects' "humble remonstrances" in making changes. For example, the outright prohibition of slave markets on Sunday and feast days, islanders' argued, would mean decreased attendance at Mass and thus increase the slaves' tendency to "libertinism." Article 9 imposing fines on freemen impregnating slave women and depriving masters of slave concubines and the resulting mulatto children was, it was argued, impractical and violated the principle that a slave could not testify against the master. Later changes in the law indicate that the monarchy came to accept these objections. In any case, these penalties did not apply if the free man wed the woman in proper Catholic form.[39]

Other measures of the code were not enforced or were unenforceable, among them the prohibition of slaves "owning" property and the requirements concerning the amounts of food and cloth to be given to them. According to island opinion, unless slaves could accumulate property and pass it on to their children, they would all run away. In the eighteenth century, the Bourbons frequently recognized the legitimacy of such arguments and did not seek to enforce the letter of the law in these respects.

The best antidote to assumptions that royal rule meant rigorous obedience in the colonies is a reading of Médéric Moreau de Saint-Méry's compilation of royal ordinances and edicts. Repeated efforts to force habitants to cultivate their claimed lands, repeated prohibitions of the king's officers engaging in trade, repeated demands that no one be allowed to leave the islands without permission, and repeated prohibitions of unauthorized vessels trading in the islands are just a few examples of the difficulty of implementing laws imposed on people far away.[40]

Beyond policies designed to improve island conditions, whether or not the habitants concurred, some measures wholly favored metropolitan interests at colonial expense. The refusal to abolish the state tobacco monopoly in France after the return of peace in 1679, despite the previous contention that wartime emergencies had necessitated it, severely damaged Saint-Domingue, where tobacco was almost the sole crop.[41] Restriction of tobacco production in France and the right to freely re-export leaf not purchased by the monopoly were the supposed quid pro quos.[42] The previously discussed triumph of metropolitan sugar refiners is another example of state preferences.

Despite a variety of impediments—metropolitan restrictions, uncertainties about slave supplies, expulsions and harassment of Jews and Huguenots, and stagnant prices for sugar—the French Windward Islands slowly moved toward "maturity" as plantation societies. Consolidation of larger estates manned by dozens of slaves became more typical, and previously unexploited windward parts of these islands (e.g., Grande-Terre, Guadeloupe) started to come under cultivation. Correspondingly, some small planters departed these islands, especially vulnerable Saint-Christophe, primarily for the "virgin" lands of Saint-Domingue. On Saint-Christophe, however, the number of whites actually increased during the 1680s, rising from 2,885 in 1682 to 3,381 in 1689. The precipitous decline of the 1690s was due to war.[43] Some reasonably reliable statistics reinforce the idea that, unlike on English Barbados, the conquest of sugar was gradual in the French islands. At Martinique between 1660 and 1688, the European population doubled, increasing from perhaps 2,489 to 5,060, while the number of slaves increased from 2,642 to 11,476. But in 1680, only about one-eighth of the habitants owned more than ten slaves. Only about 3 percent possessed more than forty slaves, although these planters owned over half of all slaves.[44] At Guadeloupe in 1687, there were 3,546 Europeans and 4,982 slaves. At Saint-Christophe, 4,470 slaves worked for 3,152 whites.[45] Still, with barely two slaves for every free person on the most advanced island, Martinique, French colonial society was far removed from the classic plantation complex of the middle eighteenth century.

In 1685, Seignelay divided the monopoly concession of West African trade. The Senegal company lost its monopoly south of the Gambia River, not only because of its failure to supply enough slaves but because of its inability to procure significant gold along the Gold Coast.[46] In its defense, the company claimed to have supplied 4,561 slaves to the Antilles, only 500 below its obligation of 2,000 per annum.[47] However, during those same years, the English Royal African Company delivered more than 15,000 slaves to Barbados and Jamaica. The new Compagnie de Guinée was granted a monopoly from south of the Sierra Leone River to the Cape of Good Hope, but it was more interested in selling slaves to colonial Spaniards, who could pay hard cash, than to French Caribbean planters, who had to resort to buying smuggled slaves. Moreover, the Dutch devastated the company's posts on the Gold Coast, preventing it from reaching its quotas.[48] And how many of the already heavily indebted habitants could afford the company's extravagant price of

5,000–9,000 pounds of sugar per slave, depending on age and gender? In neighboring English islands, the price was about 3,000 pounds of sugar. By 1692, Minister Louis Phélypeaux, comte de Pontchartrain, became so exasperated that he authorized du Casse at Saint-Domingue to acquire slaves however he could get them.[49]

Although Martinique, Saint-Christophe, and Guadeloupe were far from reaching "maturity" as monoculture slave societies, Grenada, Sainte-Lucie, Saint-Martin, and Saint-Barthélemy in the Lesser Antilles and Saint-Domingue were more "backward" by far. The smaller Lesser Antillean islands housed settlers scratching out a living by supplying provisions to the larger islands, by the truck trade (*cabotage*) among the islands or with the Caribs, and by smuggling with Dutch, English, or Danish partners. After a visit to Danish Saint Thomas in the 1690s, the Dominican Father Jean-Baptiste Labat pegged it as a cover for Dutch contraband.[50]

Guiane had great difficulty recovering from the trials of war. Some of the few colonists there (according to one source, 116 in 1677) survived by extracting raw materials and by trading with declining numbers of aborigines. Jean Hurault estimates that of some 20,000 to 30,000 in 1600, only some 4,000 to 5,000 indigenes remained in 1730.[51] Guiane sugar planters in 1682 were granted exemptions from duties on sugar imported into France in order to rebuild, and some growth occurred.[52]

By 1687, Cayenne had 321 whites and 1,700 slaves, evidence of some large sugar plantations at Cayenne. The new and able governor, the marquis de Ferolles (1679–1705), worked hard to attract Huguenots and Jews, who, along with other planters grew cotton, indigo, and sugar. However, a relative scarcity of slaves and Cayenne's unattractiveness to European merchants, who could not be sure to make a cargo there, hampered it. Four years later, a ray of hope appeared when a number of freebooters with some fortune settled at Cayenne. However, in 1688, the future governor of Saint-Domingue, Jean du Casse persuaded these adventurers to join his expedition to conquer Dutch Suriname. Du Casse also took the Guiane militia with him. Many were lost in the debacle that ensued, and du Casse brought the remainder to Martinique rather than returning them to Cayenne, as he had promised. Only 200 militiamen survived this debacle.[53]

After the Peace of Nijmegen (1678), Louis XIV put pressure on the Portuguese court to recognize French claims to the northern shore of the Amazon and the coast northeast to the Orinoco. Meanwhile, Portuguese slavers in Brazil attacked indigenes in Guiane, many of whom fled to the protection of the French at Cayenne. In 1704, Ferolles prodded habitants to enslave Aroua Indian refugees in proximity to Cayenne. Jesuit missionaries condemned these slave raids, refused to allow Mme. Ferolles to perform her Easter duties, and complained vociferously to the king. Louis dispatched a delegation of investigation led by Rémy d'Orvilliers. In the meantime Ferolles died, and d'Orvilliers replaced him. The latter ordered the release of the Aroua with compensation "insofar practicable." Guyane remained a marginal colony. Surveying the situation there in the 1680s, Bégon concluded that only *forçats* (convicts) could solve the problem of insufficient colonists, auguring a dubious future.[54]

The 1680s were not a propitious time for the French settlements at Tortuga and Saint-Domingue. Neither Pouançay (died 1683) nor his successor Cussy (1684–91) could persuade Versailles to abolish the tobacco monopoly in France, on which the habitants blamed all their woes. A current estimate is that tobacco production plummeted 40–50 percent in the decade after 1674. Some settlers abandoned their homesteads for Jamaica, while others resumed careers as pirates. But, now with peace (except in 1683–84), Paris expressed strong displeasure. In 1688, Seignelay chastised Cussy for interfering with French merchants trading with neighboring Spaniards. Versailles hoped to penetrate the Spanish empire by peaceful if illegal trade.[55] While tobacco growers complained about fat cat "tax farmers," the latter bitterly reported to Seignelay about the myriad frauds perpetrated by unscrupulous habitants. Almost all tobacco arrived in rolls of some fifty pounds, which too often camouflaged the rolling of the leaves on eight- to ten-pound wooden rods instead of the legal three- to four-pound ones. Rolls allowed the cheaters—and most were, out of hatred for the monopolists—to hide inferior leaf, the result of second and third harvesting from the same plant, a practice outlawed in Virginia since the 1630s.[56] During the curing process, only one sprinkling of salt water was permitted, but soaked leaf is obviously heavier, and one can imagine that producers away from the coast did not bother with salt water. In the long run, of course, damaged goods meant an increasingly negative reputation for Saint-Domingue's leaf (cigar lovers may appreciate the irony, given the fine ones produced in the Dominican Republic today).

During the turbulent 1690s, the bigger planters, a small minority, switched to indigo, which required more land and more slave labor.[57] In

1687, Saint-Domingue had about 3,810 Europeans and 3,358 slaves.[58] In 1697, despite du Casse's pleas that habitants needed to produce tobacco in quantity and for good prices, Pontchartrain and Louis, desperate for cash, reaffirmed the tobacco farm. Du Casse predicted what in fact occurred: the wealthier habitants survived and prospered in indigo and especially sugar production, whereas the poorer colonists had little recourse except wage labor or piracy.[59]

By the latter 1680s, the political and military structure of the French Caribbean had matured. After 1685, sovereign councils on the chief islands served as the supreme judicial bodies and enforcers of the royal laws and orders. Royal judges and attorneys handled ordinary judicial matters. The intendant oversaw all judicial and political affairs, was in charge of finance and infrastructure projects, and directed the sovereign councils. The governor-general was the overall military commander; the king's lieutenant on Martinique commanded the royal troops, and governors on each island commanded the militias. Aside from these, who were paid from the treasury, other officials received compensation in pounds of sugar or exemption from the capitation tax. For example, sovereign council members received either 1,200 pounds of sugar or exemption from the capitation tax for twelve slaves, which was worth the same amount.[60]

The Tribulations of the Nine Years' War, 1689–1697

In 1688 and 1689, France found itself at war with two great sea powers, England and the Dutch Republic, as well as the armies of the Austrian and Spanish Hapsburgs. The Nine Years' War lasted until 1697. (Historians who look beyond the European campaigns prefer "Nine Years' War" to the name "War of the League of Augsburg"; "King William's War" is also used in connection with colonial North America.) Although the colonial status quo ante prevailed at the Treaty of Ryswick, which ended the war in 1697, its terrible fiscal costs, in combination with economic difficulties and massive harvest failures, left France exhausted. Important naval defeats in the early 1690s signaled the demise of Colbert's offensive blue water naval policy, and France's Caribbean colonies were left without significant support. In any case, the royal navy had not overcome infrastructure and logistics problems that would allow lengthy Caribbean cruises. Lack of facilities to undertake repairs and local shortages of foodstuffs were the two most serious problems.[61]

The comte de Pontchartrain *pére* replaced Seignelay as secretary of state of the Marine. Long kept from the highest levels of power because of his family's connections to Fouquet, Pontchartrain had no special expertise in maritime matters. From 1693 on, his son Jérome started work in his father's office, inheriting the position in 1699.[62]

War against a Dutch and English alliance proved disastrous for France's African monopoly companies. In 1689, they transported only about 800 slaves, not enough to replace those who had died, according to the administrators. Later years saw even less activity. In early 1693, an English Royal African Company expedition from James Island in the Gambia easily captured France's principal Senegal entrepôts, Gorée and Saint-Louis. The English took all the cannon and provisions before destroying the fortresses. Even though a subsequent French expedition recaptured these places, the company's losses led to another bankruptcy and sale of assets between 1694 and 1696.[63]

At war's outbreak in America in 1689, a privately financed expedition led by Jean du Casse failed to capture Suriname, where seven Dutch ships supplemented the town's cannon. Dutch settlers at Berbiche in Guiane paid him a paltry ransom in exchange for peace, after they and their slaves had put up stiff resistance. At Saint-Domingue, a freebooter fleet under Graffe's command terrorized the north coast of Jamaica for six months. In the Lesser Antilles, Blénac coordinated militia and buccaneers from Saint-Domingue in successful attacks on English Saint Christopher and captured Dutch Saint Eustatius. Irish uprisings against English masters on Saint Christopher assisted the French triumph. Given that Grenada, Tobago, and Saint-Croix were still then French, 1690 marked the high point of France in tropical America. Blénac neglected the opportunity to conquer the weakly defended English Leeward Islands, however, and his hurry to convey his English booty to Martinique contributed to French vulnerability at Saint-Christophe. All too soon, led by their aggressive governor Christopher Codrington, the English counterattacked in 1690–91 at Saint-Christophe, Marie-Galante, Saint-Barthélemy, and Guadeloupe, heavily damaging French plantations and carrying off crucial slave labor. The victors dispossessed and transported some 1,800 habitants to Hispaniola, only a privileged few of whom allowed to relocate to Martinique. Only the lack of naval support for Codrington saved Guadeloupe, where the militia companies, meant to consist of 100 men each, may have been under strength (Labat mentions one of 80 men, "including a few mulattoes and free Negroes," and another had only 38 men, including some armed Negroes). The English naval commander forced a withdrawal from Guadeloupe, however, much to Codrington's disgust.[64]

Bitter conflicts between Blénac and the veteran intendant-general Du Maitz de Goimpy (1684–1696) led to the governor-general's demand to be replaced; others between the intendant and Captain du Casse led the latter to withdraw his men, which hurt the defense of Saint-Christophe. The English victors there ruined sugar works and led off slaves and beasts of burden, and French habitants fled to other islands. Labat blamed the loss of Saint-Christophe on the decline of the small habitants' tobacco farms. The militia there, according to him, declined from 10,000 to 2,000 by the 1690s, although these numbers are dubious.[65] For the rest of the war, the French abandoned defense of small islands such as Saint-Croix, Saint-Barthélemy, Marie-Galante, and Saint-Martin, which were too easily overrun; in fact, in 1695, the French transported all the habitants and slaves from Saint-Croix—which had flourished because it sent all its sugar to Danish Saint Thomas, according to Labat—to northern Saint-Domingue, which had suffered greatly from enemy attacks. The displaced habitants could not even bring their furniture or animals with them.[66]

In 1691, Pontchartrain sent a fleet to counter English naval forces. However, a major outbreak of yellow fever weakened the expedition and killed the new governor-general, the marquis d'Eragny.[67] Yellow fever also harmed the English fleet in 1692. The next year, a large English force under Sir Joseph Wheler and Codrington attacked Saint-Pierre, Martinique. The rough terrain, the toll imposed by armed Negro skirmishers, the impact of disease in the English ranks, and the valor of its militia saved Martinique in 1693.[68] In one of many small running engagements, two domestics of the sieur Rose led fifty-two armed slaves in an assault on an English party.[69] Still, despite this success, prospects looked particularly bleak in that *annus horribilis*, one that also saw devastating famine in France.

Wheler's defeat signaled important changes in the conduct of the war. The English attempted no further invasions of the French Windward Islands. On the French side, the minister learned the apparent lesson that, if well supplied with munitions, the colonists could defend themselves without substantial and incredibly expensive naval support and more marines. (The *troupes de la marine* were worthless for anything other than guard duty, Labat thought; he noted that their officers nonetheless despised the more effective colonial militias.)[70] Continuous work on fortifications at such key sites as Saint-Pierre and Fort Royal made Martinique, at least, nearly impregnable.[71] The costs in mounting a lengthy siege of such places made this impracticable, at least in the context of late seventeenth-century warfare. Furthermore, local privateers from Martinique wreaked havoc on enemy shipping. At war's end, the British Admiralty estimated the loss of naval and merchant ships at 4,000.[72] On the other hand, British attacks severely curtailed imports from France, raising prices for basic commodities to extraordinarily high levels.

Blénac—who should by rights be as well known as New France's Louis de Frontenac—returned to the Antilles as governor-general in 1692 and held that post until his death from dysentery in 1696. He was a harsh taskmaster and invariably made enemies of lesser officials. Although Blénac evidently treated him with respect, Labat calls his behavior "bizarre" at times and somewhat grudgingly judges him to have been a very brave and loyal royal servant, and wiser than most people acknowledged.[73]

True to form, the king attempted to pay war costs by granting monopolies in return for up-front payments. In 1692, he granted a monopoly on the sale of coffee, tea, sorbet, and chocolate, which had become "so common in our realm." The king, however, set maximum prices on these, no doubt with little effect. Louis ordered that island marines be required to work for their subsistence. Captains who did not prevent desertions and keep their companies up to par lost three l.t. per soldier per month. In 1696, Louis ordered that Saint-Domingue indigo planters pay two *sols* the pound exported to sustain island defenses. He rationalized that planters could afford this sacrifice because they did not pay the capitation tax. Perhaps aware of Saint-Domingue's reputation, the king mandated a huge fine of 1,500 l.t. for the *first* offense. It is true that the number of slaves at Saint-Domingue grew by 40 percent during the 1680s, from 2,100 to 3,358, explained in large part by the 1683 sacking of Vera Cruz, with some 1,200 slaves as part of the booty.[74]

After 1694, attention turned to the western Caribbean. The early war years at Saint-Domingue had been disastrous. Because of the decline of tobacco production, many habitants had taken to the sea as freebooters. In 1690, Father Plumier complained that "poor habitants" were abandoning farms and going off to "our enemies."[75] The effective militia declined from around 3,000 to 2,000. Severe freebooter losses, including the demise of Grammont and Graffe's shipwreck, left the French colony exposed, and the king now granted an amnesty to freebooters who had left Saint-Domingue because of the royal refusal to allow them pirating "passports."[76]

Further weakened by buccaneer losses in the failed raid on Suriname, Cussy could not repulse a strong Spanish force at the battle of Limonade, east of Le Cap in the northern sector, in 1691. The more numerous and better-armed Spanish militia routed a French militia that was notoriously undisciplined and not experienced in large-scale combat. Cussy, thirty officers, and 400–500 French were killed, leaving the unfortified Cap open to a brutal sacking. The Spanish did not recognize the right of French settlement, so they massacred captured men—Labat says they simply dispatched wounded French militiamen—and hauled off all others as prisoners. All over Saint-Domingue, severe shortages of gunpowder, of cannon, and of fortifications left the habitants almost helpless. At this battle and others during the war, buccaneer contingents proved utterly unreliable; in fact, after fleeing, they often looted French habitations.[77]

The displaced habitants of the Lesser Antilles helped fill some of the manpower gap, and the king did send food, arms, and a military engineer to help the beleaguered colony. Of some 2,000 habitants of Saint-Christophe taken to Saint-Domingue, half or more died or opted to return to Martinique. Yet, a significant contingent of seasoned young women from the evacuated island helped stabilize Saint-Domingue and contributed to improved birthrates there, which, however, did not offset losses due to war and yellow fever.[78]

News of these disasters led the minister to appoint the energetic ex-slave trader and naval captain Jean du Casse as the new governor of Saint-Domingue. Du Casse was on his own, because contrary winds and currents made communication with Martinique extremely rare, as all previous governors of Saint-Domingue had discovered. The new governor quickly placed his confidants on the sovereign council and moved to restore militia discipline. In 1694, with some 3,000 habitants and freebooters (Graffe played a leading role), backed by royal ships, du Casse led a major raid on neighboring Jamaica, which yielded about 3,000 slaves, an influx that reinforced his standing in his labor-starved colony.[79] The famous 1692 earthquake that had destroyed Port Royal, sin city of the Americas, had weakened Jamaica's defenses.

Not surprisingly, the Spanish and English allies launched a counter-

attack, which ravaged the north of Saint-Domingue. The king's lieutenant at Le Cap, the now corpulent Graffe, abandoned it and ordered
a retreat, which soon turned into a *sauve qui peut* (every man for himself) rout. The Spanish put Le Cap to the torch.[80] No help came from
a France in misery in 1695, but Graffe was replaced as commandant of
Le Cap in 1697 by Joseph Donon de Gallifet, formerly king's commandant at Saint-Croix.

The situation was so grave at Saint-Domingue that a council of war
required a list of slaves deemed to be of "good will" to assist in the fighting. Slaveholders would receive compensation in case of the death or
maiming of their property. Maimed slaves were to receive their freedom
and free health care. Slaves who captured an enemy officer or saved a
French soldier would receive their freedom.[81]

Allies in name only, however, the Spanish and English forces did not
cooperate, and bickering within the English command provided further
assistance to du Casse in defending the western sector. Disease and the
paucity of booty at the conquered towns discouraged the allies. French
losses in men, slaves, and matériel were not insubstantial, including
dozens of women and children and upwards of a thousand slaves. However, the 1695 campaign was not a permanent setback to the young
colony. In the same sense, the English burning of the administrative center, Petit-Goâve, in 1698 was a temporary setback, although the notary
records went up in smoke (much to later historians' dismay). The decision to abandon the island of Saint-Croix and remove its habitants to the
northern sector of Saint-Domingue meant relatively quick recovery for
an area tormented twice by the Spanish.[82] The king gave significant incentives to decommissioned soldiers to stay at Saint-Domingue. These
benefits included exemption from capitation tax for themselves, their
families and their slaves, "if they have any."[83]

Meanwhile, by all contemporary accounts, du Casse's fair, vigorous
governance brought increasing order and confidence to the colony. His
credit with Pontchartrain protected him from recriminations by the authorities at Martinique, and he promoted African slave imports by all
means possible, sanctioning illegal commerce with the Danish outpost
of Saint Thomas and small-scale raids on isolated Jamaican plantations.
In times of food shortages, he attempted to fix prices.[84]

Meanwhile, the mid 1690s were extremely trying years in the French
Caribbean. Slave imports were rare. A price squeeze of the worst sort occurred. Sugar prices remained low, while those of essential imports sky-

rocketed. Labat notes that in 1695 a barrel of flour (often weeviled) cost 1,500 pounds of sugar, while a barrel of wine cost 3,000.[85] A habitant might make do with cassava bread temporarily, but how could he live without wine?

French reversals in Europe led to desperate measures to remove Spain from the coalition. Without the financial ability to use the royal navy in set battles after the defeat at La Hougue in 1692, where the French fleet lost fifteen ships of the line, the king decided to outsource the maritime effort by granting letters of marque and privileges to private syndicates able to put together offensive maritime operations.[86] The crown subsidized these operations by allowing royal ships to be privatized in return for 20 percent of the prize monies. Their successful attacks on English shipping were among the many factors driving England into near bankruptcy and thus to the peace table.[87]

Three major expeditions attacked parts of Spanish America in 1696–98, the last resulting in the sacking of the walled Spanish colonial city of Cartagena de Indias, after the signing of the Treaty of Ryswick. However, these fleets did not provide direct protection to the French colonies; indeed, the Cartagena exploit drew over a 1,000 habitants from Saint-Domingue. Du Casse had argued that an attack on Jamaica or Santo Domingo would be far more valuable; in this, he reflected the views of his illustrious predecessor Bertrand d'Ogeron, but the outcome was the same. Du Casse also argued that peaceful commerce with New Spain would achieve better results.[88] However, the fleet commander, Jean-Bernard-Louis Desjean, the baron de Pointis, an experienced naval artillery officer and a typically proud nobleman, desired immediate profits for himself and his investors, not the least of whom was the king. The old hankering to pillage the Spaniards trumped protection of tobacco and sugar planters and left the colonies in precarious positions. Preying on Spaniards had for 150 years undermined French colonial projects.

Pointis and du Casse, who led some 1,100 men in the attack, quarreled from the beginning. Sources differ on the number of du Casse's troops. Labat, who knew du Casse, claims 1,500 habitants, freebooters, and slaves participated.[89] Pointis absolutely needed du Casse's freebooters and militiamen for the planned assault, but he wanted to treat them similarly to his sailors and not as the independent contractors that they had always been. Du Casse disagreed about the target of attack, preferring Portobello. Pointis insisted on Cartagena.

About 180 African slaves followed their masters in the assault, the reward for which was a letter of freedom for survivors (their masters, however, receiving indemnities for their loss). Du Casse imposed this bargain, and insisted that no master had the right to force slaves to fight without this compensation. Du Casse enfranchised fifteen or sixteen of his slaves in this manner, which meant that four or five died in battle.[90] Actually, the black troops preceded the freebooters in the initial assault, and their casualties were heavy. Louis XIV agreed with du Casse that slave troops taken prisoner would be given their freedom if returned to French custody. Among these was Vincent Olivier, who later became commander of all free colored troops in the northern sector of Saint-Domingue. A long-lived and extremely prominent member of the free colored community, he actively recruited free blacks to form a unit (*chasseurs-volontaires*) that played a prominent role in the French-led siege of Savannah in 1779 during the War of American Independence. Another freedman, Etienne Auba, born in 1683 and thus only 14 when he served at Cartagena, became a captain of the free black militia at Fort Dauphin and lived to be 98.[91]

Two positive results emerged from the Pointis expedition: first, his sailing caused the diversion to the Caribbean of an English fleet resisting a French siege of Barcelona; second, the pillage from Cartagena (and, earlier, from Jamaica) helped establish the first sugar plantations at Saint-Domingue. Eventually, that is, because Pointis absconded with the booty, and it was only after appeals that Louis ordered the payment of 1,400,000 l.t. in slaves and merchandise to the Saint-Domingue warriors.[92] Du Casse's strong attachment to Jérome de Pontchartrain no doubt helped his case. The king estimated that the Saint-Domingue contingent returned home with some 600,000 l.t. of booty, and a total of two million was thus the island's share.[93] Pontchartrain specifically authorized an agreement between Gallifet, representing Saint-Domingue, and the directors of the two African slave trade companies in 1698 to deliver 1,000 *nègres* for 250,000 l.t. Of that sum, 150,000 came from the island's share of the Cartagena booty (although it should not be assumed that the slave traders fulfilled the bargain).[94]

Among others, du Casse deployed capital gained in the raid to establish a sugar habitation.[95] Balanced against these gains was the loss of some 200 killed or badly wounded, and others captured by Dutch and English ships. Also, a subsequent English raid burned the colony's administrative center, Petit-Goâve, with du Casse escaping in his nightshirt through a window.[96]

As part of an initiative to better relations with Spain, and because of his apparently genuine outrage, the king returned church chalices and other ornaments that Pointis had looted. Furthermore, he rebuked Pointis in public for this particular theft. At Louis's behest, Pontchartrain ordered du Casse to select an able man to return the clerical loot to Cartagena and, simultaneously, to explore "avenues of commerce."[97]

Although individuals prospered during this violent decade, population figures for French tropical America abundantly demonstrate the extreme difficulties of the Nine Years' War. Indeed, the king must have agreed, because the interim governor of Saint-Domingue in 1698, Charles de Guitaud, exempted habitants from charges for weighing produce for four years. The northern sector of Saint-Domingue had lost more than two-thirds of its men, although the transferred settlers from Saint-Croix in 1696 compensated somewhat. The king promoted the reestablishment of tobacco planting by mandating that the Domaine d'Occident accept 700,000 lbs. of tobacco per annum for six years at specified prices. The edict also attempted to control all aspects of tobacco production to ensure good quality.[98] However, rising sugar prices after 1698 allowed for a relatively rapid recovery of Saint-Domingue. Du Casse was the principal champion of sugar. The introduction of experienced sugar planters from Saint-Christophe and Saint-Croix no doubt assisted this process.

The sacking of Cartagena was the last hurrah of the buccaneers. Few received their lots of the spoils. Those who survived had the choice of becoming habitants or piracy; the majority probably chose the latter profession. On more than one occasion, royal officials threatened hanging as the punishment for the recalcitrants.[99]

After the Treaty of Ryswick, Pontchartrain and du Casse intended to foster trade with Spanish America, which meant a serious crackdown on buccaneering, as well as good behavior toward Spanish Creoles. Pursuing pro Spanish policies after 1697, du Casse prohibited habitants from hunting in adjacent Santo Domingo, and also from horse theft there, as contrary to the "rights of people" and Ryswick.[100] In 1698, Pontchartrain and a group of powerful maritime officials and financiers, including Antoine Crozat, a figure well known to Louisiana scholars, launched the Compagnie de Saint-Domingue. The twelve directors pledged 1.2 million l.t. to jump-start the company. With du Casse's help, the company aimed to establish an entrepôt at the Ile de vaches (Island of cows) along the south coast, thus competing with Dutch Curaçao, English Jamaica, and Danish Saint Thomas for the lucrative trade with Spanish America. It also hoped to lure habitants there to plant sugar. As a sign that the secretary of state had lost confidence in the French slave-trading companies, and as an indicator of the new company's influence, Louis XIV allowed it to buy slaves directly from Dutch Caribbean entrepôts. He also agreed to finance the company's fortress at its headquarters and allowed it exemptions from many taxes and duties. The gold, silver, and gems expected from the trade with Spanish America could be brought into France without paying duty.[101]

War alone does not explain the tribulations of this last decade of the century. Natural disasters, never completely absent from the American Tropics, abounded in these years. Saint-Christophe suffered a terrible earthquake in 1690, which resulted in the loss of 12,000,000 pounds of sugar, not to mention the crumbling of Poincy's famous château.[102] The most renowned disasters of the Caribbean islands (though not of Cay-enne) are, of course, hurricanes, most occurring from July 1 to the end of October or even later. In 1694, a powerful storm heavily damaged Saint-Pierre and some other parts of Martinique. The high waves swept away some fifty houses at Saint-Pierre, many of which had also served as warehouses, as well 200 other structures.[103]

To the previous catalogue of killer or debilitating diseases already en-demic in the islands—for whites, especially malaria, and for underfed blacks, dysentery—was added yellow fever. Called *mal de Siam* because it arrived on French East India Company ships, this devastating disease killed Governor-general d'Eragny and badly sickened his successor, the aging Blénac, as well as Du Maitz de Goimpy.[104] Three governors-general between 1696 and 1709 died, notably Thomas-Claude Renart de Fuchsamberg d'Amblimont (1696–1700). Martinique suffered badly. Outbreaks at Fort Royal claimed 205 victims in 1692 and 111 in 1693. Further outbreaks occurred there in 1703 and 1706. New arrivals and sailors were particularly susceptible. Yellow fever passed on to the other islands, and although exact figures are unavailable, the damage must have been significant to what was presumably a population lacking resistance to the disease.[105] These natural and epidemiological difficulties only magnified the harm caused by enemy actions.

From 1697 to 1701, Jérôme de Pontchartrain drew up bold plans to strengthen the French navy and colonies in preparations for either an all-out assault on the Spanish empire or for a defense of it should Louis's grandson inherit the childless Charles II's throne. Pontchartrain officially became secretary of state for the Marine in 1699, when his father gave up the office. Louis XIV insisted that displaced colonists from Saint-Christophe return to their lands with their slaves or see them forfeited. *Gloire* always trumped the colonists' economic and security concerns. Among many other measures, Pontchartrain established the Compagnie de Saint-Domingue in 1698 to facilitate trade with the Spanish empire. Windward Island producers of sugar were so concerned about initiatives to promote sugar planting at Saint-Domingue that they protested to Paris that a glut would result in low prices.[106]

After Ryswick, the king and Pontchartrain once again turned their attention to the Caribbean. (Typically, historians of New France inadequately acknowledge the continuing Caribbean focus of France's Atlantic empire; Pontchartrain called the Canadian settlements "the worst of all" colonies.)[107] The exclusion of foreign commerce, impossible during wartime, was reaffirmed with prison time and heavy fines for both smugglers and officials who tolerated them. They demanded that once again officials conduct yearly censuses. Louis and Pontchartrain railed against officials who "pretended" to administer justice on their own authority and not according to proper legal procedure. Louis sent a marine commissary to the islands to make certain local officials were implementing his rash of orders.[108] In 1700, the court sent Inspector-general of the Marine de La Boulaye and Renaud, the engineer-general of the Marine, to Guiane and Saint-Domingue to report on all military-related matters in those isolated colonies.[109]

In 1698, Pontchartrain planned an expedition with the sieur Pierre Le Moyne d'Iberville to establish a base somewhere along the Gulf Coast that would either threaten the Spanish in northern New Spain (Mexico and Texas) or protect them if they turned out to be allies in a future war. As du Casse feared, d'Iberville in 1699 attracted some freebooter habitants to his enterprise. Even the aging Graffe, now captain of a frigate, signed on as a guide and translator. Ironically, Graffe sailed for the last time with a French fleet whose goal was to protect the American ports of France's new ally Spain.[110]

Du Casse warned Pontchartrain that by annoying the Spaniards, the Mississippi project contradicted the secretary's goal of peacefully penetrating the Spanish empire, arguing that possession of Spanish Santo Domingo was in fact the key to any effective effort to conquer the Spanish empire, either literally or commercially. All lightly populated colonies, especially Cayenne, should be closed down and the settlers trans-

ferred to Saint-Domingue, he contended. Notions that the new continental settlement would supply Saint-Domingue with the natural resources it increasingly needed—wood, cattle, and provisions—proved
largely fanciful.[111]

Subsequent events proved that Ryswick was the end of a two hundred years' war (1494–1697) between the French and Spanish monar-
chies. After Charles II's death in 1700, complicated events led to the
Bourbon assumption of the Spanish throne in the person of Philip V.
The subsequent War of the Spanish Succession surprisingly had very
positive results for Frenchmen in tropical America. Spanish-French legal and covert cooperation in the American Tropics launched a boom period for France's possessions.[112]

Colbert and Seignelay created an institutional framework to promote
the integration of France's Caribbean colonies into a unified, centralized
empire. By the time of Jean-Baptiste Colbert's death in 1683, much had
been done to establish rules that would govern future metropolitan-
colonial relations. The system would see elaboration or refinement in
future decades, especially in relationship to Saint-Domingue, but it
clearly retained Colbert's mark down to the French Revolution. While
overly praised by so many earlier historians, he hardly deserves the contemptuous dismissal of his career that has been fashionable in both so-
cialist left and anti-statist right circles.[113]

The realities of colonial development would, however, seriously
modify or even occasionally undermine policies based on the often bom-
bastic official rhetoric that insisted on the parent-child analogy of motherland and colony; that is, the authoritarian if paternalistic family model
of old France. Officials at Versailles had to formulate policies that negotiated through the often conflicting strategic and fiscal needs of the state,
metropolitan economic interests, and colonial needs. They consciously
attempted to balance these interests, primarily at the expense of foreign
commerce, to please as much as possible all concerns, including, unfortunately, those of their parasitic financier friends and clients. Often they
did a reasonably good job of reconciling the inevitable conflicts—in
peacetime. But their best plans fell prey to the god of war, when financial necessity recognizes no future concerns. Unfortunately, the proud
Mars of France, Louis XIV, provided the occasion for many such wars
and much misery, both metropolitan and colonial.

CHAPTER NINE

Island Society from the 1660s to the 1690s
The Habitants

The same set of manners will follow a nation, and adhere to them over the whole globe, as well as the same laws and language. The SPANISH, ENGLISH, FRENCH and DUTCH colonies are all distinguishable even between the tropics.

David Hume, "Of National Characters" (1742)

In the final four decades of the seventeenth century, the people of France's colonies in tropical America were different in many respects from their neighbors; indeed, the wars of Louis XIV heightened those distinctions by promoting greater dependence on the mother country. A comparison of French Caribbean islanders with their counterparts in Acadia or on the Saint Lawrence reveals environmental, ecological, and economic factors that perceptibly distinguished *Canadien* habitants from their Caribbean cousins. This chapter analyzes the reasons for this gradual divergence.

Of the many factors that contributed to the transition from the frontier era to the plantation complex era of the eighteenth century, the most obvious is the "taming" of the islands' natural environment, a consequence of growing population and more intensive soil cultivation. But the political, cultural, and psychological aspects of this transition cannot be ignored. Restricting the remaining Island Caribs to reservation islands was no doubt considered more important then than it appears in hindsight.[1] Taming the "excesses" of individualism, most apparent in the partially successful effort to rein in buccaneers and freebooters, was part of the process, as was the occasional dispatch of "good" young Frenchwomen to settle the habitants' wanderlust. Most important was the increasing commercialization of the colonial economy. As plantation agriculture grew gradually more important, poor white habitants, free blacks, and people of color, as well as the few Island Caribs were slowly but inexorably pushed to the margins of society. To be sure, a mixed small farming / pastoral economy continued to predominate in those settlements where plantation agriculture was little developed (e.g., Sainte-Lucie, Saint-Barthélemy, and Saint-Martin).

It cannot be reiterated enough that the various islands did not develop at the same rate. Saint-Christophe may have emerged from a frontier stage by the 1660s, in the sense that little undeveloped arable land remained. By 1670, Africans (4,901) outnumbered Europeans (4,450) there, which suggests that there were still many small farmers.[2] The few large planters were becoming predominant, and in combination with accelerating hostilities with the English, some migration of small men occurred, presumably to Saint-Domingue. Cayenne had only a tiny population, but the great preponderance of slaves to free settlers there— 1,507 to 175 by 1685—meant that a few plantations dominated society, more so than in any other colony. Saint-Domingue remained in a frontier stage down to the 1690s. In the mid 1680s, whites outnumbered African slaves 4,386 to 2,939 there. By 1700, however, of 13,642 people, Africans and African Americans totaled 9,082, signaling a significant shift to plantation agriculture (especially indigo and, at the very end of the century, sugar). The number of sugar works at Guadeloupe grew from one in 1644 to 113 in 1669.[3]

Lest the reader jump to the conclusion that a "sugar revolution" was under way, consider that if all the roughly 4,500 slaves on Guadeloupe were owned by those 113 owners, which is highly unlikely, they would have averaged forty slaves apiece. At Capesterre, Charles Houël and two other sugar magnates possessed over a hundred slaves each, so, yes, there were a few such people in the French islands. In the Basse-Terre region, the Dominicans on their two habitations possessed the most slaves, eighty, followed by Governor du Lion, with seventy, and the Jesuits, with sixty-seven.[4] The next largest owner had fifty-two. The great majority of *sucriers* in that area thus possessed many fewer than forty slaves. With a few exceptions, such habitants hardly qualify as "sugar magnates," substantial though they may have been. Until the mid 1680s, Guadeloupe and its dependencies, far larger than Saint-Christophe, moved at about the same very gradual pace toward planter predominance. In 1685, slaves outnumbered whites there by 5,257 to 3,670. In 1700, just 6,855 slaves lived alongside 4,466 free people, indicating a stagnant pace of development.[5]

Martinique had 111 sugar mills by 1671, and many farmers who planted sugarcane to sell to mill owners.[6] Tracy was indulging in only mild hyperbole when he complained to Colbert that planters at Mar-

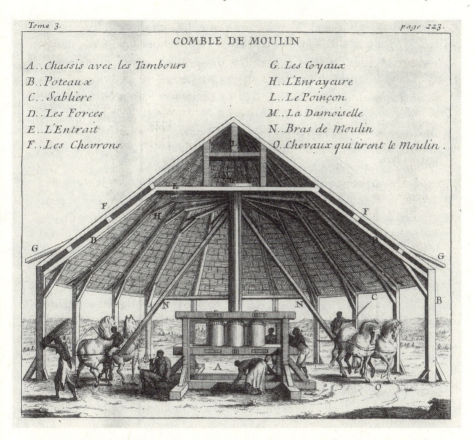

Horse-powered sugar mill. From Jean-Baptiste Labat, *Nouveau voyage aux isles de l'Amérique* (Paris, 1722), 3: opposite 223.

tinique "have practically abandoned manioc planting to make sugar."[7] By 1679, all the arable land at Martinique had been allotted, which is not to say all had been put into production.[8] Repeated royal edicts mandating that habitants either cultivate their allotted concessions or return one-third for redistribution were ignored. Labat thought that the islands' white population would have been larger if these edicts had been enforced.[9] At Saint-Christophe, there were 121 mills in 1671. Overall, perhaps 12,000 tons of sugar were produced in the French islands, equivalent to about 30 percent of the Brazilian total.[10]

According to a 1683 census, Martinique had 122 sugar works and Saint-Christophe had 90; Guadeloupe had 89, as well as 12 indigo works, the most on any island. The decline in numbers of sugar mills at Saint-Christophe and Guadeloupe may be attributed to the Dutch War, slumping prices for sugar in Europe, and the problem of obtaining slaves. Christian Schnakenbourg uses the word "crisis" to describe Guadeloupe's sugar industry from 1670 to 1700; the survivors would form the *grands blancs* caste of the following century.[11] Grenada, Saint-Croix, and Marie-Galante together had 30 sugar works. Of these islands, only Saint-Christophe had reached its peak.[12] Military disasters in the 1690s left Saint-Christophe with only 1,061 whites and 722 slaves.[13]

Labat gives us a snapshot of his parish at Guadeloupe. It contained 307 whites and 690 slaves, thus a lower than typical ratio of free to bonded people. Only five habitants were sugar planters, with the majority of free colonists engaged in smaller-scale indigo, cacao, and *roucou* production. Other parishioners were provision farmers and pastoralists.[14] He describes two other quarters of Guadeloupe as areas of mixed agriculture. Ginger and sugar were the staple or cash crops, but manioc, tobacco for local use, and vegetables were also grown, and cattle and fowl were raised. Shall we call Guadeloupe at this time a sugar island?

Labat sketches a model sugar works, with 120 slaves to work the fields, mill, and boilers. Ten of these slaves would be too old to work or too sick at any given time, and twenty-five of them would be children, available only for light tasks. Of the remaining eighty-five slaves, some forty would be needed as skilled workers—among them, masons, boilers, wheelwrights, carpenters, barrel makers, and smiths—and for odd jobs. These slave artisans were vain about their superior status and should be encouraged to be. Others, such as wagon drivers, woodcutters, and domestics required less skill. The remaining forty-five slaves did the fieldwork, assisted at harvesting time by the artisan slaves. The annual expense for these slaves was about 6,600 l.t. against a projected revenue of 44,640 l.t. Labat computes the cost of slaves' food, clothing, and medicine but not the cost of replacing them. About a hundred cattle, fifty horses, and a herd of sheep would also be needed.[15]

In another place, Labat discusses his purchase of twelve slaves in 1698 at a cost of 5,700 francs (a franc being equivalent to an *écu*, thus 3 l.t.), which amounts to 475 francs, or 1,425 l.t. per individual (17,100 l.t. total). He paid for them in muscavado at 7 l.t., 15 sols the hundredweight, or a total of 220,600 pounds of sugar. Elsewhere, Labat says that the estate produced 190,000 pounds of muscavado in 1698, as well as 40,000 pounds of the more valuable clayed sugar and 12,000 pounds of molasses, thus easily paying for his purchase in one year. On the English islands, such slaves cost only the equivalent of 100–120 francs apiece, which was, according to Labat, why they were treated so brutally there.[16]

Remembering that Labat wrote to promote island development, his discussion of sugar's profitability in favorable years illustrates why so many wealthy planters favored it. Labat computes the average profit for sugar planters in the Windward Islands at 15 percent in the "good" years, those of peace, 1698–1701, whereas an estate of similar size in France earned 5–6 percent. He also notes that sugar refiners in France much desired the good muscavado at Saint-Domingue, which sold for 3–4 l.t. the hundredweight. The fertile plains around Léogane in Saint-Domingue were a beehive of activity, he says, with both sugar estates and cacao walks emerging rapidly.[17]

Tiny Saint-Martin and Saint-Barthélemy exemplify islands and remote parts of the larger islands in which development was very slow. Saint-Barthélemy, for example, had 290 whites and forty-six slaves running cattle ranches and a few indigo works in 1671. By 1688, the respective numbers increased to 349 and seventy two, with only one-third of whites owning slaves. The largest slaveholder had ten. Owners and slaves worked side by side to eke out a living on Saint-Barthélemy's largely arid soil.[18] The inhabitants of the Saints, islets adjacent to Guadeloupe, combined mixed farming (cotton, maize, peas, manioc) with raising animals and fishing (oysters, shrimp, conch, rock lobster) in the rich nearby waters. Labat notes that while no one got rich, the habitants lived comfortably—that is, in times of peace.[19]

This very gradual maturation of most islands is in part explained by the preeminence of Martinique and its commercial capital, Saint-Pierre. Shippers almost invariably stopped there first, and Guadeloupe planters were forced to buy from middlemen there when their needs could not be supplied via foreign interlopers.[20] The predominance of tobacco at Saint-Domingue and its greater distance from trade routes meant that few French slave ships stopped there. The economic superiority of Martinique is easily demonstrated. By 1685, the number of blacks was double that of whites, 10,611 to 5,183. By 1700, there were 15,266 Africans and African Americans to 6,774 whites.[21]

All the French islands, if least of all Martinique, lagged behind English Barbados because of weak prices for sugar after 1670, the instabilities related to war, the inability of French traders to replace the Dutch, and the far superior English slave trade. The French slave trade was especially ineffective before 1700. Despite monopolies and a host of economic incentives, the French West India Company and succeeding companies failed to supply the French market; their few thousand slaves were in any case priced too high.[22] The hesitant transition to the plantation complex before 1700 was accompanied by only a slight growth of white population, from 15,271 in 1670 to 17,188 in 1700. The number of slaves increased from 15,826 in 1670 to 33,343 in 1700, a significant increase, but one dwarfed by the next century's explosive growth.[23]

The gradual growth of sugar production is explained by heavy capital costs and, from the 1670s on, unstable markets. In the early 1660s, according to Jacques Petitjean Roget, a relatively modest sugar operation needed fifty to 100 hectares of land (from about 124 to 247 acres), forty slaves and the mill, coppers, cisterns, and so on, to produce 100,000 lbs. of sugar.[24] Other than the du Parquet habitation at Saint-Pierre, in 1660, only the Jesuits and perhaps a few others had such places. The black robes employed twelve servants, presumably *engagés*, forty-five adult slaves, and thirty-two children.[25] Until after 1715, the French slave trade was almost nonexistent, and so planters depended on Dutch and English interlopers and captured Portuguese and Spanish slaves; even the Caribs were a significant source, supplying slaves captured primarily from English islands.

The gradual transition to sugar, especially at Martinique, was assisted by the increasing hurricane activity of the latter decades of the seventeenth century. Ferocious storms in 1672, 1680, 1694, 1699, and 1713 damaged the island without regard to the size of habitations, but because of the size of their estates, their many slaves, and their political influence, sugar planters were in a better position than most to obtain credit and rebuild.[26] Men of less means must have been tempted by offers to buy their habitations.

Dutertre devotes only three pages to sugar in his classic four-volume history published between 1667 and 1671. To be sure, a celebrated picture of a sugar works accompanies the text.[27] In dramatic contrast, his fellow Dominican Labat composed hundreds of pages on sugar, sugar making, and the accompanying slave system. Not only was Labat manager of a sugar works, he lived in the islands from 1695 to 1705, when sugar increasingly dominated island life.[28]

As he traveled through the islands, Labat was often the guest of wealthy planters, such as Claude Pocquet, the proud owner of three *sucreries* and over 200 slaves, and the former Guadeloupe proprietor

Houël's eldest son, the owner of 400 slaves, large herds of animals, and well-built refinery buildings. Both of these early *grands blancs* were generous men, Labat tells us, and they evidently treated him well. The bitter dispute between Labat's Dominican order and the elder Houël over the size of the original land concession was forgotten.[29]

Louis XIV used the granting of letters of nobility as a reward for valor in war, and island society included some minor nobles. However, nobles did not have exemption from capitation taxes unless they occupied an office in the sovereign councils or were militia captains. Nobles had the right to carry swords, as did all militiamen, unlike in France. Although nobility was no doubt attractive to some islanders, wealth was more important. Just as they rejected many aspects of French society, islanders refused to accept the privileged position of the nobility. Labat notes that when Houël's heirs refused to sell land without feudal rights attached, prospective buyers balked.[30]

Labat is less generous toward less successful Creole habitants, perhaps reflecting an incipient hostility between *grands* and *petits blancs*. He characterizes these Creoles as "debauched, lazy, arrogant, presumptuous liars."[31] Did he imbibe such beliefs at the well-stocked tables of his rich planter hosts? He attributes these character traits, especially "laziness," to the fecundity of the islands and to life among slaves. According to Labat, Creoles passed their time with games and food and drink. Both wealthy and modest habitants consumed prodigious amounts of wine and brandy, cheese from the Auvergne, Roquefort, and Parma, pistachios, olives, olive oil, and dried fruit.[32] Up in the morning to a shot of brandy, they took chocolate at 8 A.M. They marked the passage of hours with brandy, chocolate, and cigars (cigarillos, really). The wealthier wore wigs, silk stockings, and jewels. As for books, they bought a few of these to appear *savant*. Especially intemperate in food and drink—Labat avoids discussion of sexual proclivities—were the habitants of Saint-Domingue, perhaps reflecting their freebooter heritage.[33]

Labat mainly describes the lifestyle of better-off habitants. The poorest *petits blancs* lived more modestly. Their daily bread was either cassava cakes or potatoes served with a sauce of crushed red pepper, salt, and lemon juice. A little fish accompanied these starches. The Island Carib would have felt right at home, especially because the chief drink was the indigenous *maby*.[34]

Environmental destruction continued to spread throughout the Windward Islands and accelerated rapidly in the less developed colonies, such as Sainte-Lucie, Grenada, Saint-Croix, and Saint-Domingue, which still depended heavily on hunting for food, leather. and tortoise shell. After the French occupied Cayenne in 1664, the colonists "cut down and burned entire forests" to create farms, and no unoccupied arable land remained on Saint-Christophe.[35] At Martinique, settlers opened up the now available (1660 treaty) Island Carib lands on the windward coast, but nevertheless the sovereign council had to mandate that planters maintain adequate acreage in foodstuffs.[36] The dry Grand-Terre of Guadeloupe, previously little developed, now attracted some settlement, especially along the southern coast. However, hunters of feral pigs in the big islands now had to undertake veritable odysseys to find them.[37] Dutertre describes the hunt for tortoises, manatees, and even crabs as "totally ruined" by the 1660s.[38]

Labat notes that because of their growing scarcity, Windward Islanders used salt ponds to raise young turtles.[39] He also bemoans the decline of manatees, which he attributes to coastal human development. Manatee tasted like veal, he exclaimed, and as a "fish," it could be eaten during Lent and on Fridays.[40] Despite its frontier character, Saint-Domingue may have witnessed the most dramatic ecological change, with the slaughter of feral cattle and pigs by buccaneers, packs of wild dogs, and Spanish mulatto hunters.[41] By the 1680s, large corrals of re-domesticated pigs emerged as an alternative source of meat.[42]

French colonists and their slaves needless to say made war on snakes and rats, undesirable (to the French) meat that was fed to the slaves, and Labat entertains his readers with a bloody account of how sailors at Saint-Croix treated sharks: taking only the belly meat to eat, they cut off the dorsal fin, threw them overboard, and watched "gaily" as other sharks ripped the helpless creatures apart.[43]

Island Caribs conducted a lively truck trade with the French, either directly or via half-Carib Frenchmen living among them, exchanging hammocks, chickens, and pigs for brandy or other spirits. Their main foodstuffs beside native starches were now Old World yams and bananas. The diminishing number of Island Caribs, especially on Dominica, lived in close proximity to French habitants, and usually assisted them in struggles with the English. Prisoners taken in these conflicts or those with their traditional Arawak enemies were assimilated into Carib society. Labat identifies measles as a great killer of Caribs, which is likely a guess.[44]

As a result of Paris's increasing influence on island affairs, better information on island population is available. Better, but far from perfect, and thus a mixed blessing. Who counted the people, and whom did they want to fool? The fact that censuses were done primarily for tax purposes means probably that the number of slaves is an undercount. Habitants, except for officials, clergy, and militia officers, paid capitation taxes on all slaves and *engagés*, but on the larger plantations, where most Africans lived, it was presumably easier to hide them. For example, in 1678, Blénac ordered all captains and militia officers to assist the tax farmer's clerks in compiling an accurate census. If someone was caught hiding slaves, they were to be confiscated and sold at auction, with one-fourth of the proceeds given to the person exposing the fraud.[45] Censuses also counted settlers available for militia duty; no doubt some habitants attempted to evade the counters. Finally, censuses probably undercounted an emerging mulatto population. Plenty of opportunity existed for chicanery, and colonists of all nations do not rank high for obedience to authority. Philippe and Marie Rossignol examined a list of habitants at Guadeloupe in 1664, which had fallen into English hands during the second Anglo-Dutch War, and compared the names on it to the 1664 census found in the French National Archives. Only a minority of names on the first list appeared on the official census of the same year.[46]

The most notable change in white population was the dramatic decline of the northwestern arc islands, Saint-Christophe, Saint-Croix, Saint-Martin, and Saint-Barthélemy. In 1670, these islands contained about 30 percent of the total French population, but the Dutch and English ravaged them in the wars of the 1670s and 1690s, and refugees emigrated to the bigger Windward Islands and, especially, Saint-Domingue. The addition of settlers from Saint-Christophe and their slaves and the entire free and enslaved population of Saint-Croix no doubt played a significant role in the dynamic growth of Saint-Domingue at the very end of the century. By 1700, Saint-Domingue and the bigger Windward Islands contained 90 percent of the French Caribbean population, as compared to 70 percent in 1670.[47]

The fact that the white population was growing, if only at a very moderate rate, calls for explanation. Indentured servants, despite the government's encouragement of their migration, were clearly not the source of growth. For example, at Martinique, the number of indentured servants plunged from about one-quarter of the white population in

Estimated Populations of French Caribbean Islands, 1660–1700

Year	Island	Whites	Blacks	Colored	Source
1660	Martinique	2,783	2,642	?	Poussou, 46
	Martinique	2,753	2,644	25	Elisabeth, 27
1664	Martinique	3,293	3,018	34	Elisabeth, 27
	Saint-Domingue	900	?	?	Camus, 26
1669	Martinique	3,718	5,849	?	Roget, 1376
	Martinique	3,818	5,849	?	Elisabeth, 27
1670	Martinique	3,894	6,183	?	Roget, 1376
	Martinique	3,844	6,171	?	Elisabeth, 27
	Martinique and Grenada	4,177	6,393	?	Pritchard, 424
	Guadeloupe	3,444	4,482	?	Pritchard, 424
	Saint-Domingue	3,100	?	?	Pritchard, 424
	Cayenne (Guiana)	100	50	?	Pritchard, 424
1671	Saint-Christophe	3,333	4,468	?	Pritchard, 50
	Saint-Christophe	3,233	4,392	?	Elisabeth, 25
	Martinique	4,018	6,582	?	Elisabeth, 27
	Guadeloupe	3,331	4,267	98	Pritchard, 54
1677	Saint-Domingue	3,500	?	?	Camus, 17
1681	Saint-Domingue	4,336	2,102	210	Pritchard, 65
1682	Martinique	4,478	8,034	?	Roget, 1376
	Martinique	4,505	9,634	190	Elisabeth, 27
	Martinique	4,505	9,364	251	Pritchard, 54
	Saint-Christophe	2,885	4,301	92	Pritchard, 50
	Guadeloupe	2,998	4,109	70	Pritchard, 54
1684	Martinique	4,857	10,656	?	Roget, 1376
	Martinique	4,857	10,454	169	Elisabeth, 27
1685	Martinique	4,862	10,343	?	Roget, 1376
	Martinique	4,882	10,343	251	Elisabeth, 28
	Martinique and Grenada	5,183	10,611	358	Pritchard, 424
	Guadeloupe and Marie Galante	3,670	5,257	?	Pritchard, 424
	Saint-Christophe	4,598	5,294	?	Pritchard, 424
	Cayenne	175	1,507	?	Pritchard, 424
	Saint-Domingue	4,386	2,939	?	Pritchard, 424
1687	All islands	18,657	25,558	1,066	Pritchard, 45
1687	Martinique	5,022	10,801	315	Elisabeth, 28
	Martinique	5,019	10,801	?	Pritchard, 45
	Guadeloupe	3,546	4,982	?	Pritchard, 45
	Saint-Domingue	4,411	3,358	224	Pritchard, 66
	Saint-Domingue	4,000	?	?	Poussou, 44
1688	Martinique	5,071	11,416	290	Elisabeth, 28
1689	Saint-Christophe	3,381	4,017	ca. 200	Pritchard, 50
1692	Martinique	6,413	12,857	344	Pritchard, 54
	Martinique	6413	12,856	184	Elisabeth, 28
1694	Martinique	6,149	12,887	libres, 477	Elisabeth, 28.

(continued)

Estimated Populations of French Caribbean Islands, 1660–1700 (*Continued*)

Year	Island	Whites	Blacks	Colored	Source
1696	Martinique	6,455	13,126	libres, 505	Elisabeth, 28
	Guadeloupe	3,649	6,431	307	Pritchard, 54
1697	Martinique	6,825	13,458	libres, 505	Elisabeth, 28
1698	Martinique	6,761	13,596	libres, 557	Elisabeth, 28
1699	Martinique	6,243	13,292	libres, 533	Elisabeth, 28
1700	Martinique	6,567	14,566	libres, 507	Elisabeth, 28
	Martinique	6,567	14,566	?	Pritchard, 424
	Martinique and Grenada	6,774	15,266	533	Pritchard, 424
	Guadeloupe and Marie Galante	4,466	6,855	403	Pritchard, 424
	Saint-Christophe and dependencies	1,061	722	30	Pritchard, 424
	Cayenne	327	1,418	17	Pritchard, 424
	Saint-Domingue	4,560	9,082	?	Pritchard, 424

Sources: Michel Camus, "Correspondance de Bertrand Ogeron, gouverneur de l'île de la Tortue et de la côte de Saint-Domingue au XVIIème siècle," *Revue de la Société haïtienne d'histoire et de géographie* 43, no. 146 (March 1985); Léo Elisabeth, *La Société martiniquaise au XVIIe et XVIIIe siècles, 1664–1789* (Paris: Karthala, 2003); Jacques Petitjean Roget, *La Société d'habitation à la Martinique: Un Demi-siècle de formation, 1635–1685* (Paris: Champion, 1980); Jean-Pierre Poussou, "L'Immigration européene dans les îles d'Amérique," in *Voyage aux îles d'Amérique* (Paris: Archives nationales, 1992); James Pritchard, *In Search of Empire: The French in the Americas, 1670–1730* (Cambridge: Cambridge University Press, 2004).

Note: "Whites" refers to all Europeans. "Blacks" refers to enslaved Africans and African Americans. "Colored" refers to so-called *gens de couleur,* who were almost all mulattoes before 1701; a few were free, but probably most were slaves. Libres refers to free people who were not Europeans (Africans, African Americans, mulattoes, and Caribs). Caribs were rarely counted; when they were, they were included under colored or libre.

1671 to less than 2 percent in 1688, and it declined further during the Nine Years' War.[48] Nor probably was a surplus of births over deaths the cause. Free white migration and, perhaps, the practice of granting freedom, land, and one year's pay to miserably treated soldiers willing to become colonists helped sustain some growth.[49]

An analysis of white populations in the English and French Caribbean islands provides some interesting comparisons. According to Richard Dunn, the white population of Barbados declined from 22,000 in 1660 to 15,000 in 1700; that of Jamaica grew from 3,000 in 1660, when the colony had just been established, to 12,000 in 1680, but declined to 7,000 in 1700; that of the Leeward Islands (English Saint Christopher,

Antigua, Nevis, and Montserrat) grew from 8,000 in 1660 to 11,000 in 1680, but then declined to 7,000 in 1700.[50] In all the French colonies except for war-plagued Saint-Christophe, the white population grew gradually in the four decades after 1660, with the exception of the war years of the 1690s.[51] The usual explanation for white demographic decline in the English Caribbean is that the triumph of sugar in Barbados by 1660 and in Jamaica and the Leeward Islands by the 1680s caused a decline of the small farmer. Simultaneously, the dramatically increasing reliance on African slave labor made the indentured servant system obsolete; if French habitants had been able to procure the slaves they desired, the results might have been similar. By about 1700, British West Indian sugar production had surpassed that of Brazil and was at least two and a half times that of France's tropical colonies.[52] The stability of the French population is explained by slower economic development.[53]

Comparing frontier Jamaica and Saint-Domingue is especially instructive. Both colonies came into existence at about the same time, in the early 1660s. By 1670, however, Jamaica already had some 7,000 Europeans and 7,000 slaves, whereas Saint-Domingue had 3,100 whites and a negligible number of slaves. In 1685, Jamaica had about 11,000 whites and about 22,000 slaves. In that year, 4,560 whites and 2,939 slaves show up on the Saint-Domingue census. In contrast, from 1640 to 1700, the white population of English continental North America increased from about 26,000 to about 251,000.[54] By 1700, Jamaica's 7,000 whites lived among roughly 40,000 Africans and African Americans. The figures for Saint-Domingue in that year were 4,560 whites and 9,082 slaves.[55]

However, the rising price for sugar, the preponderance of clayed sugar produced in the more advanced French Windward Islands, and capital acquired by robbery during the Nine Years' War led to an explosion of sugar planting at Saint-Domingue. Labat suggests that the easier availability of cattle and horses there, many coming from Spanish Santo Domingo, as well as relatively abundant land, on which slaves were encouraged to raise pigs for their sustenance, were other advantages of the "big island."[56] Finally, contraband trade with neighboring Santo Domingo was large and unremitting despite occasional confiscations. Labat describes one typical scenario. A Spanish ship comes into port proclaiming a need to take on food and water or make repairs. A *pôt de vin* is given to the local official, and during the lengthy purchase of goods or repairs, cargo is surreptitiously unloaded and exchanged goods are brought on board. Then the shipmaster informs the official that he has inadequate cash and thus requests permission to pay his debts in goods. Further transactions then occur.[57] The king's chief officials at Martinique and even the local governor at Petit-Goâve are far away.

A report of 1701 counted thirty-five sugar works at Saint-Domingue, twenty more soon to be operating, and ninety in various stages of construction.[58] Gallifet, the commander at Le Cap and former governor of Saint-Croix, heavily promoted the advance of sugar in the northern plain adjacent to the town.[59] By 1715, Saint-Domingue's white population almost equaled that of Jamaica, and its black population trailed by only about 12,000. In global terms, the number of French slaves in the West Indies and Guiane grew from 33,343 to 81,593 during the predominantly war years 1700–1715. These figures alone illustrate why the year 1700 marks such a dramatic shift in the character of France's settlements in tropical America.[60]

Enough concordance between unofficial 1685 estimates and the official 1687 census provides a modicum of confidence in these figures. Africans in the French Caribbean islands had surpassed the European population in numbers, but not yet by a two-to-one ratio. However, minus Saint-Domingue, with its slim European majority, the Lesser Antilles approached a two-to-one ratio. More developed Saint-Christophe, Martinique, and Guadeloupe contained 20,253 African slaves and 11,717 whites. Furthermore, given that significant numbers of slaves worked on the 407 sugar works in these islands, numerous nodules of the kind of economy and society that would one day characterize the plantation complex had already developed. By 1700, the French West Indies and

Total Populations of French Caribbean Islands, 1687

Island	Population	Source
Martinique	16,253	Pritchard, 45
Guadeloupe	8,698	Pritchard, 45
Saint-Christophe	7,773	Pritchard, 45
Saint-Domingue	7,993	Pritchard, 66
Cayenne	2,083	Saintoyant
Marie-Galante and St. Croix	2,412	Saintoyant
Grenada	640	Saintoyant

Sources: James Pritchard, *In Search of Empire: The French in the Americas, 1670–1730* (Cambridge: Cambridge University Press, 2004); Jules Saintoyant, *La Colonisation française sous l'ancien régime (du XVe siècle à 1789)*, 2 vols. (Paris: Renaissance du livre, 1929), 1: 241.

Guiane contained 17,188 whites, 33,343 blacks, and 983 *gens de couleur*.[61] This not yet two-to-one ratio of slaves to free population demonstrates a gradual transition to a plantation complex regime. The takeoff to a mature plantation system occurred during the first fifteen years of the eighteenth century.

Tobacco cultivation in the Lesser Antilles declined after 1660 and was of minor economic importance by the time of the tobacco monopoly in 1674. Tobacco producers had acquired a negative reputation, in part due to unscrupulous mixing of second-growth and first-growth leaves.[62] In 1671, the value of sugar at Martinique was fifteen times greater than that of tobacco, and the acreage devoted to sugar was three times larger. To be sure, the number of habitations devoted to tobacco and provisions still significantly surpassed the total of sugar works. Tobacco farms were small. Soil erosion, the inferior quality of the leaf, and the pressures to transfer the limited amount of arable land to sugar damaged tobacco production. Colonial governors supported the transition; in the 1650s, du Parquet had granted three years' tax exemption to anyone switching to sugar. A 1660 memoir asserted that sugar already surpassed tobacco at Martinique. In 1659, the Martinique council first regulated the price of rum, and fines were first levied in sugar, rather than tobacco, in 1660.[63] A few years later, Colbert claimed the Dutch took 2,000,000 pounds of sugar from these islands, compared to 1,000,000 of other products.[64]

Symbolically, the triumph of sugar may be dated to 1669, when all fines at Martinique were levied in sugar. Sugar occupied more than two-thirds of the arable land, and tobacco only one-fifth, although the latter crop still employed twice as many colonists.[65] In 1664, 77 percent of habitants owned fewer than five slaves, and another 11 percent owned six to ten, hardly making them big entrepreneurs. By 1680, 69.3 percent of habitants owned fewer than five slaves, and another 12.1 percent held six to ten.[66] At Martinique in 1685, of 1,048 habitations, there were 172 plantations with sugar works; sugar, tobacco, indigo, cotton, and provision farms accounted for the rest.[67] Over three-quarters of these modest habitants owned one or more slaves. Sugar magnates thus did not monopolize French tropical society. At Martinique in 1680, only 1.2 percent of habitants owned more than sixty slaves, while 8.3 percent owned between twenty-one and fifty-nine.[68] Fewer than 10 percent of habitants thus owned enough labor to qualify as sugar planters.

The 1660s also saw rapid growth of sugar production at Guadeloupe.

In 1661, some seventy-one sugar works dotted the island, many of them established by Dutch and Portuguese Jewish refugees from Brazil. Eight years later, 113 mills produced 4,375,000 pounds of the sweetener. The declining prices for sugar in the 1670s halted this momentum, and the use of the term "sugar revolution" for Guadeloupe is a large exaggeration.[69]

The last bastion of tobacco was Saint-Domingue. Its rapidly growing population produced some 3,000,000 pounds annually by 1674.[70] After that, an oscillating pattern, but one of overall decline, characterized production there. By 1700, tobacco had become of minor importance, thanks to a combination of metropolitan policies and taste—a marked preference for Virginia leaf—and widespread fraud in the packaging of the "rolls." Habitants experimented with indigo and ginger, with some success, in part because of a 1693 royal edict exempting duties on the re-exportation of indigo.[71] By around 1700, sugar planters had begun a transformation that in thirty years turned Saint-Domingue into the classic plantation island.

The major factors slowing the ascendancy of sugar in the Lesser Antilles were the interrelated ones of capital and slaves. Unlike tobacco, sugar required significant capital to make a profitable crop. The minimum amount of land needed was twenty *carreaux*, or approximately 21.60 hectares. An emerging island custom of de facto primogeniture, in opposition to the Custom of Paris, did not arouse serious royal opposition. For example, the sovereign council of Martinique claimed authority as the final court of appeal in cases involving family disputes over inheritances. In general, junior siblings sold their share to the chief inheritor; in return, they received a note with a fixed interest rate of about 5 percent. Many of these younger siblings continued to live on the habitation.[72]

A distinction needs to be made between planters of sugarcane and planters of sugarcane with ownership of a mill (*sucrerie*). In 1671, at Martinique, half of all sugar planters did not own a mill.[73] No doubt some of these eventually became mill owners. However, if Barbados is any guide, drought, war damage, and especially disastrous hurricanes often forced these smaller planters to sell out to richer neighbors. Richard Dunn surmises that the violent 1675 storm at Barbados produced such a social transformation.[74] Most large planters were able to obtain the credit to rebuild, which often meant a two- to three-year lag in production.[75]

For these larger Caribbean planters, the heavy capital costs were in slave labor, beasts to transport the cane to the mill and to run the mill, and the industrial equipment (e.g., copper boilers, pipes, ladles) associated with processing sugar. Except for Guadeloupe, which had some water-driven mills, horses and cattle provided the energy to squeeze raw cane.[76] After milling the cane, cisterns conducted the raw juice to the boiling house, where it was distilled and crystallized in a more or less lengthy process, depending on the sugar's quality. The latter ranged from heavy, molasses-laden sugar (muscavado, or *sucre brut*) to the semi-refined clayed sugar. This form of "white" sugar became especially popular after metropolitan restrictions on colonial refining, and it had triumphed in the Lesser Antilles by 1700.[77]

This transformation occurred despite a late seventeenth-century royal edict dramatically raising duties on refined and clayed sugar, while reducing those on muscavado. The king acted at the behest of metropolitan refiners threatened by the competition. In 1696, the king also mandated that planters pay merchants with at least 50 percent muscavado, and that without added sugary liquid.[78] The number of refineries at Martinique declined from eighteen in 1698 to none in 1700.[79] Clayed sugar with its molasses "waste" product also gradually promoted another industrial task, rum distillation. These operations took much money and backbreaking labor.

At the start of every great fortune is a great theft, to paraphrase Balzac. He was not writing about sugar, but he might just as well have been, especially if political influence on concessions of island property is to be considered theft. We have already met such robber barons in earlier chapters, among them Houël; Poincy, who misappropriated Compagnie des Isles funds to establish sugar works; and the leader of the failed 1657 Compagnie de l'Amérique méridionale who appropriated company servants and provisions to establish a thriving sugar plantation.[80] Island officials took advantage of their positions to acquire the pick of newly arrived slaves at "bargain" prices. How else could Poincy have accumulated many hundred slaves, about 100 indentured servants, and three sugar works before his death?[81] Land stolen from the Caribs ended up planted with cane.

Later at Saint-Domingue, plunder from buccaneer raids, most especially the spectacular ones at Jamaica in 1694 and at Cartagena in 1697–98, fueled the transition from tobacco to indigo and sugar.[82] As noted in Chapter 8, du Casse and several lieutenants used their booty from the

Cartagena raid to buy land, slaves, and the technology necessary to produce sugar.[83] Pontchartrain's worries that the islands already produced excessive sugar were ignored, and rightly so.[84] If Labat can be believed, a hundredweight of muscavado brought only a little more than two l.t. in 1694, somewhat more than four l.t. in 1697, and twelve l.t. by 1701. Despite heightened duties, clayed sugar brought forty-four l.t. the hundredweight in 1700–1702. This rise in price was steep and stimulating to production. Muscavado, which was primarily produced at Saint-Domingue, fetched twelve to fourteen l.t. the hundredweight around 1701.[85] The last years of the seventeenth century witnessed dramatically rising prices for all types of sugar, which spurred the development of the eighteenth-century plantation complex.

No doubt some honest men and women were involved in this transformation, but their stories are mostly hidden to historians. Young men on the make who married widows/mistresses of habitations, a relatively common stepping stone to island fortunes, were an exception, discussed below. Labat notes that a French gentleman could always find an advantageous marriage at Saint-Domingue, whether to a widow or the daughter of a nouveau riche ex-freebooter.[86]

The list of Guadeloupe habitants in 1664, so expertly analyzed by the Rossignols, demonstrates that relatively few habitants had made the transition to sugar. They compared the names with a 1669 document identifying sugar planters. Of the 701 names on the first list, fewer than forty appear on the 1669 list. Who were these people? Many are not a surprise, starting with the Jesuits and Dominicans fathers who ran plantations in lieu of receiving tithes. They had all kinds of advantages—free land, royal subsidies, and exemptions from militia duty, from the capitation tax for themselves and their slaves, and from providing slave labor for public works (*corvées*) on fortifications and roads.[87] By 1669, they were producing between forty (the Jesuits) and seventy-two thousand pounds of sugar per annum. The current governor, du Lion, owned two plantations capable of making 112,000 pounds, and he co-owned another on Marie-Galante. Other sugar makers are described as councilors to the former co-proprietor, Boisseret. In the 1650s, Guadeloupe had benefited from the migration of Dutch and Portuguese Jewish planters from Brazil; by 1669, only one sugar maker is specifically so identified. Was Yzacq Duquerut a Portuguese Jew, a French Jew, or a Huguenot sugar maker, given that Isaac was such a popular name with both Jews and Huguenots? These sugar makers are described as "being capable" of producing amounts ranging from 20,000 to 140,000 pounds per annum.[88]

However the process occurred, the transition to sugar cultivation is best described as relentless. In 1661, Martinique and Guadeloupe each had a little fewer than seventy-five *sucreries;* ten years later, the figure had risen to over 100, out of some 1,100 habitations. This growth was facilitated by the import of some 1,200–1,300 slaves from Dutch Curaçao from June 1664 to April 1665, thus prior to the French West India Company making good its monopoly.[89] There were 172 sugar works in 1685, out of some 1,050 habitations. In 1664, at Martinique, 684 sugarcane planters possessed 2,750 slaves, with the twenty six who possessed over twenty slaves owning 880. It is safe to say each *sucrerie* had at least fifteen African slaves, and a very few had over fifty. These were still Lilliputian operations by the standards of a later era.

In 1671, at Guadeloupe proper, roughly 47 percent of property owners owned on average ten to eleven acres; the next 22 percent or so controlled on average thirty-one acres; the next 16 percent or so had on average sixty-four acres. These properties included uplands and ravines difficult to cultivate, and even the last group could not perhaps sustain sugar cultivation. These habitants concentrated on producing food, while some grew ginger, tobacco, and cotton. The next cohort, about 10 percent, controlled on average 143 acres; these were planters of sugarcane. Finally, the true kingpins were the approximately 5 percent who averaged 1,823 acres. These were relatives of the previous proprietors, refugees from Brazil, militia captains, and the religious orders such as the Jesuits and Dominicans. Island custom and then royal declarations exempted sovereign councilors, militia captains, and clergy from the capitation tax, a large advantage.[90] However, within this last category, three property owners stand out. Houël's concessions totaled the astounding figure of approximately 22,353 acres. Those of the former slave trader Carolof and the heirs of Boisseret each had about 16,099 acres. These three properties combined controlled nearly 47 percent of Guadeloupe proper.[91]

It is true that in those areas with easy access to port facilities, sugar production predominated in Guadeloupe. In global terms, almost 50 percent of cultivated land was devoted to sugarcane, with most of the rest in provision crops. In 1671, Guadeloupe had some 7,532 acres in sugarcane, compared to Martinique's 7,687.[92] Guadeloupe's handful of great proprietors may be designated as sugar barons, but the large majority of habitants were small farmers. In subsequent decades, Guadeloupe stagnated relative to Martinique.

By 1680, significant changes had occurred at Martinique. Reflecting the opening up of Capesterre, now there were 941 habitations, on which 6,279 slaves worked. Forty-eight sugar planters possessed over twenty slaves, with a total of 2,389, and thus an average of just over forty-eight apiece. Another seventy-three owned between eleven and twenty slaves apiece; their farms were perhaps small sugar operations, processing their sugarcane at a neighbor's mill or owning one jointly. A hundred or more slaves, the standard of the later plantation complex era, staffed only four or five plantations.[93] By 1700, Martinique boasted 242 sugar plantations, whereas Guadeloupe had 183.[94] Inasmuch as Guadeloupe had had 113 in 1669, the modest growth rate of sugar is apparent.

Many reasons explain why Guadeloupe lagged behind Martinique before 1700, but a major one was the need of many Guadeloupe planters to export their sugar through Saint-Pierre, Martinique, and to purchase European goods and African slaves there. Few ships sailed directly to Guadeloupe. Because of the absence of hard currency, first tobacco and then sugar served as the currency. Letters of credit based on sugar facilitated exchanges. Commissioners based on Saint-Pierre served as the essential links between French and foreign *armateurs* and the sugar planters. This dependence was somewhat mitigated by the ability of Guadeloupe habitants to engage in smuggling with their English, Dutch, and Danish neighbors to the northwest.

According to a 1683 memoir, the French Lesser Antilles produced some 25,000,000 pounds of sugar that year. In 1683, a rough estimate of sugar production in Barbados alone was about 30,000,000 pounds.[95] In 1700, according to a recent estimate, the French islands produced at most 10,000 tons or approximately 20,000,000 pounds, thus raising questions about the 1683 figure. On the other hand, the number of sugar works in the islands declined from 427 in 1687 to 338 in 1700.[96] Twenty million pounds in 1700 was only one-sixth of American production at that time, which suggests the magnitude of the change necessary before eighteenth-century French planters emerged as number one in sugar production.[97]

This gradual transition to sugar meant that some opportunities remained for the small farmer and skilled artisan, which helps explain why the white population of the islands increased slowly but gradually over these decades. In general, analysts of the question of why so many fewer

French than Spanish, Portuguese, and Englishmen migrated across the Atlantic justly concentrate on push factors or the lack of them. More than 400,000 English migrants left for America in the seventeenth century; 350,000 Spanish did so between 1561 and 1650; and 1.1 million Portuguese left for all overseas destinations between 1580 and 1761. In contrast, fewer than 100,000 French migrated to America in the seventeenth and eighteenth centuries.[98] French peasants had secure land tenures, with no fear of Enclosure Acts; they owned nearly half of all French land, and they had as an alternative to joblessness and famine employment in an ever-increasing royal army and navy. Underpopulated Spain across the Pyrenees was the real land of opportunity for artisans.

Colonists devoted few resources to public or private building. All profits beyond consumption were reinvested in the habitation and to acquire slaves who might generate future profits. The colonists' goals made this a rational decision. They had little of that sense of permanency and community that characterized contemporary New England or even Virginia, which at the end of the seventeenth century established the College of William & Mary. Although historians cannot determine mortality rates, plenty of anecdotal evidence points to a high one. Not a few colonists raced to keep ahead of the grim, sometimes marauding reaper and return in triumph to the healthier climate of the homeland. Hurricanes that could wipe out accumulated efforts overnight militated against investments in homes and churches. For example, the destruction at Martinique from a 1680 hurricane stupefied the new intendant Jean-Baptiste Patoulet.[99] That similar attitudes characterized English Caribbean colonists strongly favors the environmental explanation.[100] In this era, practically the only buildings made of stone were those of the religious orders, with their strong corporate sense of permanence.[101] The towns did not have much sense of civic pride. There were no schools, let alone universities, at a time when Massachusetts boasted Harvard, and Spanish colonial cities had much older colleges.

Given the shortage of capital, the only way for a habitant to prosper was to live constantly on credit and to be constantly in debt. Habitations were almost always bought on credit, and the price of land stayed high, because sellers knew the risk of debtors not being able to pay.[102] Colonial life was not for the timid. The desire to make a fortune as quickly as possible, without worrying about the instruments of doing so, notably the conditions of indentured servants and slaves, is understandable, if not excusable.

Impact of Royal Sovereignty and Royal Wars
from the 1660s to the 1690s

The reasons for the French crown's interest in asserting control over its tropical colonies, whether through a chartered company like the Compagnie des Indes occidentales or direct royal administration (after 1674), were rather straightforward: to strip the Dutch of their trade dominance and channel the islands' produce to France; to make the colonies more dependable in the event of war; and to introduce a more orderly, polished way of life there. Colbert was convinced that only good policing would stabilize these colonies for long-term growth. To accomplish these goals, the crown had the right, no, the moral duty, to intervene in the most minute aspects of everyday life.

To impose its will, the crown possessed many tools, especially after 1674, when the colonies became part of the royal domain. The king had already dispatched a lieutenant general to watch over the islands during the tenure of the Compagnie des Indes occidentales, but after the Dutch War, royal officials attempted to dominate island life. The governor-general had the greatest responsibility for providing external and internal security, but without having sufficient royal troops at his disposal, which meant that he always had to consult island officials and powerful planters. Until 1713, the governor-general and the intendant stationed at Martinique had the impossible task of governing the faraway islands of Cayenne and Saint-Domingue, a situation partially rectified in 1713, when the latter received an independent governing team.

As already briefly discussed, the intendant had control over judicial and financial affairs and supervised the sovereign councils in their registering of royal laws and implementing local regulations. The intendant oversaw the work of his lieutenants (called *commissaires ordonnateurs*) stationed at Cayenne, Guadeloupe, and Saint-Domingue. Upon direct royal control, in 1675, Louis confirmed the existence of the sovereign council at Martinique and regularized the offices attached to it. These included an attorney general, as well as the usual accompanying officials, such as registrars, financial officers, and sergeants. Besides paid officials, the council included several island notables, rich planter favorites of the royal administrators. These often were militia officers or captains in the *quartiers*. In return for their unpaid work, these councilors acquired a number of privileges (most important, they paid no capitation tax on twelve slaves or servants) and, of course, prestige. Even islanders somewhat adrift from metropolitan norms prized hierarchy and the accompanying deference. Although the king appointed local judges, the sovereign councils acted as the judge of last resort, issued orders (*réglements*) implementing royal laws, saw to domestic security, and advised the governor-general and intendant. Their advice did not have to be accepted, but island administrators took it seriously.

On a theoretical or legal level, colonial sovereign councils had little independence. Determined to prevent the appearance of bodies analogous to French *parlements*, the government made certain that councilors held their seats at the king's will; they did not purchase these offices, as was the case with their metropolitan counterparts. Given the privileges and status attached to them, these seats were sought after, and therefore a potent means of controlling the elite. Nevertheless, the council could effectively veto royal measures by failing to implement them or dragging their feet. Dictated changes in long-standing island custom provoked resistance. Versailles knew that the crown needed to consult important subjects' interests if obedience was expected. In its distant colonies, inhabited by men desperate to succeed, French absolutism proceeded by bluff and accommodation even more so than in France.[103]

From 1684 on, the king sent companies of troops to the islands, the *troupes de la marine* (marines, but not much leather in these necks). Regular garrisons were very few in this period, and the king was unable to maintain naval forces in the islands for any length of time. Although the "showing of the colors" may have impressed some colonists, island officials did not have reliable military force to impose their will, should they have been so inclined. They well knew that in time of war (or in case of internal rebellions) the colony's safety depended on a militia officered by prominent habitants, not on small numbers of chronically unpaid and underfed royal troops who were subject to frequent beatings.[104] Compromise, conciliation, and cooperation with the colonists thus constituted the obvious course. For example, the king reminded Blénac in 1681 to drill the militia, but not to imprison absentees.

By their actions, island officials displayed their dismay at the excesses and permissive character of colonial life. Starting with Tracy, they attempted to restrict such "disorders" and "irregularities" as taverns and slave markets operating on Sunday during church services; or in the case of slave markets, operating at all, for how did bondsmen acquire these goods? In law, all goods belonged to masters. In 1670, de Baas decreed that only gentlemen and the king's officers could wear swords and carry arms; all other free men could only do so when on militia duty or when hunting *marrons*. The effectiveness of this measure is unclear.[105]

Officials restricted Huguenots from open worship, Jews from working their slaves on Sunday and holy days, and slaves from carrying "offensive" weapons without written permission from their owners. Other minute restrictions of island life were attempted, all in the name of establishing good order. In 1688, the Saint-Domingue council lamented that ordinary habitants, described as "libertines," showed "disdain" for the king's edicts.[106] In 1669, de Baas issued orders to enforce closing of taverns and Negro markets during Sunday services. He complained about public blaspheming, tolerance of prostitutes, and masters and commanders "abusing" female slaves.[107] Such efforts to impose order were the impetus behind the famous *Code noir* of 1685. Informed by memoranda from Patoulet, who in turn consulted island customs, precedents, and interests, this code mainly dealt with the regulation of slavery, but also confirmed the expulsion of the islands' Jews and imposed further restrictions on Huguenots.[108]

Sovereign councils frequently expressed concern about free but poor islanders. In 1671, for example, the Martinique council condemned all "vagabonds" to indentured servitude. Upper-class councilors complained about the libertine conduct of so many young people. As an example, it condemned to servitude two young men who twice were caught engaging in "infamous and illegal acts"—a rare reference to homosexual conduct in the records.[109]

De Baas passed three ordinances in 1671 about the proper fabrication of indigo, sugar, and tobacco, and to eliminate fraudulent practices, such as packing inferior sugar in the middle of the barrel or inferior tobacco leaf in the center of the roll. These ordinances minutely detailed how colonial produce should be produced and processed. At a time when only *sucre brut* was made at Martinique, de Baas promoted superior white sugar (*cassonade blanc*) as made in Brazil. De Baas had the council elect experts among merchants and habitants to inspect produce at the royal weighing stations and to confiscate substandard goods.

State policies to curtail libertinage were only modestly successful. Royal officials recognized that regulation by fiat or excessive favoring of metropolitan over colonial interests could push habitants to leave for neighboring islands. At first, the Revocation of the Edict of Nantes in 1685 was not rigorously enforced, out of fear that affected Huguenots would leave for neighboring Protestant islands.[110] As late as 1692, Pont-chartrain *père* advised Saint-Domingue's Governor du Casse to avoid excessive harshness toward these dissenters.[111] Versailles worried that coercive approaches would make the habitants less willing to defend their islands. Because Louis could not send significant forces to support the colonies during the Dutch War and, especially, during the nearly disastrous Nine Years' War, colonial militias constituted the chief defense. Paris officialdom believed that colonists had made an enormous sacrifice by leaving France, and that they should therefore be coddled a bit. Royal officials thus never had the stomach to wield a heavy hand against colonists who manifested "don't tread on me" attitudes.

To put a more positive spin on royal policy, the king and Colbert consistently instructed the general administrators to pursue a policy of firm, fair justice toward all habitants and to treat them with kindness (*douceur*), as long as they demonstrated respect for and obedience to the king. Only that would attract and hold colonists in the islands. The administrators were to be especially concerned that island officials and militia captains "not vex [habitants] under any pretext" and allow them liberty to complain to the administrators and even to the king. The administrators were also to prevent the "vexations that the rich normally visit on the poor."[112] Overzealous officials were not to tamper with freedom of commercial exchanges. Royal naval captains were not permitted to force habitants to serve as sailors, no matter their need for manpower. The king determined to halt the island custom of particular governors and militia captains dispensing justice to habitants. Martial law was no longer justifiable. Blénac himself was not to arrest any habitant arbitrarily, except in the rare case of treason.[113]

So how did the crown take small steps toward effective control? Foreign military incursions (e.g., Martinique in 1674; Cayenne, 1667 and 1676; Saint-Christophe, 1690; Guadeloupe, 1692; Saint-Domingue, 1691 and 1695) demonstrated the insecurity of the American Tropics. Some colonists responded with a patriotism mingled with fear of the burning of their habitations and looting of their slaves. That their king was the most powerful in Europe must have given colonists a sense of security, even though his ships and troops were only occasionally of assistance. Beyond these war-related issues, colonists were not always united in opposition to royal regulation; they were divided by provincial origin and, increasingly, by gaps between rich planters and artisans, shopkeepers, provisions farmers, and day laborers.

Royal influence also slowly increased because the court accommo-
dated the interests of habitants, especially the wealthier ones, as much as
was thought possible, given often-conflicting metropolitan interests. After Colbert's death, Seignelay forcibly dispatched galley slaves, recalcitrant Huguenots, and other social "scum" to the Caribbean. These actions reflected Louis XIV's hardening attitude to religious and social
"misfits." Some 20 percent of migrants from the Angoumois region were
kidnapped from Huguenot parents and forcibly exiled to America.[114]
However, after protest from colonial officials and habitants alike, the
government had backed away from these counterproductive policies by
the end of the 1680s. To further exemplify royal paternalism, in 1687,
the king mandated that island governors review the militia every two
months, but that officials travel to the *quartiers* instead of having "busy"
colonists assemble at one central point.[115]

An important example of the dynamics of the royal-colonial relationship concerns the island custom of preventing creditors from seizing land, beasts, and slaves. Tracy and de Baas had both permitted creditors to seize slaves and beasts of burden. However, Blénac argued
successfully in 1678 that slaves and sugar works be treated as animals
were in France, otherwise the colonies would perish. The next year, a
royal ordinance prevented the tax farmer Oudiette from seizing these essential plantation assets.[116] In 1681, the king reiterated that slaves could
never be seized, "in the same way that beasts cannot be seized in my kingdom."[117] But then article 44 of the *Code noir* allowed creditors to take
slaves as "moveable" property. Two years later, presumably because of
protests, the king declared that article 44 was not applicable to wills
recorded before 1685.[118]

Employing a variety of tactics, therefore, royal authority gradually
increased, especially at the older Lesser Antilles settlements; the story
was different at the freebooter stronghold of Saint-Domingue. After
1678 and before 1683, attempts were made to rein in these ruffians, although the tobacco farm heavily damaged the habitants' ability to prosper. The renewal of war with Spain opened the floodgates once again,
and the likes of Grammont and Graffe sailed to the Spanish Main. With
the Truce of Ratisbon in late 1684, the king wished to end the giving of
freebooter commissions and threatened to fire those officials who gave
them. However, Spain's participation in the anti-French defensive alliance of the League of Augsburg (1686) once again changed the dynamics in the western Caribbean.

Neither Versailles nor colonial officials could depend on a highly structured Catholic Church to help enforce obedience in the islands. Unlike New France, the French Caribbean was not "blessed" with a bishop's presence. The regular clergy—Jesuits, Dominicans, Capuchins, and Carmelites—were not simple pawns of the establishment. They could and did appeal orders to powerful people in France and Rome. In any case, the clergy had their hands full with often unruly parishioners. The Capuchins especially, because they did not accumulate land, slaves, and sugar mills, had a difficult time of it. Things reached such a low point in the later 1680s that Seignelay ordered the governor of Saint-Domingue to select one habitant from each parish to assure support for them. The fathers had been reduced to cassava cakes and water.[119] The sovereign council in Saint-Domingue condemned "contemptuous" disobedience to the clergy and "flagrant" blasphemies; even if exaggerated, the order suggests at minimum the regularity of petty disobedience and blasphemy.[120]

Shortages of personnel plagued efforts to bring the "true religion" to a motley population of lukewarm Catholics, recalcitrant Huguenots and foreign Protestants, a few Jews, a small number of free mulattoes, and a mass of slaves who were normally baptized but uncomprehending of Christian mysteries. Labat mentions that of 690 slaves in his parish, 64 were communicants, that is, instructed Christians able to take communion; 568 had received baptism alone, and 58 (presumably newcomers) had not.[121] In 1685, a total of fifty-nine religious serviced a population of roughly 44,570 habitants in all French tropical America.[122] Even if the clerics performed their functions responsibly, which colonial officials disputed, each priest averaged 755 clients, in societies with little concentration of population and in topographies posing substantial impediments to travel. The situation worsened after 1691, when yellow fever took a toll on clerical numbers.[123] For example, the Dominican superior general died, and so did many of his colleagues.[124]

Some priests were most interested in promoting their order's economic interest, in obtaining influence at the highest level of local government, and in living as well as possible in the tropics. One such was Father Labat, who lived in the islands between 1695 and 1705. A true Renaissance polymath acquainted with all the sciences, he was determined "to be of some utility to my nation." Island officials found him very useful in strengthening fortifications, for example. During the English invasion of Guadeloupe in 1703, this priest directed cannon fire from the fort at Basse-Terre.[125] "Utility to my nation" is a reminder that he lived on the cusp of the Enlightenment (but only on the cusp: he believed in and feared sorcerers among his African slaves).[126] His pragmatism, versatility, and skepticism of received wisdom and certitude in the superiority of European civilization remind one of his contemporaries John Locke and the creator of Robinson Crusoe, Daniel Defoe.

Fortunately, the gourmand Dominican did not share some Protestants' ambivalence toward pleasures of the palate. He recounts in detail the fruits of his garden and his omnivorous experiments with island flora and fauna. He declares that snakes, monkeys, and fried bananas make excellent fare.[127] He found the Carib method of barbequing fowl by throwing the bird whole into the fire succulent, because it preserved the juices (*jus*).[128] His freebooter friends knew how to please him with cheeses, wines, and the like for serving as their confessor. Patriot that he was, Labat no doubt let them off with a few Hail Marys and a "Bon appétit!"[129]

Labat proposed mercantilist prescriptions for island and imperial growth. He chastised both "lazy," irrational habitants who wasted golden opportunities and metropolitan merchants whose cheating led to retribution by colonists. Each side felt justified in perpetuating fraud. Labat accepted the role of the government in adjudicating such quarrels and proposing top-down reforms. He enthusiastically praised Colbert, "that incomparable minister."[130] Labat's books are a primer on how colonists could improve their lot. He advocated that colonists plant cacao trees, whose chocolate would not only reduce French imports but also promote sugar production, which would in turn promote the French slave trade. The king's revenues would grow at every step in the process.[131] Labat could not imagine why the poorer parts of France did not adopt the nutritious American potato.[132]

Like Colbert, the conventional Catholic Labat valued a person's usefulness more than the character of his religious beliefs. He tells the reader about his determination to hire a skilled Lutheran refiner from Hamburg despite his superior's opposition. Labat wryly comments that he was "indifferent that the resulting sugar be either Lutheran or Catholic, as long as it was very white."[133] In a visit to Danish Saint Thomas, he encountered some refugee French Huguenots. The difference in religion, he opines, did not prevent their hearts from being French.[134] He describes in some detail his amicable relations with his rich, Huguenot neighbor at Guadeloupe, who had encountered persecution from Labat's predecessor. The Huguenot behaved properly, including bringing his slaves to Catholic services. Labat suggests that a good example and charity were the best tools of evangelization. In turn, his neighbor deeded him land to increase his homestead. From these sentiments, one may surmise that Labat's attitude toward the Revocation of the Edict of Nantes was lukewarm.

Labat's tolerance of Protestant neighbors did not apply to the English. During his stay overseas, France fought its ancient enemy for about seven years. He rails against English treatment of Island Caribs and of their African slaves. He did admire the English for their commercial and industrial virtues; for example, they made a superior muscavado. However, his vitriol usually prevailed. Discussing the eating habits of sharks, he claims they always preferred fish to humans, but if they attacked people, they preferred blacks to whites, and then, among Europeans, English to French. He hypothesizes that humans with the strongest scent attracted them first, and that Britons' diet, rich in red meat, accounted for their more alluring smell to sharks.[135]

At Guadeloupe, Labat's neighbors treated him very generously and with respect. They helped him with his garden and gave him chickens and other small gifts. They agreed to pay for an extension of the church. When his superiors appointed him Dominican superior at Martinique in 1704, however, Labat expressed regret and concern. He regarded the people of Martinique as "libertines" who reacted badly if a cleric chastised their bad behavior.[136]

In his book *In Search of Empire: The French in the Americas, 1670–1730* (2004), James Pritchard launches scathing attacks on the proposition that Colbertism had any positive impact on colonial population growth, social formation, and economic growth. Touché Father Labat. Aspects of Pritchard's argument are useful correctives to some previous overly laudatory accounts. However, he swings the pendulum too far in the anti-statist direction. He notes, for example, that the government could not prevent the return of emigrants to France. True enough, but the ministers understood that if the colonies acquired the reputation of being prisons, long-term growth would be seriously impeded. The French crown's unwillingness or inability to employ coercion against the habitants (with the notable exceptions of Jews and Huguenots and the unfortunate brief experiment of transporting *forçats* in the 1680s) promoted their loyalty to the king. Just as important, even if motivated by shortage of adequate tools of coercion, the king's willingness to allow the colonists to live without *taille* and tithe, salt taxes and personal *corvées*, inheritance taxes and prohibitions of hunting and fishing—in short without all the grievous and annoying encumbrances of France—must have been a stimulant for habitants to settle permanently, marry, and pass on the fruits of their labors to their children. Only someone with ideological blinders can fail to recognize that Louis XIV intended to be a father to his faithful, that is, Catholic, colonial subjects; or that the supremely pragmatic Colbert did not always prefer metropolitan to colonial interests or pursue policies that colonial elites could not stomach.

Becoming Creoles

Despite sketchy statistics, which in 1696 drew royal disapproval of the failure to maintain baptismal, marital, and death records, some generalizations about island peoples may be offered here. First, the diversity of the European population was remarkable. The Rossignols' population list of 1664 contains Flemish, English (at least four), Portuguese, Savoyards, Italians, Germans, and two dozen Irishmen. The European population increased slowly overall, with Saint-Domingue having the quickest development, because of its attractiveness to small farmers and adventurers. Martinique saw its white population double.[137] Although migration from France was probably largely responsible for the increases, in the older colonies, a more settled, family-oriented life became prevalent. Saint-Domingue remained the quintessential frontier colony of young, mobile men, with only a scattering of women. In 1680, women constituted 10 percent of the population, and twenty years later, 20.9 percent.[138]

Significant numbers of non-Catholics lived in the islands. At least seven heads of household with a total of twenty-three persons at Martinique were Jews. At least 22 percent of all sugar planters were Protestants, primarily French and Dutch.[139] Until 1682, Jews had free exercise of religion, but Huguenots did not. The latter's repeated efforts to get permission for civil marriage were consistently rebuffed; their only alternatives were to return to France to get married, or formally convert to Catholicism.[140]

In these decades, free people or indentured servants coming from France were primarily single males. Even though the indentured servant system had gained notoriety in France, the 1660s were years of significant departures for tropical America, as indeed they were for freemen. The Compagnie des Indes occidentales encouraged both types of migration. Especially effective was the loan of passage fees, to be repaid with the harvesting of the first crop. The number of under-age indentured servants shipped during this decade led the king to try to enforce a minimum age of eighteen.

After 1660, the islands' population became more female and younger. At Martinique, in 1660, males capable of fighting constituted 58 percent of the population, and 77 percent of the male segment. By 1685, such men constituted just 34 percent of a population that had doubled, and 60 percent of the male population. This trend continued through the eighteenth century.[141]

Whether free or servant, those who survived the "seasoning" period and who established a respectable habitation were then able to acquire wives, either on the spot or in France. Among the list of habitants at Guadeloupe in 1664, men identified as carpenters, tailors, surgeons, barrel makers, tobacco rollers, and fisherman were not rare, and were probably former indentured servants.[142] At Martinique, at least, growth of nuclear families and thus the creolization of the population characterized the decades between 1660 and 1700. Léo Elisabeth demonstrates that in 1664, children constituted 24.7 percent of the white population; in 1680, that figure rose to 35.5, and in 1694 to 40.9. The latter figure was the highest percentage of any year down to 1826.[143] Jacques Petitjean Roget has shown that 271 husbands, wives, and children lived on 100 Martinique habitations in 1660. In 1684, that number had jumped to 366. Overall, about 57 percent of free men supported families in 1665, compared to 73 percent in 1680. The number of children per household increased from an average of 1.74 in 1665 to 2.01 in 1680. These averages are skewed because 28 percent of households were without children. The percentage of bachelor habitants, in 1664 more than a third in the older sections of Martinique and over a half in newly exploited Capesterre, fell markedly by 1680, to about a quarter in both areas. Meanwhile, the number of unrelated whites on those habitations had fallen from 113 to 90, whereas the number of slaves more than doubled, from 431 to 965.[144]

Overall, "white" society at Martinique was only modestly reproducing itself by 1680, because of the percentage of bachelors, small family size, and some migration of poorer whites. More than 80 percent of families had from one to four children, and families with just one or two constituted more than 50 percent in both the 1664 and 1680 censuses. In 1680, families averaged 2.77 children.[145] There was indeed a slight increase in family size between these years, but less than one might expect. Multiple factors were at work, including high mortality rates for both adults and children, more similar to the rates for European commoners than for continental North America. Fully 43 percent of masters living in 1664 had either died or left Martinique by 1680. Martinique was a society with rapid turnover and more opportunity for success or failure than in France. Nevertheless, the successful habitants in established areas grew relatively older, because their average age increased from 38 to 43; those in the newer areas averaged about four years younger in 1664, but the average in 1680 was only about a year younger.[146]

Looking at white population structure and trends to 1700, a few further observations are useful. Except at Saint-Domingue, women reached near parity with men by 1690. In the 1680s, more than 600 women from French poorhouses (*hôpitaux*) had been sent to the islands.[147] Next, there were roughly twice as many children as women by the 1680s. Of course, not all women were married, so the number of children in married households was more than two. For example, at Saint-Barthélemy in 1681, married women averaged 3.2 children.[148] In a sample of Martinique parishes, Elisabeth finds that Creole women born between 1645 and 1670, married before 1691, and living into their fifties averaged seven children.[149] In a survey of two parishes between 1660 and 1709, he finds an average of four children for married women. These numbers are low compared to those of New France or New England, but they were close to the norm of rural Europe.[150]

Saint-Domingue remained a male-dominated society. In 1681, only 435 free women were available for 1,421 "heads of households" and some 2,000 free and indentured servants, the large majority of them male.[151] True to Saint-Domingue's frontier character, the old practice of *matelotage* remained more vigorous there than elsewhere. One such was the sieur de Gallison, *matelot* and heir of the former governor Pouançay. By 1685, the wealthy Gallison had been named to the superior council.[152]

Just as in the frontier period, habitants lived isolated on their farms. Nevertheless as the population grew, as more wealth was accumulated, and as more families took root, the desire for imported goods naturally increased. So did the size and, more important, the functions of towns. Louis's wars increased the need for better, stone fortifications.[153] To dispense justice, the king sent out governors, intendants, lieutenants, and judges, who established themselves in the *bourgs*—in the case of Martinique at Fort Royal, the locus of royal government, although Saint-

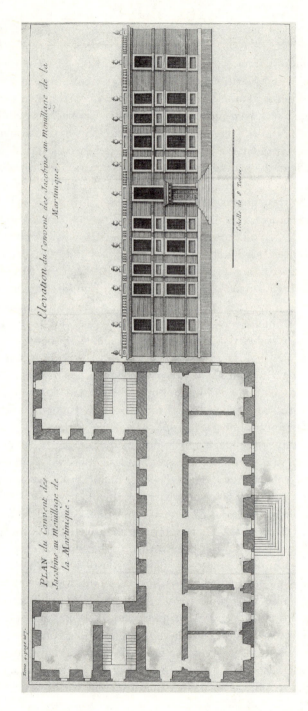

Plan of the Convent des Jacobins on Martinique.

Pierre remained overwhelmingly the commercial capital, its easily accessible roadstead being ideal for smuggling. Illegal commerce occurred in all Martinique ports except Fort Royal.[154]

The missionary orders were based in the towns, especially the Jesuits and the Dominicans, who must have been galled at having such a high percentage of Huguenots as their neighbors; in Basse-Terre, Guadeloupe, some 20 percent of the population in 1671 were Huguenots, as compared to 7 percent on the island overall. French and foreign Calvinists controlled one-third of the sugar works.[155] Commercial agents of chartered companies, as well as those of private firms, established warehouses for storage of colonial products they exchanged for European commodities. At Basse-Terre, Guadeloupe, in 1671, there were a hundred merchants, sixty-five artisans, and apprentices living in these *magasins*. Rounding out this picture were the inevitable taverns to accommodate transient sailors, indentured servants, and the few free blacks. Some towns became noted for specialized functions. For example, there were some 2,000 corsairs among Saint-Pierre's population of about 5,000.[156]

Former indentured servants who acquired skills could establish themselves in these small colonial towns. Because habitants had barely begun the practice of training slaves to be coopers, masons, carpenters, tobacco spinners, sugar boilers, and surgeons, the service of such artisans was in high demand. Labat repeatedly complains about their "arrogance," presumably the result of their ability to command high wages. They had the right to squat on crown land fifty paces along the coast, as long as they accepted that they would have to leave if the monarch needed it.[157]

As these colonial societies matured, it is not surprising that transatlantic trading links became denser. The habitants themselves procured commodities for resale on return visits to France. They continued to associate with metropolitan merchants. In return for credit, habitants sent colonial produce to their partners, which then allowed for further advances. For example, in 1673, Jacques Yvon, sieur de Landes, a habitant of Saint-Domingue and companion of d'Ogeron's, signed a contract with a merchant of Nantes, Hubert Antheaume. The latter agreed to send indentured servants and commodities (brandy, wine, textiles, butter, and wheat) to Yvon for sale on the island. After Antheaume recovered the capital advanced, the two were to split profits or losses. That Yvon established the first sugar works at Saint-Domingue around 1680 suggests the profits were far greater than the losses. As he prospered,

Yvon moved seamlessly from commerce to the life of a planter and king's official. He became the king's lieutenant at Léogane. Gabriel Debien, who traces the ascent of Yvon, believes that almost all colonial fortunes were accumulated either in this way or by freebooting or marrying a rich widow (as did Yvon), and not by habitants patiently plowing back their small annual profits into their farms.[158]

The historian Anne Perotin-Dumon has provided a remarkable portrait of Basse-Terre, Guadeloupe, in this period. She traces the strong links between sugar refiners and factors in this tiny *bourg* (320 people in the 1670s) and Huguenot firms in La Rochelle, which in turn had links with Amsterdam. This Protestant mercantile international was not put out of business by Colbert's anti-Dutch policy, because ships of the Compagnie des Indes occidentales only rarely appeared at Guadeloupe. Planters of Guadeloupe and Marie-Galante looked to Dutch Saint Eustatius for slaves and goods. Governor du Lion, who accused de Baas of illicit commerce, stocked his plantations with slaves bought from the Dutch. Habitants' wants now included salt beef, lard, salt fish, wheat, olive oil, wax candles, soap, tools for making sugar and manioc, cloth, hats, ribbons, paper and pens and, *bien sûr*, copious amounts of wine and brandy.[159]

This snapshot of rural and urban island life presents a picture not startlingly different from the demographic situation in France, with one major exception—women. Demographic equilibrium as a result of large numbers of single people (both male and female), of high mortality rates due to disease, and of a low average number of children per family also characterized seventeenth-century French society. Dutertre writes with sadness that so many young children became languid, yellow-tinted, and then died.[160] No doubt a man might get richer in the islands than by farming in the cold climates of New England or the Saint Lawrence valley, but the chance of reproducing himself and enjoying the fruits of his work in old age surrounded by wife, children, and grandchildren were much less.

Exceptions to the rule were not rare, perhaps most famously Sieur Guillaume Dorange. Thanks to Labat, the life of Pierre du Buc can be sketched. After killing a gentleman, he was able to skip from France to the Antilles. He gained the trust of d'Esnambuc at Saint-Christophe and accompanied du Parquet to Martinique after 1635. He distinguished himself in skirmishes against the Caribs and eventually established himself on former Carib lands at the Bay of Trinity. He became one of the first *sucriers* in that area. Du Buc fought and suffered wounds in the war of 1666–67. Although he must have been in his seventies, he fought against the English at Guadeloupe and Martinique in the early 1690s. Louis XIV ennobled him in 1701. He left forty-two children and grand-children.[161]

Dysentery was a persistent killer. Labat almost died of it in 1699.[162] Scientists today distinguish between epidemic dysentery and the less dangerous endemic form. It is impossible to specify what forms were present then. The organisms responsible for epidemic dysentery pass from person to person, or via food and water. Bloody diarrhea is the most obvious symptom, along with fevers and abdominal cramps. Today, 10 to 20 percent of attacked individuals in poor countries die, especially children under two, elderly people, and those suffering from malnutrition.[163] Other diseases that afflicted tropical colonists included worms, smallpox, and venereal disease. In 1699, for example, smallpox killed many slaves, and in the previous year many white women.[164]

The disease environment worsened after 1690 with the introduction of yellow fever, which the bite of the *Aedes aegyptus* mosquito transmits to humans. After five days of incubation, the fever causes violent head and body aches, along with digestive hemorrhaging. In that era, death or recovery occurred after about eight days. Yellow fever may have appeared at Guadeloupe before 1650.[165] Labat says that the disease ravaged the islands for eight years, and discusses how it devastated swampy Léogane in Saint-Domingue. When he got it, the constant vomiting made it impossible for him even to take communion; he almost died of it in 1697. He notes that Creoles were almost never made sick by it.[166]

Prudence cautions that myths about the islands as a paradise for (European) women be treated with skepticism.[167] Island males, no matter how liberated from many traditional beliefs, did not abandon the patriarchal views of old France. That is, God created woman as inferior to man; the passions not reason dominate women's nature, opposite to the male; therefore, women cannot control their sexual urges, particularly after they had tasted that fruit in marriage; and masterless women threaten good order.[168] Beyond these beliefs, frontier insecurities had produced a society that emphasized military readiness, not therefore the type of society conducive to female equality. The exceptionally misogynist de Baas complained to Colbert that women made the colonists soft, and these "demons" badgered men to return to France.[169] Duter-

tre blames the Martinique tumults of 1665 on island women infuriated
that the new Compagnie des Indes occidentales had not stocked fancy
goods.[170]

Free Caribbean women nevertheless led better lives than their sisters
in France, far too many of whom struggled desperately to gain their daily
crust of bread, and so many of whom were confined to the drudgery of
domestic servitude, or, worse, ended up as prostitutes or confined in
poorhouses. By far the largest number of abandoned babies were female.
Old age held terrors for women without independent means—the great
majority—and charges of witchcraft plagued old "crones."[171] Women in
general had greater opportunities to achieve a decent existence in the islands than they did in France.

The ratio between the sexes gradually improved over the century. As
always, the figures for Martinique are best documented. In 1660, white
women composed only 22 percent of the population. By 1671, that figure had risen to one-third. By the early 1680s, almost 40 percent of the
population was female; by 1697, that had reached 47 percent and thus
rough gender equivalence.[172] At Saint-Barthélemy, in 1671, men outnumbered women by 161 to 129.[173] The occasional female indentured
servant did not remain celibate very long, given these ratios. A few men
married black and mulatto women, for example, Jean Salomon of Guadeloupe, whose widow, Marie, is described as a *mulatresse*.[174] Most white
women were sooner or later married to masters of habitations or, if widowed, owners themselves.[175]

Unlike France, the islands were a sellers' market for women and apparently contained few unmarried adult women. Convent life was not an
option. Michel Houël, who lived with his wife, a daughter aged eight
from a first marriage, and a daughter aged seven from his current wife,
must be considered a fortunate man.[176] Satisfying the sexual needs of
men was not the most important consideration, as modern readers might
think. As important was the need to have legitimate heirs to whom to
pass on one's hard-earned earthly goods. The relative shortage of women
led to the islands' version of the charivari, or shivaree, mock serenading
of newly married couples. The sovereign council at Martinique in 1683
formally banned such attempts to humiliate older, wealthier men marrying the cream of the crop of younger women.[177]

Who were these island women? Although some were Creoles in the
1660s, a majority came from the commoner classes of the homeland. At
Martinique, married women on average were younger than their spouses

by some nine years, unusual by seventeenth-century standards among commoners.[178] In the 1664 census, they averaged thirty years of age, and in that of 1680, thirty-four. However, a number of well-off widows wed younger men and, in three Martinique cases, males more than twenty years younger. If most island women were originally poor, they were most certainly not all women of ill repute as metropolitan legend claimed. In fact, women of loose morals, and in four cases their pimp husbands, were unceremoniously returned to France.[179]

Few of the 965 women at Martinique in 1680 had arrived on organized convoys from France, although about 100 were shipped in 1665 and 1667 to women-starved Cayenne and Saint-Domingue.[180] After the Dutch War, Colbert did dispatch some respectable young women from the *hôpitaux* with some initial success. French opinion stubbornly held that these were prostitutes, and the king had to reprimand a bishop who requested that the prostitutes in his diocese be shipped to the islands.[181] In 1685, Blénac complained to Seignelay that recently arrived young women "were extremely ugly, many among them were debauched, and others ruined, so that the planters and soldiers . . . do not want to marry them."[182] He insisted that there were enough Creole females at Martinique to satisfy demand, an assertion supported by census figures.[183]

As in France, blended families were numerous, and for the same reasons. Death, not divorce, was the chief culprit in that era. For example, the Irishman Jacques Galgan lived in Guadeloupe with his wife Helène Destriches, her daughter aged six, and their two-year-old daughter.[184] Single parents simply did not have the resources to raise children alone, and the isolation of the habitations must have been a strong force promoting remarriage.

Another example of blended families and multiple marriages is Marie Anne Dieulevant. Born in France in 1654, she first married a long-settled habitant at Saint-Domingue, a militia captain and presumably well-off planter. They had one daughter. After his death in 1690, Marie Anne married again, resulting in the birth of a son. After that husband's death, she married the ex-freebooter Laurent de Graffe, with whom she had a daughter. According to legend, the now wealthy Marie Anne had had a quarrel with Graffe and showed up at his plantation pistol in hand. The aging Graffe demonstrated that he had not lost his famous bravado by telling her to pull the trigger. He impulsively asked for her hand and, supposedly, the marital contract was drawn up on the spot. This acquisition was far more valuable to the buccaneer captain than any previous conquest. To be sure, his marital bliss must be deemed problematical, because Marie Anne's temper was renowned.[185]

Although biographical information is rare, it is apparent that free women led active, involved lives on the habitations. They were neither the plantation mistress of later stereotype nor submissive, humble help-mates of male desires. They had to be strong to survive and prosper in a difficult environment. Portrayals of upper-class French colonial women that emphasized physical fragility and the need to be guarded against the hazards of plantation life—the sun, disease, and black male lust, whether real or imagined—lay in the distant future.

Women who survived their husbands, a frequent occurrence given the age differential, normally inherited a habitation. For example, at Gua-deloupe in 1664, the widow of Jean Dupré lived in a *case* with two men, the wife of one of them, and two children, one of whom was her daugh-ter, whose marriage record has been identified.[186] Suitors eager for a head start or who wanted to round out their own possessions besieged better-off, younger widows. Labat laughs heartily at a man who married a rich widow and now haughtily drove about in a carriage. Three years earlier, he had been a cooper on a merchant vessel. Not all widows re-married, but given the need to manage a labor force consisting of in-dentured servants and African slaves, a second marriage was a likely choice. On Saint-Barthélemy in 1681, of fifty-nine women living with children, fifty seven were married, with only two widows, a ratio very un-like that in contemporary France.[187]

Some island women married a number of times. Take the case of Madeleine Garet, born in 1637. At eighteen, she married a Martinique habitant eleven years older than she was and gave him two children. By 1664, they had a modest *place* with two *engagés* and one mulatto and three African slaves, a rather typical spread of that era. Widowed, she appar-ently remarried a prosperous man, because at his death she owned a 250-acre habitation planted with sugarcane. This estate brought her some 5,000 l.t. annually. She remarried again, this time a man five years older, with whom she had a child. Although a man of small means, his lucky catch allowed him to end his life as a militia lieutenant and as warden of his parish church. This husband also having died, Madeleine remained a widow until her death in 1728 at the amazing age of ninety-one.[188] For her at least, the islands were frontiers of fortune.

Perhaps because widows either remarried quickly or had adequate means to remain single, the curse of poor widows in France being suspected or accused of witchcraft was apparently absent.[189] Also rare or absent were the busybody clerics and lawyers so involved with the blight of European witch hunts. Dutertre does relate the story of one such trial at Martinique, for which he blamed an Italian agent provocateur. He adds that public opinion blamed judicial authorities for allowing the proceedings against the unfortunate woman to go forward.[190]

By the end of the seventeenth century, better-off Creole girls had the opportunity of acquiring an education. Under the tutelage of Jesuits, the Ursuline nuns established a convent school at Saint-Pierre, where, for a dowry of 4,000 to 5,000 francs, rich families could give their daughters a "proper," metropolitan type of education and protect them from libertines.[191]

Habitants faced enormous difficulties in achieving a rapid accumulation of funds before returning home in triumph. Given the dangers and hardships they had to face, probably only a minority of habitants prospered and passed on substantial property to their heirs.[192] Nevertheless, whatever their condition, the few rich *grands blancs* and the struggling *petits blancs* alike all lived better than indentured servants and slaves, the focus of the next chapter.

CHAPTER TEN

Island Society from the 1660s to the 1690s
The World of Coerced Labor

Indentured servants, the dominant European element before 1664, diminished gradually in importance thereafter; especially on those Windward Islands moving toward the wealthier man's crops—indigo, cotton, and sugar. The picture is clear at Martinique, where the number of white bondsmen declined dramatically in relation to the African slave population.[1] In part, the decline resulted from the many indentured servants who returned to France or who died. Nevertheless, numerous single, relatively poor males still arrived in the Caribbean, with some 15,000 leaving the port of La Rochelle between 1660 and 1715.[2] The peak years for such departures were difficult ones in France, especially 1660–66 and 1683–86.[3] Debien attributes the dramatic numbers of the early 1660s to royal promotion of colonization, but the social misery index of that same era should not be discounted. The price of wheat skyrocketed in parts of France between 1660 and 1664 before returning to previous levels in the later 1660s.[4]

The character of the indentured servant system changed gradually from the 1650s on. Previously, masters had often known and recruited their servants in France. Bertrand d'Ogeron de la Bouëre best exemplifies such recruiting after 1660, but he was an exception to the practice of impersonal recruitment of servants for sale to the highest bidder across the Atlantic. One consequence was growing social disdain for such recruits in the islands.[5]

The majority of recruits after 1660 were unskilled servants who migrated to Saint-Domingue. This undeveloped colony was the only one where an ex-servant could hope for a grant of land; some freed servants there received a buccaneer rifle instead of tobacco.[6] Saint-Domingue also appealed to ex-servants who hoped that a move far away would wash away the stain of servitude.[7] This island also benefited from d'Ogeron's reputation for good treatment of servants. Nevertheless, chroniclers railed against the system, and the extremely popular, picaresque tale of

Alexandre Exquemelin, who survived a brutal master before taking off with the buccaneers, was a best seller.[8]

The more settled Windward Islands attracted mainly skilled male servants, because slaves increasingly did unskilled labor.[9] Metalworkers, carpenters, joiners, and coopers to service the sugar works, surgeons to heal sick slaves, barrel makers, sugar refiners, and masons were especially prized. These workers were able to negotiate better conditions, such as a higher clothing allowance before embarkation, the right to eat at the master's table, higher wages, and a guaranteed return to France. The cost of these servants and their reputed arrogance eventually pushed planters to train slaves in skilled occupations.

The war of 1666–68 slowed the pace of recruitment, so much so that the crown acted to ensure its continuance for reasons of internal and external island security. That explains Colbert's bold but futile reduction of servants' terms to eighteen months.[10] All contracts from 1671 on included a clause that the servant renounced his right to the eighteen-month stipulation.[11] Though the Dutch War (1672–78) saw a dramatic decline in the number of servants shipped, Colbert absolutely rejected Governor-general Jean-Charles de Baas's plea that the Paris poorhouses provide coerced labor.[12] Louis and Colbert thus promoted the inherently contradictory policies of promoting the growth of slave-grown sugar and the continuing migration of poor whites to maintain the racial balance deemed necessary for colonial self-protection.

The 1670s saw a drastic decline in the number of *engagés* in the islands,[13] in the case of Martinique from 969 in 1671 to 201 in 1678.[14] After the Dutch War and after Colbert's death, another spurt of emigration occurred in the years 1683–86, but some of these migrants were coerced Protestants. Influenced by the former island intendant Michel Bégon, subsequently intendant of the galleys, Seignelay allowed shipments of galley slaves, especially to underdeveloped Cayenne and Saint-Domingue. In the early 1680s, to enable them to find American husbands, the king provided generous trousseaux to poor young women taken from the *hôpitaux*, some of whom were of less than virtuous character in the opinion of prudes such as the intendant Jean-Baptiste Patoulet.[15] Most Protestants forcibly sent found ways to escape island prisons, often with the help of sympathetic habitants.[16] Ultimately, outcries from island officials about the counterproductivity of this type of emigration stopped this overtly coercive labor regime.

In 1698, after the Nine Years' War had meant the virtual cessation of indentured servant emigration, Louis and the Pontchartrains required all ships to transport a certain number of *engagés*, depending on their tonnage. At Martinique, only four domestics or indentured servants were left by that time. During the next four years, 664 domestics appear on the census rolls.[17] Admittedly, fraudulent evasion of this royal provision was probably the rule rather than the exception. However, at Nantes, the years 1697–1701 witnessed significant levels of emigrants. Although the resumption of war in 1702 slowed the sending of indentured servants, the flow began again after 1710, and it was strong in the immediate postwar years. About one-third of the indentured servants from Nantes in these years were skilled workers, who demanded decent wages and living conditions.[18]

Despite the efforts of royal officials, from Lieutenant General Alexandre Prouville de Tracy forward, who protested the poor treatment of fellow Christians and Frenchmen, as well as the arbitrary practice of increasing the thirty-six-month contract on this or that pretext, young, primarily male servants were for the most part beyond the protection of law.[19] "One shakes with indignation at the way the *engagés* are treated," the comte de Blénac exclaimed. "I wouldn't treat my dog like that, no matter how angry I was!" Only 50 of some 600 recent arrivals had evidently survived the three-year term, and he saw no benefit in such a wasteful system.[20] Disease in addition to labor conditions played a part in such apparently high mortality rates. The word "apparently" is apropos, because masters had every reason not to inform the secular or clerical authorities about servants' early deaths.[21]

Exquemelin provides a gruesome picture of indentured servitude, which his personal experiences no doubt strongly colored. He had been indentured as a skilled surgeon, but his master at Tortuga refused to allow him to practice his trade and instead forced him to work at "base" tasks. After a difficult year, he grew very ill and received little food except eggs brought to him by a "poor Negro slave." His master imprisoned him for days in a dark hole, and he nearly starved to death. Only the intervention of d'Ogeron permitted his escape. Exquemelin compares indentured servants to galley slaves, although he admits that some buccaneer masters treated their servants reasonably well.[22]

No doubt servants found life very difficult in the islands, especially the first year. Tropical diseases took their toll on all the newly arrived, but servants also toiled long hours in the hot sun. Working twelve hours a day was hardly the same in the Caribbean as in France. Most servants suffered from protein deficiencies, because they had little fresh meat and few vegetables to supplement the manioc, potatoes, and bananas that were their staple diet. Some desperate servants could not resist the temptation to borrow money from their masters, and thus did not have adequate funds to pay their return passage. Probably, skilled servants were the only ones able to return.

Most habitants and most of the declining number of *engagés* lived in rural areas on rough-hewn farms, but some lived in towns. The proximity of a good harbor superseded all other considerations in choice of sites for a habitation. Thus, the sheltered harbor at Fort Royal, Martinique (Fort-de-France today), the capital after 1692, outweighed the "bad air" of the surrounding mosquito-laden swamplands. The shortage of fresh water delayed but did not prevent the growth of Pointe-à-Pitre, Guadeloupe. The same can be said of Port-au-Prince, the later capital of Saint-Domingue and of Haiti today. These pre-plantation era towns had unpaved streets, roaming animals, and the noisome filth caused by the indiscriminate dumping of "night soil" (human wastes) despite laws against such practices. The canal at Fort Royal, Martinique, acquired the nickname of the "caca" river.[23] Servants living in these bourgs were especially susceptible to malaria and yellow fever.

Some *engagés* escaped servitude, with the rough coast of Saint-Domingue as a favorite refuge; others were recruited to work on the tobacco habitations there or to assist the buccaneers in their hunts for feral cattle and pigs. Often these servants were promised a hunting rifle instead of tobacco as their wage, so that, after three years, they could become buccaneers.[24] One such was Exquemelin, who provided one of the most famous accounts of their lives. He asks his reader to envision gritty men with long, "frizzy" hair contained by a hat, wearing a cloak of crude cloth, setting off for the hunt. Bands of twelve men with their valets hunt together for protection against the Spanish. They are equipped with the famous long buccaneer rifle and fifteen to twenty pounds of powder, carried in calabashes sealed with wax against humidity. All carry mosquito nets, which they hang in crudely built huts at the site of the hunt.

Using hunting dogs to locate the cattle, they kill or wound these beasts, and the valets immediately cut their hamstrings. According to Exquemelin, some masters and servants ran so fast that they could catch the cattle and disable them by cutting the hamstrings. A mulatto named Vincent de Rosiers made almost all his kills that way, thus saving balls and precious powder. After the master sucked the marrow from the four great bones, he left a valet to cut off the hide and proceeded to the next kill, until all the servants had one animal to prepare. The valet had to transport a hide weighing some 100 pounds back to the camp. Returned to the huts in the evening, the party ate some of the fresh meat with a sauce consisting of water, salt, lemon, and pimentos. Potatoes, which had been placed in the ashes to catch the fat of the grilling meat, ordinarily accompanied the meat. Alternatively, they cooked green bananas like carrots or roasted the mature fruit, served with sugar and orange juice.[25] A round of tobacco and perhaps some rum or other spirit ended another day for master and servant alike.

Some buccaneers specialized in killing pigs. Exquemelin writes that they cured long strips of meat overnight before smoking it on a wooden barbecue grill. Pig bones and fat were put into the fire to thicken the smoke. The processed meat was sold in sixty-pound packets for six pieces of eight (about eighteen l.t.), and large pots of pig fat brought the same amount. Exquemelin describes the meat in ecstatic terms, although its flavor diminished greatly after a month or two.[26]

After the Nine Years' War, the king attempted to revitalize the institution of the indentured servant by assigning a quota of servants to be transported by all Caribbean-bound vessels. In 1699, a royal edict mandated that servants transported to the islands had to be over eighteen and healthy.[27] The next year, the intendant at Martinique, concerned about abuses of indentured servants, mandated the specific amount of food and clothing to be given them, and prohibited the practice of ending their contracts early to get rid of sick servants. Masters were either to care for these servants or pay a fee to the hospital for that purpose.[28] Abuses continued mostly unpunished despite these measures; in contrast, offenses such as theft of masters' property could result in capital punishment.[29]

Just as had earlier writers, Labat writes that indentured servants received as bad treatment as slaves. Servants and slaves on tobacco farms at Saint-Domingue lived an equally hellish existence. During the harvesting, drying, and de-stalking season, they got only four to five hours' sleep and had to use some of that time searching for frogs and crabs to supplement their meager food rations.[30]

By the 1660s, almost everyone from Colbert to the humblest small slaveholder in the Caribbean agreed that for Europeans, Africans constituted the wealth of the Indies, the sine qua non of a brighter future. In an order that removed the 5 percent duty on "Guinée negroes" brought to the islands, the king agreed "there is nothing that contributes more to the augmentation of the colonies . . . than the laborious work of Negroes."[31] Unlike indentured servants, Africans remained in slavery in perpetuity. Moreover, contemporaries believed that they were somewhat easier to manage than the often rowdy, defiant *engagés*—who were Christian Europeans, after all, with some customary rights—and they probably survived longer than the latter too. Indentured servants were nonetheless still considered valuable in skilled positions, as commanders of the African workforce or as sugar refiners or tobacco finishers, but they were never plentiful enough or willing to submit to hot and grueling labor on the burgeoning sugar plantations. Africans were not given a choice.

Colonists sought desperately to augment their holdings in slaves by hook or by crook, and in relative terms they succeeded, but at a high price to all concerned. Around 1680, a slave cost anywhere from c. 800 to 1,500 l.t., depending on factors ranging from age to gender to physical health. In 1698, Labat bought twelve slaves at an average price of 1,425 l.t.[32] No wonder, then, that the prospect of plundering foreigners of their slaves motivated contemporary colonial militias to fight, that slave ships and Iberian slaves in general were among the favorite targets of buccaneers, and that colonists illegally traded for slaves with Caribs who captured runaways or stole them from other Europeans.

The high price of African slaves reflected strong European demand and their relative scarcity in the French Caribbean islands. In the years 1662–1713, French slavers are estimated to have brought only 8,494 Africans to America, or in any case somewhere between 7,000 and 15,000.[33] Le Havre and La Rochelle were the only significant French ports participating in the slave trade during the era of the monopoly companies (the Compagnie des Indes occidentales, the Compagnie du Sénégal, and the Compagnie de Guinée).[34] Nantes, after 1700 the most important French slave-trading port, was practically absent from this nefarious commerce at the time.[35] From 1672, the colonists could rely much less on their most dependable suppliers, the Dutch.[36] The remarkable fact that English slavers carried 71,332 of the 89,316 slaves transported to America in the 1670s, and 106,801 out of 157,677 slaves brought during the 1680s, suggests the ultimate provenance of bonded newcomers in French colonies.[37]

The capture of Gorée in Senegambia from the Dutch in 1677 did give the French a toehold in northwestern Africa, but the last decades of the century were ones of failure for the French slave trade. Although slaves from Senegambia constituted about a quarter of the French slave trade total in the seventeenth century, that number is 1,719.[38] The incompetence of company officials and specially designated merchants for this trade would be laughable except for the consequences for slaves who ended up in their hands. For example, one Antoine Taruant of Clermont in central France had a contract with the habitants of Saint-Domingue to provide 2,000 slaves, but he managed to transport only 438. Taruant demonstrated that he had sent ships to Guinea in 1698, which cost him over 683,000 l.t. to outfit. His captains bought 1,857 slaves (thus nearly the 2,000 quota), but 837 died during the Middle Passage. His ships were in such bad shape that 567 of the survivors had to be sold at Martinique. Because Taruant persuaded the king of his enormous losses, Louis ordered that he repay the habitants 100,000 l.t., less than the amount they had put up for the venture.[39]

However they arrived in the French islands after 1660, probably the majority of slaves now originated in the Gulf of Guinea, the area Europeans named the Slave Coast. Thus slaves from Angola no longer predominated. European slave traders increasingly found their cargoes along the Slave Coast, which was the probable home of many of the contraband slaves supplied to the French by English traders. Labat attempted to learn the language of the majority of his order's slaves, the "Aradas" of the Slave Coast.[40]

Only after 1700–1701 did the French slave trade, entering into an era of greater freedom from company monopolies and with access to Spanish American markets because of the contract (*asiento*) granted to the French by Bourbon Spain, become more dynamic. Once again, the turn of the eighteenth century was a time of dramatic changes in the relationship between France and its tropical American colonies. Without a significant national slave trade, Colbert's dream of an integrated, self-sufficient colonial empire remained a chimera.

However French habitants obtained them, there were almost 16,000 slaves in the Greater Caribbean by 1670, slightly more than half of the total population. The 1660s had been a decade of significant growth; for example, the number of slaves at Martinique increased from 2,644 in 1660 to 5,849 in 1669.[41] The Dutch War slowed the pace of growth, as demonstrated in the Martinique censuses. Between 1671 and 1682, the number of slaves increased from 6,183 to 8,039. Just two years later, there were 10,656, thus a greater increase than in the previous decade.[42]

By 1685, there were some 25,000 African slaves in the Greater French Caribbean (including Guiane). That number increased modestly by 1700 to 33,343, as compared to 17,188 whites.[43] It is important to reiterate that such numbers are estimates. Militia captains, whose duty it was to count their neighbors, both African and European, often were too busy with their own plantations and other duties to devote too much time to a tedious job, and sometimes they undercounted slaves or counted young adults as children to avoid the capitation tax.

In contrast to the modest growth in French slave numbers, in 1700, the English Royal African Company and the private entrepreneurs who followed in its wake had furnished Barbados with most of its 40,000 slaves, more than in all the French colonies combined. More pertinently, given its recent transition to sugar, Jamaica, which had had a little over 9,000 African slaves in the 1670s, had 40,000 by 1700.[44] Its future rival Saint-Domingue dramatically lagged behind in the last decades of the seventeenth century.

When the number of slave imports into a plantation colony can be known with some reasonable certainty, then their survival rate can be approximately measured. For example, it is estimated that some 264,000 slaves were imported into the English West Indian colonies between 1640 and 1700, but that the total number of slaves in 1700 was only about 100,000.[45] No doubt a significant number were reexported to Spanish and French colonies and an unknown number lost to French and Dutch raiders. Nevertheless, English West Indies' slaves almost certainly had a negative rate of growth. Using eighteenth-century figures, different authorities have estimated annual negative growth rates for slaves in all European colonies as ranging from 5.4 to 6 percent.[46]

Can anything useful be deduced about the situation of the French colonies? As indicated above, 33,343 slaves toiled in French tropical America in 1700. The very poorly organized French slave trade averaged less than one ship annually between 1643 and 1700. Forty-nine French slaving voyages in the seventeenth century are estimated to have imported at most 15,000 slaves.[47] Yet Philip Curtin in his famous census of the European slave trade estimates some 124,500 imports to the French islands in just the years 1675–1700, a total that appears greatly exaggerated. If it is accurate, then the negative growth rate was significantly greater than it was for the English plantation colonies. Official French correspondence for the years 1670–1700 reports the arrival of only about 6,000 African slaves.[48] Admittedly, the smuggling of slaves from Dutch Saint Eustatius or Curaçao or from various English islands was widespread, but gauging the volume of it is impossible. For example, the census suggests roughly 6,500 slaves at Guadeloupe in 1700, yet French slavers brought only 802 slaves there during the seventeenth century.[49]

Given this irregularity of supply, the African cultural backgrounds of French slaves in these decades were presumably more diverse than in the preceding period, when Dutch suppliers brought, it is surmised, a majority of "Angolans." The small number of slaves arriving from Senegambia aboard French slave ships had little in common with the Angolans who predominated prior to the 1660s. Similarly, the slave population was at least as diverse as in the eighteenth century, when French slavers provided a significant percentage of the overall trade. If seventeenth-century colonists were already accepting notions about different African "nations,"[50] they had little opportunity to select ethnic groups to cater to their stereotypes. Although the differences can be overstated, this wide diversity of ethnic and cultural backgrounds presumably made the formation of a Creole Afro-Caribbean culture a painfully slow process.[51] The ethnic and linguistic diversity mandated learning a French-African lingua franca. Also the practice of bringing slaves from different plantations together for catechism instruction perhaps allowed incipient building of communities. According to Labat, Creole Christian slaves were more "content" than bossales. Creoles rarely committed suicide, for example.[52]

For the decades before 1690s, we have scant information about African birthrates and almost none about mortality rates, unless one accepts Curtin's estimates and concludes that the growth rate on the French Caribbean islands was even more negative than in the English plantation colonies.[53] Also, if the volume of the slave trade is guesswork, then the ratio of Creole to African-born slaves cannot be known. Given the rather rapid growth of the African population after 1660, in combination with the small proportion of pre-adolescent slave children in the French colonies, it may be concluded that African-born bossales were in the majority.

Arlette Gaultier suggests that the birthrate for Africans and African Americans at Martinique and Guadeloupe in the years 1669–85 was fifty-one per thousand per annum, a rate higher than in Europe and in West Africa, although she also suggests an abnormally high mortality rate.[54] Dutertre marvels at African women's fecundity, comparing it to that of Jewish wives during the Egyptian captivity. He asserts that on Lieutenant General Philippe Longvillier de Poincy's estates in 1660, there were 160 children between four and ten out of a total population of 700 to 800 "Angolans."[55]

No matter how approximate the census data are, they do not support the impression given by Dutertre. Considering that men probably constituted more than 60 percent of all slaves exported from Africa, a remarkable gender balance quickly emerged among slaves. In 1664, men outnumbered women two to one at Martinique, but a rough gender balance was reached just five years later. In 1664, slave children (1,032) actually outnumbered slave women (691) at Martinique and constituted 33.8 percent of the total slave population, a figure never to be surpassed in the era of slavery. In twelve censuses between 1664 and 1700, Léo Elisabeth counts 29,862 children for 25,160 working female slaves. There are too many caveats to conclude that female slaves had on average one living child apiece. Compared with Saint-Domingue in roughly comparable decades, the number of slave children at Martinique was relatively high. At Saint-Domingue, there was only about one child for every two adult slave women.[56] Even in smaller colonies with few plantations like Saint-Barthélemy, where conditions of slaves working on cattle ranches or small habitations can be assumed to have been not as onerous, in 1681, slave mothers averaged about 1.6 children.[57] The apparent conclusion is that more established slave communities on the older islands with higher percentages of Creole slaves fostered more stable families; however, the situation for families everywhere was deplorable, suggesting that any increase in slave populations may be explained by new arrivals.

Given the supply uncertainties and the high costs of slaves, rational owners had every motivation not only to keep slaves alive as long as they were productive but also to foster their reproduction. Royal officials in the 1680s and 1690s complained that the islands had only 50 percent of the slaves they needed for full development.[58] Did slaveholders take the rational long view of their business or were they driven to get rich quickly and get out?

Some evidence from the mid eighteenth century suggests that on plantations owned by religious orders, sufficient numbers of children were born not only to satisfy internal needs but also to sell the surplus.[59] Labat provides a guide for rational Christian owners, who should treat their slaves as their children, which of course at that time meant rigorous punishment of all faults. Arbitrary punishments should never occur,

African women preparing manioc. From Jean-Baptiste Labat, *Nouveau voyage aux isles de l'Amérique* (Paris, 1722), 1: opposite 379.

or slaves would sulk in protest or even flee the habitation. Instead, their behavior should be controlled by shaming them. Labat assigns "women's work," such as collecting cane trash, to "bad" male slaves. Two suits of clothes and basic foodstuffs (especially manioc, grown, of course, by the slaves themselves) must be provided. Rum should never be denied a slave "who needs it," presumably because of fatigue. Labat condemns the Spanish and English system of giving free time on Saturdays so that slaves could provide for themselves; what if bad weather prevented their work, and what about the "lazy" slaves who refused to work on their free time? Theft and *marronage* were the inevitable results.[60]

Labat adopted an interesting approach to royal ordinances that, although well intentioned, were not obeyed for good economic reasons; good for the masters, that is. For example, the king mandated that forty ounces of salt meat be given weekly to each slave. In wartime, such meat was simply unavailable, and in peacetime, masters considered the expense exorbitant. Labat writes that "reasonable" masters planted yams and potatoes as a substitute, but admits that their number was "small." Militia officers, themselves usually large sugar planters, were "lax" in enforcing this requirement.[61]

Unfortunately, slaveholders in a rush to fortune were not usually the most rational of people. Historians today can only hypothesize at explanations for the deficit of slave children. No doubt excessive work, poor nutrition, and disease are part of the explanation, as was the case of sixty slaves of Labat's neighbor, all dead in a six-day period. Labat attributes the deaths to the "bloody flux" and venereal disease, and thus in part blames the slaves' "intemperance and indiscretion" in addition to the master's poor treatment.[62] More problematic is the slave woman's role in refusing to generate new life in such debilitating conditions through birth control, abortion, and infanticide.

Most slaves produced sugar, tobacco, provisions, and some cotton and indigo, the reason they were purchased. From the 1660s on, they were increasingly likely to do the grueling tasks related to sugar production. At Martinique, in 1664, 1,605 out of 2,750 slaves worked on farms possessing fifteen or fewer Africans, thus primarily on tobacco and provision grounds. Just 245 worked on what might be called plantations (with more than forty slaves). The premise is that sugar cultivation required more than fifteen slaves even supposing the owner milled his cane at a neighbor's sugar works. Deep cane holes had to be dug, the young shoots needed constant weeding, and some fifteen months later, the mature cane had to be cut rapidly, bound into bundles, and transported as quickly as possible to the mill. At harvest time, slaves' lives were hellish, with the only compensation in some cases being extra rations of tafia— a rough rum. There followed the multiple processes of crushing the cane, boiling the juice, curing it in earthen pots, and, finally, transporting it to a port. Sugar was a capital- and labor-intensive industrial crop, not a small man's crop.[63] In contrast, tobacco required tedious but ex-

hausting attention. Once it was planted, extensive weeding and worm-
ing were needed, and then the leaf had to be cut, transferred to drying
sheds, washed with salt water, and, finally, rolled for transport by skilled
workers.

Slaves also cleared ground, built huts and other structures, worked
provision grounds, maintained livestock, and provided domestic service,
among other tasks. Some armed slaves hunted and others fished for their
owners. Although their lives were not as regimented as those of their
eighteenth-century successors, slaves in the late seventeenth century had
less opportunity to become drivers or skilled plantation artisans, roles
still primarily filled by Europeans. The scope of French island slaves'
employment appears to have been less extensive than that of slaves in
other frontier and pre-plantation societies, such as Virginia, Carolina,
and Louisiana, especially in herding, lumbering, and hunting.

On one unusually large plantation in late seventeenth-century Martinique, 200 slaves worked in a variety of tasks depending on age, gender, and health. Eleven slaves worked in the owner's household, a highly
unusual figure, indicating the presence of the master's family. The plantation infirmary occupied forty slaves, only twelve of whom were sick.
Only 25 of the 200 were infants and children, an atypically low ratio.
Nineteen slaves were involved in food production or pastoral activities.
Five artisans are listed. Forty-one of the weakest slaves, the aged and
nursing mothers, constituted a gang doing "light" labor. The remaining
eighty-four performed the hard field labor associated with the sugar
regime.[64] Except perhaps for Saint-Domingue slaves, opportunities not
to be under the master's eye appear to have been fewer on these small islands. Still, master-slave relations were so relatively relaxed in these years
that officials became alarmed and sought to instill more order and discipline.

By 1680, the number of slaves at Martinique had increased to 6,279,
of whom 2,275 worked on habitations with fifteen or fewer slaves. In
contrast to 1664, now about 1,900, or a bit less than one-third, slaved on
plantations with more than forty fellows.[65] Martinique, now the most
developed French island, was moving steadily if not spectacularly in the
direction of the dominance of sugar magnates.

A few slaves lived and worked in the tiny island *bourgs*, where they
presumably performed a wide variety of tasks. If urban Jewish families of
Martinique in 1664 are any indicator, urban masters held from two to six
slaves, with an average of four.[66] Students of slave systems generally con-

sider urban slaves to be a privileged minority, with more diverse occupations and greater freedom of movement; but, to reiterate, there were few such slaves.

The record is mixed concerning French treatment of slaves in this era. The variables suggest how complicated the issue is. Were slaves treated differently in urban and rural settings? In rural areas, the type of crop worked and the size of the habitation were no doubt important. Conditions differed in times of war and peace, and in seasons of dryness and wetness. Who can doubt that slaves suffered even more than their masters when hurricanes or earthquakes devastated islands? In 1681, two monstrous hurricanes created terrible food shortages in English Saint Christopher,[67] and the French of Saint-Christophe, and even more their slaves, presumably also suffered grievously. Were priests and militia captains, who were supposed to enforce protective measures, in contact with a slave's habitation? What about the character of the master himself? One solid conclusion is that the slaves of religious orders were better off than most.

Most masters viewed Africans primarily as means of production and as inferior in all ways to themselves. No surprise there, given their exploitation of peoples who were so physiologically and culturally different. A few Compagnie des Indes occidentales propagandists presented a picture of happy slaves, at least as content as French peasants.[68] Priest chroniclers expressed views of Africans ranging from disdain to abhorrence to outrage at their "pagan" customs; that is, until they accepted saving grace, which "whitened" their sins. Chance remarks by officials may or may not reflect masters' views. D'Ogeron gifted Colbert de Terron with a young African woman, "who it appears has no bad inclinations."[69] Dutertre and de Baas pitied these people because of the terrible treatment meted out to them. De Baas complained to Colbert that "these miserable wretches" could not survive twenty-hour days fed on only vegetables (yams, potatoes, cassava). He argued for the importation of Irish salted beef to allow them to continue with such Herculean labors. "I confess, My Lord [Colbert], that I have a great deal of weakness in the matter of carrying out your orders, for slaves are human beings, and human beings should not be reduced to a state which is worse than beasts."[70] La Barre commented to Colbert on the short life span of the "skinny" Africans who survived the Middle Passage. They died "very frequently, suffering without a doubt."[71]

On the other hand, racism—the idea that physiology determines cul-

tural behavior, and thus that despised customs are not subject to change
—was foreign to seventeenth-century culture and heretical to the Church.
All French slaves, unlike English and Dutch bondsmen, received baptism, if not already baptized in Africa; many heard catechism lessons, and
some were legally married.[72] Some received burial in sacred ground.
Dutertre lauded the systematic religious training that Poincy supplied to
his 160 slave adolescents and expressed much optimism about their spiritual progress. In 1664, Tracy reaffirmed the requirement to baptize and
marry all slaves.[73] In 1671, in an ordinance mandating specific fees for
religious services, the king decreed that those provided to slaves be
gratis, because otherwise these charges would constitute a tax on planters. Jean de Clodoré asserts around the same time that masters always
arranged for Negroes to marry whom they pleased, even persons on
other estates, and that they did not separate families.[74]

Labat presents a detailed program for treating slaves. That slaves'
well-being guaranteed masters' profits governed his views. Treat the
newly arrived with patience and charity, he writes, so that they can overcome their grief. Feed and wash them under the care of an established
slave family. However, do not let them eat or sleep with Christians until
they become jealous and demand baptism. Slaves who become Christians and who pick up Creole pidgin come to accept their status and make
the best of it. If they ask for something, then explain why such is impossible, but send them away with a bagatelle (a little present). If they deserve punishment, administer it directly; do not threaten punishment or
they will run off. If they do run off, do not punish them if they return
within twenty-four hours. If they stay away longer than that, take away
something they value, such as their chickens, rather than using violence.
Allow them their little holidays and dances, except for the "lascivious cal-
enda," a sexually suggestive dance. Do everything possible to keep them
on the plantation during holidays, including the distribution of spirits.
Do everything to encourage them to bring their garden products to market, and never take away what they have earned. In other words, Labat
wants them to buy into the slave system.[75]

Creole slaves, who are "every bit as refined as whites," need different treatment. In general, they are trustworthy; indeed, they sometimes
take up their masters' quarrels against slaves of another estate. Creoles
can be used as "valets" and are the better choices for skilled positions.
However, Labat warns that these slaves are very adept at pretending

simple-mindedness and naïveté to whites who do not know them—the Sambo or Quashee personality.[76]

Compared to mid eighteenth-century practices, these and similar observations suggest such benign treatment of slaves as to generate a healthy skepticism. Yet, since no one in France cared much about how masters treated slaves, what was the point in these contentions about the character of French slavery? To be sure, Labat wished to portray a harmonious and orderly society based on good Christian practices. No contemporary English observer was similarly inclined. With some exceptions, overt defenders of slavery did not appear until attackers of the institution emerged, well after 1750.

Christianization did not prevent masters from acting brutally toward slaves, although authorities and priests sometimes intervened. Priests routinely intervened with masters to mitigate the consequences of short-term flight (*petit marronage*).[77] Some went beyond attempting to help slaves to bolder statements about the institution's injustice. A Capuchin father, member of the only order to refuse to benefit from slave labor, protested slave executions at Saint-Pierre, Martinique, by burying condemned slaves in red clothing to indicate their status as martyrs. It is not known what happened to him.

However, the ability to mitigate the harshness of bondage related to the priests' workload. In the mid 1680s there were approximately 44,000 souls in the French islands, served by about fifty clergy, or about 880 people per priest. True, this ratio was far better than that of the 1730s, when about sixty clergy tried to serve 187,000 people, or 3,130 people per priest.[78] Given the difficulty of land communication, it is not surprising that priests such as Dutertre testified to how fatiguing parish and evangelical duties were. The successes of individuals described below must be understood in this context.

The Jesuits took the lead in converting slaves. They assigned a priest as special curate for this group (called the *curé des négres*). The first known curate was Father Louis Charpentier at Saint-Christophe. Before his death in 1669, he had baptized about a third of the slaves under his supervision.[79] A successor was the zealous Father Jean Mongin, who provides us with precious details concerning his evangelical strategies and efforts. With 2,400 souls in his custody, he drew a profile of his "dear *nègres*," including information about their background, family life (if any), and, especially, their religious and moral state. Mongin knew who was baptized, who was ready for the more esoteric knowledge that undergirded the other sacraments, and who backslid. Unlike his near contemporary Labat, Mongin avoided close relations with habitants, being aware of how they could impede his spiritual oeuvre. No doubt many resented his evangelization, which disrupted work schedules. Mongin refused baptism to slaves recently arrived from Africa, even if they requested it. The Jesuit insisted that they learn the catechism and settle down with one marriage partner. When he first approached slaves with this latter proposition, he admits, they treated it with mocking hilarity.

After one year, Mongin took stock of his work. Now he had 2,522 charges, and the efficacy of his insistence on wedlock was indicated by 128 newly married people. There were "123 adults baptized and 103 children, of whom 42 were praying in paradise for the others, because half of the infants die here."[80] Of the rest, 562 took communion at Easter, meaning they could be considered good Christians, 511 knew the principal doctrines, the last step before full acceptance, and 626 knew their prayers. That left 597 in what the Jesuit considered total religious ignorance. On special occasions, he arrived bearing gifts. Gathering together his beloved flock, Mongin queried each one about the religious progress made since the last visit. To those who had progressed, a reward was given, and those who had not supposedly felt covered with shame. When his charges backslid, Mongin reminded them of their English counterparts, who did not receive baptism, did not go to church, and were not given proper burial.[81] However, only thirteen Jesuits worked in the islands in 1685.[82]

A Jesuit relation from about 1710, probably authored by Guillaume Moreau, curé des nègres at Guadeloupe from 1706 to 1710, tells the story of a clever French slave who fell into the possession of the English at Antigua in 1690 and became a trusted and privileged servant to his new master there. However, since the English did not permit slaves Christian service, this well-trained Catholic eventually escaped with family and friends to Guadeloupe to partake of the spiritual life. The slave insisted to the author that he and fellow Catholic captives had maintained worship in the spiritual desert of Antigua and had baptized their children and married according to the traditions they had known among the French. The Jesuit marvels that while the slave's material life worsened in Guadeloupe, it was more than made up for by the possibility of salvation.[83] It is not clear whether this slave had Jesuit masters; it is clear that he was either very sincere or told the Jesuit what the priest wanted to hear.

Labat notes that before he took over a Dominican plantation, the slaves had suffered under poor management. Thirty-five slaves were able to work, but eight to ten of the elderly were sick, and fifteen children were malnourished. Labat changed all of that by treating the slaves firmly but rationally.[84] He soon established a trusting relationship with some elderly male slaves, making an effort to acquire a basic knowledge of their language and engaging them in good-natured bantering. Following his own rules, he punished "all faults" immediately, of course.

Master-slave relations developed ad hoc, with precedents becoming customs and customs acquiring the force of law over time. Some customs became colonial laws in early decades, and many found their way into the famous *Code noir*.[85] Early on, island governors and sovereign councils regulated masters' and slaves' behavior in the name of the common good of owners and the state. As noted earlier, du Parquet pushed through measures preventing slaves being made to work on Sundays and holy days. In 1665, the Martinique sovereign council passed a law compensating owners for slaves turned in for crimes, so as to combat leniency for masters' fear of losing valuable property.[86] The council acted occasionally against "cruel and unusual punishment" imposed by deranged masters. For example, in 1670, it removed from office a militia lieutenant who had mutilated some slaves. A year later, it fined a master 500 pounds of sugar for burning a female slave's "shameful parts," adding that a reoccurrence would merit corporal punishment; admittedly, such punishments were derisory.[87] How many masters behaved so horribly cannot be known.

Royal officials also intervened in these matters as early as 1664, when Tracy condemned indentured servants for "debauching" slave women and forced masters to nurse sick slaves, among a variety of measures.[88] He and his successors censored masters' laxness in controlling slave movements and in allowing access to weapons.[89] Missionaries still retained the zeal and the clout to make life difficult occasionally for masters who flouted these regulations.

Punishments of slaves hinged on the received "wisdom" of always punishing for offenses and never otherwise. Masters administered ad hoc reprisals for misdemeanors and, before the measure to compensate them for public executions of slaves, even for capital offenses. Any European could beat or even kill a slave caught in theft after dark. Public punishments ranged from cutting of appendages, such as noses and ears, to the public humiliation of the iron collar, accompanied by a vice propping the mouth open "sweetened" by fiery hot red pepper, to capital punishment. Dutertre found the vice punishment especially effective because the victims' "shame" subjected them to slave children's laughter. He also tells the "amusing" story of a slave who, having already lost one ear, begged Poincy to give him a substitute punishment instead of removing his other ear, because he would have no place to carry a cigar when working.[90] In 1682, enough mutilated slaves existed to have the intendant Patoulet rule their masters free of the capitation tax for them.[91]

The Martinique council issued extensive regulations governing punishments. Some examples will allow the reader to judge the system. First, a slave caught stealing pigs, sheep, or chickens worth less than 100 pounds of sugar received punishment from the owner; more than that and offenders became subject to public reprisal. A second offense meant the removal of an ear. The master was responsible for compensating the owner of the stolen property. Second, in case of cattle or horse theft, punishment for a first offense was removal of a leg; a second offense merited death. The master once again compensated the owner. Next, slave fugitives for fifteen days received a whipping and branding. A slave missing for four to six months had one hamstring cut. The master had to inform the officer of the *quartier* that such punishment had been inflicted, presumably to guard against owners' reluctance to damage valuable property. Numerous regulations aimed to deter illicit trade between slaves and whites, apparently an endemic problem. Free people who bought from slaves not having written permission to sell were subject to heavy fines for the first offense and capital punishment for a second. Does the severity of punishment suggest that this measure was aimed at free people of color? No slave could travel at night without the master's permission. Finally, for slaves who dared lift a hand against any European, the punishments were gruesome. Hanging and strangling awaited the slave who struck a white, and if the white died as a result, the offender was broken on the wheel, a horrible exit.[92] Such laws do not tell us how frequently these punishments were inflicted, however, which depended far too much on the will of the masters.

On its surface, the *Code noir* appears to be a relatively humane set of slave laws, if any such laws can be so dignified. It prevented masters from engaging in "excessive" and "arbitrary" behavior toward slaves; mandated work-free Sundays and holy days, not insignificant in a Catholic culture; established precise guidelines for feeding and clothing bondsmen, a growing problem given the scramble to turn over all arable land to the production of staples; insisted upon slaves' spiritual integration into the larger community; and tried to protect African women from sexual aggression. However, any humanitarian aspects were tertiary to the primary one of guaranteeing public order and the secondary one of promoting prosperity. Metropolitan and island authorities nonetheless attempted to restrain planters from overexploitation of slaves in their frenzied quest for short-term profit.[93]

Clearly, the authorities were increasingly concerned about maintaining order in a society with a gradual, mounting demographic dominance of slaves. And they were concerned that habitants exhibited too much laxness in disciplining slaves. An article of the code in principle established a fund to compensate owners for the loss of slaves to the judicial process. No doubt shocking to officialdom was the fact that some slaves carried offensive weapons and swords, no less. The code should be viewed in the context of an absolutist France intent on removing vagabonds, beggars, prostitutes, witches, and "lunatics" from public space.

Even more astounding, no doubt, was the visible evidence of colonists' consorting with African or African American women, the product of which was a small, but growing, mulatto group, or what from the eighteenth century forward are referred to as "people of color," to take account of various degrees of "racial" mixture.[94] Island customs granted mulattoes freedom by a certain age, especially when the father was master of the slave mother and was willing to accept responsibility.[95] In 1680, Blénac reported that the custom at Martinique was to free mulatto males at twenty years and females at fifteen.[96] Some mulattoes, for example, Manuel Rodrigues at Guadeloupe, owned habitations.[97] Island judges seem mainly to have been concerned when a white man damaged someone's property by impregnating a slave woman of whom he was not the owner.[98]

Starting in 1674, metropolitan officials expressed alarm at the problem and the lack of uniform legal codes to regulate it. Patoulet, who provided Colbert with much of the information for the *Code noir*, was among those officials who believed that the islands' customs toward mulatto children encouraged the *libertinage* of African women, who seduced whites to produce free offspring.[99] Europeans of that era believed women's sex drives were voracious, and that "primitive" cultures such as those of West Africa were far less sexually constrained; in that context, the intendant's anxieties are more comprehensible.[100]

In any case, shorn of its offensive discourse, the official point of view may not be far off the mark. It is generally assumed that coercion of female slaves, whether direct or indirect, explains mulatto children, but little evidence is available. Many advantages might accrue to the mother of such a baby. In parts of West Africa, for a female slave to be impregnated by a free father meant freedom for her and the child.[101] That said, the relatively small number of known mulattoes in the latter decades of the seventeenth century suggests a good dose of bureaucratic hysteria about the "problem."

The code attempted to reduce the negligence of the master class. The attitudes expressed are not surprising, when at home the state stepped in to punish children whose parents failed to do so. For example, the master could still free his mulatto child, but only if he married the mother (article 9). However, marriage to a white father not her master did not change the status of either mother or child.[102] The code granted full rights to all freed Negroes and mulattoes, while simultaneously imposing different and more severe punishments on them. Article 58 commanded that freedmen maintain a special respect for their former masters and their families. Paradoxically, French law considered slaves both as commodities without standing in the civil community and as people morally responsible for their behavior.

The code's success in regularizing procedures in relation to mulattoes and reducing what was deemed islanders' laxity in these matters is hard to judge. We do not know to what extent these laws were enforced. For example, late in 1688, the Saint-Domingue council mandated that the code be read in parish churches; "some" colonists were refusing to obey it because it had not been read in public.[103] It appears that the provision mandating that a white master marry a slave woman he had impregnated was not rigorously enforced. Historians argue that those provisions that wealthier habitants approved of or did not hotly oppose were accepted; all others were implemented indifferently, or not at all. For example, an edict stated that if it were proven that a master had impregnated his slave, both mother and child were to be confiscated; however, according to Labat, this was just another royal edict that was unenforceable because of local opposition. He notes that to avoid trouble with parishioners, many curates simply did not report these births.[104] The governor-general and intendant could not be everywhere, and the bigwigs of the sovereign councils and local militia officers were themselves prosperous planters.

For the last fifteen years of the seventeenth century, an intriguing dispute concerned the efforts of the Domaine d'Occident monopoly to collect capitation taxes from free blacks and mulattoes. In general, all Europeans except officials and all masters of slaves paid this tax, but by long-standing island custom, white Creoles did not. The Domaine d'Occident and on occasion the king asserted, however, that this privilege did not apply to freedmen; indeed, the former argued that all people of color, including those born free, should pay the tax. Free people of color and freedmen stood in opposition, and were often supported by white Creoles and local island officials concerned about social harmony. Prior to 1700, people of color won the argument, and at that date there were only two legal statuses in French tropical America, free and slave.[105]

The sentiment of the chief slaveholding habitants toward mulattoes apparently remained in favor of freeing them at age twenty or twenty-one. Can there be much doubt that most of these *gens de couleur* were the offspring of slaveholders? In 1697, du Casse recommended to Pontchartrain that the *Code noir* be amended to free all mulattoes at majority age (twenty-one). Du Casse may have believed that they would be natural supporters of the slave system.[106]

As compared to "mature era" plantation complexes, stronger incentives toward milder treatment of slaves existed in these pre-plantation decades. Eighteenth-century planters could count on a dependable slave supply; not so, the habitants. Louis XIV and Colbert tried to stifle Dutch slaver interlopers without substituting an effective French slave trade. Although they did somehow arrive, obtaining new slaves was a haphazard process, and it would have been as unreasonable to destroy or harm a slave as it would a horse. If one worked one's slaves to an early death, their replacement was far from certain.

The hazards of slave labor inevitably led to a variety of more or less serious "accidents," especially in the dangerous sugar industry. The typical eighteen-hour days during the months of harvesting and preparing the cane left slaves exhausted. Slaves had to procure food during their "rest" hours. Some but not all masters supplemented food rations during this difficult labor regime.[107] Boiler men suffered horrible burns. Especially dangerous was feeding cane into the sugar mill, a task for slave women.[108] Labat tells the story of one poor woman whose sleeve was caught in the mill. Her body was dragged into the machine until her head was cut off and dropped by the mill. Labat draws from the story only the practical lesson that in order to prevent such accidents resulting from inattentiveness caused by long hours of work, these women should be made to smoke and sing.[109]

Unfortunately, there were plenty of unreasonable masters. To cite just a few more examples, in 1670 the Martinique council stripped an officer of his commission for mutilating his slaves.[110] Commentators such as Labat note such cases but point out that other nations, especially the English, were so much crueler. They treated their slaves like beasts, or worse, chaining some "criminals" in baskets on trees to bake in the hot sun until they died. Some English masters cut off the hands and heads of "criminals" as a deterrent. Others fed slave offenders bound hand and foot into the sugar mill.[111] Labat was a patriot, however, and his fulminations against the English should be taken with a grain of salt.

Labat does admit that terrible punishments occasionally occurred in the French colonies, as during a nearly general revolt at Martinique that was not unmasked until the last moment. In general, however, the fewer French slaves, their religious training, and perhaps more charitable masters meant a more humane system, at least in Labat's opinion. Throughout his volumes, Labat strongly makes the case that the humane master not only fulfills his Christian duties but profits from his kinder treatment of slaves, who responded better to the carrot than to the stick.[112]

After 1675, the sovereign councils had authority over more serious slave "crimes," thus, de jure at least, limiting the master's power. Not that the sovereign councils were "soft on crime." In one case, in 1679, one council did admit to some "indulgence" when it punished some thirty slaves who had stolen a boat and tried to escape. The men "only" had their left legs removed, and the women had their noses razed and their foreheads branded. The councilors warned, however, that capital punishment would imposed for similar future offenses.[113]

In this period, most masters were in daily contact with slaves. It would be naïve to suggest that familiarity bred better relations, but it remains true that the most discontented eighteenth-century slaves lived on absentee plantations run by managers whose only concern was to squeeze out quick profits in order to establish themselves as plantation masters. In the frontier and pre-plantation eras, there must have been much less paranoia about slave upheavals because of the relative demographic equilibrium and the fact that habitants had demonstrated fierce military valor, something lacking in their eighteenth-century counterparts. The slaves themselves possessed few unifying forces, not even language, because Creole was probably not fully developed.[114] They suffered from a variety of diseases, from rampaging yaws to smallpox to dysentery, which along with periodic food shortages must have discouraged systematic resistance.[115]

The above must again be placed in the context of the crude demographic picture presented earlier. The ratio of roughly one slave child for every two adult slave women at Saint-Domingue and roughly one for every slave female elsewhere cannot be explained away easily. In the official censuses, the free colored population was small and not broken down into gender and age groups. Officially, there were somewhat fewer than 1,000 in 1700;[116] anecdotal evidence suggests that significant numbers of *gens de couleur* were registered in baptismal records as whites. Rare were communities of free blacks and mulattoes as occurred at the *Fond des nègres* at Saint-Domingue.[117] After 1700, when free colored children were counted, they constituted about half of the *gens de couleur*. As elsewhere in the world of Atlantic slavery, these children were almost always the offspring of white fathers and enslaved females. Even if a certain percentage of black females became the sexual property of white masters or overseers, that does not entirely account for the low birthrates of enslaved females.

A small number of blacks acquired freedom.[118] Valiant military service for males, domestic service for women, which must often have included sexual "favors," and the ability to squeeze money out of an oppressive economy were the principal roads to freedom. According to the *Code noir*, a female slave who married her master became free, as did her children. If the master refused to marry his slave concubine, he was fined 2,000 pounds of sugar and in theory had the woman and his children confiscated. According to articles 57 and 59, freedmen had the same rights as free French subjects, although they were to demonstrate respect for their former masters (article 58). To be sure, other articles punished the manumitted severely for helping runaway slaves or for laundering stolen goods (article 39). In this period, far fewer legal restrictions on masters manumitting their slaves existed than was the case in the eighteenth century. Article 55 said that all masters over twenty years of age could grant freedom to their slaves if they wished. To be sure, pressure was building in the islands to limit the number of free mulattoes and *nègres* because of their growing numbers and their supposed immorality. Serious restrictions, however, did not occur until the eighteenth century.[119]

Labat tells of a successful freedman named Louis Galère, who ran a boat service between Saint-Pierre and Fort Royal, Martinique, charging passengers three l.t. He did so well that he owned twenty slaves, who manned his three or four large canoes.[120] Scholars of Atlantic slave systems will not be the least surprised that a freedman owned slaves.

Historians can provide little more than impressions about the "quality of life" of late seventeenth-century French slaves. So many variables are involved, ranging from the character and economic status of the master to the type and intensity of work to the regularity of supplies from Europe and to rainfall amounts in any particular year. Diet was naturally the slaves' most immediate concern, and Dutertre, for one, connects nutritional levels to the wetness or dryness of the season and the year. According to him, slaves received inadequate food from most masters and had to supplement their basic rations. They could expect a bit of meat or salt fish with their potatoes or maize or cassava or their preferred yams. At heaviest work times, most notably during the frenetic months of processing sugar from January to June, slaves might receive extra food and tafia. The master supplied vegetables from slave-worked provision grounds, although the move to sugar tempted some to cut corners. In the second half of the century, the Brazilian system of giving slaves a "free" day to take care of their own food needs encountered stiff official resistance but was not unknown.

During this era, Africans had some advantages over those of the eighteenth century in supplying their food needs. Land was more available for their small gardens, which produced herbs, vegetables, and tobacco. Although less so than in the frontier era, wild products—fish, shellfish, and crabs, as well as fruit and nuts—were also more available than in the eighteenth century.[121] Most important, before 40 official holy days were suppressed in 1728, slaves had about 100 free days a year (52 Sundays plus other holy days), comparable to the number of days off enjoyed by many modern Americans. Time devoted to gardens, to fishing and hunting, and to exchange of goods was correspondingly much greater.[122] Despite royal prohibitions, some masters gave slaves half days on Saturdays in lieu of some or all of the required foodstuffs legally mandated. Finally, unless the regulations cited above amounted purely to official paranoia, as elsewhere, slaves resorted to appropriation of European goods to supplement their food supply and acquire other items, especially cloth, tobacco, and spirits. For example, the Saint-Domingue council in 1692 attempted to halt slaves trading and bartering goods out of fear that these were their masters' property.[123] At the risk of historical anachronism, is it unreasonable to assume that these "thieves" believed they were simply retrieving the fruits of their unjustly coerced labor?

All of the above should not give the impression that slaves were well fed, or that they did not suffer from malnutrition, especially in wartime. The usual supplement of salt fish or meat to the weekly manioc allotment became more problematical, not that a manioc diet was a healthy one. But without the fish/meat protein, deficiencies became worse, and slaves found it necessary to hunt crabs at night by the light of cane trash torches.[124] The low birthrates of slave women and the low survival rate of children are symptomatic of poor nutrition. Island chroniclers noted that slaves found any form of food palatable. Discussing the inedibility of a particular type of turtle, Labat notes that slaves, "for whom all is good," ate them.[125]

Unfortunately, the scant and impressionistic evidence does not permit many safe generalizations about the living conditions of African slaves in the French Caribbean. Slave families lived in very crowded huts, which Dutertre estimates at about sixty square feet of living space. The Cartesian Labat built his slave huts in a row separated by twenty feet. If he is not exaggerating, his slave families enjoyed 450 square feet of living space.[126] Slaves had few items of furniture and slept on beds of intertwined branches covered with leaves. Contemporaries noted that they frequently bathed in rivers, so in this respect at least they had better hygiene than their masters. They certainly wore far less than masters, who typically equated status and clothing.[127] According to Dutertre, slaves suffered from many sicknesses, including yaws, dropsy (edema), and violent headaches; yet he claims that they were less often sick than Europeans.[128]

How did Africans react to this changing economic and political environment? Dutertre professed to believe that they were happy when treated well and morose, even suicidal, when poorly treated, but such observations should be viewed very cautiously. Dutertre's incredulous wonder that slaves viewed themselves as superior to Europeans in every way, and especially in physical beauty, is also typical.[129] Beyond such impressions, shards of evidence suggest that different African groups fiercely tried to maintain miniature communities within the larger social system, and apparently most owners were quite willing to accommodate their efforts. If an Angolan wished to marry an Angolan of the same habitation, and that made them content and productive, then so much the better. In any case, masters apparently believed that African males would not work without sexual outlets, and the even gender balance of the late seventeenth century indicates that they acted on that belief.[130] Owners may have turned their eyes away from the common African custom of polygamy for prestigious males. The real problem arose when potential partners lived on different plantations, but some owners switched slaves to accommodate their sexual preferences to ensure smoothness of production.[131]

At this time, relatively few Africans lived on estates large enough to support the creation of autonomous communities, and in combination with missionary zeal and presents, this may explain the surface successes of Christianity. Truly Christianized slaves were a small minority, but without the eighteenth-century massive influx of Africans from similar cultural backgrounds to reinforce traditional beliefs and customs, a syncretic Christianity might well have sunk even deeper roots in Caribbean soil. Catholic missionaries were old hands at this game, and surely the Africans were not tougher raw material than the Germans and Slavs of a thousand years earlier. Besides, the minority of Africans who cooperated with the missionaries and accepted at least the externals of Catholicism in good faith were making a rational decision, given the circumstances.[132]

In other ways, Africans sought to shape their own communities, environments, and destinies. Most slaves had access to small gardens in which they grew the tobacco of which they were so fond, and foods they found especially delectable, such as plantains and yams. They traded surplus items on market days, and the most industrious acquired some wealth that might be used one day to purchase emancipation, or to supply more immediate needs, such as liquor to deaden pain.

Opportunities for improving one's condition were not rare in the latter half of the seventeenth century. Masters furious at the high wages and "insolence" of European artisans started training some of their bondsmen to perform the former's tasks.[133] African slaves "of good will" were recruited in emergencies to control those of "bad intentions" and to fight in colonial wars. Labat praises their courage at Martinique in 1693, Cartagena in 1697–98, and Guadeloupe in 1703.[134] If crippled in combat, they received freedom and public support. Emancipation could result from especially heroic acts, such as capturing an enemy flag or officer; significant monetary rewards compensated other, less dramatic deeds, such as returning French deserters.[135]

Labat was not in the least reluctant to arm his slaves to protect the Dominican plantation against English coastal raids during the Nine Years' War. He seems to have been certain of their loyalty because of what he considered his just and fair treatment. He and his white sugar refiner alternated nightly guard duty in the company of six armed slaves. Historians of slave systems have often noted this willingness of *some* slaves to fight for masters, if for nothing else not to be removed from a situation with which they were familiar.[136] However, Labat also cautions that one should hide one's possessions during wartime or "bad" slaves would steal them.[137]

Some male slaves thus possessed some advantages in the struggle for freedom and survival. Their increasing importance in the skilled and pastoral positions on the habitations meant less time in the fields. Later, during the eighteenth century, this sexual division of labor became so marked that often 60–80 percent of field laborers were women.[138]

We know little for certain about the forms of accommodation and resistance to the system in these early days. Surely, most slaves made necessary accommodations to an oppressive system, and then tried to work in and around it. To understand the master's commands, some French words had to be assimilated. The polyglot character of African groups was another factor in the apparently slow emergence of island Creole dialects. Perhaps Creoles, those born into slavery and who most likely knew no other than the emerging Creole language, were probably less likely to violently reject their servile condition.[139] In general, these slaves were more trusted and received more favorable duties than the alienated, newly arrived Africans. Those slaves most interested in courting the favor of masters no doubt strove to imitate their language insofar possible.

Like European peasants, once they had acquired "customary rights," such as that of market day, African slaves resisted the rolling back of those "rights." Metropolitan authorities and some colonial officials professed amazement that slaves could trade goods when in law they could own nothing.[140] In 1697, the council at Saint-Domingue prohibited the purchase of goods from slaves without written permission from their masters, especially horses and indigo. The prohibition discusses how slaves fenced goods from *quartier* to *quartier* to prevent detection. The crucial issue for slaves was how to achieve some private space and decisions within the oppressive public space of slavery. They certainly committed petty thefts and did as little work as possible. They rarely tattled on each other, and they often hid thieves and *marrons;* if caught, some acted stupefied and blamed the devil.[141]

Occasionally, a brave slave might simply say no to the oppressors. Dutertre relates the story of the "virgin of the islands," a young slave woman who refused to marry because she did not want to bring a child into such a world of misery.[142] She perhaps gives some credence to the notion that female slaves, subject to both the economic and sexual whims of masters, suffered more greatly in slavery than their male counterparts. It would be useful, of course, to have more examples of these "natural rebels."[143]

Labat opines that French slaves at Saint-Domingue received harsher treatment than those in the Lesser Antilles. He explains that the opportunity to flee to Spanish Santo Domingo underlay this harsher regime. For example, only at Saint-Domingue were slaves routinely branded, a procedure horrifying to Lesser Antillean Creole slaves. Saint-Domingue slaves passed from owner to owner so frequently that, according to Labat's "humorous" rendition, their branded bodies resemble "those obelisks of Egypt."[144] He might have noted that the far more relaxed political and clerical environment of Saint-Domingue encouraged more inhumane master conduct.

Contemporary commentators noted that slaves loved to laugh at their owners' foibles, but in indirect ways, designed to avoid retribution. Labat claims that slaves had mocking nicknames for all whites, according to their perceived major faults. They hooted at poor white beggars.[145] They mocked fellow slaves' vices by saying they swore like whites, stole like them, or were drunkards like them.[146] One of Labat's slaves teased him for eating salad, food for cows and horses.[147] Like the Caribs, slaves thought Europeans ugly. Intending to astonish his readers, Dutertre writes that Africans considered black to be beautiful, that they actually preferred flattened noses and "frizzy" hair, a look Dutertre compared to the head of Medusa.[148]

With caution, we may assume that the better-known forms of eighteenth-century resistance were present earlier. The chroniclers refer to slaves' "laziness," some "nations" being lazier than others. Labat, for example, cautions sugar planters to plant perfectly straight cane rows to detect napping or hiding Negroes.[149] Pretenses of ignorance, petty or grand theft, breaking of tools, and arson no doubt occurred, although the frequency of these practices eludes the historian.

Did seventeenth-century slaves commit suicide or infanticide or induce abortions, as they were accused of doing in the succeeding century? Gaultier's previously cited evidence for high slave birthrates might suggest a negative answer but for census evidence indicating small numbers of children, which, however, may be explained by childhood illnesses and malnutrition.[150] Some contemporaries noted intense parental love of Africans for their children, so much so, according to Labat, that a shrewd owner could gain their loyalty and good behavior by treating the little ones well.[151]

Did slaves resort to poison to wreak vengeance on Europeans or other slaves, as mid eighteenth-century owners so frequently charged? This charge does not resonate much in seventeenth-century sources. True, Labat reports rumors that thirty slaves were lost to poison on a neighbor's plantation, but that is at the very end of the century.[152] Missionary writers mention the existence of sorcerers and wise women, whose herbal remedies some habitants used, but they do not connect them with the dispensation of poisons. The first local laws specifying the crime of poisoning are from the early 1720s. The *Code noir* of 1685 does not mention slave poisonings. Perhaps our sources are defective or the paranoia of eighteenth-century Europeans was absent in earlier generations.[153]

Did slaves engage more in short-term (*petit*) *marronage* or the long-term variety? Here, some evidence is available. *Petit marronage* was endemic, and resolved without excessive stress and punishment, often through clerical intervention. Labat insisted that maroons seeking his help first work a half day in his garden.[154] Long-term *marronage* by individuals or, far more troubling, communities created greater anxieties. In 1665, the maroon band at Martinique of Francisque Fabulé, a black Spartacus of Herculean proportions, provoked such tumults that the sovereign council negotiated his "surrender" by freeing him and providing a tribute in tobacco; furthermore, it promised not to punish his followers.[155] They made peace in 1665 in what a later historian calls "a necessary capitulation" on the part of the French. Martinique's Governor Robert de Clodoré hired Fabulé to round up those of his men who refused to submit, which apparently he did with some success. Clodoré even made him general of an armed band of slaves during the war with England in 1666–67. In 1671, however, the council at Martinique imprisoned Fabulé for supposedly corrupting slaves into becoming *marrons*, among other offenses. Eventually, in 1671, in what may have been a setup, this giant ex-slave was sent to the galleys.[156]

After "a large number of Negro maroons committed many disorders and violent actions" in 1671, the Martinique sovereign council condemned to death slaves of ten years' "service" who after that time became fugitives for more than three years.[157] Two years later, de Baas ordered that slaves have written permission to be outside their habitations. A few years later, the council ordered that boats be chained to prevent escapes. Specific bounties for returned slaves were established.[158] At the end of the century, according to Labat, the bounty was 500 pounds of sugar for each individual returned. Similarly, the Saint-Domingue council mandated the chaining of small boats.[159] Around 1700, permanent maroon communities existed in the mountainous interiors of Guadeloupe and Martinique.[160]

The most serious problems of *marronage* occurred at Saint-Domingue. Labat claims that probably 600–700 well-armed maroons lived in the interior of the French colony. They had established a vibrant trade with French hunter habitants, exchanging hides and smoked meat for ammunition and cloth.[161] Windward Island slaves who escaped to Carib islands risked recapture or sale to other Europeans. However, at Carib-controlled Saint Vincent, the mixed group called Black Caribs had achieved autonomy from former Carib masters by around 1700, and they may have accepted new refugees. Saint Vincent, to the windward of the French islands, was not an easy place to reach. Barbados presumably supplied its new recruits.[162]

Another form of *marronage* was taking passage on a ship returning to France. As captains were often short of crew for return passage, it must have been tempting to exchange free passage for labor. Indirect evidence for the practice comes from royal ordinances condemning it with severe fines and even prison terms for guilty captains.[163]

As for rebellions, a few relatively minor tumults broke out in this period, and were mainly connected to maroon bands. Anxieties led the authorities to display the quartered body of one Séchoux who was found guilty of conspiring to lead a band of maroons to refuge with the Caribs.[164] In 1671, the Martinique attorney general complained about the number of bands of refugee slaves, and rewards for their capture were increased. Habitants were granted permission to cut the slave's hamstring in cases of recidivism.[165] In 1677, the Martinique council instituted a list of punishments for maroons according to the length of their absence. In the same year, one Petit-Jean from Angola had his leg removed in front of assembled slaves.[166] In 1678, Blénac reported "a fairly large uprising" of slaves from the Gold Coast. Ten or twelve died in the resistance, nine were executed, and another thirteen awaited judgment.[167] Perhaps the executed exhibited the combination of defiance and stoicism of the slave at Fort Royal who requested tobacco while being burned and who kept smoking as the lower half of his body was consumed.[168]

A possible slave conspiracy occurred at Saint-Domingue in 1691, exactly one hundred years before the massive upheaval that doomed the French regime there and allowed for the creation of the first black republic, Haiti. With Spanish forces from neighboring Santo Domingo threatening Le Cap, two slaves and an indentured servant purportedly conspired to kill all the habitants' dependents while the militia was off fighting. A court martial condemned the slaves, Janot Marin and Pierrot, to burial alive; the sixteen-year-old indentured servant, Louis Blaise, was burned after being knocked on the head, In 1697, a conspiracy of "a number" of slaves may have occurred at Port-de-Paix, Saint-Domingue; at least one slave was executed. As usual with such conspiracies, the truth is impossible to tease out of scanty, biased accounts.[169]

Seventeenth-century chroniclers rarely mention slave revolts or even conspiracies to revolt. How are we to explain this difference considering the relative frequency of revolts at Barbados? Was the higher ratio of slaves to free people at Barbados the reason for the difference? Or was it that peaceful conditions at Barbados through much of the century had left the English there more complacent and less vigorous in the pursuit of arms? Or does the partial Christianization and possibly less inhumane treatment of French slaves explain the rarity of overt rebellion? These are difficult issues to address given the state of the documentation.

As the number of slaves at Saint-Domingue increased significantly in the 1690s, a decade of war, the habitants apparently became more ambivalent about these aliens in their midst. On the one hand, growing fear is apparent, as at Le Cap after the debacle of 1691 and the supposed slave conspiracy referred to above. The commandant there gave carte blanche to habitants to slay any slave suspected of "treason."[170] On the other hand, in the midst of the war crisis of 1695, discussed in Chapter 8, island officials actively recruited slaves deemed to be well disposed toward their masters. Promises of freedom in case of serious injury or for capturing enemy officers, as well as for saving a Frenchman, perhaps motivated the recruits. Slave soldiers also received thirty l.t. for each enemy head or French deserter brought in. Masters were to receive 450 l.t. for each slave who died in combat.[171] With the return of peace by 1699, the sovereign council issued an order that prohibited slaves from having access to horses and certain arms, including rifles and large clubs. Only slave commanders and those authorized to hunt for their masters were exceptions. The penalty for the first offense was the clipping of the offender's ear. The council itself was to decide the penalty ad hoc for a second offense.[172] Historians of slave systems in the Americas recognize this pattern of increasing harshness of slave codes when populations of Europeans and Africans became increasingly unbalanced.

Were African slaves of the French in this era better or worse off than Africans enslaved in their homelands? Whereas all seventeenth-century chroniclers believed those in Christian hands were more fortunate, almost all modern historians assert the contrary. Indeed, the question itself has more than a whiff of heresy. Such a comparative study, although it would have to navigate very carefully indeed to avoid charges of insensitivity, might help illuminate conditions on both sides of the Atlantic. Perhaps the information about French slavery in the American Tropics herein might provide modest help to the brave person who undertakes such a project.

In conclusion, then, despite the manifest social flaws of this pre-plantation-complex era and documented cruelties, attributable in part to disease, to human greed, and to the uncertainties of life without a developed civil society, the condition of coerced laborers in the seventeenth-century French Caribbean was perhaps not as unbearably grim as that of those in the English West Indies. Moreover, worse conditions were endured by their own eighteenth-century African and African American successors on the plantation islands.

Conclusion

In late spring of 2006, the Harvard Program in Atlantic History sponsored a seminar on the transformations of the Atlantic World at the end of the seventeenth century. I agree with the seminar's theme, that fundamental changes occurred in the French Caribbean around 1700. When the smoke cleared after the War of the Spanish Succession (1702–13; called Queen Anne's War in North America), it became apparent that the war years had seen a dramatic growth in the Caribbean colonial economy. How could that be when France faced the mighty British empire, which, in conjunction with its continental allies, finally thwarted the continental ambitions of the aging Sun King?

I can only point here to a few reasons for the strange prosperity of the French Caribbean during wartime. (Should time and patience allow, a putative sequential volume will cover the eighteenth century to 1789.) Aware that the mighty British navy dominated the French in the wars spanning from 1744 to 1815, readers might assume such maritime hegemony in an earlier era. True, the British royal navy won some important engagements in European waters (e.g., at Vigo in 1703), but its worldwide commitments left the British unable to dominate the Caribbean. A monumental naval battle opposing huge fleets such as that of the Saints (Les Saintes, 1782) was far in the future. The French alliance with Spain, the proximate cause of the war, ended the dangerous Anglo-Spanish alliance in the Caribbean that had so threatened Saint-Domingue in the Nine Years' War. French naval and privateer ships (especially from Saint-Malô in northern France and Martinique) harassed British colonial shipping. In short, the French in the Caribbean suffered little from this war.

Especially for Saint-Domingue habitants, the alliance with Spain facilitated exchanges with adjacent Santo Domingo and other parts of Spain's American empire. Under Pontchartrain, too, a struggling settlement was established in these years on the Gulf Coast, first at Biloxi (1699) and then at Mobile (1702). It barely survived the war years, in contrast to the Caribbean colonies. Still, contacts with Spanish Pensacola and Mexico helped the "Louisiana" colonists. Such French and Spanish contacts also provided needed food and beasts to power the French Caribbean islands' burgeoning sugar mills. They apparently more than offset the decrease in shipping from France.

The French monopoly of providing slaves to the Spanish empire (the *asiento*) and illicit smuggling of slaves help explain the astonishing growth of slavery in the French Caribbean after the turn of the century. James Pritchard estimates there were some 33,343 slaves in 1700; in 1715, the figure was 81,593.[1] The explosion of sugar making at the large, virgin-soil colony of Saint-Domingue transformed the buccaneer paradise into a plantation hell for slaves in a remarkably short time.[2] As I have argued throughout this volume, the development of the sugar complex in the French Caribbean occurred only in the first three decades of the eighteenth century.

How had the American Tropics changed as a result of French exploration, exploitation, and colonization in the sixteenth and seventeenth centuries? Although it was by no means a pristine wilderness, because of Native American manipulation of the environment, there is no denying that the coming of Europeans, soon accompanied by their African slaves, profoundly transformed the Greater Caribbean. Even in the sixteenth century, when the impact of transient European settlers, sailors, and marauders was less dramatic, they nevertheless exchanged ironware, "trinkets," and spirits for native produce and tobacco. Did the Old World passersby also transfer their plethora of germs and viruses? Perhaps, but no evidence is available on this issue.

From the start of the era of colonization, the European and African impact on Caribbean ecosystems and on the indigenous population dramatically accelerated. Island Caribs found themselves reduced to a few reservation islands by 1660. After that, they attempted to play Europeans off against each other to maintain some independence.[3] Although little evidence exists, it is likely that European and African diseases decreased the indigenous population. By around 1700, Labat had to hire guides to find an Island Carib village on Dominica. At that same date, "Yellow" Caribs found themselves in a struggle with Black Caribs for control of Saint Vincent. Island Caribs had valiantly struggled to maintain their customary lifestyle, but the future must have looked bleak for them by 1700.

Europeans attempted to rid the Caribbean islands of "vermin" and "pests," and to create on them frontiers of fortune. They rapidly shot edible birds and animals, most notably feral pigs, and cut down valuable trees, such as mahogany. They attempted to make of the islands little Frances insofar possible. How disheartening that wheat, grapes, and olives did not prosper in this climate. They planted soil-destroying tobacco, and then, from the 1650s on, attempted to put as much land as possible into sugar. The mountainous topography of such islands as Martinique and Saint-Domingue put limits on exploitative practices, to be sure. Not until the coffee revolution of the 1730s were island uplands seriously transformed.

It can hardly be doubted that the (great?) majority of French migrants to these tropical "paradises" found them frontiers of misfortune. Scattered census records strongly indicate a high turnover for these European immigrants. Many, especially indentured servants, died in miserable conditions. Others found a way to return to France, although how many is unclear. However hyperbolic, missionary chroniclers' stupefaction about how inhumanely masters treated indentured servants cannot simply be dismissed. That some former *engagés* survived and prospered is not in doubt, but they were a small minority. Even if they did survive, they and their descendants had to struggle to overcome the prejudice against their origins.

Free habitants had a better chance of finding fortune. Still, it is highly likely that only a minority of them prospered, married, lived reasonably long lives, and passed on their property to their widows and heirs; here the contrast with their Canadian cousins is most stark. The majority of islanders no doubt either returned to Europe or succumbed to the difficult disease environment, to wars with Caribs and European foes, or to various accidents. The most prosperous, whether due to luck or political influence or talent, became sugar planters in the second half of the seventeenth century, filled offices in the local churches and sovereign councils, and perhaps acquired minor titles of nobility. To this minority, the American Tropics were indeed frontiers of fortune. Those of their Creole children who remained in the islands were better equipped than their forebears physiologically and economically to prosper there and became the *grands blancs* of the eighteenth century.

The African slaves of the French, a two-to-one majority by 1700, never found the American Tropics a frontier of fortune. Even though they may have been slightly less unfortunate than their eighteenth-century successors, as this book has suggested, at least half their children died before adulthood; the fact that contemporary European children of the lower classes did not have a much better chance in life does not diminish the horror of the African experience. That some Africans and African Americans coped with their situation by pleasing their masters and offering military and other services to the establishment cannot be doubted, nor is it surprising. Bantering with the likes of a Father Labat must have given limited pleasure. "Volunteering" to serve as cannon fodder for Pointis and du Casse at Cartagena in desperation for freedom demonstrates the slaves' limited options. That some male slaves achieved their freedom by these means, or female slaves by offering their domestic services to perhaps lonely masters, a kind of semi-freedom to be sure, does not start to mitigate or excuse the injustices and inhumanity of the slave system. These were the fortunate few, albeit their new lives were lived in a crucible of angst that their newfound freedom was fragile indeed. The few who genuinely accepted Roman Catholic Christianity could hope for eternal bliss in heaven, where their masters (if any made it) would exist in equality with them in the presence of God. That the English and the Dutch refused to provide such an outlet is not much of a tribute to French practices.

I cannot end without reiterating my obligations to the historians who have made this volume possible. Whatever merit it may possess is largely due to early chroniclers and historians such as the Dominicans Dutertre and Labat, the almost omniscient Moreau de Saint-Méry, the nineteenth-century writer Adrien Dessalles and the early twentieth-century scholar Stewart Mims. The notes show how dependant I am on such contemporary historians as Michel Camus, Gabriel Debien, Richard Dunn, Léo Elisabeth, Philippe Hrodej, Gérard Lafleur, Abdoulaye Ly, Jean-Pierre Moreau, Sue Peabody, Jacques Petitjean Roget, and Alisa Petrovich, as well as so many other researchers in the field. Special thanks go to James Pritchard, whose masterful *In Search of Empire* made my task much less difficult. I trust that my labors, now almost forty years long, reflect the importance of their contributions.

Notes

Preface

1. Michel de Montaigne, *Essays*, trans. M. Cohen (Baltimore: Penguin Classics, 1961), 108.

2. Gabriel García Márquez's affirmation that the "natural geographical space of Brazil is the Caribbean" supports the idea of considering all French activities in tropical America as of a piece. Cited in Oruna D. Lara, *Caraïbes en construction: Espace, colonisation, résistance*, 2 vols. (Épinay-sur-Seine: Centre de recherches Caraïbes-Amériques, 1992), 1: 234.

3. Médéric Moreau de Saint-Méry, *Loix et constitutions des colonies françaises sous le vent . . .*, 6 vols. (Paris: Quillau, 1785–90). Few scholars have apparently read through his six volumes. There is a modern edition of his *Description . . . de Saint-Domingue* with an excellent introduction by Blanche Maurel and Etienne Taillemite (Paris: Larose, 1958; also 1984). The magnificent collection of his materials is housed at the French colonial archives, the Centre des archives d'outre-mer (cited below as CAOM), formerly Archives nationales, Section Outre-mer (ANSOM), now in Aix-en-Provence.

4. See, e.g., Jacques Dampierre, *Essai sur les sources de l'histoire des Antilles françaises, 1492–1664* (Paris: Picard et fils, 1904); Stewart Mims, *Colbert's West India Policy* (New Haven, Conn.: Yale University Press, 1912); and Charles Cole, *Colbert and a Century of French Mercantilism* (New York: Columbia University Press, 1939; reprint, Hamden, Conn.: Archon Books, 1964).

5. James Pritchard, *In Search of Empire: The French in the Americas, 1670–1730* (Cambridge: Cambridge University Press, 2004); Bernard Moitt, *Women and Slavery in the French Antilles, 1635–1848* (Bloomington: Indiana University Press, 2001); see also Kenneth J. Banks, *Chasing Empire across the Sea: Communications and the State in the French Atlantic, 1713–1763* (Montreal: McGill-Queen's University Press, 2002).

6. Montaigne, *Essays*, 275.

7. James McClellan III, *Colonialism and Science: Saint-Domingue in the Old Regime* (Baltimore: Johns Hopkins University Press, 1992), 18–19, 111–12.

8. Growing interest in comparative slave studies, owing, among other reasons, to the work and inspiration of the late Gabriel Debien, who was very helpful to me and other American scholars, led to the emergence of scholarly groups

such as the Association of Caribbean Historians, the French Colonial Historical Society, and various institutes in France (Bordeaux, Nantes, La Rochelle).

9. W. J. Eccles, *France in America* (New York: Harper & Row, 1972); id., *France in America*, rev. ed. (Markham, Ont.: Fitzhenry & Whiteside; East Lansing: Michigan State University Press, 1990). Dr. Eccles informed me that he had to fight his publisher to get the space he did obtain for the West Indies. In the preface to the revised edition, he writes: "Eighteen years have elapsed since this book was first written. During that time a great deal of research has been done by many scholars, including myself, which caused me to view several aspects of the history of the period in a new light." These words unfortunately do not apply to the French West Indies.

10. W. J. Eccles, *The French in North America, 1500–1783* (East Lansing: Michigan State University Press, 1998). For a more elaborate critique, see Philip P. Boucher, "W. J. Eccles's *France in America* from a Caribbeanist's Perspective," *British Journal of Canadian Studies* 11 (1997): 72–77.

11. Montaigne, *Essays*, 56.

Introduction

1. Pierre Pluchon and Lucien Abenon, eds., *Histoire des Antilles et de la Guyane* (Toulouse: Privat, 1982). Two essays by Paul Butel in this volume do give a brief overview of the seventeenth century.

2. See, e.g., works by Richard Dunn, Philip Curtin, and Ira Berlin cited below and listed in the online bibliography at www.philipboucher.com. The phrase "plantation complex" comes from Philip Curtin, *The Rise and Fall of the Plantation Complex: Essays in Atlantic History* (New York: Cambridge University Press, 1990).

3. On "false starts," see Eccles, *France in America* (1990), chap. 1.

4. I use "Island Carib" or "Carib" here because these terms are most familiar to general readers. Apologies to anthropologists and ethnohistorians who prefer terms the indigenous people used to describe themselves, such as "Kalinago." By the eighteenth century, it does not make much sense to call people of color mulattoes, because many were not, but in the early period, people of color were indeed mulattoes, almost all being the first-generation offspring of European males and African females.

5. For western historiography, see, e.g., Gordon Lewis, *Main Currents in Caribbean Thought: The Historical Evolution of Caribbean Society in Its Ideological Aspects, 1492–1900* (Baltimore: Johns Hopkins University Press, 1983; reprint, University of Nebraska Press, 2004), 17. No doubt it is very difficult for a scholar trained in European, specifically French, history, and who has immersed himself in French-language sources, to escape a "Eurocentric" approach completely.

6. The first chapter of Banks, *Chasing Empire*, intended as an overview of France's American colonies before 1700, contains a plethora of factual errors, but

in all fairness, Banks has told me that his editor insisted on last-minute addition of such materials.

7. *Voyage aux îles d'Amérique* (Paris: Archives nationales, 1992.) To be sure, there are many fine, accurate essays in this volume, and references to it will be frequent below, where it is cited as AN catalogue, *Voyage aux îles*. Based on materials he found in the Spanish archives, Jean-Pierre Moreau, *Les Petites Antilles de Christophe Colomb à Richelieu, 1493–1635* (Paris: Karthala, 1992), 181–82, also has the English colonizing Barbados before Saint Christopher.

8. My catalogue of an exhibition held at the John Carter Brown Library, Philip P. Boucher, *Les Nouvelles Frances: France in America, 1500–1815* (Providence, R.I.: John Carter Brown Library, 1989), trans. as *Les Nouvelles Frances: La France en Amérique, 1500–1815* (Sillery, Quebec: Éd. du Septentrion, 2004), offers a very brief account.

9. Michel Devèze, *Antilles, Guyanes, la mer des Caraïbes, de 1492 à 1789* (Paris: SEDES, 1977).

10. For a sound analysis of these issues relative to the British Caribbean, see Richard Dunn, *Sugar and Slaves: The Rise of the Planter Class in the English West Indies, 1624–1713* (New York: Norton, 1973), chaps. 8 and 9.

11. See, e.g., Orlando Patterson, *The Sociology of Slavery: An Analysis of the Origins, Development and Structure of Negro Slave Society in Jamaica* (Rutherford, N.J.: Fairleigh Dickinson University Press, 1967).

12. See, e.g., Charles Frostin, *Les Révoltes blanches à Saint-Domingue aux XVIIe et XVIIIe siècles: Haïti avant 1789* (Paris: Éditions de l'école, 1975), and other works of his listed in the online bibliography, www.philipboucher.com.

13. David Eltis, *The Rise of African Slavery in the Americas* (Cambridge: Cambridge University Press, 2000), 9, table 1–1.

14. Historians of Africa vigorously debate about the conditions of slavery in various regions of West Africa, and even whether the term "slavery" should be used, given the images it evokes. See, e.g., John Thornton, *Africa and Africans in the Making of the Atlantic World* (Cambridge: Cambridge University Press, 1992), 72–129.

Chapter 1. At the Dawn of French Colonization: The Greater Caribbean

1. The population of French Guiana was 199,509 as of December 2006, according to the CIA World Factbook, www.cia.gov/cia/publications/factbook/geos/fg.html (accessed February 27, 2007). And see Neil Sealey, *Caribbean World: A Complete Geography* (Cambridge: Cambridge University Press, 1992), 196.

2. Depending on the period, French possessions included Tobago; Martinique and its dependencies, Sainte-Lucie (Saint Lucia), Grenada, and the Grenadines; Guadeloupe and its dependencies, the Saintes and Marie-Galante; the French part of today's St. Kitts (Saint Christopher), called by the French Saint-

Christophe, and its dependencies, part of Saint-Martin, Saint-Barthélemy, and Saint-Croix. Further complicating this picture, the English called St. Kitts and its dependencies Leeward Islands (that is, below the wind).

3. McClelland, *Colonialism and Science*, chap. 1.

4. Guadeloupe here means the island proper of Guadeloupe and its nearly connected partner Grande-Terre, as well as Marie-Galante, the Saints, and Desirade. Guadeloupe is butterfly-shaped and consists of two islands, Guadeloupe proper and Grande-Terre, which are separated by a salt river. No two sources agree on these measurements. The *L'Historial antillais* ed. Jean-Luc Bonniol (Pointe-à-Pitre, Guadeloupe: Société Dajani, 1981), 533, has Martinique at 1,091 sq. km. In December 2003, the Saints, Desirade, Saint-Barthélemy, Marie-Galante, Saint-Martin, and Petite-Terre voted for independent status from Guadeloupe proper.

5. David Watts, *The West Indies: Patterns of Development, Culture and Environmental Change Since 1492* (Cambridge: Cambridge University Press, 1987).

6. Ibid., 12. Others are Saint Thomas, Anguilla, Barbuda, and Tobago.

7. The Carib name for Dominica was Wai'tukubuli (original spelling, Ouaitoucoubouli), which meant "Tall is her body" according to Lennox Honychurch, "Aspects of Carib/Kalinago Culture," www.lennoxhonychurch.com/article.cfm?id=389 (accessed February 27, 2007), 3–4.

8. The town of Saint-Pierre has not recovered its former prominence, and its population is under five thousand. *Hammond's Global World Atlas* (Maplewood, N.J., 1988), 160.

9. For this paragraph, see Watts, *West Indies*, 9–13. McClelland, *Colonialism and Science*, 27, counts five serious earthquakes at eighteenth-century Saint-Domingue.

10. *Hammond's World Atlas*, 82.

11. McClelland, *Colonialism and Science*, 27.

12. *Histoire des Antilles et de la Guyane*, ed. Pierre Pluchon and Lucien Abenon (Toulouse: Privat, 1982), 15.

13. Alexandre Moreau de Jonnés, *Histoire physique des Antilles françaises; savoir: La Martinique et les îles de la Guadeloupe* (Paris: Migneret, 1822), 106. For his complete list, see pp. 110–16.

14. McClelland, *Colonialism and Science*, 73–77.

15. Jean-Baptiste Dutertre, *Histoire générale des isles Antilles . . .* 4 vols. (Paris: T. Jolly, 1667–71), 2: 29. Dutertre published an earlier, one-volume *Histoire générale des isles* (Paris: J. Langlois and E. Langlois, 1654). I cite this version as *Histoire* (1654); the later edition is cited as *Histoire générale*.

16. Moreau de Jonnés, *Histoire physique*, 350–51.

17. Watts, *West Indies*, 37.

18. Ibid., 15, 66–68.

19. Moreau de Jonnés, *Histoire physique*, 170–75, 274.

20. Dutertre, *Histoire générale*, 2: 319.

21. See, e.g., ibid., 2: 289.

22. Douglas Taylor and Walter Hodges, "The Ethnobotany of the Island Carib of Dominica," *Webbia* 12 (1957): 588. The scientific name of the plant is *Bixa orellana*. The daily application of *roucou* promoted a reddish-bronze tint.

23. See Philip P. Boucher, "The Caribbean and the Caribs in the Thought of Seventeenth Century French Colonial Propagandists: The Missionaries," *Proceedings of the French Colonial Historical Society*, ed. James Cooke 4 (1979): 17–32, and "French Images of America and the Evolution of Colonial Theories," *Proceedings of the Western Society for French History* 6 (1979): 220–28.

24. See Guillaume Coppier, *Histoire et voyage des Indes occidentales* (Lyon: I. Huguetan, 1645) for the negative perspective. The Caribs' name for themselves was transcribed by the Dominican Father Raymond Breton as "Callinago," but the preferred spelling today is Kalinago.

25. For details, see the first chapter of Philip P. Boucher, *Cannibal Encounters: Europeans and Island Caribs, 1492–1763* (Baltimore: Johns Hopkins University Press, 1992).

26. For the next pages, I rely on the principal primary sources, as well as on a number of valuable books: Peter Hulme, *Colonial Encounters: Europe and the Native Caribbean* (London: Methuen, 1986); Gérard Lafleur, *Les Caraïbes des Petites Antilles* (Paris: Karthala, 1992); Moreau, *Petites Antilles;* Laurence Verrand, *La Vie quotidienne des Indiens Caraïbes aux Petites Antilles (XVIIe siècle)* (Paris: Karthala, 2001); and Doris Garraway, *The Libertine Colony: Creolization in the Early French Caribbean* (Durham, N.C.: Duke University Press, 2005), chap. 1.

27. Verrand, *Vie quotidienne*, 95–101, chronologically cites seventeenth-century chroniclers' depictions of Island Carib material and spiritual culture. In some cases, such as funerary rites, contemporaries demonstrate significant concurrences about Carib practices.

28. For an introduction to the debates, see Boucher, *Cannibal Encounters*, 1–11.

29. Caribs told missionaries that they had been on the islands for ten generations, which carbon-14 dating confirms, according to Robert Divonne's introduction to Adrien Le Breton's contemporary *Historic Account of Saint Vincent, the Indian Youroumaÿn, the Island of the Karaÿbes* (Mayreau Island: Mayreau Environmental Organization, 1998).

30. Raymond Breton's manuscript writings are available in *Les Caraïbes, La Guadeloupe . . . d'après les relations du R. P. Breton*, ed. Joseph Rennard (Paris: Ficker, 1929).

31. Raymond Breton, *Dictionnaire caraïbe-françois* (Auxerre: G. Bouquet, 1665); see Douglas Taylor, *Languages of the West Indies* (Baltimore: Johns Hopkins University Press, 1977), which summarizes the work of dozens of technical articles.

32. Among others, see C. J. M. R. Gullick, *Myths of a Minority* (Assen, Netherlands: Van Gorcum, 1985).

33. Douglas Taylor and B. J. Hoff, "The Linguistic Repertory of the Island Carib in the Seventeenth Century: The Men's Language, a Carib Pidgin?" *International Journal of American Linguistics* 46 (1980): 301–12.

34. Breton spent about five years living with the Caribs of Dominica and nineteen years in all in the islands (1635–54). No other missionary of that era lasted even ten years in the islands. See a modern edition of his *Relations de l'Ile de Guadeloupe*, 2 vols. (Basse-Terre: Société d'Histoire de la Guadeloupe, 1978).

35. See, e.g., Kenneth F. Kiple and Kriemhild C. Ornelas, "After the Encounter: Disease and Demographics in the Lesser Antilles," in *The Lesser Antilles in the Age of European Expansion*, ed. Robert Paquette and Stanley Engerman (Gainesville: University Press of Florida, 1996), 56.

36. For sixteenth-century Spanish–Island Carib conflicts, see Joseph Boromé, "Spain and Dominica," *Caribbean Quarterly* 12, 4 (1996): 30–46; Moreau, *Petites Antilles.*

37. Caribs made fermented drinks from sweet potatoes, as well as palm and hog plum wine. For fascinating details, see Taylor and Hodges, "Ethnobotany."

38. Le Breton, *Historic Account*, 9–13.

39. Moreau, *Petites Antilles*, 121.

40. See, e.g., Jacques Bouton, *Relation de l'établissement des français depuis l'an de 1635 en l'isle de la Martinique* (Paris: Cramoisy, 1640), 130. The predominance of Spanish words undermines the view that hatred alone characterized Island Carib–Hispanic relationships.

41. Boucher, *Cannibal Encounters*, 16–17.

42. After the French gained control of most of Guadeloupe and Martinique by the 1650s, Dominica became the home of evicted Caribs, who may have numbered from 4,000 to 5,000 there.

43. The term *karbay* is of Tupi-Guarini origin according to Honychurch, "Aspects of Carib/Kalinago Culture," 5.

44. The anonymous author of a manuscript account of a freebooter voyage to Martinique shrewdly guessed that the Caribs did not really know the cause of their ancient hatred of the Arawaks, but that custom dictated the cycle of war and vengeance. See *Un Flibustier français dans la mer des Antilles, 1618–1620*, ed. Jean-Pierre Moreau (Paris: Seghers, 1990), 217. Perhaps he had read Montaigne's famous essay "Cannibals," which comes to a similar conclusion about Tupi-Guarini wars.

45. Verrand, *Vie quotidienne*, 69–73, is good on the issue of captaincy.

46. See Boucher, *Cannibal Encounters* for an evaluation of these sources; and see also Robert Myers, "Island Carib Cannibalism," *New West India Guide / Nieuwe West-Indische Gids* 58 (1984): 147–85. Most current French authors, not being familiar with such English-language sources, gullibly reflect seventeenth-

century contemporary views on the topic. See, e.g., Verrand, *Vie quotidienne*, 217–22.

47. *Flibustier français dans la mer des Antilles*, 20–22, 137.

48. See Jean Hallay, "La Martinique et les Antilles au XVIIe siècle, relation du P. Jean Hallay de la Compagnie de Jésus," *Nouvelle revue retrospective* 17 (1902): 74. Other meals were family-based and less formal. See Verrand, *Vie quotidienne*, 150–51.

49. On males making basketry, see Jean-Baptiste Labat, *Nouveau voyage aux isles*, 6 vols. (Paris: P. F. Giffart, 1722), 2: 50–51. Unlike some sources who had little direct contact, the author of *Flibustier français dans la mer des Antilles* describes Carib males as constantly busy (183–84). The younger men played a vigorous and amazing ball game requiring "inimitable" acrobatic skills (184–85).

50. See the very sympathetic account of Le Breton, *Historic Account*, 13–16.

51. Ibid., 17–19.

52. *Flibustier français dans la mer des Antilles*, 185–87.

53. See, e.g., Hallay, "Martinique et les Antilles au XVIIe siècle," 74.

54. *Flibustier français dans la mer des Antilles*, 154.

55. Dutertre, *Histoire* (1654), 422; Charles de Rochefort, *Histoire naturelle et morale des isles . . .* (Rotterdam: A. Leers, 1665), 509.

56. Verrand, *Vie quotidienne*, 133–35. See his list of cultivated plants on p. 137.

57. See Dutertre, *Histoire* (1654), 424–25, for a longer list of goods they traded, which includes domesticated poultry and wild pigs, neither of which Caribs ate.

58. For something of an exception, see Le Breton, *Historic Account*, 20–21.

59. For these and other details, see *Flibustier français dans la mer des Antilles*, 207–15.

60. See Boucher, *Cannibal Encounters*, 36.

61. Hallay, "Martinique et les Antilles au XVIIe siècle," 81.

62. *Flibustier français dans la mer des Antilles*, 193–98.

63. Le Breton, *Historic Account*, 26–27, gives the above description without negative editorializing.

64. *Flibustier français dans la mer des Antilles*, 179–80. On the next page, he notes how he was starting to understand their language. Of all Carib beliefs and practices, this writer was most offended by these "fantasies" and "superstitions." Breton does not mention this paradisiacal myth.

65. Significant conversions could be realized if the Indians could only be settled and "reduced," the Jesuit Hallay believed ("Martinique et les Antilles au XVIIe siècle," 83).

66. Dutertre, *Histoire générale*, 2: 501.

Chapter 2. French Challenges to Iberian Hegemony in America up to 1625

1. On this tragic encounter, see Carl Sauer, *The Early Spanish Main* (Berkeley: University of California Press, 1966).

2. Moreau, *Petites Antilles*, esp. 28–40.

3. In 1493, the Spanish Borgia Pope Alexander VI divided the world between the Portuguese and Spanish. The two crowns agreed on a somewhat different division the following year at Tordesillas.

4. Charles Bréard, *Documents relatifs à la marine normande . . . pour les Antilles* (Rouen: A. Lestringant, 1889). See also Gayle Brunelle, *The New World Merchants of Rouen, 1559–1630* (Kirksville, Mo.: Sixteenth Century Journal Publishers, 1991).

5. See inter alia Boucher, *Cannibal Encounters*, 20–22; Olive Dickason, "The Brazilian Connection: A Look at the French Techniques for Trading with Amerindians," *Revue française d'histoire d'Outre-mer* 71 (1984): 129–46.

6. Laurent Vidal, "La Présence française dans le Brésil colonial au XVIe siècle," *Cahiers des Amériques latines"* 34 (2000–2002): 22.

7. Jean Meyer, "Nantes au XVIe siècle," in *La France et la mer au siècle des grandes découvertes*, ed. Philippe Masson and Michel Vergé-Francheschi (Paris: Tallandier, 1993), 93.

8. See Frederick Baumgartner, "Adam's Will: Act II Henry II and French Overseas Expeditions," *Proceedings of the French Colonial Historical Society*, ed. Philip Boucher, 11 (1985): 137–49.

9. Frank Lestringant has made a brilliant career out of studying these expeditions. See, e.g., his *Le Huguenot et le sauvage: L'Amérique et la controverse coloniale en France, au temps des guerres de religion* (Paris: Klincksieck, 1990).

10. Quoted in Paul Hoffman, *The Spanish Crown and the Defense of the Caribbean, 1535–1585: Precedent, Patrimonialism and Royal Parsimony* (Baton Rouge: Louisiana State University Press, 1980), 68.

11. For a well-researched if hagiographical biography of Villegaignon, see Arthur Heulhard, *Villegaignon: Roi d'Amérique* (Paris: Leroux, 1897).

12. For Coligny's evolving attitudes to the reform movement, later known as the Huguenot Cause, see Lilian Creté, *Coligny* (Paris: Fayard, 1985), 73–76.

13. For French images of Brazil, see Boucher, *Cannibal Encounters*, 21–22. Not all the letters attributed to Vespucci were his.

14. Villegaignon called the native women "whores." Cited in Frank Lestringant, *L'Expérience huguenote au nouveau monde, XVIe siècle* (Geneva: Droz, 1996). Lestringant's publications are essential to a new understanding of this era; perhaps most of all his *Le Huguenot et le sauvage*. See esp. 283–304 for an invaluable

chronology of events, coupled with a list of French and European writings on America between 1493 and 1615.

15. Vidal, "Présence française," 27.

16. Among others, see Ch. André Julien, *Les Voyages de découverte et les premiers établissements (XVe–XVIe siècles)* (Paris: Presses universitaires de France, 1948), 206–10, and Lestringant, *Huguenot et le sauvage.*

17. French and Tupinambá resistance on the coast north of Rio continued until the 1570s.

18. A handy reference is Frederick Baumgartner, *France in the Sixteenth Century* (New York: St. Martin's Press, 1995).

19. Ribaut argued that his intentions and those of France were peaceful colonization, but one may well be skeptical. See Jean Ribaut, *The Whole and True Discoverye of Terra Florida* (Deland: Florida State Historical Society, 1927), 53–60, a reprint of the 1563 English version, the French original having disappeared.

20. A useful translation of the important primary documents is *Laudonnière and Fort Caroline: History and Documents,* trans. Charles Bennett (1964; reprint, Tuscaloosa: University of Alabama Press, 2001).

21. The 1560s was an exceptionally dry decade and thus hardly likely to have seen abundant harvests. See Brian Fagan, *The Little Ice Age: How Climate Made History, 1300–1800* (New York: Basic Books, 2000), 96.

22. Woodbury Lowery, *The Spanish Settlements Within the Present Limits of the United States: Florida, 1562–1574* (New York: Russell & Russell, 1959), 122.

23. John McGrath, *The French in Early Florida: In the Eye of the Hurricane* (Gainesville: University Presses of Florida, 2000), 52.

24. Lowery, *Spanish Settlements,* 142–43.

25. Here I am following the analysis of McGrath, *French in Early Florida,* 123–24.

26. Laudonnière's *L'Histoire notable* (1586) is available in *Les Français en Amérique pendant la deuxième moitié du XVIe siècle,* ed. Suzanne Lussagnet and Ch. André Julien (Paris: Presses universitaires de France, 1958); also in English in René Goulaine de Laudonnière, *Three Voyages,* trans. and ed. Charles Bennett (Gainesville: University Presses of Florida, 1975).

27. Those familiar with the Roanoke voyages of the 1580s will recognize some striking parallels with the Florida ones of the 1560s: Coligny/Ralegh and the Calvinist/Puritan character of enterprises aimed at outflanking the Spaniards in America; the exploratory voyages; the failed first colonial effort due in part to Laudonnière's and Ralph Lane's mishandling of relations with local indigenes; the critical role of tempests in aborting these enterprises (September 13–15, 1565, and June 10–13, 1586); the monarchs' tepid support, inasmuch as immediate prospects were less than striking; and the difficulty of resupplying these outposts because of crises at home. Finally, Coligny and Ralegh, those champi-

ons of international Protestantism, were killed in part for their aggressive opposition to Spain.

28. Almost exactly two decades later, Sir Francis Drake arrived at Roanoke to resupply the English colony. However, after suffering losses to a tropical storm in early June, he transported the colonists home only days before relief ships arrived.

29. Even though McGrath subtitled his book *In the Eye of the Hurricane*, I prefer to use the word "tempest," because tropical storm winds (i.e., under 74 mph) could have easily ravaged Ribaut's ships.

30. Since Spanish archival evidence was not published until the nineteenth century, French, primarily Huguenot, views have long held sway. The modern, revisionist view may be found in Eugene Lyon, *The Enterprise of Florida* (Gainesville: University of Florida Press, 1976) and McGrath, *French in Early Florida*.

31. See Boucher, *Nouvelles Frances*, 13–16, for a succinct account of these polemics; or, for a lengthy one, Lestringant, *Huguenot et le sauvage*.

32. One can read these and other sixteenth-century accounts in *Français en Amérique*, ed. Lussagnet and Julien.

33. André Thevet, *La Cosmographie universelle . . .* 2 vols. (Paris: P. L'Huillier, 1575); and Jean de Léry, *Histoire d'un voyage . . .* (La Rochelle: Antoine Chuppin, 1578). Janet Whatley has translated Léry as *History of a voyage to the land of Brazil, otherwise called America* (Berkeley: University of California Press, 1990).

34. See, e.g., Guillaume du Bartas, *La Seconde sepmaine* (Antwerp: Mersmann, 1591), bk. 7, 88. "You, France, open your bosom to me, mother, you do not wish / That in strange countries, a vagabond I grow old / You do not wish that a Brazil pride itself with my bones."

35. Nicholas Le Challeux, *Discours de l'histoire de Floride*, in *Français en Amérique*, ed. Lussagnet and Julien, 204.

36. Cited in Boucher, *Nouvelles Frances*, 16.

37. See Sue Peabody, *"There are no Slaves in France": The Political Culture of Race and Slavery in the Ancien Régime* (New York: Oxford University Press, 1996).

38. *Copie d'une lettre . . . par les capitaines des galleres* (La Rochelle: Jean Portau, 1583) as printed in Paul Gaffarel, *Histoire du Brésil français* (Paris: Maissoneuve, 1878), 493–501.

39. Brunelle, *New World Merchants*, 44–48.

40. See, e.g., Laudonnière in *Français en Amérique*, ed. Lussagnet and Julien, 41–42. Also Russ Managhni, "Sassafras and Its Role in Early America, 1562–1662," *Terrae Incognitae* 29 (1997): 10–21. To sixteenth-century people, it was axiomatic that God would place a remedy in America for what was believed to be an American disease.

41. Moreau, *Petites Antilles*, 89.

42. Mickäel Augeron, "Coligny et les Espagnols à travers la course (c. 1560–1572): Une politique maritime au service de la Cause protestante," in *Coligny, les Protestants et la mer*, ed. Martine Acerra and Guy Martinière (Paris: Presses de l'Université de Paris–Sorbonne, 1997), 167.

43. Michel Vergé-Francheschi, "L'Admirauté de France dans la deuxième moitié du XVIe siècle: Un enjeu entre catholiques et protestants," in *Coligny, les Protestants et la mer*, ed. Acerra and Martinière.

44. Iberian America did not get a breathing spell, however, because English and Dutch corsairs swarmed there in the 1580s and 1590s. See, e.g., Kenneth Andrews, *The Spanish Caribbean: Trade and Plunder, 1530–1630* (New Haven, Conn.: Yale University Press, 1978); Cornelius Ch. Goslinga, *The Dutch in the Caribbean and on the Wild Coast* (Gainesville: University of Florida Press, 1971).

45. Jean Mocquet, *Voyages en Afrique, Asie, Indes Orientales et Occidentales* (Rouen: Chez Jacques Cailloué, 1645). The best source for this Brazilian episode is Andrea Daher, *Les Singularités de la France équinoxiale: Histoire de la mission des pères capucins au Brésil (1612–1615)* (Paris: Honoré Champion, 2002).

46. Walter Ralegh, *The Discovery of Guiana* (1596; reprint, Amsterdam: Da Capo Press, 1968).

47. Mocquet, *Voyages*, 115.

48. On the interest in sugar, see Claude d'Abbeville, *Histoire de la Mission des pères capucins en l'isle de Maragnan* (Paris: Huby, 1614), 208.

49. Mocquet, *Voyages*, 97–101.

50. See Guillaume de Vaumas, *L'Éveil missionaire de la France* (Lyon: Imprimerie Express, 1942), 53–55, for these events. The French were not the only ones interested in Brazil. Extensive Dutch and English activities in the same area have been documented. On the Dutch, see Goslinga, *The Dutch in the Caribbean*; on the English, Joyce Lorimer, *English and Irish Settlements on the River Amazon, 1550–1646* (London: Haklyut Society, 1989). La Ravardière's fleet skirted Tobago on its return and saw herds of wild goats there (Mocquet, *Voyages*, 137). Mocquet's account was translated by Nathaniel Pullen as *Travels and voyages into Africa, Asia, and America, the East and West-Indies, Syria, Jerusalem, and the Holy-land* (London, 1696). Is this perhaps a source for Robinson Crusoe's goats? To be sure, Alexander Selkirk's island in the South Pacific also had goats.

51. The pope's price for annulling a previous marriage was that Henri wed the strongly Catholic princess of Tuscany. Henri performed his marital duty, and Marie was pregnant within the first months of marriage. See Baumgartner, *France in the Sixteenth Century*, 233–34.

52. Vidal, "Présence française," 32.

53. The reader limited to English may consult Boucher, *Nouvelles Frances*, 17–22; or John Hemming, *Red Gold: The Conquest of the Brazilian Indians* (Cambridge, Mass.: Harvard University Press, 1978).

54. See Claude d'Abbeville, *Histoire de la mission*, 71–73.

55. The standard money of account was the *livre tournois* (l.t.), which equaled twenty *sols* of hard money. Each *sol* in turn was worth twelve *deniers*. The silver *écu* of some forty-two grams of silver was valued in the seventeenth century at three l.t., so each l.t. was the equivalent of about fourteen grams of silver. The gold *louis* was worth twenty-four l.t. In the islands, the *livre sucrier* (l.s) came to be worth one-third less than the l.t. In all the islands, but especially at Saint-Domingue, the Spanish peso (*piastre*, or in English piece of eight), worth approximately three l.t., circulated in much greater volume than any other currency.

56. Daher, *Singularités*, 59.

57. Fortunately, not all copies of Yves d'Evreux's book about the colony, *Suitte de l'histoire des choses mémorables advennues en Maragnan és années 1613 et 1614* (Paris: Huby, 1615), were destroyed; the New York Public Library has one of the two extant. For a modern edition with notes, see *Voyage au nord de Brésil. Fait en 1613 et 1614*, ed. Hélène Clastres (Paris: Payot, 1985).

58. For a contemporary Portuguese account, see Lorimer, *Early English and Irish Settlements*, 168.

59. Goslinga, *Dutch in the Caribbean*, 417. *Galibi* and *Caraibe* are slightly different formulations of the same word.

60. A serious study of French failures to establish a colony in Guiana, largely because of the Galibis' hostility, raises deep questions about the myth of superior French conduct toward indigenous populations of America.

61. Warner and his men had earlier failed to plant in the Amazon valley.

62. AN catalogue, *Voyage aux îles*, 41.

63. Moreau, *Petites Antilles*, 160.

64. Printed in AN catalogue, *Voyage aux îles*, 128. According to the contract of association of 1626, Roissey and d'Esnambuc are described as having conducted operations in the Antilles for fifteen years.

65. Bréard, *Documents relatifs à la marine normande*, 212. Roissey sold the sugar for more than 15,000 l.t.

66. On the charter, see Moreau de Saint-Méry, *Loix et constitutions*, 1: 18–19. My book is greatly indebted to this invaluable compilation of primary documents.

Chapter 3. Frontiers of Fortune?
The Painful Era of Settlement, 1620s to 1640s

1. Prosper Cultru, *La Colonisation d'autrefois: Le Commandeur de Poincy à Saint-Christophe* (Paris, 1915), 7, admonished against exaggerating the role of the state, writing: "Before Colbert, nothing was done in the seventeenth century on the question of colonization but by actions of individuals, however weak and indecisive these were: the support of the state, magnificent when one reads just

preambles to edicts, is reduced to very little when one looks at the facts on the ground."

2. For a brief overview of Richelieu's colonial policy, see Philip P. Boucher, *The Shaping of the French Colonial Empire: A Bio-Bibliography of the Careers of Richelieu, Fouquet and Colbert* (New York: Garland, 1985). For a longer survey, see L.-A. Boiteux, *Richelieu: Grand Maître de la navigation et du commerce de France* (Paris: Ozanne, 1955).

3. Claude Aboucaya, *Les Intendants de la Marine sous l'Ancien Régime* (Gap: Louis-Jean, 1958), 31.

4. At the beginning of the century, one *livre tournois* (l.t.) was worth about ten grams of silver. Throughout the seventeenth century, the English pound contained a little over 100 grams of silver. Alain-Philippe Blérald, *Histoire économique de la Guadeloupe et de la Martinique, du XVIIe siècle à nos jours* (Paris: Karthala, 1986).

5. The Athenian general and statesman Pericles (r. 461–429 B.C.E.) persuaded Athenians to fortify and protect their city and to attack the Spartan enemy via maritime raids on their home territory.

6. A major famine occurred in France in 1630–31, the first one since 1596–97. Robin Briggs, *Early Modern France, 1560–1715* (Oxford: Oxford University Press, 1977), 38.

7. For excerpts from Rasilly's memorandum of 1626, see Jules Saintoyant, *La Colonisation française sous l'ancien régime (du XVe siècle à 1789)*, 2 vols. (Paris: La Renaissance du livre, 1929), 1: 82–83.

8. Armand Jean du Plessis, Cardinal de Richelieu, *Mémoires . . .* in *Nouvelle collection des mémoires . . .* ed. Michaud and Poujalet, 3 vols. (Paris: Féchoz & Letouzey, 1881), 1: 438.

9. Cultru, *Colonisation*, 10–11.

10. Boiteux, *Richelieu*, 293.

11. The charter can be examined in Dutertre, *Histoire générale*, 1: 209–15. The 7,000 figure is cited in the charter itself.

12. On Barbados, see Dunn's admirable *Sugar and Slaves*, chaps. 2 and 3.

13. The most accessible English account is Nellis Crouse, *French Pioneers in the West Indies, 1624–1664* (New York: Columbia University Press, 1940).

14. The term "sneak attack" is Dunn's in *Sugar and Slaves*, 119. For European–Island Carib relations throughout these years, see Boucher, *Cannibal Encounters*, chap. 2.

15. On the treaty, see Dutertre, *Histoire générale*, 1: 18–20.

16. Moreau, *Petites Antilles*, 196. He cites Spanish sources for these numbers.

17. Dutertre, *Histoire générale*, 1: 62. Dutertre, *Histoire* (1654), 24, claims that the English were so terrified of the French that they would "rather fight two devils than one Frenchman."

18. D'Esnambuc established the custom of a three-year term to mitigate the hostility of bonded servants toward masters hoping to emulate the longer terms of English bonded servants. Boiteux, *Richelieu*, 288.

19. One such was Guillaume Coppier, who published an account of his travels and travails under the title *Histoire et voyage des Indes occidentales*.

20. D'Esnambuc's letter is printed in Maurice de Lavigne de Sainte-Suzanne, *La Martinique au premier siècle de la colonisation (1635–1742)* (Nantes: Chantreau, 1935), 207–8.

21. For the case against overly simplistic attributions of Native American susceptibility to imported epidemic diseases, see David S. Jones, "Virgin Soils Revisited," *William and Mary Quarterly*, 3rd ser., 11, no. 4 (October 2003): 703–42.

22. Dutertre, *Histoire* (1654), 114.

23. Jacques Bouton, *Relation de l'établissement des François* (Paris: Cramoisy, 1640), 40. The Jesuit Bouton published the first major account of the French islands. Du Parquet carried six or seven pistols. Joseph Rennard, *Tricentenaire des Antilles, Guadeloupe-Martinique, 1635–1935* (Fort-de-France, Martinique: René Cottrel, 1935), 105.

24. Matthieu du Puis, *Relation de l'establissement d'une colonie Françoise dans la gardeloupe de l'Amérique* (Caen: Marin Yvon, 1652; reprint, Basse-Terre, Guadeloupe: Société d'histoire de la Guadeloupe, 1972), 23–24, 28.

25. Dutertre, *Histoire générale*, 2: 84–92, esp. 92. These events can also be followed in Adrien Dessalles, *Histoire générale des Antilles*, 5 vols. (Paris, 1847), 1: 72–75. De l'Olive has his defenders. See Henry Renault du Motey, *Guillaume d'Orange et les origines des Antilles françaises* (Paris: Picard, 1908), 148.

26. Du Puis, *Relation*, 41–45.

27. Rochefort, *Histoire naturelle et morale*, 316–21, 321–22.

28. See Boucher, *Cannibal Encounters*, 42–43, and Dutertre, *Histoire générale*, 1: 75; and for more detail on these early years at Martinique, see Jacques Petitjean Roget, *La Société d'habitation à la Martinique: Un Demi-siècle de formation, 1635–1685*, 2 vols. (Paris: Champion, 1980).

29. Joseph Rennard, *Histoire religieuse des Antilles françaises* (Paris: Larose, 1954), 15–17.

30. See David Allen, "The Social and Religious World of a Knight of Malta in the Caribbean, c. 1632–1660," *Libraries and Culture* 25, no. 2 (1990): 147–57.

31. The registers of the Compagnie des Isles are in CAOM, F2A19. Pages from these registers about the company's relations with early missionaries are reproduced in Rennard, *Tricentenaire des Antilles*, 225–33.

32. Letters are in Moreau de Saint-Méry, *Loix et constitutions*, 1: 72.

33. Abbé J. Leber and Gabriel Debien, "La Propagande et le recrutement pour les colonies d'Amérique au dix-septième siècle," *Conjonction* 48 (1953): 80.

34. Gabriel Debien, *Les Esclaves aux Antilles françaises (XVIIe–XVIIIe siècles)* (Basse-Terre, Guadeloupe: Société d'histoire de la Guadeloupe, 1974), 252.

35. See Allen, "Social and Religious World," 149.

36. Boiteux, *Richelieu*, 307. In 1635, the price dropped from 100 l.t. the hundredweight to fifty; in 1637, it declined to forty l.t.; by late 1639, it had dropped to less than twenty.

37. Du Motey, *Guillaume d'Orange*, 30–31. See also Poincy's often disingenuous account of these affairs to the Compagnie des Isles in Rennard, *Tricentenaire des Antilles*, 110–12.

38. On the inflating costs of war, see Geoffrey Parker, *The Military Revolution: Military Innovation and the Rise of the West, 1500–1800* (Cambridge: Cambridge University Press, 1996); on the French army, see John Lynn, *Giant of the Grand Siècle: The French Army, 1610–1715* (Cambridge: Cambridge University Press, 1997).

39. Briggs, *Early Modern France*, 38.

40. For this paragraph, see *France in Crisis, 1620–1675*, ed. P. J. Coveney (Totowa, N.J.: Rowan & Littlefield, 1977).

41. For an overview of the seventeenth-century "crisis," see Geoffrey Parker and Lesley M. Smith, *The General Crisis of the Seventeenth Century*, 3rd ed. (New York: Routledge, 1997).

42. For a good overall view of these social conditions, see George Huppert, *After the Black Death: A Social History of Early Modern Europe*, 2d ed. (Bloomington: Indiana University Press, 1998).

43. For Richelieu's vast wealth, see Joseph Bergin, *Cardinal Richelieu: Power and the Pursuit of Wealth* (New Haven, Conn.: Yale University Press, 1985). At his death, the cardinal was worth at least 20 million l.t. See also *State and Society in Seventeenth Century France*, ed. Raymond Kierstead (New York: New Viewpoints, 1975) on the "system."

44. Hubert Méthivier, "A Century of Conflict: the Economic and Social Disorders of the '*Grand Siècle*,'" in *France in Crisis*, ed. Coveney, 70.

45. According to Cosimo Brunetti, in 1660, tobacco worth fifty l.t. the hundredweight paid a duty of ten l.t.; sugar worth thirty l.t. the hundredweight paid seventeen and a half l.t. In Holland, although prices for colonial produce were substantially lower, the only duty was five *sous* the hundredweight (one l.t. = twenty sous). "Cosimo Brunetti: Three Relations of the West Indies, 1659, 1660," ed. Susan Heller Anderson, *Transactions of the American Philosophical Society* 59, pt. 6 (1969): 31, n. 95.

46. Mims, *Colbert's West India Policy*, 40.

47. Dutertre, *Histoire générale*, 2: 463–64.

48. Ibid. Although the role of the Dutch in launching the sugar revolution in Barbados has recently been downplayed, they were vital to the development

of the French industry. Thanks to Carla Pestana for her comments on previous exaggeration of the Barbados-Dutch connection.

49. According to Dutertre, *Histoire* (1654), 172–73, Poincy learned the secrets of making sugar from a Portuguese who was pardoned for a capital crime in return for divulging them.

50. Ibid., 162–64.

51. Rennard, *Tricentenaire des Antilles*, 118–19.

52. For greater detail, see Dutertre, *Histoire* (1654), 299–304. Poincy, a man "of singular piety," later told the Carmelite Maurile de Saint Michel that removing the Capuchins "caused him pain." See Maurile de Saint Michel, *Voyage des îles Camercanes, en l'Amérique . . .* (Le Mans: H. Olivier, 1652), 45.

53. In a wonderful print of Poincy's estate, the slaves' accommodations are called the *ville d'Angole*, or Angolan village. Rochefort, *Histoire naturelle et morale*, opposite p. 52.

54. Dutertre, *Histoire* (1654), 328–37.

55. Thoisy did eventually win lawsuits against Poincy and Houël awarding him 90,000 and 61,715 pounds of tobacco respectively. See Dutertre, *Histoire générale*, 1: 392–94.

56. Dutertre, *Histoire* (1654), 380–85. Poincy was to readmit those he exiled and restore their property.

57. Ibid., 393–94.

58. *Histoire de l'Isle de Grenade en Amérique, 1649–1659: Manuscrit anonyme de 1659,* ed. Jacques Petitjean Roget (Montreal: Presses universitaires de Montréal, 1975), p. 12. The company registers detailing its financial agonies are reproduced in Rennard, *Tricentenaire des Antilles,* 117–21.

59. Mims, *Colbert's West India Policy,* 42, cites a letter from Houël to Boisseret claiming that he could produce 100,000 pounds of sugar and much tobacco by 1650, but this was bravado, because his efforts to establish sugar mills that could produce white sugar had failed. See Chapter 5 above.

60. Dutertre, *Histoire générale,* 1: 40.

61. Dessalles, *Histoire générale,* 1: 156 says 73,000 l.t.

62. Ibid., 443.

Chapter 4. Frontiers of Fortune?
The Era of the Proprietors, 1649 to 1664

1. See the text of the king's *arrêt* in Moreau de Saint-Méry, *Loix et constitutions,* 1: 98–99.

2. Unlike Saint-Christophe, Saint Martin / Sint Maarten remains in the joint possession of the French and Dutch.

3. On proprietary rule as superior to that of the Compagnie des Isles, see Dutertre, *Histoire* (1654), 468.

4. See, e.g., Rochefort, *Histoire naturelle et morale,* 339.

5. Gabriel Debien, "Les Engagés pour les Antilles, 1634–1715," *Revue d'histoire des colonies* 37 (1951): 158–70.

6. Dutertre, *Histoire* (1654), 468.

7. Robert Batie, "Why Sugar? Economic Cycles and the Changing of Staples in the English and French Antilles, 1624–54," *Journal of Caribbean History* 8–9 (1976): 40. For evidence of growth, see Mims, *Colbert's West India Policy*, 45.

8. Peter Moogk, *La Nouvelle France: The Making of French Canada — A Cultural History* (East Lansing: Michigan State University Press, 2000), 108–9, suggests that some two-thirds of servants in New France returned, apparently a much higher rate of return than for English servants.

9. Jan Rogozinski, *A Brief History of the Caribbean from the Arawak and the Carib to the Present* (New York: Meridian Books, 1994), 19. This "estimate" is, however, largely guesswork.

10. Pierre Pelleprat, *Relation des missions . . . dans les isles* (Paris: S. Cramoisy, 1655), 16–17.

11. Rochefort, *Histoire naturelle et morale*, 344.

12. Cosimo Brunetti, a contemporary commentator, claimed that a hundred Martinique militiamen could defeat three or four hundred European infantry, and that twenty-five could take on three hundred Caribs. "Cosimo Brunetti," ed. Anderson, 29.

13. Dutertre, *Histoire générale*, 2: 439–44.

14. See, e.g., Pelleprat, *Relation*, 9.

15. Dutertre, *Histoire générale*, 1: 463

16. Ernst van den Boogaart, "Un Second Brésil au territoire des Caraïbes," in *La France-Amérique (XVIe–XVIIIe siècles): Actes du Colloque international d'études humanistes*, ed. Frank Lestringant (Paris: Champion, 1998), 279–80.

17. Ambushes of Carib pirogues by Martinique fishing vessels in the Grenadines also played a role in pushing the Caribs to war. *Histoire de l'Isle de Grenade . . . anonyme*, ed. Petitjean Roget, 61, 63.

18. Perhaps because he had returned to France, Dutertre discusses these events neither in his 1654 *Histoire* nor in the 1667 edition.

19. Dutertre, *Histoire générale*, 1: 433.

20. *Histoire de l'Isle de Grenade . . . anonyme*, ed. Petitjean Roget, 18–19.

21. Dutertre, *Histoire générale*, 1: 462–63.

22. For eulogies of the almost universally admired du Parquet, see *Histoire de l'Isle de Grenade . . . anonyme*, ed. Petitjean Roget, 155–56.

23. Dutertre, *Histoire générale*, 3: 536.

24. *Histoire de l'Isle de Grenade . . . anonyme*, ed. Petitjean Roget, 22–23. "Indian" Warner attacked isolated habitations on Sunday morning, when he knew from his Christian upbringing that the colonists would be at church, according to this author, the Dominican Bénigne Bresson, who depicts Warner as a dangerous, duplicitous charmer. Ibid., 185–87.

25. For further details, see Boucher, *Cannibal Encounters*, 48–53.

26. Petitjean Roget, *Société d'habitation*, 2: 1160.

27. Boiteux, *Richelieu*, 339.

28. On these earlier efforts, see Jean Hurault, *Français et Indiens en Guyane, 1604–1972* (Paris: Union générale d'éditions, 1972), 65–67. Hurault was the first French scholar to use the British Museum Sloane ms. 3662, which provides interesting details of early Guiana.

29. A settlement in Guiana fell to Indian attacks due to "so many injustices" committed by the French, according to Jean-Baptiste Labat, *Voyage du chevalier Des Marchais en Guinée, isles voisines et à la Cayenne. Fait en 1725, 1726, 1727*, 4 vols. (Paris: Saugrain l'aîné, 1730), 4: 355.

30. Hurault, *Français et indiens*, 74–75.

31. We have only Brétigny's detractors' version of events. See, e.g., Paul Boyer, *Veritable relation . . . de voyage . . . que Monsieur de Brétigny fit* (Paris: Rocolet, 1654).

32. A few French did continue a precarious existence in the fort. See Henri Castonnet des Fosses, *La Colonisation de la Guyane française* (Angers: Lachèse & Dolbeau, 1888), 45–46.

33. CAOM, C14 1, fols. 10–12.

34. On this company and the relevant primary and secondary sources, see Philip P. Boucher, "A Colonial Company at the Time of the Fronde," *Terrae Incognitae* 11 (1979): 43–58.

35. I made this mistake in my 1974 University of Connecticut dissertation "France 'Discovers' America," 200; so have many others, including Le Ber and Debien, "Propagande," 71. In 1651, Scarron, hitherto a bitter critic of Cardinal Mazarin, started receiving a 3,000 l.t. pension from Fouquet, a key Mazarin ally.

36. Scarron's wife at the time, nicknamed "la Belle Indienne" (the beautiful Indian) because of her connection with the Antilles, was the Martinique-born future morganatic wife of Louis XIV, Madame de Maintenon.

37. For these facts, see Antoine Biet, *Voyage de la France équinoxiale* (Paris: F. Clousier, 1664), 10–19.

38. CAOM, C14 1, fol. 5.

39. *Projet d'une compagnie pour l'Amérique* (Paris, 1651).

40. The Jesuit Relations can now be found on-line at http://puffin.creighton .edu/Jesuit/relations (accessed March 3, 2007).

41. For details of company personnel, see Boucher, "Colonial Company," 48–49.

42. These sordid events can be followed in Biet, *Voyage*, 19, 44–51.

43. Henri Ternaux-Compans, *Notice historique sur la Guyane française* (Paris: Firman Didot, 1843), 58–59.

44. Jean de Laon, sieur d'Aigremont, *Relation du voyage . . . du Cap de Nord* (Paris: P. David, 1654). The volume is dedicated to the duchesse d'Aiguillon.

45. This rare poster, entitled *La Descente par les françois en la Terre Ferme de l'Amérique*, can be viewed at the John Carter Brown Library. Thanks to Susan Danforth for bringing it to my attention.

46. The original of this document is in the Archives des affaires étrangères, Paris, in the series Mémoires et documents, Amérique, vol. 4, fols. 459–60.

47. Cited in Boucher, "Colonial Company," 54.

48. Hallay, "La Martinique et les Antilles au XVIIe siècle," 91.

49. Pelleprat, *Relation*, Dedication.

50. Blaise François de Pagan, *Relation historique et géographique* . . . (Paris: C. Besogne, 1656).

51. Nicholas Sanson, *L'Amérique en plusieurs cartes* (Paris: [N. Sanson], 1657), Dedication.

52. Thomas Gage, *A new survey of the West India's* . . . (London: E. Cotes, 1655).

53. For details on this little-known company, see the little-known Philip P. Boucher, "Shadows in the Past: France and Guiana, 1655–1657," *Proceedings of the French Colonial Historical Society* 6 (1981): 13–26.

54. On Colbert's management of Mazarin's investments and for his early career, see Philip P. Boucher, "Comment se forme un ministre colonial: L'initiation de Colbert 1651–1664," *Revue d'histoire de l'Amérique française* 37, no. 3 (1983): 431–51.

55. Dutertre, *Histoire générale*, 1: 489.

56. Petitjean Roget, *Société d'habitation*, 1: 480–95.

57. On these events, see Boucher, "Shadows in the Past."

58. Battling gout, the governor overexerted himself putting down a small anti-tax sedition. Dessalles, *Histoire générale*, 1: 183.

59. "Cosimo Brunetti," ed. Anderson, 29.

60. For this shabby story, see Dutertre, *Histoire générale*, 1: 535–37.

61. For Fouquet's interest, see Philip P. Boucher, "Reflections on the 'Crime' of Nicholas Fouquet: The Fouquets and the French Colonial Empire, 1626–1661," *Revue française d'histoire d'Outre-mer* 72 (1985): 13.

62. Houël's quarrels can be followed in Dessalles, *Histoire générale*, 1: 184–87, or in Crouse, *French Pioneers*, 249–58.

63. Dutertre, *Histoire générale*, 3: 240.

64. For an older but excellent account of Poincy's life in the islands, see Prosper Cultru, *La Colonisation d'autrefois: Le Commandeur de Poincy à Saint-Christophe* (Paris, 1915).

65. The effort to colonize it was a disaster. Of 500 men only 150 remained. Dessalles, *Histoire générale*, 1: 229.

66. Fouquet's tax was one of the inspirations for the 1660 English Navigation Act, which specifically placed an equivalent duty on all French goods. "Cosimo Brunetti," ed. Anderson, 37n40.

67. For all this and more, see Boucher, "Reflections on the 'Crime.'"

68. Bibliothèque nationale, Manuscrits français, vol. 8022, fols. 159–61 verso.

69. Fouquet's close ties to the Jesuits and his support of missions and religious good works may all, of course, have been devices to shield his personal conduct. For an example of Fouquet's patronage of religious orders, see St. Vincent de Paul, *Correspondance, entretiens, documents,* ed. Pierre Coste, 14 vols. (Paris: Lecoffre, 1920–25), 8: 430. The intense spirituality of his mother and wife, as well as his own in prison, should be part of any evaluation.

70. Louis XIV betrays such emotions in a letter about Fouquet's arrest cited in *Archives de la Bastille; d'après des documents inédits,* ed. Louis Ravaisson-Mollien and François Ravaisson (Geneva: Slatkine, 1975), 362–64. It was one thing to pardon a princely traitor like the Grand Condé, but the son of a noble of the robe could hardly expect the same lenience.

71. Nicholas Foucquet, *Défenses de M. Fouquet . . . ,* 15 vols. (Paris, 1665), 3: 349.

72. For all this as well as the relevant literature, see Boucher, "Reflections on the 'Crime.'"

73. See Alisa Petrovich, "Revisioning Colbert: Jean-Baptiste Colbert and the Origins of French Global Imperial Policy, 1661–1683" (Ph.D. diss., University of Houston, 1997) for a good exposition of these ideas.

74. Cited in Pierre Adolphe Cheruel, *Mémoires sur la vie publique et privée de Fouquet . . . ,* 2 vols. (Paris: Charpentier, 1862), 1: 324.

75. Germaine Martin, *Histoire du crédit en France sous le règne de Louis XIV* (Paris: Larose, 1913), 110.

76. The commission is in Moreau de Saint-Méry, *Loix et constitutions,* 1: 87–88.

77. On Colbert's early years in office, see Boucher, "Comment se forme un ministre colonial"; on Colbert's relations with d'Ogeron, see *Correspondance de Bertrand d'Ogeron, 1662–1675,* ed. Michel Camus (Port-au-Prince, Haiti: Les Ateliers Fardin, 1985), 92.

78. See Boucher, "Comment se forme un ministre colonial."

79. *Correspondance administrative sous le règne de Louis XIV . . . ,* ed. G. B. Depping 4 vols. (Paris: Imprimerie nationale, 1850–55), 1: 648.

80. The first intensive analysis of Colbert's dependence on Fouquet's ideas and initiatives was Boucher, "Comment se forme un ministre colonial."

81. Roland Lamontagne, "L'Influence de Colbert sur l'oeuvre de Jean Talon," *Revue de l'histoire de l'Amérique française* 4 (1952): 42–61.

82. CAOM, C8B1, 13.

83. Colonial companies had difficulty recruiting agents to run their affairs overseas, and those willing to go acted as if their employer owed them. See, e.g.,

Jean de Clodoré, *Relation de ce qui s'est passé dans les isles . . .* 2 vols. (Paris: Clousier, 1671), 1: 16.

84. See Richard Bonney, *Political Change in France Under Richelieu and Mazarin, 1624–1661* (Oxford: Oxford University Press, 1978), 209.

85. CAOM, C8B1, 13.

86. Hurault, *Français et indiens,* 77.

87. The links between this Compagnie de Guiane and the Compagnie des Indes occidentales françaises of a year later were first detailed in Mims, *Colbert's West India Policy,* 68–71.

Chapter 5. Frontier-Era Free Society: The 1620s to the 1660s

1. John McCusker's figures are cited in Christian Huetz de Lemps, "Indentured Servants Bound for the French Antilles in the Seventeenth and Eighteenth Centuries," in *"To Make America": European Emigration in the Early Modern Period,* ed. Ida Altman and James P. P. Horn (Berkeley: University of California Press, 1991), 201n23.

2. For this figure, as well as for other extremely useful estimates of island population, see Pritchard, *In Search of Empire,* 424.

3. See, e.g., William Cronon, *Changes in the Land: Indians, Colonists, and the Ecology of New England* (New York: Hill & Wang, 1983).

4. Dunn, *Sugar and Slaves,* 87.

5. Pritchard, *In Search of Empire,* 424. Cayenne was an anomaly in this respect. Its tiny European population of 327 held 1,418 slaves, more than a one-to-four ratio.

6. See, e.g., the writings of Ira Berlin, John Garrigus, Edmund Morgan, Dan Usner, and Peter Wood in the online bibliography, www.philipboucher.com.

7. See, e.g., Peter Kolchin, *Unfree Labor: American Slavery and Russian Serfdom* (Cambridge, Mass.: Harvard University Press, 1987) and the sources Kolchin cites in his useful *American Slavery, 1619–1877* (New York: Hill & Wang, 1993), 265–66.

8. On the social mobility of seventeenth-century Frenchmen, see Leslie Choquette, *Frenchmen into Peasants: Modernity and Tradition in the Peopling of French Canada* (Cambridge, Mass.: Harvard University Press, 1997), Introduction, and Moogk, *Nouvelle France,* chap. 4. This myth of the Frenchman reluctant to give up home, hearth, and garden for new opportunities in Europe and beyond the seas is probably rooted in the fact that few French left for the Americas in the great European migration of the nineteenth and early twentieth centuries.

9. Robert Jütte, *Poverty and Deviance in Early Modern Europe* (Cambridge: Cambridge University Press, 1994), 34. Jan de Vries, *The Economy of Europe in an*

Age of Crisis, 1600–1750 (Cambridge: Cambridge University Press, 1976) is still the best one-volume survey of the European economy in that era.

10. See, e.g., Emmanuel Le Roy Ladurie, *Times of Feast, Times of Famine: A History of Climate Since the Year 1000*, trans. Barbara Bray (1971; rev. ed., New York: Noonday Press, 1988).

11. Paul Bondois, "La Misère sous Louis XIV: La Disette de 1662," *Revue d'histoire économique et sociale* 12 (1924): 59–62.

12. Richard Bonney, *The European Dynastic States, 1494–1660* (Oxford: Oxford University Press, 1991), 368–69.

13. On the conditions of that era, see, e.g., Huppert, *After the Black Death*, or Jütte, *Poverty and Deviance*.

14. Cited in Jütte, *Poverty and Deviance*, 26.

15. Bonney, *European Dynastic States*, 383.

16. Huppert, *After the Black Death*, 73, citing Pierre Goubert's classic *Beauvais et le Beauvaisis de 1600 à 1730* (Paris: S.E.P.V.E.N., 1960).

17. For some of the nuances of this difficult issue, see Bonney, *European Dynastic States*, 426–28. Price inflation was less on yearly average than today but affected the essentials of life, especially bread. The cheapness of our basics—wheat, rice, potatoes, sugar, salt, oil, and even meat—would have astounded the common man of that era.

18. Huppert, *After the Black Death*, 74–75.

19. Ibid., 80.

20. See, e.g., ibid., chap. 7, esp. 87–88, on the "barefoot men" of the 1639 Normandy rebellion.

21. Ibid., 105–9.

22. Moreau de Saint-Méry, *Loix et constitutions*, 1: 553.

23. For a laundry list of "inconveniences," ranging from nausea and terrible thirst to lack of privacy, to fearsome storms and disheartening calms, see Dutertre, *Histoire générale*, 2: 44–45, who blames most of the early deaths at Guadeloupe on rotten shipboard food and drink (1: 78).

24. *Correspondance . . . d'Ogeron*, ed. Camus, 93–101.

25. André Chevillard, *Les Desseins de . . . Richelieu pour l'Amérique* (Rennes: Durand, 1659), 28–29.

26. Biet, *Voyage*, 351.

27. For similar problems among English North Americans, see among others Karen Kupperman, *Settling with the Indians: The Meeting of English and Indian Cultures in America, 1580–1640* (Totowa, N.J.: Rowan & Littlefield, 1980).

28. Rochefort, *Histoire naturelle et morale*, 339.

29. Ibid., and Dutertre, *Histoire générale*, 2: 420.

30. Maurile de Saint Michel, *Voyage*, 63; Pelleprat, *Relation*, 7–8.

31. Alexandre Exquemelin, *Histoire des avanturiers qui se sont signalez dans les Indes*, 2 vols. (Paris: J. Le Febvre, 1686), 1: 162.

32. In 1660, Cosimo Brunetti claimed that feral pigs were still abundant at Martinique. "Cosimo Brunetti," ed. Anderson, 26.

33. See Labat, *Nouveau voyage,* 2: 231, on the spread of sand, 2: 286–87; 3: 4–6, on the agouti; 3: 11, on the rarity of mahogany.

34. James Axtell, *After Columbus: Essays in the Ethnohistory of Colonial North America* (Oxford: Oxford University Press, 1988), chap. 11.

35. For details, see Boucher, *Cannibal Encounters,* chap. 2, where I first called these men *coureurs des îles,* Caribbean counterparts to the famous Canadian *coureurs de bois.* I have since seen the phrase adopted, without mention of the source.

36. Rochefort, *Histoire naturelle et morale,* 321.

37. I am extrapolating from English data. See Batie, "Why Sugar?" reproduced in *Caribbean Slavery in the Atlantic World: A Student Reader,* ed. Verene Shepherd and Hilary McD.Beckles (Princeton, N.J.: Markus Wiener, 2000), 210–11.

38. For this paragraph, see Christian Schnakenbourg, "Note sur les origines de l'industrie sucrière en Guadeloupe au XVIIe siècle (1640–1670), *Revue française d'histoire d'Outre-mer* 55, no. 200 (1968): 275–81. Some muscavado was produced at Guadeloupe in this era.

39. Dutertre, *Histoire générale,* 2: 450.

40. Anne Perotin-Dumon, *La Ville aux îles, la ville dans l'île: Basse-Terre et Pointe-à-Pitre, Guadeloupe, 1650–1820* (Paris: Karthala, 2000), 723. This is by far the best work on French colonial towns in the Caribbean.

41. "Cosimo Brunetti," ed. Anderson, 27.

42. The company granted exemptions from all taxes to artisans willing to practice their craft in the *bourgs.* Perotin-Dumon, *Ville aux îles,* 724.

43. For the difficulties of establishing sugar cultivation at Guadeloupe, see Schnakenbourg, "Note sur les origines," 267–83.

44. Ibid., 290–91.

45. W. R. Menkman, *De Nederlanders in het Caraibische zeegebied, waarin vervat de geschiedenis der Nederlandsche Antillen* (Amsterdam: Van Kampen & Zoon, 1942), 73. Thanks to Wim Klooster for the reference.

46. Perotin-Dumon, *Ville aux îles,* 213–16.

47. Moogk, *Nouvelle France,* 91; Choquette, *Frenchmen into Peasants,* 100–105.

48. Gérard Lafleur, *Les Protestants aux Antilles françaises du vent sous l'ancien régime* (Basse-Terre, Guadeloupe: Société d'histoire de la Guadeloupe, 1988), is by far the best source. He shows that the Protestants were especially numerous and powerful at Guadeloupe, and that they had strong ties with the Dutch. See p. 153.

49. See Garraway, *Libertine Colony.* This literary critic jumps to some astonishing conclusions, but she demonstrates a knowledge of early French Caribbean history possessed by few historians.

50. Boiteux, *Richelieu*, 313.

51. Ibid., 307.

52. L. P. May, *Histoire économique de la Martinique (1635–1763)* (Paris: Riviére, 1930), 27.

53. Dutertre, *Histoire générale*, 2: 474.

54. Léo Elisabeth, *La Société martiniquaise aux XVIIe et XVIIIe siècles, 1664–1789* (Paris: Karthala, 2003), 471.

55. For examples of these associations, see L. Merle and G. Debien, "Colons, marchands et engagés à Nantes au XVIIe siècle," *Revue de "La Porte Océane"* 9, no. 101 (December 1953): 7.

56. Hallay, "Martinique et les Antilles au XVIIe siècle," 78. Cosimo Brunetti in 1660 talks of habitants who had accumulated up to eight or ten thousand *livres de rentes*, that is, interest from investments. "Cosimo Brunetti," ed. Anderson, 28.

57. Alison Games, *Migration and the Origins of the English Atlantic World* (Cambridge, Mass.: Harvard University Press, 1999).

58. Kenneth Kiple, *The Caribbean Slave: A Biological History* (Cambridge: Cambridge University Press, 1984), 165.

59. Ibid., 15–17.

60. Rochefort claims that Basse-Terre, Saint-Christophe, was a town of fine brick houses, but one must be careful with this propagandistic account. *Histoire naturelle et morale*, 48–49.

61. For the best early account, see Dutertre, *Histoire générale*, 2: 450–51.

62. See Poincy's letter to the company in Rennard, *Tricentenaire des Antilles*, 103–4.

63. Rochefort, *Histoire naturelle et morale*, 52–56.

64. Maurile de Saint Michel, *Voyage*, 119.

65. For the 1639 convoy, see Lebers and Debien, "Propagande," 80.

66. Du Motey, *Guillaume d'Orange*, 129.

67. According to Dutertre, *Histoire générale*, 2: 454. No doubt, "attractiveness" is culturally conditioned and dependent on factors such as male-female ratios.

68. Ibid., 2: 455–56.

69. Ibid., 1: 329.

70. Ibid., 2: 462.

71. When the Compagnie des Isles attempted to introduce *lods et ventes*, the colonists flew into rebellion. Many made a living by preparing land to sell to newcomers. Ibid., 2: 440–41.

72. Ibid., 2: 446.

73. For the debate on the oppressiveness of feudal dues, see Robert C. H. Sweeney, "What Difference Does a Mode Make? A Comparison of Two Seven-

teenth-Century Colonies: Canada and Newfoundland," *William and Mary Quarterly* 53, no. 2 (April 2006): 284–87.

74. Dutertre, *Histoire générale*, 2: 474.

75. Petitjean Roget, *Société d'habitation*, 2: 1162.

76. Dampierre, *Essai sur les sources*, 224.

77. Boiteux, *Richelieu*, 297.

78. Dutertre, *Histoire générale*, 2: 445–46, characterizes island justice as "good and brief," and applauds the absence of lawyers.

79. Moreau de Saint-Méry, *Loix et constitutions*, 1: 55–56; see also Michel Vergé-Franceschi, "Le Rôle stratégique des îles," in AN catalogue, *Voyage aux îles*, 131.

80. The official document can be found in Dutertre, *Histoire générale*, 1: 312–14.

81. Rochefort, *Histoire naturelle et morale*, 54. Rochefort's panegyric of Poincy, which emphasizes the commander's fairness to all colonists including Protestants, is on p. 46.

82. Dutertre, *Histoire générale*, 1: 320.

83. *Histoire de l'Isle de Grenade . . . anonyme*, ed. Petitjean Roget, 169.

84. Rennard, *Tricentenaire des Antilles*, 232–33. Rennard reproduces documents from Compagnie des Isles registers in CAOM F2 A19.

85. Sylvain Auroux and Francesco Queixalos, "La Première description linguistique des Antilles françaises: Le Père Raymond Breton (1609–1679)," in *Naissance de l'ethnologie? Anthropologie et missions en Amérique, XVIe–XVIIIe siècle*, ed. Claude Blanckaert (Paris: Cerf, 1985), 109.

86. For the late 1640s, one contemporary author said there were twelve Jesuits, three Dominicans, and three Carmelites. Antoine Godeau, *Oeuvres chrestiennes et morales en prose*, 2 vols. (Paris: Pierre Le Petit, 1658), 2: 165. For the terrible physical toll on the Carmelites, see Maurile de St. Michel, *Voyage*, 324–27.

87. To give an idea of the difficulties of working with contemporary writings, Pelleprat, *Relation*, 25, claims that the Jesuits alone converted 12,000–13,000 Huguenots, when that was the likely total of the entire European population.

88. This paragraph owes much of its conceptualization to E. L. Jones, "The European Background," in *The Cambridge Economic History of the United States*, 3 vols., ed. Stanley L. Engerman and Robert E. Gallman (Cambridge: Cambridge University Press, 1966), 1: 105–6.

Chapter 6. Frontier-Era Society: The World of Coerced Labor

1. Gabriel Debien, in his "Les Engagés pour les Antilles," and Leslie Choquette, *Frenchmen into Peasants*, among others, extensively employed these archival sources.

2. In the introduction and elsewhere in *Sugar and Slaves*, Richard Dunn discusses this phenomenon in the English Caribbean context.

3. More than half the English migrants to the Americas from 1630 to 1700 were indentured servants. The numbers involved dwarf the French ones, even if the latter cannot be known. For the far better known English case, see Henry A. Gemeny, "Market for Migrants: English Indentured Servitude and Emigration in the Seventeenth and Eighteenth Centuries," in *Colonialism and Migration; Indentured Labor Before and After Slavery*, ed. P. C. Emmer (Dordrecht: Martinus Nijhoff, 1986), 38.

4. Moogk, *Nouvelle France*, 108.

5. Huetz de Lemps, "Indentured Servants," 201n23. There were about 33,000 English, 26,000 of them at Barbados, compared to perhaps 15,000 to 16,000 French.

6. Between 1620 and 1642, some 80,000 English "swarmed" out of their island home. Of these about 58,000, or more than 70%, crossed the Atlantic. Carl Bridenbaugh, *Vexed and Troubled Englishmen, 1590–1642* (New York: Oxford University Press, 1968), 395. Henry Gemery and James Horn say 60% in "British and French Indentured Servant Migration to the Caribbean: A Comparative Study of Seventeenth-Century Emigration and Labor Markets," in International Union for the Scientific Study of Population, Conference on the Peopling of the Americas, Vera Cruz, Mexico, May 18–23, 1992, *Proceedings*, 294.

7. Bridenbaugh, *Vexed and Troubled Englishmen*, 397–400.

8. Jean Tanguy, "Les Engagés Nantais pour les Antilles," in *Actes du 97e Congrès national des sociétés savantes* (Nantes, 1972), 53–54.

9. Bridenbaugh, *Vexed and Troubled Englishmen*, chap. 11.

10. Moogk, *Nouvelle France*, 100; Debien, "Engagés pour les Antilles," 83–84.

11. L. Merle and G. Debien, "Colons, marchands et engagés à Nantes au XVIIe siècle," *Revue de "La Porte Océane"* 10, no. 102 (January 1954): 12.

12. Debien, "Engagés pour les Antilles," 52–53.

13. Choquette, *Frenchmen into Peasants*; Moogk, *Nouvelle France*.

14. Tanguy, "Engagés Nantais," 60.

15. All the sources cited above note the rarity of female servants.

16. Tanguy, "Engagés Nantais," 60, 62.

17. Ibid., 61.

18. See the chart in Frédéric Mauro, "French Indentured Servants for America, 1500–1800," in *Colonialism and Migration*, ed. Emmer, 96.

19. Moogk, *Nouvelle France*, chap. 4. On servants leaving La Rochelle and Bordeaux respectively, see Debien, "Engagés pour les Antilles," 83–84, and Huetz de Lemps, "Indentured Servants."

20. Figures for La Rochelle demonstrate that for every servant embarking for New France, five went to the Caribbean. However, those who explain the

preference for the islands as a consequence of their favorable image in France have not read the travel book authors. See, e.g., Huetz de Lemps, "Indentured Servants," 173, 180.

21. See the chart in Mauro, "French Indentured Servants," 99.

22. Debien, "Engagés pour les Antilles," 158–70.

23. L. Merle and G. Debien, "Colons, marchands et engagés à Nantes au XVIIe siècle," *Revue de "La Porte Océane"* 10, no. 103 (February 1954): 10.

24. Tanguy, "Engagés Nantais," 63n21, 64.

25. The coastal cities did not themselves produce large numbers of servants. Huetz de Lemps, "Indentured Servants," 197, speculates that abundant maritime-related employment kept these urban residents at home.

26. Tanguy, "Engagés Nantais," 65.

27. Ibid., 64.

28. Lebers and Debien, "Propagande," 80. The revolt of the barefoot men of Normandy occurred in these years.

29. Debien, "Engagés pour les Antilles."

30. Merle and Debien, "Colons, marchands" (February 1954), 9.

31. For a striking comparison of the occupations of British and French indentured servants see Gemery and Horn, "British and French Indentured Servant Migration," 296, table 4.

32. Jean-Pierre Poussou, "L'Immigration européene dans les îles d'Amérique," in AN catalogue, *Voyages aux îles*, 54.

33. Moogk, *Nouvelle France*, 107.

34. See, e.g., Dutertre, *Histoire générale*, 1: 4. Rochefort, *Histoire naturelle et morale*, 288–89, lavishes praise on d'Esnambuc for his humane treatment of these servants.

35. Dutertre, *Histoire générale*, 1: 16. For a scathing indictment of French shippers who brought too many passengers in crowded, dirty conditions, see Maurile de Saint Michel, *Voyage*, 328.

36. For these trickeries, see inter alia Pelleprat, *Relation*, 21, and Chevillard, *Desseins de . . . Richelieu*, 84. However, Debien cautions not to exaggerate the number of kidnappings. "Engagés pour les Antilles," 172–73.

37. Dutertre, *Histoire générale*, 2: 464–65. See also Poincy's outraged letter to the Compagnie des Isles about this affair, reproduced in Rennard, *Tricentenaire des Antilles*, 108–9.

38. For examples, see Pelleprat, *Relation*, 20–21; Chevillard, *Desseins de . . . Richelieu*, 84.

39. Dutertre, *Histoire générale*, 2: 478–80. The symptoms—fatigue, fevers, thirst, and yellow bile—may suggest that malaria was one of the diseases involved.

40. Rochefort, *Histoire naturelle et morale*, 2–3.

41. Huetz de Lemps, "Indentured Servants," 177.

42. Dutertre, *Histoire générale*, 2: 469–70.

43. Labat, *Nouveau voyage*, 1: 227–29. He lived to be more than ninety years old.

44. For his later exemplary life, see ibid., 5: 11–12.

45. See, e.g., Maurile de Saint Michel, *Voyage*, 290. For a more detailed exploration of missionary views, see Boucher, "Caribbean and the Caribs," 17–32, or the excluded chapters on my web site, www.philipboucher.com.

46. In her recent *Libertine Colony*, Doris Garraway argues that libertinage characterized French Creole society in both the seventeenth and eighteenth centuries. Her case is far stronger for the latter century.

47. A good analysis is Eltis, *Rise of African Slavery*, esp. chap. 3.

48. Chevillard, *Desseins de . . . Richelieu*, 84.

49. Rochefort, *Histoire naturelle et morale*, 30. See also Dutertre, *Histoire générale*, 2: 427–28.

50. On the Caribbean Church, see Rennard, *Histoire religieuse des Antilles françaises*.

51. Dutertre, *Histoire générale*, 1: 19.

52. Petitjean Roget, *Société d'habitation*, 2: 1500.

53. See Peabody, *"There are no Slaves in France."*

54. Cited in Huppert, *After the Black Death*, 116.

55. Dutertre, *Histoire générale*, 2: 483.

56. "Unthinking decision" is Winthrop Jordan's famous formulation in *White over Black: American Attitudes Toward the Negro, 1550–1812* (Baltimore: Penguin Books, 1969), chap. 2 title.

57. Patterson, *Sociology of Slavery*, 9.

58. Dan Usner, *Indians, Settlers and Slaves in a Frontier Exchange Economy: The Lower Mississippi Valley Before 1783* (Chapel Hill: University of North Carolina Press, 1992).

59. Lucien Peytraud, *L'Esclavage aux Antilles françaises avant 1789* (Paris: Hachette, 1897), 8. Boiteux, *Richelieu*, 288, mentions "about" 500 at Saint-Christophe in 1635 but does not cite a source.

60. For an example of an English slave trader operating at Guadeloupe, see Petitjean Roget, *Société d'habitation*, 1: 484. The English sold prime slaves for 17,000 pounds of tobacco apiece.

61. Thornton, *Africa and Africans*, 118.

62. Dutertre, *Histoire* (1654), 275.

63. CAOM C8 1, July 1664.

64. There is no contemporary documentation to support this version. The story has its source in the popular work of Labat, *Nouveau voyage*, 4: 114.

65. Unless a contemporary document is uncovered to support this assertion, it should be assessed as unproven and used with caution.

66. Rochefort, *Histoire naturelle et morale*, 335–36, fancifully trivializes the eventual dominance of sugar over indigo by writing that habitants loved candied pineapple and ginger, as well as orange and lemon jams; in contrast, they hated the rotten smells of the decaying plants necessary to make indigo dye.

67. See, e.g., Pacifique de Provins, *Briève relation . . .* (Paris: N. and Jean de La Coste, 1646), 13.

68. Rochefort, *Histoire naturelle et morale*, 341.

69. Poincy reminds us that after the Crusades, his order, the Knights of Malta, developed Cyprus as the first "sugar island." Lana, *Caraïbes en construction*, 140–41.

70. Petitjean Roget, *Société d'habitation*, 2: 1167–68. Of the slaves at the main plantation, three were household domestics and fifteen were artisans, including four sugar makers. Students of slave systems will note the high ratio of children to female slaves on Poincy's smallest plantation. It was very rare to have more children than females on any Caribbean plantation at any time.

71. Rochefort's estimate of 300 Poincy slaves for the early 1650s may be based on information from the *bailli* directly. *Histoire naturelle et morale*, 54.

72. Dunn, *Sugar and Slaves*, 68, for Modyford; for Hilliard, Paul Butel, *Les Caraïbes au temps des flibustiers* (Paris: Aubier Montaigne, 1982), 175.

73. At least according to Rochefort, *Histoire naturelle et morale*, 40, Houël had 100 *nègres*; also Batie, "Why Sugar?" 219.

74. Perotin-Dumon, *Ville aux îles*, 111.

75. Rochefort, *Histoire naturelle et morale*, 48, 333, calls sugar plantations the "true silver mines" of the islands and names the most important sugar makers at Saint-Christophe, starting with Poincy, of course, and including the latter's nephews, his militia captains, and Guadeloupe's former governor Auger.

76. See, e.g., Batie, "Why Sugar?" 1–41.

77. Unlike relatively flat Barbados, the French Windward Islands had few wind- and water-driven mills; less mountainous Guadeloupe was a partial exception.

78. Petitjean Roget, *Société d'habitation*, 2: 1187.

79. Robert L. Stein, *The French Sugar Business in the Eighteenth Century* (Baton Rouge, Louisiana State University Press, 1988), 41.

80. "Cosimo Brunetti," ed. Anderson, 28. Another more precise estimate is 2,686 slaves. See Elisabeth, *Société martiniquaise*, 85.

81. Elisabeth, *Société martiniquaise*, 85, 110.

82. Dutertre, *Histoire générale*, 2: 483, 1: 500, 2: 501, claims variously that there were more Africans than Europeans in the French Caribbean islands by the 1650s; that there were more slaves than colonists at Guadeloupe in 1656; and that more than 15,000 of the slaves had been baptized. Writing in the mid 1650s, Pelleprat, *Relation*, 54, asserts that there were from 12,000 to 13,000 baptized Africans in the islands. These numbers are exaggerations to impress the faithful

at home. Batie, "Why Sugar?" 225n115, suggests 13,000 free colonists and 10,000 slaves, but says either figure could be off by some 2,000. Without a citation, Stein, *French Sugar Business*, 41, claims that there were 12,000 whites at Guadeloupe and 3,000 slaves in 1656. His figure for whites is highly unlikely; Pritchard, *In Search of Empire*, 424, estimates, based on official censuses, that there were fewer than 3,500 whites at Guadeloupe in 1670.

83. Petitjean Roget, *Société d'habitation*, 2: 1002.

84. Ibid., 1164.

85. Herbert Klein, *The Atlantic Slave Trade* (Cambridge: Cambridge University Press, 1999), 139, for an analysis of the Cambridge University Press database on CD-ROM, *The Trans-Atlantic Slave Trade*, ed. David Eltis et al. (1999).

86. This and other material about the health conditions of Africans on both sides of the Atlantic is indebted to Kiple, *Caribbean Slave*. See pp. 12–13 for this paragraph.

87. Patterson, *Sociology of Slavery*, 74.

88. The phrase "jacks of all trades" is Peter Wood's in *Black Majority: Negroes in Colonial South Carolina from 1670 Through the Stono Rebellion* (New York: Knopf, 1974), 104.

89. Dutertre, *Histoire générale*, 2: 526–28, says that as long as masters provided adequate food and drink, as well as opportunities to socialize with kin, slaves were "content."

90. E.g., Maurile de Saint Michel, *Voyage*, 36.

91. Dutertre, *Histoire générale*, 2: 493.

92. See, e.g., Pelleprat, *Relation*, 55.

93. Petitjean Roget, *Société d'habitation*, 2: 1128.

94. Patterson, *Sociology of Slavery*, 99.

95. I am enormously simplifying Kiple's sophisticated analysis. See his *Caribbean Slave*, chaps. 5–9.

96. Dutertre, *Histoire générale*, 3: 375. Geophagy causes no serious harm as long as the clay is clean. European observers professed horror at the practice and used it to reinforce negative perceptions of Africans.

97. John Thornton, *Africa and Africans*, 118, suggests that the Angolan share of the slave trade before 1650 was about 65%. The data on the Cambridge University Press CD-ROM *The Trans-Atlantic Slave Trade* (1999), are of little value in understanding the development of seventeenth-century slavery in the French colonies. Only about 7,000 slaves are known to have been brought to Martinique, Guadeloupe, Saint-Domingue, and Saint-Christophe in that century, and none from "Angola." Obviously, only a small minority of Africans arriving in the French islands came via the French slave trade. See Sue Peabody, "'A Dangerous Zeal': Catholic Missions to Slaves in the French Antilles, 1635–1800," *French Historical Studies* 25, no. 1 (Winter 2002): 64, table.

98. See the famous print in Rochefort, *Histoire naturelle et morale*, opposite p. 52.

99. Ira Berlin, *Many Thousands Gone: The First Two Centuries of Slavery in North America* (Cambridge, Mass.: Harvard University Press, 1998), chap. 2. Dutertre, *Histoire générale*, 2: 502, confirms that many were formally Christian but claims that they were not well instructed.

100. *Histoire de l'Isle de Grenade . . . anonyme*, ed. Petitjean Roget, 157–58.

101. Dutertre, *Histoire générale*, 1: 61.

102. Kiple, *Caribbean Slave*, 118.

103. Moreau de Saint-Méry, *Loix et constitutions*, 1: 61; also Dutertre, *Histoire générale*, 2: 513–14. In 1660, Cosimo Brunetti indicated that planters used both methods. "Cosimo Brunetti," ed. Anderson, 29.

104. Dutertre, *Histoire générale*, 2: 501–3. Typically, he castigates the Dutch and English for never baptizing their slaves.

105. These were likely "Atlantic Creoles" given their origination. Dutertre, *Histoire générale*, 2: 502–3, is quite explicit that slaves taken from the Portuguese or Spanish were "usually Christian."

106. Moreau de Saint-Méry, *Loix et constitutions*, 1: 83.

107. Dutertre, *Histoire générale*, 2: 472.

108. Ibid., 2: 509.

109. Debien, "Les Esclaves," in *Histoire des Antilles*, ed. Pluchon and Abenon, 141.

110. The central West African coast became the major focus of the trade from the 1670s to the 1770s. For a discussion of different African cultural zones, see Thornton, *Africa and Africans*, 183–92.

111. Ibid., 191.

112. Rochefort, *Histoire naturelle et morale*, 342.

113. For one orientation to the evolution of Creole languages in the French islands, see Ellen Schnepel, "The Language Question in Guadeloupe: From the Early Chroniclers to the Post-War Generation," *Plantation Society in the Americas* 5 (1998): 61–94.

114. Maurile de St. Michel, *Voyage*, 80.

115. Dutertre, *Histoire générale*, 1: 153. Assisted by fellow slaves, one very large refugee avoided capture for three years.

116. E.g., Maurile de Saint Michel, *Voyage*, 39.

117. Jacques Adelaide-Merland, *Les Antilles françaises de leur découverte à nos jours* (Fort-de-France, Martinique: Desormeaux, 2000), 15; Dutertre, *Histoire générale*, 1: 500–503.

118. Moreau de Saint-Méry, *Loix et constitutions*, 1: 83.

119. Dutertre, *Histoire générale*, 2: 498.

120. Historians of slavery in the seventeenth and the early part of the eigh-

teenth century do not have available the documents, especially newspapers, that have helped historians such as Gerald Mullin and Philip Morgan to better understand African American responses to slavery. Mullin, *Flight and Rebellion: Slave Resistance in Eighteenth-Century Virginia* (New York: Oxford University Press, 1972); Morgan, *Slave Counterpoint: Black Culture in the Eighteenth-Century Chesapeake and Lowcountry* (Chapel Hill: University of North Carolina Press, 1998).

121. For relevant contemporary quotations about their "laziness," see Petitjean Roget, *Société d'habitation*, 1: 493.

122. Dutertre, *Histoire générale*, 2: 497.

123. Maurile de Saint Michel, *Voyage*, 36; Petitjean Roget, *Société d'habitation*, 1: 491–92.

124. Dutertre, *Histoire générale*, 2: 513, 460.

Chapter 7. The Transformation from Settlements to Colonies Begins: The 1660s to the 1670s

Pierre-Régis Dessalles, *Annales*, avant propos. This is vol. 3 of his grandson Adrien Dessalles's *Histoire générale*.

1. Dutertre, *Histoire générale*, 3: 23; Joseph-Antoine Le Febvre de La Barre, "Mémoire sur les projets de la compagnie qui se forme pour le Cap du Nord," CAOM C14 1, fol. 85 suite.

2. See Mims, *Colbert's West India Policy*; Nellis Crouse, *The French Struggle for the West Indies, 1665–1713* (New York: Columbia University Press, 1943); Joseph-Antoine Le Febvre de La Barre, *Description de la France équinoctiale . . .* (Paris: Ribou, 1666), 4–9.

3. See, e.g., John Wolf, *Louis XIV* (New York: Norton, 1968), and François Bluche, *Louis XIV*, trans. Mark Greengrass (New York: Franklin Watts, 1990). These two major biographies say almost nothing about France overseas.

4. "First rate" ships boasted over seventy-six cannon; second rate had sixty-four to seventy-six; third raters carried between fifty and sixty-four; ships of the fourth rate wielded thirty-six to fifty; and, finally, fifth raters had twenty to thirty-six.

5. On all aspects of the royal navy under Louis XIV, see Daniel Dessert, *La Royale: Vaisseaux et marins du Roi-Soleil* (Paris: Fayard, 1996); for the annual list of royal ships, see 301–2, table.

6. Banks, *Chasing Empire*, 23. Louis spent about eleven million l.t. on the navy, compared to fifty-four million on the army.

7. Briggs, *Early Modern France*, 41.

8. Méthivier, "A Century of Conflict," in *France in Crisis*, ed. Coveney, 65.

9. Schnakenbourg, "Note sur les origines," 293–95. The number of sugar works at Guadeloupe actually fell from seventy-one in 1661 to sixty-five in 1667.

10. Stein, *French Sugar Business*, 98.

11. See Dunn, *Sugar and Slaves*, chaps. 2 and 3.

12. For the English figures, see citations in Huetz de Lemps, "Indentured Servants," 201n23. By 1678, there were 10,408 whites in the English Leewards. Dunn, *Sugar and Slaves*, 127. There are no solid estimates for the French in 1660, but in 1670, there were 15,271. Pritchard, *In Search of Empire*, 424.

13. Colbert praised his conduct in adjusting "himself to an austere life, which so few know how to do." CAOM C81, letter of Colbert to Tracy, September 22, 1664, cited in Mims, *Colbert's West India Policy*, 61.

14. On April 17, 1664, the king ordered the proprietors to bring their contracts before the council of commerce. Moreau de Saint-Méry, *Loix et constitutions*, 1: 98–99.

15. For his ordinance, see Dutertre, *Histoire générale*, 3: 71–76. For all his regulations, see Moreau de Saint-Méry, *Loix et constitutions*, 1: 117–22.

16. For the career of "Indian" Warner, see Boucher, *Cannibal Encounters*, chap. 3.

17. Dutertre, *Histoire générale*, 4: 145–46.

18. Boiteux, *Richelieu*, 211.

19. In so doing, Colbert thus took the advice of the directors of the Compagnie de Guiane on how to promote the larger Compagnie des Indes occidentales. CAOM F3, 21, fols. 43–54.

20. These can be followed in Moreau de Saint-Méry, *Loix et constitutions*, 1: 94–133.

21. Mims, *Colbert's West India Policy*, 80, says two merchants were on the initial subscription list of the Compagnie de Guiane.

22. Joseph Rennard, *Baas, Blénac, ou les Antilles françaises* (Fort-de-France, Martinique: Alexandre, 1935), 50.

23. Daniel Dessert, "Le Lobby Colbert: Un Royaume ou une affaire de famille?" *Annales: Economies, Sociétés, Civilisations* 30 (1975): 1303–36.

24. Mims, *Colbert's West India Policy*, 81.

25. See the letter of one bishop to Colbert about his prompt obedience to the king's order in May, *Histoire économique de la Martinique*, 306–7.

26. For the text of the company's charter, see Dutertre, *Histoire générale*, 3: 33–47.

27. Leber and Debien, "Propagande," 83–85.

28. *Correspondance administrative*, ed. Depping, 3: 428.

29. Biet, *Voyage;* La Barre, *Description*.

30. For more details, see Boucher, "French Images of America and the Evolution of Colonial Theories," 220–28.

31. *Correspondance . . . d'Ogeron*, ed. Camus, 22–23. Jéremie Deschamps du Rausset settled his claims for a paltry 15,000 l.t., but only received c. 10,000. Impoverished, he eventually returned to Tortuga. Pierre Bardin, "Aux débuts de la

Tortue et de l'île de Saint-Domingue," *Généalogie et Histoire de la Caraïbe* 128 (July–August 2000): 2914.

32. For the earlier sale figures, see Dutertre, *Histoire générale*, 1: 443.

33. Mims, *Colbert's West India Policy*, 74.

34. Rennard, *Baas, Blénac*, 50–51.

35. Ibid., 51.

36. Abdoulaye Ly, *La Compagnie du Sénégal* (Paris: Présence africaine, 1958), 95–96.

37. Ibid., 103.

38. Ibid.

39. Ibid., 109–10.

40. Dutertre, *Histoire générale*, 4: 282, avers that he "could not understand why it has not been abandoned" given its awful climate.

41. Eccles, *French in North America*, 91–92.

42. See Cole, *Colbert and a Century of French Mercantilism*, and Petrovich, "Revisioning Colbert."

43. Carl and Roberta Bridenbaugh, *No Peace Beyond the Line: The English in the Caribbean, 1624–1690* (New York: Oxford University Press, 1972), 182.

44. See his memoir to Colbert as cited in Saintoyant, *Colonisation française*, 1: 224.

45. Ly, *Compagnie du Sénégal*, 93n16.

46. Dutertre, *Histoire générale*, 3: 167.

47. Bibliothèque nationale, NAF, no. 9323, fol. 251, as cited in Rennard, *Baas, Blénac*, 21.

48. Dessalles, *Histoire générale*, 3: 123–33. Pierre-Régis Dessalles describes La Barre as rash and quick to judgment, overly sensitive when criticized, and confrontational with the council. This evaluation is likely true considering other parts of his career. See, e.g., Boucher, "Comment se forme un ministre colonial," 440–41.

49. Dutertre, *Histoire générale*, 4: 82. "Necessity and misery pushed them to the precipice."

50. On these events, see ibid., 81–89.

51. Ibid. Dutertre blames a tobacco roller (*torqueur*) for inciting the riots.

52. Despite his valiant service, Clodoré suffered the ignominy of summary dismissal as governor in 1668 by La Barre. Clodoré found vindication in France, and La Barre was recalled.

53. Moreau de Saint-Méry, *Loix et constitutions*, 1: 87–88.

54. Contemporary chroniclers such as Dutertre provide information, as do the eighteenth-century historians Father P. F. X de Charlevoix, *Histoire de l'isle espagnole ou S. Domingue* (Paris: Guerin, 1730–31), and Moreau de Saint-Méry, *Description . . . de l'isle Saint-Domingue.* An excellent annotated edition of Ogeron's correspondence is *Correspondance . . . d'Ogeron,* ed. Camus, 1–188.

55. Moreau de Saint-Méry, *Loix et constitutions*, 1: 158.

56. Louis awarded letters of nobility to four key leaders of the victory. Dessalles, *Histoire générale*, 1: 385.

57. Later in 1666, a destructive hurricane hammered the victorious French at Saint-Christophe. Petrovich, "Revisioning Colbert," 296.

58. Dutertre, *Histoire générale*, 4: 113–18.

59. Dessalles, *Histoire générale*, 1: 361.

60. Dutertre, *Histoire générale*, 4: 180–81.

61. The Dutch Admiral Cuyssens joined Clodoré in accusing La Barre of cowardice concerning this lost opportunity. AN catalogue, *Voyage aux îles*, 73.

62. *Histoire des Antilles*, ed. Pluchon and Abenon, 101.

63. Watts, *West Indies*, 243, says that Antigua and Montserrat lost 1,300 slaves to the French.

64. Petrovich, "Revisioning Colbert," 296–97. Company directors evaluated the losses at around 400,000 lt. It was later estimated that total company losses were more than two million lt.

65. *Correspondance administrative*, ed. Depping, 3: 522.

66. Dessalles, *Histoire générale*, 1: 489.

67. Ibid., 1: 532. On the fortunes of the Compagnie des Indes occidentales françaises, see Mims, *Colbert's West India Policy*.

68. Mims, *Colbert's West India Policy*, 165–72.

69. Moreau de Saint-Méry, *Loix et constitutions*, 1: 174–75.

70. Jacob Price, *France and the Chesapeake: A History of the French Tobacco Monopoly, 1674–1791, and its Relationship to the British and American Tobacco Trades*, 2 vols. (Ann Arbor: University of Michigan Press, 1973), 1: 5.

71. These very illuminating royal letters are cited in Rennard, *Baas, Blénac*, 59. See also ibid. for other information about de Baas.

72. Cole, *Colbert and a Century of French Mercantilism*, 74.

73. Gaston Martin, *Nantes au XVIIIe siècle: L'ère des négriers (1714–1774)* (Paris: Alcan, 1931), 314.

74. Rennard, *Baas, Blénac*, 44.

75. Ly, *Compagnie du Sénégal*, 119–20.

76. Ibid., 126–27; Peytraud, *Esclavage aux Antilles françaises*, 41; Petrovich, "Revisioning Colbert," 420–21; Watts, *West Indies*, 261; Philippe Hrodej, *L'Amiral du Casse: L'Élévation d'un Gascon sous Louis XIV*, 2 vols. (Paris: Librairie de l'Inde, 1999), 1: 44.

77. Moreau de Saint-Méry, *Loix et constitutions*, 1: 197.

78. William Doyle, *The Old European Order, 1660–1815*, 2d ed. (Oxford: Oxford University Press, 1992), 53; Watts, *West Indies*, 262; Mims, *Colbert's West India Policy*, 274–75; Pritchard, *In Search of Empire*, 167.

79. Moreau de Saint-Méry, *Loix et constitutions*, 1: 368–69. For details, see Stein, *French Sugar Business*, 95.

80. Moreau de Saint-Méry, *Loix et constitutions*, 1: 395–96; Stein, *French Sugar Business*, 150; Petrovich, "Revisioning Colbert," 514n114.

81. An excellent source is Stein, *French Sugar Business*. See pp. 8–10 for this paragraph.

82. Pritchard, *In Search of Empire*, 169–70, estimates that French production increased by about 50% between 1675 and 1683, reaching about half the English Caribbean total of 18,000 tons.

83. Moreau de Saint-Méry, *Loix et constitutions*, 1: 226–27.

84. Cited in Cole, *Colbert and a Century of French Mercantilism*, 260.

85. See Lafleur, *Protestants aux Antilles*, 98.

86. CAOM, B2, fol. 135, as cited in Mims, *Colbert's West India Policy*, 337.

87. Charles Plumier, *Description des plantes de l'Amérique* (Paris: Imprimerie royale, by J. Annison, 1693), Preface. Plumier praises Michel Bégon as someone "well known to savants."

88. Leber and Debien, "Propagande," 85.

89. Price, *France and the Chesapeake*, 1: 79.

90. Cited in *Correspondance . . . d'Ogeron*, ed. Camus, 81.

91. On all of this, see ibid., 116–50; and see also Frostin, *Révoltes blanches à Saint-Domingue*.

92. Pritchard, *In Search of Empire*, 282–83.

93. William J. Eccles, *Canada Under Louis XIV, 1663–1701* (Toronto: McClelland & Stewart, 1968), 105–6.

94. *Correspondance . . . d'Ogeron*, ed. Camus, 11–14.

95. AN catalogue, *Voyage aux îles*, 152.

96. For the two years between April 1670 and April 1672, the month of the declaration of war, see Moreau de Saint-Méry, *Loix et constitutions*, 1: 194–262, or sixty-eight pages; for the next twenty-four months, April 1672–April 1674, Moreau needed only twenty-eight pages, 1: 253–81.

97. I am indebted to Pritchard, *In Search of Empire*, chap. 6, for this section.

98. On these events, see Boucher, *Cannibal Encounters*, 73–74.

99. Petrovich, "Revisioning Colbert," 314; Moreau de Saint Méry, *Loix et constitutions*, 1: 195–96.

100. CAOM, C8 A1, de Baas to Colbert, February 8, 1674, as cited in Ly, *Compagnie du Sénégal*, 39.

101. The number of rated ships grew from just nine in 1661 to 120 in 1672. Pritchard, *In Search of Empire*, 48; also Jean Meyer, "Louis XIV et les puissances maritimes," *Dix-septième siècle* 123 (1979): 161.

102. *Correspondance . . . d'Ogeron*, ed. Camus, 165.

103. Pritchard, *In Search of Empire*, 24.

104. The famous former buccaneer and author Alexandre Exquemelin accompanied this fleet as a surgeon. Michel-Christian Camus, "Une Note critique

à propos d'Exquemelin,' *Revue française d'histoire d'Outre-mer* 77, no. 286 (1990): 80.

105. Inexplicably, Goslinga, *Dutch in the Caribbean*, 475, describes Fort Royal as "heavily defended."

106. Rennard, *Baas, Blénac*, 113; Goslinga, *Dutch in the Caribbean*, 476.

107. Rennard, *Baas, Blénac*, 76–77.

108. Cited in ibid., 32.

109. Martin, *Histoire du crédit*, 89.

110. Moreau de Saint-Méry, *Loix et constitutions*, 1: 296.

111. Jean-Baptiste Colbert, *Lettres, instructions et mémoires de Colbert*, 8 vols., ed. Pierre Clément (Paris: Imprimerie imperiale, 1861–62), 3, pt. 2: 552–53.

112. Moreau de Saint-Méry, *Loix et constitutions*, 1: 299.

113. Ibid., 1: 292–93.

114. CAOM, C8 AI, de Baas to Colbert, 8 February, 1674, as cited in Ly, *Compagnie du Sénégal*, 39.

115. To be fair, Lézy retrieved some of his reputation by his actions at the recapture of Cayenne and the assault on Tobago.

116. For a revisionist view of d'Estrées career, see Pritchard, *In Search of Empire*, 282–83.

117. For the most detailed biography of Blénac, see André Baudrit, *Charles de Courbon, comte de Blénac (1622–1696)* (Fort-de-France, Martinique: Mémoires de la Société d'histoire de la Martinique, 1967).

118. Rennard, *Baas, Blénac*, 140.

119. Ibid. This was the bloodiest naval engagement of Louis's reign, according to Dessert, *La Royale*, 209, who blames d'Estrées habitual impetuosity.

120. Ly, *Compagnie du Sénégal*, 143–53.

121. Dessert, *La Royale*, 189–91.

122. Ibid., 327, lists the *Terrible* as shipwrecked, but Dessert does not include this catastrophe in his list of Louis XIV's naval battles. See p. 332.

123. Peter Galvin, *Patterns of Pillage: A Geography of Caribbean-based Piracy in Spanish America, 1536–1718* (New York: Peter Lang, 2000), 154–55.

124. Despite their importance, Wolf, *Louis XIV*, never mentions the battle of Tobago and the disaster off Curaçao.

125. Recent analyses have tended to exonerate d'Estrées. See, e.g., Dessert, *La Royale*, 189–91, 249–52.

126. Ibid., 251.

Chapter 8. The Sun King Asserts Control: The 1680s to the 1690s

1. Dessalles, *Annales*, in Dessalles, *Histoire générale* 3: 185–91, 223–24. Moreau de Saint-Méry, *Loix et constitutions*, 1: 336–38.

2. For many more details, see Price, *France and the Chesapeake*, 1: 20–21.

3. For a highly laudatory appraisal of Seignelay's work as minister, see Dessert, *La Royale*, 282–83.

4. For his commission, see Moreau de Saint-Méry, *Loix et constitutions*, 1: 318–21. From here on the term "administrators" will be used when the governor-general and the intendant acted in unison.

5. Baudrit, *Charles de Courbon*, 97–103.

6. See Boucher, *Cannibal Encounters*, 87, 90–92.

7. E.g., Cristóbal Diatristán de Acuña, *Nuevo descubrimiento del gran río de las Amazonas* (Madrid, 1641), trans. Marin de Gomberville as *Relation de la rivière des Amazones* (Paris: C. Barbin, 1682).

8. Moreau de Saint-Méry, *Loix et constitutions*, 1: 343–44.

9. Galvin, *Patterns of Pillage*, 155. Grammont served as king's lieutenant at Tortuga.

10. Michel Camus, "Un Flibustier reconverti: Laurent de Graffe," *Revue de la Société haïtienne d'histoire et de géographie* 46 (1988): 57, puts the number of slaves Graffe took from Vera Cruz at from 1,200 to 1,300. Many stories are told of Graffe's origins. Although Exquemelin, cited ibid., 54, depicts him as having blond hair, his surname may reflect the Spanish Latin American adjective *grifo*, meaning "kinky, woolly," denoting African ancestry (Clifford, *Lost Fleet*, 130–31). J. H. Parry and P. M. Sherlock, *A Short History of the West Indies*, 2d ed. (London: Macmillan, 1963), 91, spell his name "de Graaf" and assume that he was Dutch.

11. Cited by Charlevoix, *Histoire de l'isle Espagnole*, 2: 145.

12. Clifford, *Lost Fleet*, 206.

13. Camus, "Flibustier reconverti," 53.

14. Hrodej, *Amiral du Casse*, 135.

15. Saintoyant, *Colonisation française sous l'ancien regime*, 1: 101.

16. Mims, *Colbert's West India Policy*, 236.

17. Moreau de Saint-Méry, *Loix et constitutions*, 1: 314–17.

18. Hrodej, *Amiral du Casse*, 54–55.

19. CAOM C6, 1, April 9, 1680, cited in Petrovich, "Revisioning Colbert," 528n353. See also Ly, *Compagnie du Sénégal*, 161–68.

20. Petrovich, "Revisioning Colbert," 363. For an interesting account of a French slaving voyage of this era, see Jean Barbot, *Journal d'un voyage de traite en Guinée, à Cayenne et aux Antilles fait par Jean Barbot en 1678–89*, ed. Gabriel Debien, Marcel Delafosse, and Guy Thilmans (Dakar: IFAN, 1979).

21. Bibliothèque nationale, NAF, no. 9339, 96 v, as cited in Petrovich, "Revisioning Colbert," 363; also, Ly, *Compagnie du Sénégal*, 165–68.

22. Watts, *West Indies*, 247.

23. Ly, *Compagnie du Sénégal*, 175n2, 176–79.

24. See, e.g., Moreau de Saint-Méry, *Loix et constitutions*, 1: 464.

25. Rennard, *Baas, Blénac*, 215–18.

26. See, e.g., Moreau de Saint-Méry, *Loix et constitutions*, 1: 515.

27. Dessalles, *Annales*, in Dessalles, *Histoire générale*, 3: 205–6. Somehow, despite having eleven children, Blénac gained enough money from his office to purchase many noble estates in France. Baudrit, *Charles de Courbon*, 13.

28. Moreau de Saint-Méry, *Loix et constitutions*, 1: 483, 520, 586, 588.

29. Ibid., 1: 342.

30. Baudrit, *Charles de Courbon*, 78.

31. Tracy and de Baas had earlier ruled that creditors could pursue these assets. See, e.g., Moreau de Saint-Méry, *Loix et constitutions*, 1: 221–23. The prohibition was reiterated in 1681. Ibid., 347

32. Jacques Petitjean Roget, "Les Femmes des colons à Martinique," *Revue d'histoire de l'Amérique française* 9 (1955–56): 222–23.

33. See Barbot, *Journal*, 254.

34. Gérard Lafleur, "Les Juifs aux îles françaises du vent (XVIIe–XVIIIe siècles)," *Bulletin de la société d'histoire de la Guadeloupe*, 65–66 (1985): 82–115.

35. Moreau de Saint-Méry, *Loix et constitutions*, 1: 474.

36. For the debate about the influence of Roman law, see Vernon V. Palmer, "The Origins and Authors of the *Code noir*," in *An Uncommon Experience: Law and Judicial Institutions in Louisiana, 1803–2003*, ed. Judith Kelleher Schafer and Warren M. Billings (Lafayette: Center for Louisiana Studies, University of Southwestern Louisiana, 1997), 331–59, and Alan Watson, "The Origins of the *Code Noir* Revisited," *Tulane Law Review*, March 1997, 1–15.

37. Palmer, "Origins and Authors of the *Code noir*," 343.

38. Yvonne Bézard, *Fonctionnaires maritimes et coloniaux sous Louis XIV: Les Bégon* (Paris: Michel, 1932), 46.

39. Dessalles, *Annales*, in Dessalles, *Histoire générale*, 3: 290–92.

40. Moreau de Saint-Méry, *Loix et constitutions*, 1: 518–19, 533–34, 559, 640.

41. See Price, *France and the Chesapeake*, 1: 30–32.

42. Moreau de Saint-Méry, *Loix et constitutions*, 1: 345.

43. Pritchard, *In Search of Empire*, 50.

44. Petitjean Roget, *Société d'habitation*, 2: 1381–83. Pritchard, *In Search of Empire*, 45, gives 5,019 whites, 10,801 blacks, and 433 "coloured" for 1687.

45. Pritchard, *In Search of Empire*, 45.

46. Ly, *Compagnie du Sénégal*, 188–90. The company defended itself by noting that it could not collect even half the six million l.t. the colonists owed it. Hrodej, *Amiral du Casse*, 64.

47. Hrodej, *Amiral du Casse*, 64.

48. Ibid., 67–68, 74.

49. Ly, *Compagnie du Sénégal*, 197–201; Moreau de Saint-Méry, *Loix et constitutions*, 1: 514.

50. Labat, *Nouveau voyage*, 5: 317.

51. CAOM C14 1, fol. 219; Hurault, *Français et Indiens*, 353–73.

52. However, Pritchard, *In Search of Empire*, 44, cites a 1677 report of Patoulet's claiming that 319 colonists, 1,374 black slaves, and 48 Indian slaves inhabited Cayenne. If true, then the 1687 figure demonstrates very little growth.

53. Hrodej, *Amiral du Casse*, 90–91. See also the interesting contemporary account *À la Guyane à la fin du XVIIe siècle: Journal de Goupy des Marets (1675–1676 et 1687–1690)*, ed. G. Debien (Dakar: Université de Dakar, 1965).

54. Hurault, *Français et Indiens*, 88; Bézard, *Fonctionnaires*, 74.

55. Moreau de Saint-Méry, *Loix et constitutions*, 1: 463–64.

56. Price, *France and the Chesapeake*, 1: 86. Though outlawed, the practice also remained a problem in the Chesapeake. Thanks to Carla Pestana for this observation.

57. Ibid., 89.

58. Guy Lasserre, "La Guadeloupe: Étude géographique" (thesis, Université de Bordeaux, 1961), 1: 232–33. Pritchard's numbers are a match for the slaves, but he has 4,411 whites in 1687. *In Search of Empire*, 66.

59. Hrodej, *Amiral du Casse*, 242–43, 246–47.

60. Labat, *Nouveau voyage*, 1: 242–43.

61. Christian Buchet, *La Lutte pour l'espace Caraibe et la façade Atlantique de l'Amérique centrale et du sud (1672–1763)* (Paris: Librairie de l'Inde, 1991), 1051–54.

62. For details, see Charles Frostin, "La Famille ministérielle des Phélypeaux: Esquisse d'un profil Pontchartrain (XVIe–XVIIIe siècles)," *Annales de Bretagne* 86 (1979): 117–40.

63. Ly, *Compagnie du Sénégal*, 207–14.

64. Hrodej, *Amiral du Casse*, 88–89, 91, 93–94; Thomas A. Spencer, *A True and Faithful Relation of . . . Expedition against the French in the West Indies* (London: Robert Clavel, 1691), 11; Labat; *Nouveau voyage*, 2: 419, 424. And see also Bruce P. Lenman, *Britain's Colonial Wars, 1688–1783* (Harlow, Eng.: Pearson, 2001), 22–24.

65. Labat, *Nouveau voyage*, 4: 534–37.

66. Ibid., 2: 243.

67. Hrodej, *Amiral du Casse*, 116.

68. Pritchard, *In Search of Empire*, 310.

69. Rennard, *Baas, Blénac*, 206–7.

70. Labat, *Nouveau voyage*, 4: 410–11; 5: 18.

71. Ibid., 5: 501. On the other hand, Labat found the fortifications at Le Cap deplorable (ibid., 131).

72. *Histoire des Antilles*, ed. Pluchon and Abenon, 103.

73. Labat, *Nouveau voyage*, 1: 194, 207–9.

74. Moreau de Saint-Méry, *Loix et constitutions*, 1: 506–7, 524–27, 554; Hrodej, *Amiral du Casse*, 132–33.

75. Philippe Hrodej, "Saint-Domingue en 1690. Les Observations du père Plumier, botaniste provençal," *Revue française d'histoire d'Outre-mer* 84, no. 317 (1997): 97–98. However, the white population remained relatively stable in the censuses of 1681 (4,336) and 1687 (4,411). Pritchard, *In Search of Empire*, 65.

76. Moreau de Saint-Méry, *Loix et constitutions*, 1: 496–97.

77. Labat, *Nouveau voyage*, 5: 96.

78. Hrodej, "Saint-Domingue," 107–8; Baudrit, *Charles de Courbon*, 119–20; Hrodej, *Amiral du Casse*, 133–34.

79. Dessalles, *Histoire générale*, 2: 161. The figure may in fact have been higher, and du Casse and his officers may have become rich from the enterprise. Hrodej, *Amiral du Casse*, 167.

80. Laurent de Graffe, the king's lieutenant at Le Cap, received the blame, and rightly so, according to du Casse and most historians, but he was largely exonerated when called to France for an accounting. Without mentioning the king's verdict, Pritchard, *In Search of Empire*, 319, is scornful of Graffe's timid leadership, and Hrodej, *Amiral du Casse*, 186; Camus, "Flibustier reconverti," 68–69, agree.

81. Moreau de Saint-Méry, *Loix et constitutions*, 1: 528–30.

82. Hrodej, *Amiral du Casse*, 185; Moreau de Saint-Méry, *Loix et constitutions*, 1: 570–71; Dessalles, *Histoire* générale, 2: 187.

83. Moreau de Saint-Méry, *Loix et constitutions*, 1: 573.

84. Hrodej, *Amiral du Casse*, 141–42, 157; Moreau de Saint-Méry, *Loix et constitutions*, 1: 586–89.

85. Labat, *Nouveau voyage*, 1: 133. He specifies that a hundredweight of sugar brought only forty to fifty sols in 1694, half of what it brought when peace was restored. Ibid., 3: 319.

86. Dessert, *La Royale*, 332.

87. Lenman, *Britain's Colonial Wars*, 24.

88. Hrodej, *Amiral du Casse*, 152.

89. Labat, *Nouveau voyage*, 5: 105.

90. Hrodej, *Amiral du Casse*, 236.

91. Stewart R. King, *Blue Coat or Powdered Wig: Free People of Color in Pre-Revolutionary Saint-Domingue* (Athens: University of Georgia Press, 2001), 69–70.

92. Moreau de Saint-Méry, *Loix et constitutions*, 1: 574.

93. Pritchard, *In Search of Empire*, 331.

94. Moreau de Saint-Méry, *Loix et constitutions*, 1: 577.

95. Gallifet and the sovereign council president Le Maire also established large plantations. Labat, *Nouveau voyage*, 5: 165, 69; Hrodej, *Amiral du Casse*, 238, estimates du Casse's share from Cartagena as between 400,000 and 600,000 l.t.

96. Hrodej, *Amiral du Casse*, 223–24.

97. Moreau de Saint-Méry, *Loix et constitutions*, 1: 581–83.

98. Pritchard, *In Search of Empire*, 424; Dessalles, *Histoire générale*, 2: 216; Hrodej, *Amiral du Casse*, 187, 197; Moreau de Saint-Méry, *Loix et constitutions*, 1: 592–93.

99. Hrodej, *Amiral du Casse*, 234; Moreau de Saint-Méry, *Loix et constitutions*, 1: 645, 673.

100. Moreau de Saint-Méry, *Loix et constitutions*, 1: 624.

101. Ibid., 1: 614. See 610–18, for the patent letters of this company.

102. Rennard, *Baas, Blénac*, 238.

103. Ibid., 237.

104. Baudrit, *Charles de Courbon*, 37, claims Blémac died of dysentery, however.

105. Pritchard, *In Search of Empire*, 432; Liliane Chauleau, *La Société de la Martinique au XVIIe siècle (1635–1713)* (Caen: Ozanne, 1966), 129, 239–40.

106. Ly, *Compagnie du Sénégal*, 22. For Jérôme de Pontchartrain's plans for continental North America, see Dale Miquelon, "Envisioning the French Empire: Utrecht, 1711–1713," *French Historical Studies* 24, no. 4 (Fall 2001): 653–77.

107. Dale Miquelon, "Les Pontchartrain se penchant sur leurs cartes de l'Amérique: Les Cartes et l'impérialisme, 1690–1712," *Revue d'histoire de l'Amérique française* 59, nos. 1–2 (2005): 55.

108. For all this, see Moreau de Saint-Méry, *Loix et constitutions*, 1: 599–603, 581, 583–88, 596, 650, 654–55, 657, 661. Louis professed himself "fatigued" by news that his officers had whipped or otherwise abused habitants. For his part, Pontchartrain was "furious" in 1700 that an officer had struck a habitant with a stick. Ibid., 644. Although pompous and vain, to be sure, Louis nevertheless had compassion for the weak.

109. For their detailed instructions, see ibid., 630–33.

110. Camus, "Flibustier reconverti," 74–75.

111. Hrodej, *Amiral du Casse*, 257–58, 280–81.

112. See the population statistics for 1715 in Pritchard, *In Search of Empire*, 424.

113. For an anti-statist perspective, see ibid., 18, 146, 191, 234–37, 279.

Chapter 9. Island Society from the 1660s to the 1690s: The Habitants

David Hume, "Of National Characters" (1742), in *Essays Moral, Political, and Literary*, ed. Eugene F. Miller (Indianapolis: Liberty Classics, 1987), 205. www .econlib.org/LIBRARY/LFBooks/Hume/hmMPLo.html (accessed March 6, 2007).

1. Barry Higman contends that the aboriginal populations did not have "a significant impact on the overall pattern of growth" of the British West Indies.

"British West Indian Economic and Social Development," in *The Cambridge Economic History of the United States*, ed. Engerman and Gallman (Cambridge: Cambridge University Press, 1996) 1: 305. Antiguans tormented by Carib raids in the 1660s and 1670s would have disagreed vehemently.

2. Pritchard, *In Search of Empire*, 424.

3. Stein, *French Sugar Business*, 42. Like almost all historians, Stein views the development of a sugar and slave society as a rapid process, too much so in my view.

4. Schnakenbourg, "Note sur les origines," 304.

5. Pritchard, *In Search of Empire*, 424.

6. Schnakenbourg, "Note sur les origines," 295.

7. Dutertre, *Histoire générale*, 3: 98–99.

8. CAOM C8 B2, Blénac to Colbert, 23 Sept. 1679, cited in Ly, *Compagnie du Sénégal*, 26–27.

9. Labat, *Nouveau voyage*, 3: 44–45.

10. Schnakenbourg, "Note sur les origines," 295.

11. Ibid., 298–99.

12. CAOM, C8 B17, Recensement des Isles de l'Amérique, April 12, 1683, cited by Ly, *Compagnie du Sénégal*, 47.

13. Pritchard, *In Search of Empire*, 424.

14. Labat, *Nouveau voyage*, 1: 252.

15. Ibid., 3: 416–429, 431, 342, 457. Labat devotes 345 pages to sugar, which was as far as I know the most extensive treatment up to that time. See ibid., 120–465.

16. Ibid., 4: 113; 4: 211; 5: 41–42.

17. Ibid., 3: 399; 5: 183. Hurricanes devastated earlier efforts to plant cacao in the Windward Islands. Ibid., 6: 33, 55. Always the pharmacist, Labat describes chocolate as a panacea. For his recipe for hot chocolate, mix two ounces of dark chocolate with three to four ounces of sugar, add a whole egg and cinnamon powder, and finish with boiling water or milk; in the latter case, omit the egg (ibid., 75).

18. Yolande Lavoie, Carolyn Fick, and Francine-M. Mayer, "A Particular Study of Slavery in the Caribbean Island of Saint Barthélemy: 1648–1846," *Caribbean Studies* 28, no. 2 (1995): 370–74.

19. Labat, *Nouveau voyage*, 2: 456.

20. Labat notes that after peace returned in 1697, an English ship from Antigua came at night to trade with his neighbors. Ibid., 2: 293.

21. Pritchard, *In Search for Empire*, 424. Elisabeth, *Société martiniquaise*, 85, 110, has slightly different figures: 6,582 whites and 14,566 enslaved people.

22. In contrast, the English slave trade in this era flourished. Between 1672 and 1713, the Royal African Company transported almost 100,000 slaves to the

Americas. K. G. Davies, *The Royal Africa Company* (London: Longmans, Green, 1957), 299.

23. Pritchard, *In Search of Empire*, 424.

24. Petitjean Roget, *Société d'habitation*, 2: 1163.

25. Ibid., 1164.

26. Chauleau, *Société de la Martinique*, 12.

27. Dutertre, *Histoire générale*, 2: 122.

28. Labat, *Nouveau voyage*, 2: 120–416.

29. Ibid., 1: 171, 181; 2: 475. Labat makes it clear that ex-officials or their heirs predominated among the big sugar planters. Ibid., 496, 512.

30. Ibid., 425.

31. Ibid., 3: 383.

32. Ibid., 460, 514–15.

33. Ibid., 6: 85–86; 3: 521; 5: 206–8.

34. Ibid., 1: 397–99. To make *maby*, Labat says, take water, clarified sugar syrup, twelve sweet potatoes, and quartered ripe oranges and let ferment for thirty hours.

35. Dutertre, *Histoire générale*, 2: 10. Rochefort, *Histoire naturelle et morale*, 99, notes the shortage of valuable types of trees on occupied islands. See also Labat, *Nouveau voyage*, 3: 451; La Barre, *Description*, 7, 13.

36. Moreau de Saint-Méry, *Loix et constitutions*, 1: 194.

37. Dutertre, *Histoire générale*, 2: 291; Labat, *Nouveau voyage*, 2: 394; 4: 222–23. For Labat's exotic recipe for stuffing and roasting a whole wild pig, see 4: 214–33.

38. Dutertre, *Histoire générale*, 3: 97.

39. Labat, *Nouveau voyage*, 1: 309.

40. Ibid., 2: 200, 204. Whales and turtles were also "fish" in this sense.

41. By the 1680s, wild cattle had become "very rare." Moreau de Saint-Méry, *Loix et constitutions*, 1: 436. See also Exquemelin, *Histoire des avanturiers*, 113 to the effect that the wild dogs traveled in packs of 400 to 500.

42. See examples in Martine Pacton, "Flibustiers et administration royale en 1685 (documents)," *Conjonction: Revue franco-haïtienne*, nos. 174–75 (1987): 172.

43. Labat, *Nouveau voyage*, 5: 44.

44. Ibid., 4: 305, 309, 366.

45. Moreau de Saint-Méry, *Loix et constitutions*, 1: 308.

46. Philippe and Marie Rossignol, "À propos d'une liste des habitants de la Guadeloupe datée du Octobre 30, 1664," *Bulletin de la Société d'histoire de la Guadeloupe*, nos. 65–66 (1985): 29–30.

47. Pritchard, *In Search of Empire*, 52.

48. Elisabeth, *Société martiniquaise*, 30.

49. Rennard, *Baas, Blénac*, 130. Sixty-nine soldiers married in 1680–81 and were thus relieved of service.

50. Dunn, *Sugar and Slaves*, table 26, 312.

51. Pritchard, *In Search of Empire*, 424. The white population of 1685 was 18,012, and in 1700, it was 17,188.

52. For these figures see Dunn, *Sugar and Slaves*, 205.

53. A decline of roughly 1,000 whites in the French islands from 1685 to 1700 is largely explained by the collapse of the Saint-Christophe population, which went from 4,598 to 1,061. Pritchard, *In Search of Empire*, 424.

54. Jerome Reich, *Colonial America* (Englewood Cliffs, N.J.: Prentice-Hall, 1984), 237.

55. According to Hrodej, *Amiral du Casse*, 273, there were 4,800 whites in 1700.

56. Labat, *Nouveau voyage*, 5: 187–90.

57. Ibid., 217–19.

58. Ly, *Compagnie du Sénégal*, 48.

59. He did so by example. By 1716, he owned over 3,800 acres. Hrodej, *Amiral du Casse*, 252.

60. For the above figures, see Dunn, *Sugar and Slaves*, 312, and Pritchard, *In Search of Empire*, 424. For the transition to sugar at Saint-Domingue, see, e.g., Hrodej, *Amiral du Casse*, 248–53.

61. Pritchard, *In Search of Empire*, 424.

62. Labat, *Nouveau voyage*, 4: 530.

63. Dessalles, *Annales*, in Dessalles, *Histoire générale*, 3: 78.

64. CAOM C8 2, fol. 1, cited in Mims, *Colbert's West India Policy*, 45.

65. Jacques de Cauna, "La Création des grands domaines," in AN catalogue, *Voyages aux îles*, 179–80.

66. Elisabeth, *Société martiniquaise*, 44.

67. Just as in Brazil, small men planted sugar to be milled at neighboring sugar works. Petitjean Roget, *Société d'habitation*, 2: 1398; and see also van den Boogaart, "Second Brésil," 282.

68. Elisabeth, *Société martiniquaise*, 44. These planters owned 55.3% of all slaves.

69. Alain Buffon, *Monnaie et credit en économie coloniale: Contribution à l'histoire économique de la Guadeloupe, 1635–1919* (Basse-Terre: Société d'histoire de la Guadeloupe, 1979), 42.

70. *Correspondance . . . d'Ogeron*, ed. Camus,14; Price, *France and the Chesapeake*, 1: 83.

71. Moreau de Saint-Méry, *Loix et constitutions*, 1: 522–23.

72. Elisabeth, *Société martiniquaise*, 48.

73. Ibid., 39.

74. Dunn, *Sugar and Slaves*, 93–95. For a more in-depth analysis of the role of hurricanes in the British West Indies, see Matthew Mulcahy, "Weathering the Storms: Hurricanes and Risk in the British Greater Caribbean," *Business History Review* 78 (Winter 2004): 635–63.

75. Mulcahy, "Weathering the Storms," 693–94.

76. Labat found water mills much more efficient. *Nouveau voyage*, 3: 396.

77. Stein, *French Sugar Business*, 66–67; Moreau de Saint-Méry, *Loix et constitutions*, 1: 556, 591.

78. Labat, *Nouveau voyage*, 3: 312–13, gives examples of this fraud, which he describes as payback for merchants' inflated prices for goods.

79. Elisabeth, *Société martiniquaise*, 39.

80. Dutertre, *Histoire générale*, 1: 493. Despite all the funds the Compagnie des Isles invested in its sugar works, Houël never apparently dispatched any sugar. In 1646, he and company agents incurred another 12,000 l.t. charged to the company. Rennard, *Tricentenaire des Antilles*, 120.

81. Rochefort, *Histoire naturelle et morale*, 53.

82. The rapidity of the transformation to sugar is shown indirectly by a Saint-Domingue council edict of 1696 taxing tavern owners fifty pieces of eight instead of sugar as prescribed in an earlier ordinance. The council noted that "no sugar is made here." Moreau de Saint-Méry, *Loix et constitutions*, 1: 545.

83. Banks, *Chasing Empire*, 31.

84. Moreau de Saint-Méry, *Loix et constitutions*, 1: 582.

85. Labat, *Nouveau voyage*, 3: 319–20, 322–23.

86. Ibid., 5: 172.

87. See, e.g., Moreau de Saint-Méry, *Loix et constitutions*, 1: 283.

88. Rossignol and Rossignol, "À propos d'une liste," 31–79.

89. Wim Klooster, *Illicit Riches: Dutch Trade in the Caribbean, 1648–1795* (Leiden: KITLV Press, 1998), 109.

90. See the king's confirmation of this island custom in Moreau de Saint-Méry, *Loix et constitutions*, 1: 470–71.

91. Christian Schnakenbourg, "Le 'Terrier' de 1671 et le partage de la terre en Guadeloupe au XVIIe siècle," *Revue française d'histoire d'Outre-mer* 67, nos. 246–47 (1980): 42–43, 49. At the top end, property was much less concentrated on Martinique, whose topography was less suited to enormous properties.

92. Ibid., 49.

93. See Petitjean Roget, *Société d'habitation*, 2: 1382, table.

94. Cauna, "Création," 179–80.

95. Memoir in AN catalogue, *Voyages aux îles*, 39; for Barbados estimate, see Dunn, *Sugar and Slaves*, 202–3.

96. Pritchard, *In Search of Empire*, table 3.1, p. 171. Prices started to rise after 1696, and so did the number of *sucreries*. See ibid., table, 3.2, p. 172.

97. Ibid., 170.

98. Ibid., 16–17.

99. Patoulet's report to Colbert is cited in Baudrit, *Charles de Courbon*, 34.

100. Dunn, *Sugar and Slaves*, 287–88.

101. Danielle Bégot, "Architectures créoles," in AN catalogue, *Voyage aux îles*, 269–70.

102. Buffon, *Monnaie et credit*, 11–12.

103. Roger Mettam, *Power and Faction in Louis XIV's France* (New York: Basil Blackwell, 1988), 9–12.

104. Rennard, *Baas, Blénac*, 127–30.

105. Dessalles, *Annales*, in Dessalles, *Histoire générale*, 3: 139–40. For Tracy's regulations, see Moreau de Saint-Méry, *Loix et constitutions*, 1: 238–43.

106. Moreau de Saint-Méry, *Loix et constitutions*, 1: 475–76.

107. Ibid., 180–82.

108. Ibid., 388. According to Pritchard (*In Search of Empire*, 27), 226 Jews, including 132 slaves, were expelled from Martinique.

109. Moreau de Saint-Méry, *Loix et constitutions*, 1: 220–21.

110. Gérard Lafleur, "Religion et société aux Antilles françaises," in AN catalogue, *Voyage aux îles*, 291–92. For the expulsion of the Jews, see Lafleur, "Les Juifs aux îles françaises du vent (XVIIe–XVIIIe siécles)," *Bulletin de la Société d'histoire de la Guadeloupe*, nos. 65–66 (1985): 77–131.

111. Moreau de Saint-Méry, *Loix et constitutions*, 1: 514.

112. CAOM B9, fol. 89v. Such rhetoric makes one almost nostalgic for "absolutist" monarchy.

113. Moreau de Saint-Méry, *Loix et constitutions*, 1: 298; Baudrit, *Charles de Courbon*, 87.

114. Pritchard, *In Search of Empire*, 27–28.

115. Dessalles, *Histoire générale*, 1: 461–62.

116. Moreau de Saint-Méry, *Loix et constitutions*, 1: 221–23, 324–25.

117. Ibid., 355–56.

118. Ibid., 460.

119. Ibid., 477–78.

120. Ibid., 475.

121. Labat, *Nouveau voyage*, 1: 230.

122. Pritchard, *In Search of Empire*, 424; for the number of priests, see Rennard, *Histoire religieuse*, 62–63.

123. Labat, *Nouveau voyage*, 5: 138. He says that in 1702 there were only five clerics in Saint-Domingue. Ibid., 205.

124. Ibid., 2: 2; 4: 15.

125. Ibid., 1: 292–93; 2: 489; 6: 144–45.

126. See Garraway, *Libertine Colony*, 168–70.

127. Labat, *Nouveau voyage*, 1: 347, 418, 423; 4: 101–2; 5: 13.

128. Ibid., 2: 93.

129. Ibid., 1: 216–18, 225.

130. Ibid., 3: 483–502.

131. Ibid., 6: 89

132. Ibid., 2: 348. Labat experimented with growing potatoes at La Rochelle.

133. Ibid., 3: 383.

134. Ibid., 5: 332.

135. Ibid., 2: 45; 1: 467–68.

136. Ibid., 6: 350, 465.

137. Petitjean Roget, *La Société d'habitation*, 2: 1376.

138. Pritchard, *In Search of Empire*, 66, table 1.10.

139. Elisabeth, *Société martiniquaise*, 181.

140. Ibid., 182.

141. Ibid., 470.

142. Rossignol and Rossignol, "À propos d'une liste," 38, 40, 44.

143. Elisabeth, *Société martiniquaise*, 83.

144. Petitjean Roget, *Société d'habitation*, 2: 1401–3.

145. Ibid., 1403.

146. Elisabeth, *Société martiniquaise*, 36, has demonstrated a dramatic increase of Creoles in militia companies between the years 1664 and 1680.

147. Baudrit, *Charles de Courbon*, 77.

148. Lavoie, Fick, and Mayer, "Particular Study of Slavery," 376.

149. Elisabeth, *Société martiniquaise*, 111.

150. Ibid., 118.

151. Pritchard, *In Search of Empire*, 61.

152. Pacton, "Flibustiers et administration royale," 172.

153. Local officials used requisitioned slaves to build these fortifications. Thus the wealthier habitants paid this forced labor tax. Labat notes that these island roosters used every trick to reduce this burden. 5: 415.

154. Banks, *Chasing Empire*, 79.

155. Perotin-Dumon, *Ville aux îles*, 103.

156. Ibid., 102. Labat, *Nouveau voyage*, 1: 77, counts 2,400 Europeans and an equal number of "Negroes and children" in Saint-Pierre.

157. Ibid., 2: 568; 2: 571; 3: 3, for just some examples of Labat's antagonism toward artisans.

158. Merle and Debien, "Marchands, colons" (February 1954), 6–11.

159. Perotin-Dumon, *Ville aux îles*, 113–17.

160. Dutertre, *Histoire générale*, 2: 459.

161. Labat, *Nouveau voyage*, 1: 481–85. Du Buc reminds me of Pierre Boucher of New France.

162. Ibid., 4: 14–15. According to Stein, *French Sugar Business*, 31, this was amoebic dysentery.

163. "Epidemic Dysentery Health Update," *International Newsletter on the Control of Diarrhoeal Diseases*, supplement to no. 55 (December 1993–February 1994): 1–12.

164. Labat, *Nouveau voyage*, 4: 251.

165. Kiple and Ornelas, "After the Encounter," 60. Their account of how difficult it was to have conditions on slave ships that would serve to convey the virus from Africa to the Caribbean is very useful. See pp. 58–59.

166. Labat, *Nouveau voyage*, 1: 435; 5: 204; 1: 435.

167. Authors such as Dutertre contrast Indian women treated as beasts of burden with what they considered to be pampered French women. See Dutertre, *Histoire générale*, 2: 382.

168. Merry Wiesner, *Women and Gender in Early Modern Europe* (Cambridge: Cambridge University Press, 1993; 2d ed., 2000), provides a convenient synthesis on early modern women.

169. CAOM C7 A1, 4 as cited in Petrovich, "Revisioning Colbert," 498.

170. Dutertre, *Histoire générale*, 3: 235–36.

171. For an overview of early modern witchcraft, see Brian P. Levack, *The Witch-Hunt in Early Modern Europe* (1987; 3d. ed., New York: Pearson Longman, 2006).

172. Elisabeth, *Société martiniquaise*, 116.

173. Lavoie, Fick, and Mayer, "Particular Study of Slavery," 373, table 1.

174. Rossignol and Rossignol, "À propos d'une liste," 73.

175. Island custom prevented relatives of the deceased husband from contesting a childless widow's inheritance. Dutertre, *Histoire générale*, 2: 455–56.

176. Rossignol and Rossignol, "À propos d'une liste," 49.

177. Dessalles, *Annales*, in Dessalles, *Histoire générale*, 3: 269–70, 355. Whether sexual imbalances explain the occasional bestiality is uncertain. In 1697, one Jacques Le Bas was burned alive for being caught in flagrante with his mare.

178. See Huppert, *After the Black Death;* Wiesner, *Women and Gender in Early Modern Europe;* and Beatrice Gottlieb's *The Family in the Western World: From the Black Death to the Industrial Age* (New York: Oxford University Press, 1993), 60–62.

179. Petitjean Roget, *Société d'habitation*, 2: 1414–15.

180. Jean-Pierre Poussou, "L'Immigration européene," in AN catalogue, *Voyage aux îles*, 55.

181. Petitjean Roget, "Femmes des colons," 222.

182. CAOM C8 4, fol. 60.

183. Pritchard, *In Search of Empire*, 50, 54, tables 1.5 and 1.6. Not so at Saint-Domingue; see ibid., 66, table 1.10. By 1686, women outnumbered men 196 to 150 at Saint-Barthélemy, according to Lavoie, Fick, and Mayer, "Particular Study of Slavery," 373, table 1.

184. Rossignol and Rossignol, "À propos d'une liste," 51.

185. Camus, "Flibustier reconverti," 70–72.

186. Rossignol and Rossignol, "À propos d'une liste," 47.

187. Labat, *Nouveau voyage*, 5: 20; Lavoie, Fick, and Mayer, "Particular Study of Slavery," 376. One example of a wealthy widow who remained unmarried was Mme. de Gourselas, who owned multiple plantations and at least 100 slaves. Rennard, *Baas, Blénac*, 160.

188. Petitjean Roget, *Société d'habitation*, 2: 1409–11.

189. Witch trials were diminishing in France, and Louis XIV stopped them in 1683. Levack, *Witch-Hunt*, 184.

190. Dutertre, *Histoire générale*, 2: 447–49.

191. Labat, *Nouveau voyage*, 1: 82.

192. Ibid., 3: 158–61; 1: 104, 157.

Chapter 10. Island Society from the 1660s to the 1690s: The World of Coerced Labor

1. Petitjean Roget, *Société d'habitation*, 2: 1377; and see also Elisabeth, *Société martiniquaise*, 30, table.

2. Gemery and Horn, "British and French Indentured Servant Migration," 290, remark on the larger percentage of skilled servants in the French migration as opposed to the English.

3. Debien, "Engagés pour les Antilles", 74, 140, and the graph on 248–49. In 1663, the Paris authorities threatened capital punishment for anyone forcibly spiriting people away to America. Moreau de Saint-Méry, *Loix et constitutions*, 1: 93.

4. See the chart in Mauro, "French Indentured Servants," 100.

5. Debien, "Engagés pour les Antilles," 185–86.

6. Ibid., 140–48.

7. Elisabeth, *Société martiniquaise*, 223–24.

8. On Exquemelin, see Camus, "Note critique," 79–90.

9. Debien, "Engagés pour les Antilles," 145–47.

10. Moreau de Saint-Méry, *Loix et constitutions*, 1: 190–91. In the document, the king implores masters to feed their servants adequately and to treat them well.

11. Debien, "Engagés pour les Antilles," 64. For examples of servants who renounced their "rights," see Merle and Debien, "Marchands, colons" (January 1954), 11.

12. Debien, "Engagés pour les Antilles," 241–42.

13. See the chart in Mauro, "French Indentured Servants," 99, extrapolated from Debien's studies.

14. Debien, "Engagés pour les Antilles," 242. He cites English historians to the effect that Barbados and Virginia saw similar declines.

15. Ibid., 180–82.

16. Ibid., 192–93.

17. Elisabeth, *Société martiniquaise*, 30.

18. However, only refiners and surgeons could guarantee that their work would be only in their skills. Françoise and Jean-Marie Lore, *Les Engagements à Nantes ver les îles d'Amérique de 1690 à 1734* (Saint-Herblain: J.-M. Loré, 1987), 8–11. Altogether there were 2,827 contracts signed in these forty-four years.

19. Colbert praised Tracy for "forcing payments to poor servants and artisans at the hands of the little tyrants [i.e., masters] who have grown rich by the sweat of these poor wretches" (CAOM, C81 letter of September 22, 1664, quoted in Mims, *Colbert's West India Policy*, 61). For Tracy's regulations intended to protect servants against abusive masters, see Moreau de Saint-Méry, *Loix et constitutions*, 1: 119.

20. CAOM, C8A3, November 19, 1681.

21. For evidence of this deceptiveness, Moreau de Saint Méry, *Loix et constitutions*, 1: 543–44.

22. Exquemelin, *Histoire des avanturiers*, 1: 184–90.

23. For this paragraph, see Danielle Bégot, "Villes et urbanisme," in AN catalogue, *Voyage aux îles*, 259–65.

24. Debien, "Engagés pour les Antilles," 224.

25. Labat, *Nouveau voyage*, 3: 112.

26. For the above paragraphs, see Exquemelin, *Histoire des avanturiers*, 1: 147–68. Labat, *Nouveau voyage*, 5: 231, agreed. On a visit there, he ate four pounds of fresh meat. He comments that he either had a good appetite that night or that the meat was just so succulent he could not stop.

27. Moreau de Saint-Méry, *Loix et constitutions*, 1: 638–39. Shipowners were transporting servants under the age of twelve. Repeated ordinances indicate a continuing problem of enforcement. See ibid., 2: 107.

28. Ibid., 1: 639–40.

29. Ibid., 640.

30. Labat, *Nouveau voyage*, 1: 109; 4: 513–14.

31. Moreau de Saint-Méry, *Loix et constitutions*, 1: 197.

32. Labat, *Nouveau voyage*, 4: 111.

33. See the table in Peabody, "'A Dangerous Zeal,'" 64, which draws on the Cambridge University Press database on CD-ROM, *The Trans-Atlantic Slave Trade* (1999). Pritchard, *In Search of Empire*, 11n38, updates the CD-ROM's figures. Eltis, *Rise of African Slavery*, 166, table 7–1, documents the dramatic increase of the English slave trade from 1662 and 1713. For the more general picture, see also Thornton, *Africa and Africans*, 118–20.

34. According to an older study cited in Ly, *Compagnie du Sénégal*, 80, fifty-five ships left for West Africa between 1671 and 1692, but not all were engaged in the slave trade.

35. Ibid., 75.

36. Thornton, *Africa and Africans,* 120, notes, however, that all the slaves on the Remire plantation in Cayenne between 1685 and 1690 were Dutch-supplied.

37. Eltis, *Rise of African Slavery,* 166, table 7–1.

38. Peabody, "'A Dangerous Zeal,'" 64. Senegambia provided all of Saint-Domingue's 1,132 slaves brought in by French traders.

39. Moreau de Saint-Méry, *Loix et constitutions,* 1: 665.

40. Labat, *Nouveau voyage,* 4: 136–37.

41. Elisabeth, *Société martiniquaise,* 27.

42. Petitjean Roget, *Société d'habitation,* 2: 1376. Elisabeth in *Société martiniquaise,* 27, has 6,582 for 1671, 9,364 for 1682, and 10,454 for 1684.

43. See Pritchard, *In Search of Empire,* 424.

44. Patterson, *Sociology of Slavery,* 95, table 1; Dunn, *Sugar and Slaves,* 312.

45. Dunn, *Sugar and Slaves,* 314.

46. Pritchard, *In Search of Empire,* 12–13.

47. James Pritchard's updating, ibid., 11n38, of the totals given by *The Trans-Atlantic Slave Trade: A Database on CD-ROM,* ed. Eltis et al.

48. Ibid., 11–13.

49. Ibid., 424, and Peabody, "'A Dangerous Zeal,'" 64.

50. Dutertre and Pelleprat preferred Cape Verde (Senegambian) slaves. Dutertre, *Histoire générale,* 2: 496; Pelleprat, *Relation,* 55.

51. See, however, the grouping of West Africans into three broad cultural units in Thornton, *Africa and Africans,* 185–92.

52. Labat, *Nouveau voyage,* 6: 327–28.

53. Pritchard, *In Search of Empire,* 13, uncritically accepts Curtin's estimate and concludes that more than 75% of the slaves coming into French plantation colonies thus arrived on foreign ships.

54. Arlette Gaultier, *Les Soeurs de Solitude: La Condition féminine dans l'esclavage aux Antilles du XVIIe au XIXe siècles* (Paris: Éditions Caribéenes, 1985), 76.

55. Dutertre, *Histoire générale,* 2: 505, 518. The discussion in Chapter 6 suggests that Poincy owned fewer than 400 slaves.

56. Pritchard, *In Search of Empire,* 50, 54, 64, tables 1.5, 1.6, and 1.8.

57. For the problems of working out this ratio, see Lavoie, Fick, and Mayer, "Particular Study of Slavery," 375–76.

58. Ly, *Compagnie du Sénégal,* 53.

59. Elisabeth, *Société martiniquaise,* 97; according to Debien, *Esclaves,* 214–15, "religious communities . . . were about the only ones to own plantations on which births balanced deaths."

60. Labat, *Nouveau voyage,* 3: 436, 459, 332–33, 420, 442–43.

61. Ibid., 3: 339–40.

62. Ibid., 6: 343. Labat blames surgeons whose mercury "remedy" for venereal disease led to many deaths.

63. For excellent treatments of sugar production, see Dunn, *Sugar and Slaves*, chap. 6, and Sydney Mintz, *Sweetness and Power: The Place of Sugar in Modern History* (New York: Penguin Books, 1986), chap. 2.

64. Stein, *French Sugar Business*, 56.

65. Petitjean Roget, *Société d'habitation*, 2: 1381.

66. Lafleur, "Juifs aux îles," 98. The sample is only five families however.

67. Mulcahy, "Weathering the Storms," 646.

68. Clodoré, *Relation*, 1: 43–46.

69. *Correspondance . . . d'Ogeron*, ed. Camus,139.

70. CAOM, C8A 1, November 20, 1672.

71. CAOM, C7 A1, 29, as cited in Petrovich, "Revisioning Colbert," 304.

72. All the slaves the Dutch sold to the Remire plantation at Cayenne between 1685 and 1690 were baptized Kongos. Thornton, *Africa and Africans*, 120. Father Mongin at Saint-Christophe even went to court to get permission of slaves to marry against their masters' consent. Peabody, "'A Dangerous Zeal,'" 68–69.

73. Dutertre, *Histoire générale*, 2: 510–11; 3: 73–75.

74. Moreau de Saint-Méry, *Loix et constitutions*, 1: 231–34; Clodoré, *Relation*, 1: 44–46. In contrast, Patterson, *Sociology of Slavery*, 87, contends that marriage was "out of the question" for Jamaican slaves.

75. Labat, *Nouveau voyage*, 3: 443–59; 4: 142–62; 6: 327–28. Lewis, *Main Currents in Caribbean Thought*, 66, calls Labat "the epitome of racial bigotry," which is a stretch. A good master, which Labat obviously considered himself to be, always prefers *douceur* to violence, he says. Labat, *Nouveau voyage*, 3: 459. Africans had natural virtues—bravery, stoic attitudes toward misfortune, love of their fellows, and humor—as well as vices, the most important of which was sensuality, he thought. He blames their vices on the devil, so Christianization could in principle eliminate these. Sample his vol. 4: 147–90 and judge for yourself.

76. Labat, *Nouveau voyage*, 4: 188.

77. Ibid., 1: 350.

78. For the 1685 population, Pritchard, *In Search of Empire*, 424; for the 1730s, see Peabody, "'A Dangerous Zeal,'" 75.

79. Peabody, "'A Dangerous Zeal,'" 62n23.

80. Father Jean Mongin quoted in Marcel Chatillon, "La Christianisation des esclaves au XVIIe siècle d'après les *Lettres* du R.P. Mongin," in *France-Amérique*, ed. Lestringant, 333. Myriam Cottas estimates 49% mortality of children 0–10 in the eighteenth century. "La Martinique: Babylone fertile ou terre stérile," *Annales de Démographie Historique (1992)*: 201.

81. Chatillon, "Christianisation," 335.

82. Peabody, "'A Dangerous Zeal,'" 73.

83. This story is recounted in ibid., 73–74.

84. Labat, *Nouveau voyage*, 1: 114.

85. See the Martinique sovereign council 1677 "Rules for slaves [*nègres*]" and the Guadeloupe council's regulation of 1680 that all children born of slave women, including those with free white or Indian fathers remained slaves. Ly, *Compagnie du Sénégal*, 42–43.

86. Some slaveholders resisted a common fund to reimburse masters of executed slaves.

87. Moreau de Saint-Méry, *Loix et constitutions*, 1: 148, 203, 224–25.

88. Ibid., 117–22; Dutertre, *Histoire générale*, 3: 72.

89. Dutertre, *Histoire générale*, 3: 74–75.

90. Ibid., 2: 522, 531, 533.

91. Moreau de Saint-Méry, *Loix et constitutions*, 1: 365.

92. Ibid., 203–4, 307.

93. For the code with a commentary, see Louis Sala-Molins, *Le Code noir ou Le Calvaire de Canaan* (Paris: Presses universitaires de France, 1987; 4th ed., 2006). For an English translation by John Garrigus, see www.vancouver.wsu .edu/fac/peabody/codenoir.htm (accessed March 12, 2007). Thanks to Sue Peabody and John Garrigus.

94. The term "mulatto" refers to the offspring, generally first-generation, of a European, almost always a male, and an African.

95. A 1670 Martinique law prohibited priests from naming fathers of mulatto children without their permission. Dessalles, *Histoire générale*, 1: 513.

96. Elisabeth, *Société martiniquaise*, 241.

97. Rossignol and Rossignol, "À propos d'une liste," 72.

98. Fathers of mulatto offspring who did not own the mother paid a fine of 1,000 pounds of sugar to the church and a similar amount to the owner. Elisabeth, *Société martiniquaise*, 242.

99. See Dutertre on the freeing of mulattoes at the age of twenty-one. *Histoire générale*, 2: 512–13. Blénac did not share Patoulet's views and pointed to the Iberian model of widespread racial intermingling to support his case. In response, the puritanical Patoulet cited Iberian Americans' "abominable vices." Cited in Elisabeth, *Société martiniquaise*, 242. See more recently, Guillaume Aubert, "'The Blood of France': Race and Purity of Blood in the French Atlantic World," *William and Mary Quarterly*, 3d ser., 61, no. 3 (July 2004): 463–64. Patoulet's memorandum is in CAOM, F3, 248, fol. 68.

100. See, e.g., Wiesner, *Women and Gender in Early Modern Europe*, chap. 1.

101. Gwendolyn Midlo Hall, *Africans in Colonial Louisiana: The Development of Afro-Creole Culture in the Eighteenth Century* (Baton Rouge: Louisiana State University Press, 1992), 53.

102. Labat, *Nouveau voyage*, 2: 115–18, tells the story of a white slave driver who, after raping a mulatto slave woman, tried to marry her. Fortunately for him

a powerful patron helped him to buy the woman and her three small children for 1,800 l.t. Labat then married the couple.

103. Moreau de Saint-Méry, *Loix et constitutions*, 1: 476.

104. Labat, *Nouveau voyage*, 1: 121; 2: 125.

105. Elisabeth, *Société martiniquaise*, 248–52, devotes interesting and original pages to this issue.

106. Moreau de Saint-Méry, *Loix et constitutions*, 1: 579–80.

107. Labat supplied extra food for the very practical reason that malnourished slaves could not otherwise cope. He recommends a large plate of manioc cooked in bouillon, along with a little salt meat, potatoes, and yams. He also undertook the feeding of slave children to relieve parents of that anxiety. *Nouveau voyage*, 3: 211, 216.

108. For an interesting analysis of the multiple tasks and dangers involved in feeding sugarcane into the mill, see Bernard Moitt, "Women, Work and Resistance in the French Caribbean During Slavery, 1700–1848," in *Engendering History: Caribbean Women in Historical Perspective*, ed. Verene Shepherd, Bridget Brereton, and Barbara Bailey (New York: St. Martin's Press, 1995), 163–64.

109. Labat, *Nouveau voyage*, 3: 206–9.

110. Moreau de Saint-Méry, *Loix et constitutions*, 1: 203.

111. Labat, *Nouveau voyage*, 1: 450–51, 3: 459, 5: 357–58.

112. Ibid., 4: 402–4.

113. Moreau de Saint-Méry, *Loix et constitutions*, 1: 327.

114. However, Thornton, *Africa and Africans*, 197, warns against the traditional view that the multiplicity of African languages prevented rapid development of slave communities. See, e.g., his description of the Remire estate at Cayenne, where fifty-seven slaves can be assigned to four linguistic groups.

115. Debien, "Les Esclaves," in *Histoire des Antilles*, ed. Pluchon and Abenon, 152–54.

116. Pritchard, *In Search of Empire*, 424.

117. Labat, *Nouveau voyage*, 5: 244. He claims they cultivated the finest chocolate in the world.

118. I decided to place these remarks about free blacks in this chapter on coerced labor rather than in the previous chapter on free people because freedmen suffered not only social discrimination but also some legal restrictions.

119. Léo Elisabeth, "The French Antilles," in *Neither Slave nor Free: The Freedmen of African Descent in the Slave Societies of the New World*, ed. David W. Cohen and Jack P. Greene (Baltimore: Johns Hopkins University Press, 1974), 135–71, esp. 139–40. By 1724, when an amended version of the *Code noir* was established for Louisiana, mixed marriages were no longer permitted.

120. Labat, *Nouveau voyage*, 1: 195–96.

121. Dutertre, *Histoire générale*, 2: 512–15.

122. Elisabeth, *Société martiniquaise,* 147. He suggests a connection between these suppressions and worsening slave mortality after that date. With less time to devote to gardens, the slave diet may have become more monotonous and nutritionally deficient.

123. Moreau de Saint-Méry, *Loix et constitutions,* 2: 512–15.

124. Labat, *Nouveau voyage,* 2: 357–58.

125. Ibid., 1: 308. Labat mentions earth eating, which he thought affected primarily Gold Coast slaves. Ibid., 446. Opposite 2: 349 is an illustration of Africans hunting the bird known as the *diable* at the summit of the Soufrière, the highest mountain on Guadeloupe.

126. Ibid., 4: 170.

127. For comparative purposes, see Dunn, *Sugar and Slaves,* chaps. 7 and 8.

128. Dutertre, *Histoire générale,* 2: 515–18.

129. Ibid., 2: 496–97.

130. For comparative purposes, see Dunn, *Sugar and Slaves,* 251.

131. Or so Clodoré, *Relation,* 1: 43–46, claims.

132. I am not suggesting that there were no sincere converts. Labat on a number of occasions mentions communicants, or those eligible for all the sacraments. See, e.g., *Nouveau voyage,* 2: 417.

133. Dutertre, *Histoire générale,* 2: 500.

134. Labat, *Nouveau voyage,* 4: 184. Labat says that of a company of sixty at Guadeloupe, thirty were slaves of the Dominicans.

135. Moreau de Saint-Méry, *Loix et constitutions,* 1: 529. Masters of slaves slain in combat received public compensation.

136. Labat, *Nouveau voyage,* 4: 70–73; 2: 290, 429.

137. Ibid., 1: 144–45.

138. Moitt, "Women, Work and Resistance," 161–62.

139. Linguists distinguish between pidgins to foster minimal communications and Creole, a blending of French and African grammatical rules and words. See, e.g., Schnepel, "Language Question in Guadeloupe," 68–69.

140. Moreau de Saint-Méry, *Loix et constitutions,* 1: 505–6. The council of Saint-Domingue asserted that goods slaves traded were often their masters' property.

141. Labat, *Nouveau voyage,* 4: 174.

142. Dutertre, *Histoire générale,* 2: 505.

143. Beckles, "Sex and Gender," in *Engendering History,* 137.

144. Labat, *Nouveau voyage,* 5: 256.

145. Ibid., 4: 173, 175.

146. Ibid., 178.

147. Ibid., 186.

148. Dutertre, *Histoire générale,* 2: 522.

149. Labat, *Nouveau voyage,* 3: 144–46.

150. Kiple, *Caribbean Slave*, chap. 8.

151. Labat, *Nouveau voyage*, 5: 357–58.

152. Ibid., 4: 198; 6: 329. For the only other mention of poisonings in my Labat notes, see 4: 205–6.

153. Yves Debbasch, "Le Crime d'empoisonnement aux îles pendant la période esclavagiste," *Revue d'histoire d'Outre-mer* 51 (1963): 137–54.

154. Labat, *Nouveau voyage*, 1: 350.

155. Dessalles, *Annales*, in Dessalles, *Histoire générale*, 3: 109. He says the band numbered 400–500.

156. Ibid, 3: 110; Elisabeth, *Société martiniquaise*, 57.

157. Moreau de Saint-Méry, *Loix et constitutions*, 1: 248–49.

158. Ibid., 1: 327 and 248–49.

159. Labat, *Nouveau voyage*, 1: 132–33; Moreau de Saint-Méry, *Loix et constitutions*, 1: 468.

160. Labat, *Nouveau voyage*, 1: 133.

161. Ibid., 5: 256–57.

162. Ibid., 4: 436, 443.

163. Ibid., 1: 524–26.

164. Ibid., 3: 113.

165. Ibid., 3: 112.

166. Ibid., 3: 113.

167. Baudrit, *Charles de Courbon*, 83.

168. At least according to Labat, *Nouveau voyage*, 4: 183.

169. Moreau de Saint-Méry, *Loix et constitutions*, 1: 500–502. For the 1697 conspiracy, see ibid., 564–66.

170. Ibid., 502.

171. Ibid., 528–30.

172. Ibid., 622–23.

Conclusion

1. Pritchard, *In Search of Empire*, 424.

2. For the connections between exploding number of slaves and the hardening of racist attitudes at the beginning of the eighteenth century, see Elisabeth, *Société martiniquaise*, 259–80.

3. For the details of the gradual decline of these indigenous peoples, see Boucher, *Cannibal Encounters*.

Index

Page numbers followed by *f* indicate figures; page numbers followed by *t* indicate tables.